# HANDBOOK ON IRISH GENEALOGY

*The Great Famine : Hardship in Ireland caused by the failure of the potato crop in 1847.*

# HANDBOOK ON IRISH GENEALOGY

How to trace your ancestors
and relatives in Ireland

Sixth Edition
Revised and Edited
by

Donal F. Begley
Irish Genealogical Office

Genealogy Bookshop, 3 Nassau Street, Dublin 2, Ireland

© Heraldic Artists Ltd. 1984

First Impression 1970
Second Impression 1973
Third Impression (Enlarged Edition) 1976
Fourth Impression 1978
Fifth Impression 1980
Sixth Impression (Revised Edition) 1984

Library of Congress Washington
Copyright Certificate

ISBN 0 9502455 9 3

A Publication in the Heraldry and Genealogy Series by
HERALDIC ARTISTS LTD., 3 Nassau Street, Dublin 2.

Printed in Ireland by Mount Salus Press Ltd., Dublin 4.

# CONTENTS

# ABBREVIATIONS

| | | | |
|---|---|---|---|
| A.H. | Analecta Hibernica | IR£. | Irish Pound |
| app. | approximately, appendix | £. | Pound Sterling |
| Bapt. | Baptisms | Kild. J. | Kildare Journal |
| B.C.G. | Burke's Colonial Gentry | Knt. | Knight |
| Bp. | Bishop | L.P. | *Lodge's Peerage* |
| B.L. | British Library | M. | Manuscript Reference |
| B.M. | British Museum | Marr. | Marriage |
| Bt. | Baronet | mid. | middle |
| c. | *circa,* century, comments | Misc. | Miscellaneous |
| C. | Century, Copyright reserved | Ms. | Manuscript |
| | | Mss. | Manuscripts |
| Ch. | Church | n.d. | no date |
| Chas. | Charles | N.L.I. | National Library of Ireland |
| Co. | County | | |
| Cos. | Counties | O. | Original |
| d. | died, pence | P. | Positive (microfilm) |
| dau. | daughter | p. | page |
| dioc. | diocese | pp. | pages |
| DKPRI | Deputy Keeper of Public Records in Ireland | pr. | printed |
| | | pr. pr. | privately printed |
| D.K.rep. | Deputy Keeper report | P.R.I. | Public Record Office Ireland |
| do. | source as before | | |
| ed. | edited | P.R.O. | Public Record Office (of Ireland) |
| Edw. | Edward | | |
| e.g. | for example | PRONI | Public Record Office of Northern Ireland |
| esq. | esquire | | |
| Geo. | George | R.C.B. | Representative Church Body |
| G.O. | Genealogical Office | | |
| G.P.O. | General Post Office | R.C.C. | Roman Catholic Curate |
| G.R.O. | General Register Office | re. | with reference to |
| Hen. | Henry | Regs. | Registers |
| H.M.S.O. | His (Her) Majesty's Stationery Office | R.I.A. | Royal Irish Academy |
| | | s. | shilling |
| Ho. | House | S.P.O. | State Paper Office |
| H.S.L. | Huguenot Society of London | St. | saint, street |
| | | T.C.D. | Trinity College Dublin |
| i.e. | that is | temp. | temporary |
| I.M.C. | Irish Manuscripts Commission | Tr. | Transcript |
| | | viz. | namely |
| Ir. | Irish | Vol. | Volume |
| Ir.B. | Irish Builder | Vols. | Volumes |
| Irl. | Ireland | | |

# INTRODUCTION

This book is intended for those with an interest in their Irish ancestry. Its purpose is to give them as briefly as possible the facts about genealogical research in Ireland. Today a growing number of people feel the need to seek out their family origins however humble these may have been. Why this should be so at the present time need not concern us here. In any case nothing could be more natural than for civilised man to take an interest in his ancestors. For each of us this interest has a personal origin. Man is an inheritor as well as a transmitter and people are curiously actuated to know what kind of people their forebears were — how and where and when they lived and what they did. For this is the kind of knowledge that enables them to understand themselves — and others — all the better and instils in them a deeper appreciation of the land of their forebears.

In ancestry research as in other types of research a proper approach is essential if worthwhile results are to be achieved. Much of course will depend on the amount of information already known about an ancestor. As a general rule it is advisable to check first records at central level before moving on to local sources.

Various avenues of approach appropriate to what is already known about an ancestor are suggested in the course of this book. There are sections on record offices, shipping lists, wills, land records, parish church registers and gravestone inscriptions. Included also is a map section containing thirty two maps — one for each county — reproduced from Samuel Lewis's Atlas of Ireland, 1837. These maps highlight state parishes and baronies into which counties were formerly divided. It is essential for the family chronicler to appreciate the importance of such vital government records as tithe, valuation, voter and census listings.

This guide is specifically designed to enable people of Irish descent to undertake on their own the work of tracing their ancestors so that by personal involvement in their own research they can experience the joy of exploration and the thrill of discovery as they journey back in time to make their acquaintance with quaint and lovable characters that only Ireland would have produced in a day that has been.

Martin O'Beirne
July 1984

| No. of Sheet of the Ordnance Survey Maps. | Townlands and Towns. | Area in Statute Acres. | | | County. | Barony. | Parish. | Poor Law Union in 1857. |
|---|---|---|---|---|---|---|---|---|
| | | A. | R. | P. | | | | |
| 32 | Boceshil . . . | 80 | 2 | 2 | Leitrim . . | Mohill . . . | Mohill . . . | Mohill . |
| 87 | Bofara . . . | 132 | 1 | 28 | Mayo . . | Murrisk . . . | Aghagower . . | Westport . |
| 9, 10 | Bofealan . . . | 78 | 1 | 28 | Cavan . . | Tullyhaw . . | Templeport . . | Bawnboy . |
| 47, 59 | Bofeenaun . . | 659 | 0 | 10a | Mayo . . | Tirawley . . . | Addergoole . . | Castlebar . |
| 101, 102 | Bofickil . . . | 420 | 2 | 12 | Cork, W.R. . | Bear . . . | Kilcatherine . . | Castletown . |
| 25 | Bog . . . | 190 | 0 | 36 | Waterford . | Decies without Drum | Kilbarrymeaden . | Kilmacthomas . |
| 70 | Bogagh . . . | 214 | 0 | 31 | Donegal . . | Raphoe . . . | Raphoe . . . | Strabane . |
| 21 | Bogagh . . . | 168 | 1 | 24 | Londonderry . | Tirkeeran . . | Clondermot . . | Londonderry . |
| 90 | Bogagh Glebe . | 596 | 1 | 15 | Donegal . . | Banagh . . . | Kilcar . . . | Glenties . |
| 91 | Bogare . . . | 687 | 1 | 5 | Kerry . . | Dunkerron South . | Kilcrohane . . | Kenmare . |
| 53 | Bogay . . . | 91 | 2 | 7 | Donegal . . | Kilmacrenan . . | Aghanunshin . . | Letterkenny . |
| 47, 55 | Bogay Glebe . . | 156 | 1 | 29 | Donegal . . | Raphoe . . . | Allsaints . . . | Londonderry . |
| 55 | Bogbane . . . | 148 | 3 | 28 | Tyrone . . | Dungannon Middle . | Killyman . . | Dungannon . |
| 26 | Bog Commons . | 93 | 1 | 32 | Kilkenny . . | Kells . . . | Coolaghmore . . | Callan . |
| 35 | Bogderries . . | 412 | 0 | 14 | King's Co. . | Eglish . . . | Eglish . . . | Parsonstown . |
| 47 | Bog East . . | 105 | 3 | 25 | Wexford . . | Forth . . . | Mayglass . . | Wexford . |
| 27, 33 | Bogesky . . . | 305 | 1 | 31 | Cavan . . | Upper Loughtee . | Lavey . . . | Cavan . |
| 12, 21 | Boggagh . . . | 139 | 1 | 2 | Waterford . | Coshmore & Coshbride | Lismore & Mocollop | Lismore . |
| 11, 12 | Boggaghbaun . | 626 | 1 | 29 | Waterford . | Coshmore & Coshbride | Lismore & Mocollop | Lismore . |
| 36 | Boggagh (Conran) . | 150 | 1 | 26 | Westmeath . | Clonlonan . . | Kilcleagh . . | Athlone . |
| 11, 12 | Boggaghduff . . | 453 | 1 | 9 | Waterford . | Coshmore & Coshbride | Lismore & Mocollop | Lismore . |
| 36 | Boggagh Eighter . | 234 | 3 | 24 | Westmeath . | Clonlonan . . | Kilcleagh . . | Athlone . |
| 36 | Boggagh (Fury) . | 106 | 1 | 12 | Westmeath . | Clonlonan . . | Kilcleagh . . | Athlone . |
| 36 | Boggagh (Malone) . | 89 | 2 | 39 | Westmeath . | Clonlonan . . | Kilcleagh . . | Athlone . |
| 13, 17 | Boggan . . . | 267 | 1 | 16 | Carlow . . | Forth . . . | Ballon . . . | Carlow . |
| 17 | Boggan . . . | 230 | 3 | 39 | Carlow . . | Forth . . . | Barragh . . | Carlow . |
| 17 | Boggan . . . | 460 | 2 | 24 | Kilkenny . . | Crannagh . . | Tullaroan . . | Kilkenny . |
| 5 | Boggan . . . | 119 | 2 | 22 | Meath . . | Lower Kells . . | Moybolgue . . | Kells . |
| 40, 42 | Bogganfin . . | 163 | 1 | 31 | Roscommon . | Athlone . . . | Kilmeane . . | Roscommon . |
| 49, 52 | Bogganfin . . | 292 | 2 | 4 | Roscommon . | Athlone . . . | Kiltoom . . . | Athlone . |
| 49, 52 | Bogganfin . . | 105 | 3 | 15 | Roscommon . | Athlone . . . | St. Peter's . . | Athlone . |
| 52 | BOGGANFIN T. | — | | | Roscommon . | Athlone . . . | St. Peter's . . | Athlone . |
| 50, 53 | Bogganstown . . | 211 | 0 | 15 | Meath . . | Dunboyne . . | Dunboyne . . | Dunshaughlin . |
| 43, 44 | Bogganstown . . | 395 | 3 | 31 | Meath . . | Upper Deece . . | Culmullin . . | Dunshaughlin . |
| 42, 43 | Bogganstown Lower | 37 | 2 | 8 | Wexford . . | Forth . . . | Drinagh . . | Wexford . |
| 42 | Bogganstown Upper | 26 | 1 | 35 | Wexford . . | Forth . . . | Drinagh . . | Wexford . |
| 105, 115 | Boggaun . . . | 98 | 1 | 31 | Galway . . | Loughrea . . | Kilchreest . . | Loughrea . |
| 21 | Boggaun . . . | 108 | 3 | 18 | Leitrim . . | Carrigallen . . | Oughteragh . . | Bawnboy . |
| 11 | Boggaun . . . | 984 | 1 | 30 | Leitrim . . | Drumahaire . . | Cloonlogher . . | Manorhamilton . |
| 23 | Boggaun . . . | 102 | 1 | 39 | Tipperary, N.R. | Ikerrin . . . | Killavinoge . . | Roscrea . |
| 30 | Boggaunreagh . | 86 | 0 | 3 | King's Co. . | Garrycastle . . | Reynagh . . | Parsonstown . |
| 32 | Boggauns . . | 416 | 0 | 26 | Galway . . | Ballymoe . . | Kilbegnet . . | Glennamaddy . |
| 32 | Boggauns . . | 420 | 0 | 3 | Galway . . | Killian . . . | Killian . . . | Mountbellew . |
| 95 | Boggra . . . | 184 | 1 | 14 | Cork, W.R. . | Kinalmeaky . . | Templemartin . . | Bandon . |
| 59 | Boggy . . . | 678 | 1 | 28 | Mayo . . | Tirawley . . . | Addergoole . . | Castlebar . |
| 11 | Boggyheary . . | 90 | 2 | 2 | Dublin . . | Nethercross . . | Killossery . . | Balrothery . |
| 46, 47, 59 | Boghadoon . . | 1,197 | 0 | 0 | Mayo . . | Tirawley . . . | Addergoole . . | Castlebar . |
| 27, 31 | Boghall . . . | 344 | 0 | 11 | Kildare . . | Offaly West . . | Harristown . . | Athy . |
| 8, 9 | Boghil ' . . . | 371 | 1 | 23 | Clare . . | Corcomroe . . | Kilfenora . . | Ennistymon . |
| 18, 19 | Boghilboy . . | 228 | 1 | 1 | Londonderry . | Coleraine . . | Desertoghill . . | Coleraine . |
| 3, 7 | Boghill . . . | 341 | 2 | 39 | Londonderry . | North East Liberties of Coleraine . | Coleraine . . | Coleraine . |
| 68, 69 | Boghilmore Island . | 8 | 0 | 1 | Galway . . | Moycullen . . | Moycullen . . | Galway . |
| 12, 13 | Boghlone . . | 306 | 3 | 31 | Queen's Co. . | Maryborough East . | Clonenagh & Clonagheen | Mountmellick . |
| 16 | Boghouse . . | 77 | 2 | 36 | Carlow . . | Idrone East . . | Fennagh . . | Carlow . |
| 63, 64, 73, 74 | Boghtaduff . . | 931 | 3 | 4 | Mayo . . | Costello . . . | Castlemore . . | Castlereagh . |
| 45 | Bogland . . . | 109 | 3 | 34 | Wicklow . . | Arklow . . . | Arklow . . . | Rathdrum . |
| 99 | Bogpark . . . | 138 | 0 | 4 | Galway . . | Clonmacnowen . . | Clontuskert . . | Ballinasloe . |
| 98 | Bogside . . . | 35 | 2 | 0 | Donegal . . | Banagh . . . | Killaghtee . . | Donegal . |

*Facsimile copy of page 157 indicating exact location of Boggaun, Co. Tipperary.*

# CHAPTER 1

# *Tracing Ancestors and Relatives in Ireland*

If you have Irish blood in you, you will almost certainly be proud of the fact. Indeed you may wish to add to the pleasure of your holiday in Ireland by indulging in a spot of ancestor hunting in the land of your forebears.

Let's say, for example sake, your grandfather Patrick Ryan left Boggaun, Co. Tipperary for America in the year 1847. Before coming to Ireland you had the good sense to inspect his gravestone in Calvary Cemetery in New York which shows that he died on February 7, 1888 aged 61 years. It is clear therefore that he was born in 1827 and was 20 years of age when he landed in New York.

The first important step is to determine the exact location of Boggaun. From *The Alphabetical Index to the Townlands and Towns of Ireland,* a copy of which any good library will have, we learn that Boggaun is the name of a townland in the County Tipperary, barony of Ikerrin, civil parish of Killavinoge and Poor Law Union of Roscrea. A word of explanation on Irish topographical divisions may be helpful at this point. A townland is the smallest administrative division of land in Ireland, with an average area of three hundred and fifty acres.

Parishes are of two kinds, civil and ecclesiastical. The civil parish, as the name implies, is a state unit of territorial division for census and valuation purposes. The ecclesiastical parish is the normal unit of local Church administration and generally embraces a number of civil parishes.

The baronies, over three hundred in all, represent divisions of great antiquity based on the Gaelic clan and family holdings.

The Poor Law Unions were constituted under the Poor Law Act of 1838 when the country was divided into districts or unions in which the local rateable people were financially responsible for the upkeep of the poor in each area. The Unions comprised multiples of townlands within an average radius of ten miles, usually with a large market town as centre in which the 'Poor House' was located. Many of these 'Poor Houses' may still be seen and a few are still in use — for other purposes of course.

In researching placenames it is sometimes useful to recall that people in the country habitually abbreviate the names of places in their locality. County Kerry people, for example, will frequently refer to their local market town of — longford or — dorney or —civeen as the case may be. Needless to remark, such abbreviated forms of placenames will not be found in standard topographical sources. If, however, to these abbreviated forms we prefix the elements 'Bally',

## PARISH OF KILLAVINOGE.

| No. and Letters of Reference to Map | | Names. | | Description of Tenement. | Area. | | | Net Annual Value. | | |
|---|---|---|---|---|---|---|---|---|---|---|
| | | Townlands and Occupiers. | Immediate Lessors. | | A. | R. | P. | Land. | Buildings. | Total. |
| | | **BALLYSORRELL, BIG.** *(Ord. Ss. 29 & 30.)* | | | | | | £ s. d. | £ s. d. | £ s. d. |
| 1 | | John Maher, | Frederick Lidwell, Esq. | Moory pasture, | 11 | 1 | 26 | 4 15 0 | — | 4 15 0 |
| 2 | | John Maher, | Frederick Lidwell, Esq. | Land, | 94 | 0 | 2 | 59 5 0 | — | 59 5 0 |
| - | a | Michael Trehy, | John Maher, | House, offices, & garden, | 0 | 2 | 24 | 0 10 0 | 1 0 0 | 1 10 0 |
| 3 | A a | Thomas Bennett, | Frederick Lidwell, Esq. | House, offices, and land, | 20 | 1 | 27 | 11 10 0 | 1 15 0 | 13 5 0 |
| - | B | Thomas Bennett, | Frederick Lidwell, Esq. | Land, | 32 | 1 | 33 | 8 10 0 | — | 8 10 0 |
| - | A b | John Cormack, | Thomas Bennett, | House, | | | | — | 0 15 0 | 0 15 0 |
| - | c | Margaret Russell, | Thomas Bennett, | House and garden, | 0 | 0 | 18 | 0 1 0 | 0 14 0 | 0 15 0 |
| 4 | | Frederick Lidwell, Esq. | In fee, | Land, | 37 | 2 | 5 | 13 15 0 | — | 13 15 0 |
| - | a | Margaret Henley, | Frederick Lidwell, Esq. | House, | | | | — | 0 10 0 | 0 10 0 |
| - | b | Margaret Ahern, | Frederick Lidwell, Esq. | House, | | | | — | 0 5 0 | 0 5 0 |
| - | c | Catherine Fogarty, | Frederick Lidwell, Esq. | House and garden, | 0 | 1 | 31 | 0 5 0 | 0 10 0 | 0 15 0 |
| 5 | | Martin Carroll, | Frederick Lidwell, Esq. | Land, | 62 | 1 | 30 | 30 15 0 | — | 30 15 0 |
| - | a | Vacant, | Martin Carroll, | House and offices, | | | | — | 1 0 0 | 1 0 0 |
| 6 | a | Michael Kerin, | Fredk. Lidwell, Esq. | House, offices, & land, | 31 | 3 | 13 | 6 10 0 | 1 0 0 | 7 10 0 |
| | b | Patrick Carey, | | House and land, | | | | 6 10 0 | 0 10 0 | 7 0 0 |
| 7 | | William Ryan, | Frederick Lidwell, Esq. | House and land, | 20 | 2 | 27 | 11 10 0 | 0 15 0 | 12 5 0 |
| 8 | a | Patrick Healy, | Frederick Lidwell, Esq. | House, offices, & land, | | | | 15 0 0 | 1 0 0 | 16 0 0 |
| | b | Daniel Lahy, | Frederick Lidwell, Esq. | House and land, | 79 | 1 | 27 | 3 15 0 | 0 5 0 | 4 0 0 |
| | c | Michael Maher, | Frederick Lidwell, Esq. | House and land, | | | | 3 15 0 | 0 10 0 | 4 5 0 |
| | | Fredk. Lidwell, Esq. | In fee, | Land, | | | | 7 10 0 | — | 7 10 0 |
| - | | Patrick Healy & parts. | Frederick Lidwell, Esq. | Bog, | 122 | 0 | 38 | 0 10 0 | — | 0 10 0 |
| - | d | Thomas Carroll, | Frederick Lidwell, Esq. | House and garden, | 0 | 0 | 12 | 0 1 0 | 0 14 0 | 0 15 0 |
| 9 | | Gt. S. & W. Railway Co. | In fee, | Land and railway, | 9 | 2 | 3 | 6 5 0 | — | 6 5 0 |
| | | | | Total, | 523 | 0 | 36 | 190 12 0 | 11 3 0 | 201 15 0 |
| | | **BALLYSORRELL, LITTLE.** *(Ord. Ss. 23, 24, 29, & 30.)* | | | | | | | | |
| 1 | | William Bennett, | Dudley Byrne, Esq. | House and land, | 1 | 0 | 0 | 0 10 0 | 0 15 0 | 1 5 0 |
| 2 | A a | Dudley Byrne, Esq. | Philip Gowan, Esq. | House, offices, and land, | 133 | 0 | 19 | 70 5 0 | 16 10 0 | 86 15 0 |
| - | B | Dudley Byrne, Esq. | Philip Gowan, Esq. | Land, | 113 | 3 | 26 | 52 5 0 | — | 52 5 0 |
| - | | Dudley Byrne, Esq. | Philip Gowan, Esq. | Bog, | 107 | 3 | 20 | 0 10 0 | — | 0 10 0 |
| - | A b | William Kirwan, | Dudley Byrne, Esq. | House and garden, | 0 | 0 | 30 | 0 2 0 | 0 5 0 | 0 7 0 |
| 3 | | Daniel Dwyer, | Dudley Byrne, Esq. | House and land, | 7 | 2 | 24 | 3 10 0 | 0 5 0 | 3 15 0 |
| 4 | | Gt. S. & W. Railway Co. | In fee, | Railway, | 5 | 1 | 24 | 4 0 0 | — | 4 0 0 |
| | | | | Total, | 369 | 0 | 23 | 131 2 0 | 17 15 0 | 148 17 0 |
| | | **BOGGAUN.** *(Ord. S. 23.)* | | | | | | | | |
| 1 | | James Ryan, | George Goold, Esq. | Land, | 29 | 0 | 7 | 15 10 0 | — | 15 10 0 |
| 2 | | Jeremiah Commerford, | George Goold, Esq. | House and land, | 38 | 1 | 27 | 18 0 0 | 0 15 0 | 18 15 0 |
| 3 | | Michael Quinlan, | George Goold, Esq. | Land, | 12 | 3 | 29 | 5 15 0 | — | 5 15 0 |
| - | | Michael Quinlan, | George Goold, Esq. | Bog, | 4 | 0 | 12 | 0 1 0 | — | 0 1 0 |
| 4 | | George Redding, | George Goold, Esq. | House and land, | 18 | 0 | 4 | 7 15 0 | 0 15 0 | 48 11 0 |
| | | | | Total, | 102 | 1 | 39 | 47 1 0 | 1 10 0 | 48 11 0 |
| | | **CLONBUOGH.** *(Ord. Ss. 24 & 30.)* | | | | | | | | |
| 1 | | Earl of Carrick, | In fee, | Bog, | 88 | 3 | 10 | 0 10 0 | — | 0 10 0 |
| 2 | A a | William Rorke, | Earl of Carrick, | House, offices, and land, | 70 | 1 | 29 | 31 10 0 | 4 10 0 | 36 0 0 |
| - | B | William Rorke, | Earl of Carrick, | Land, | 41 | 2 | 1 | 31 10 0 | — | 31 10 0 |
| - | A b | Vacant, | William Rorke, | House and offices, | | | | — | 2 0 0 | 2 0 0 |
| - | A c | Mary Flynn, | William Rorke, | House, | | | | — | 0 10 0 | 0 10 0 |
| - | B a | Mary Flynn, | William Rorke, | House, | | | | — | 0 5 0 | 0 5 0 |
| - | b | Edward Long, | William Rorke, | House and garden, | 0 | 1 | 33 | 0 5 0 | 0 5 0 | 0 10 0 |
| - | c | Catherine Neale, | William Rorke, | House and garden, | 0 | 1 | 16 | 0 5 0 | 0 5 0 | 0 10 0 |
| 3 | A | William Rorke, | Earl of Carrick, | Land, | 24 | 3 | 34 | 11 10 0 | — | 11 10 0 |
| - | B | William Rorke, | Earl of Carrick, | Land, | 6 | 3 | 35 | 3 5 0 | — | 3 5 0 |
| - | A a | Patrick Burke, | William Rorke, | House, | | | | — | 0 5 0 | 0 5 0 |
| - | A b | Henry Doyle, | William Rorke, | House, | | | | — | 0 5 0 | 0 5 0 |
| 4 | | Patrick Cahill, | Earl of Carrick, | Land, | 6 | 2 | 14 | 3 10 0 | — | 3 10 0 |
| 5 | | Patrick Doolan, | Earl of Carrick, | House and land, | 1 | 3 | 34 | 1 5 0 | 0 5 0 | 1 10 0 |
| 6 | | Patrick Brennan, | Earl of Carrick, | Land, | 3 | 3 | 7 | 2 5 0 | — | 2 5 0 |

*Extract from Sir Richard Griffith's Valuation of Ireland, Co. Tipperary c. 1850, showing details of holding of James Ryan.*

'Abbey' and 'Cahir' respectively, then the resulting Ballylongford, Abbey-dorney and Cahirciveen can easily be located even in an elementary map of County Kerry.

The name of the native townland of the emigrant ancestor is occasionally preserved in family tradition albeit in extremely corrupt form. In instances where the corruption is so severe as to render identification of the townland impossible then the technique of recognition should be tried as a last resort. The secret here is to realise that each barony of the *General Valuation of Ireland* (see below) is prefixed by a number of alphabetical lists of townlands occurring in that barony. The average county will contain ten to twelve baronies. In fingering the townland lists for a county the eye must be trained to single out the townland name which approximates most closely to a given corrupt form.

The name of the local landlord's residence or 'Big House' as it was popularly called, was frequently employed by 19th century emigrants to indicate their home place. In view of the social and economic circumstances of the time it is easy to understand how the name of the 'Big House' could, and often did, obliterate the name of the townland on which it stood. For a list of such houses and their locations one could do worse than turn to *Atlas and Cyclopedia of Ireland.*

It may be worth observing that the names of some of the great Irish houses built in the 18th and 19th centuries — Highfield Ho., Bellevue Ho., Rockfield Ho. and so forth — were simply anglicised versions of the names of the townlands where they were located. Thus by process of inversion, we surmise that the above named houses were situated in the townlands of *Ardacha, Knockan* and *Gortnacairrge* respectively.

Should it become necessary to do some map reading in the course of your research, it is useful to know that the Government's Ordnance Survey Office has published a set of twenty-five sectional maps covering the entire country on a scale of one half inch to the mile. These maps are available from most leading booksellers.

We return to the subject of our search — Patrick Ryan. Having established that Boggaun occurs in the civil parish of Killavinoge, we now turn to *A Topographical Dictionary of Ireland* by Samuel Lewis, in order to learn a little about the area from which Patrick Ryan came. Lewis' article reads as follows —

> Killavinoge or Clonmore, — a parish, in the union of Roscrea, barony of Ikerrin, county of Tipperary, and province of Munster, 4 miles (N.E.) from Templemore, on the road from that place to Rathdowney; containing 3557 inhabitants. It comprises 8160 statute acres, including a considerable quantity of bog; and contains the residence of Dromard. It is a rectory and vicarage, in the diocese of Cashel, forming part of the union of Templemore; the tithe rent charge is £227/18/6, and there is a glebe of 36 acres. In the Roman Catholic divisions the parish forms part of the district of Templemore, and contains a chapel.

| Towns-Lands | | Occupiers Names | Quantity of Land | | | Rate per acre | | Amount | | |
|---|---|---|---|---|---|---|---|---|---|---|
| | | | A | R | P | s | d | £ | s | d |
| Graffin | | Brought forward | 221 | 2 | 19 | | | 27 | 16 | 9½ |
| | 68 | John Lahy & | 7 | 1 | " | 3 | 4 | 1 | 4 | 2 |
| | 9 | Thos. Darmudy | 1 | 2 | " | 3 | 4 | " | 5 | " |
| | 70 | Wm. Maher & Michl. Cormick | 10 | 2 | 5 | 3 | 4 | 1 | 15 | 1 |
| | 1 | Andrew Kennedy | 4 | 1 | 5 | 1 | 11 | " | 8 | 2½ |
| | 2 | James Guilfoyle | 4 | 2 | 5 | 2 | 7 | " | 11 | 8½ |
| | 3 | Wm. Meara | 4 | 2 | 25 | 3 | 4 | " | 15 | 6 |
| | 4 | Timy. Ryan | 4 | " | 20 | 3 | 4 | " | 13 | 9 |
| | 5 | Wid. Kennedy & Wid. Lahy | 3 | 1 | 30 | 2 | 7 | " | 8 | 10½ |
| | 6 | John & Michl. Guider½ | 11 | " | " | 2 | 7 | 1 | 8 | 5 |
| | 7 | Jas ⅔ & Wm ⅓ Brien | 15 | 3 | 4 | 2 | 7 | 2 | " | 9½ |
| | 8 | James Dooley | 1 | " | " | 3 | 4 | " | 3 | 4 |
| | 9 | Patk. Kilmartin | 3 | " | " | 2 | 7 | " | 7 | 9 |
| | 80 | Widow Whelan | 2 | 2 | 20 | 1 | 11 | " | 5 | " |
| | 1 | ⅙ Widow Key / ⅙ Wm. Dulahunty / ⅙ John Tracy / ⅓ Roger & Pat. Tracy / ⅙ Edmond Tracy | 53 | " | 20 | 1 | 11 | 5 | 1 | 10 |
| | 2 | Brien Fitzpatrick | 10 | 2 | " | 1 | 11 | 1 | " | 1½ |
| | 3 | Edward Mackey | 4 | 1 | " | 1 | 4 | " | 5 | 8 |
| | 4 | John & Widow Whelan | 28 | 1 | 10 | 1 | 11 | 2 | 14 | 3 |
| | 5 | James Whelan | 7 | " | 10 | 1 | 4 | " | 9 | 5 |
| | 6 | Dennis Whelan | 13 | " | " | 2 | 7 | 1 | 13 | 7 |
| | 7 | John Strahan | 3 | 3 | 30 | 1 | 11 | " | 7 | 7 |
| | 8 | John Whelan | 12 | " | " | " | 7 | " | 7 | " |
| | | | 427 | 2 | 3 | | | £50 | 3 | 8 |
| Buggawn | 9 | John Howley | 6 | " | " | 1 | 11 | " | 11 | 6 |
| | 90 | James Monaghan | 4 | " | " | 1 | 11 | " | 7 | 8 |
| | 1 | Frank Lewis | 2 | " | " | 1 | 11 | " | 3 | 10 |
| | 2 | Frank Lewis & John Roddan | 3 | " | " | 1 | 11 | " | 5 | 9 |
| | 3 | John Roddan | 4 | " | " | 1 | 11 | " | 7 | 8 |
| | 4 | John & Michl. Tracy | 12 | 1 | 12 | 3 | 4 | 2 | 1 | 3½ |
| | 5 | Michl. Dulahunty | 12 | 1 | 12 | 2 | 7 | 1 | 11 | 1 |
| | 6 | Benjn. Rawlins & J. Tracy | 10 | 2 | 22 | 1 | 11 | £1 | " | |
| | | | 54 | 1 | 6 | | | £50 | 0 | 0 |

*Extract from Tithe Composition Applotment Book, parish of Killavinogue, Co. Tipperary, 1827 showing details of Ryan family holding.*

**Civil Records**

Our search now leads us to an examination of the great property surveys of the last century with a view to tracing the family of Patrick Ryan. The best known of these was the General Valuation of Ireland, the most comprehensive of its kind ever undertaken in Ireland. The Tenement Act of 1852 envisaged one uniform valuation of all property in Ireland based on the productive capacity of the land and the economic rent of the buildings. The purpose of the valuation was to establish a fair and equitable basis for local taxation. The eminent Dublin geologist Richard Griffith was appointed Commissioner of Valuation and he was assisted in his task by an official body of valuers, surveyors, draughtsmen and clerks. Occasionally local small farmers and labourers were drafted on to the official team at a rate of pay of one shilling and six pence per week.

The returns of the Valuation running to over 200 volumes — one for each barony — were published by the Government mainly in the 1850's. The printed particulars include the name of the individual property holder, his townland or street address, the name of his immediate landlord, a description of his holding, as well as, of course, details of the valuation assessments. Only major libraries and record offices would have anything approaching complete sets of this invaluable work.

Significantly from the point of view of our search for the family of Patrick Ryan, the valuation returns for the townland of Boggaun list one James Ryan, in all probability the father of Patrick, who named his first born in the New World James, doubtlessly following the time honoured Irish custom of naming the eldest son after his paternal grandfather and the second son after his maternal grandfather. The eldest and second daughters were similarly named after the paternal and maternal grandmothers. James occupied Lot 1 amounting to slightly over twenty nine acres with a valuation of £15/10/0. Since the initial rate of tax struck was six pence per £1 valuation, his yearly contribution to the Union Exchequer was between seven and eight shillings. By reference to records in the Irish Valuation Office, 6 Ely Place, by St. Stephen's Green, it is possible to trace the name of the present day owner of the plot once held by James Ryan.

An earlier record of the Ryan family holding will be found in the Tithe Composition Applotment Book for the parish of Killavinogue dated 1827. This land survey had its origin in an Act of Parliament of 1823 providing for tithes due to the Established Church to be paid in money rather than in kind, as had been the case previous to that date. The new method of tithe payment involved a valuation of the entire country, parish by parish, when the amount of tithe payable by each individual landholder was fixed, based on the average price for wheat and oats in each parish over the seven years preceding 1821. The record of this great survey is contained in the Tithe Applotment Books.

**KILLAVINOGE PARISH**, Ikerrin Barony, Roscrea and Thurles Unions,
Co.Tipperary (North Riding).
Griffith's Valuation Year 1851 (G) ; Tithe Applotment Book Year 1827 (T)
G2 etc. = number of holders recorded

| | | | | | | | | | |
|---|---|---|---|---|---|---|---|---|---|
| Ahern | G2 | T | Egan | G | T | M'Coy | G | |
| Anderson | G | | Everit | G | T | Mackey | G | T |
| | | | Everitt | G | T | Maguire | | T |
| Bannon | G3 | T | | | | Maher | G29 | T |
| Barber | | T | Fanning | G2 | | Mahon | | T |
| Barrett | G | | Feely | | T | Malone | G | T |
| Bennett | G2 | T | Fermoyle | G | T | Mara | G2 | |
| Bergin | G2 | T | Fitzpatrick | G9 | T | Marshall | | T |
| Birmingham | G | | Fleming | G | | Martin | G5 | |
| Boohan | G2 | T | Flynn | G4 | T | Mason | | T |
| Bowe | G | | Fogarty | G7 | T | Meara | | T |
| Bray | G | | Franklin | G | T | Meehan | G3 | T |
| Breen | | T | | | | Molloy | G | |
| Brennan | G | | Gantley | G | T | Monihan | G2 | T |
| Brien | G3 | T | Gavin | G | T | Moore | | T |
| Brierton | G2 | | Ginder | G3 | | Morrissey | G2 | T |
| Broderick | G | T | Glackin | | T | Motan | G | |
| Brute | | T | Gleeson | G | | Murphy | G4 | T |
| Bruton | | T | Gorman | G2 | T | | | |
| Bryan | G3 | | Grady | | T | Neale | G | |
| Burke | G4 | T | Grant | G | | New | G | |
| Butler | G4 | T | Greed | G5 | T | | | |
| Byrne | G | | Grimes | | T | Phelan | G5 | |
| | | | Guider | | T | Pine | G2 | T |
| Cahill | G2 | T | Guilfoil | G5 | T | Prendergast | G | T |
| Cantwell | | T | Guinane | G | T | Price | G | |
| Carey | G2 | T | | | | Purcell | G | |
| Carroll | G6 | T | Hanihill | G2 | | | | |
| Carthy | G | | Hanlan | | T | Quigly | | T |
| Clarke | G2 | | Hanrahan | | T | Quinlan | G | T |
| Cleary | G | T | Hargrove | G | | Quinlisk | G3 | T |
| Coady | G2 | T | Harrington | G3 | T | Quinn | G3 | T |
| Collins | G | | Harrohill | | T | | | |
| Commerford | G4 | T | Healy | G2 | | Rawlins | | T |
| Connell | G | | Henley | G | | Redding | G2 | T |
| Connolly | G | | Hennessy | G | | Reeds | G | |
| Coonan | G2 | T | Holmes | | T | Reeves | G | |
| Cooney | G | | Howley | | T | Riordan | | T |
| Corbet | G2 | T | | | | Roe | G | T |
| Corcoran | G2 | | Joyce | G2 | T | Rorke | G | T |
| Cormack | G5 | T | | | | Russell | G | T |
| Costigan | | T | Kavanagh | G | | Ryan | G27 | T |
| Coyle | G | | Kealy | G2 | | | | |
| Cunningham | G | | Keary | G | | Scanlon | G2 | T |
| | | | Keeffe | G | | Scott | G | |
| Darmody | G2 | T | Kenihan | G2 | T | Shaughnessey | G | |
| Davy | G | | Kenna | | T | Shelly | G3 | T |
| Deegan | G2 | T | Kennedy | G3 | T | Spooner | G | |
| Delahunt | G10 | | Kerin | G | | Spunner | G2 | |
| Delahunty | G2 | | Keys | G5 | T | Steel | G | |
| Delany | G4 | T | Kilmartin | | T | Straham | | T |
| Dohan | G2 | | Kinally | | T | Sullivan | G3 | T |
| Donnellan | G | T | Kinna | G3 | | | | |
| Doohan | G3 | T | Kirwan | G6 | T | Talbot | G | |
| Doolan | G2 | | Knowlan | | T | Tierney | G4 | T |
| Dooley | | T | | | | Tracy | G10 | T |
| Doolin | G | | Laffan | G2 | T | Trehy | G | |
| Dooney | G | | Lahy | G5 | T | Tynan | G | |
| Doosey | G | | Landrigan | G2 | T | | | |
| Downey | G | | Lanigan | G3 | T | Vaughan | G | T |
| Doyle | G3 | T | Lannigan | G | T | | | |
| Duane | G | | Lewis | | T | Walsh | G | |
| Dullenty | G | T | Lidwell | G3 | T | Whelan | G4 | T |
| Dunn | G3 | T | Long | G3 | T | | | |
| Dunne | G | T | Loughlin | G | | | | |
| Dwyer | G3 | T | Loughnane | G2 | T | | | |
| | | | Lowry | G | | | | |

*Surname Index for the parish of Killavinog(u)e in the barony of Ikerrin, Co. Tipperary.*

The Tithe books, numbering some two and a half thousand manuscript volumes, range in date from 1823 to 1837. Each parochial tithe book is set out in tabular form under a number of headings, including the following: denomination or townland, landholders or tenants, area of holding, valuation and amount of tithe payable. The tithe valuation was the first comprehensive register of people in relation to the tenancy and working of the land of Ireland and its value is heightened by the loss of the 1821 census in the fire at the Four Courts building in Dublin in 1922. The books for the counties of the Republic can be consulted in the reading room of the Public Record Office, Dublin; those for the six counties of Northern Ireland were transferred to the Public Record Office, Belfast in 1924. It should be noted, however, that a microfilm copy of the northern books is available for public consultation at the National Library, Dublin.

Surname compilations for each of the 32 counties based on the returns of the two valuations referred to above are now available in the major libraries and if you know the name of the particular county from which your forebears came you will be able, by consulting the relevant County Index, to determine with reasonable accuracy the part of that county in which your people formerly resided.

If perchance your people happened to reside in one of the numerous small towns throughout the country then a good source to consult is Slater's *Directory of Ireland 1846.*

To help you visualise the interplay of placename and surname over the centuries in Ireland, *A Genealogical and Historical Map of Ireland,* widely available, shows, among other things, the distribution and location of Irish family names barony by barony.

**Local Visit**

We now come to look for a record of the birth of Patrick Ryan. By Government order under the Compulsory Registration Act 1863 general civil registration of births, marriages and deaths became effective on 1st January, 1864. The Registrar-General was and still is charged with the custody of vital statistics in Ireland. His office is located at 8-11 Lombard St. East, Dublin 2, and there is a search room for the accommodation of the public. But since the subject of our search Patrick Ryan was born about 1827, the civil records are clearly far too late in time to be of any assistance in determining his exact date of birth. In this event we must now direct our attention to the local parish church in which Patrick Ryan was baptised.

For most people a visit to the actual place or places associated with one's ancestors is normally a matter of great curiosity and interest. Living tradition is a powerfully potential source of information in the Irish countryside and the older inhabitants in the locality should be consulted. So too should the electoral lists publically displayed in all Post Offices containing as they do the names of all persons over eighteen normally resident in the locality. The lists are compiled according to townlands and special attention should be paid to the townland associated with one's ancestors since occurrence there today of the family name sought is a strong pointer to the existence of living relatives.

Where a visit to Ireland is not possible remember that a letter seeking family connections in the Emerald Isle is always a good news item for the editor of a local provincial newspaper. One could also consider placing a suitable announcement in the appropriate paper covering the area from which one's ancestors came. A list of such newspapers covering all Irish counties, together with the name of the town in which each is published, will be found below.

On the occasion of a local visit every effort should be made to find the family gravestone in the local cemetery since many of these stones are genealogical tablets in themselves containing as many as four generations of the same family.

Church registers are normally in the custody of the parish priest of each parish (Catholic) and the Rector (Protestant or Church of Ireland). Clearly it is necessary to know the religion of the subject of a search in order to avoid having to inspect a double set of records.

---

## Irish Provincial Newspapers

| County | Name of newspaper & where Published |
|---|---|
| Antrim | *Belfast Newsletter*, Belfast |
| Armagh | *Guardian*, Armagh |
| Carlow, | *The Nationalist and Leinster Times*, Carlow |
| Cavan | *Anglo-Celt*, Cavan |
| Clare | *The Clare Champion*, Ennis |
| Cork | *Weekly Examiner*, Cork |
| Derry | *Derry Journal*, Derry |
| Donegal | *Donegal Democrat*, Ballyshannon |
| Down | *Leader*, Dromore |
| Fermanagh | *Impartial Reporter*, Enniskillen |
| Galway | *Connaught Tribune*, Galway |
| Kerry | *Kerryman*, Tralee |
| Kildare | *Leinster Leader*, Naas |
| Kilkenny | *Kilkenny Journal*, Kilkenny |
| Leitrim | *Leitrim Observer*, Carrick-on-Shannon |
| Laois | *Leinster Express*, Portlaoise |
| Limerick | *Limerick Leader*, Limerick |
| Longford | *Longford Leader*, Longford |
| Louth | *Dundalk Democrat*, Dundalk |
| Mayo | *Western People*, Ballina |
| Meath | *Meath Chronicle*, Navan |
| Monaghan | *Monaghan Argus*, Monaghan |
| Offaly | *Midland Tribune*, Birr |
| Roscommon | *Roscommon Herald*, Boyle |
| Sligo | *Sligo Champion*, Sligo |
| Tipperary | *Tipperary Star*, Thurles |
| Tyrone | *Dungannon Observer*, Dungannon |
| Waterford | *Munster Express*, Waterford |
| Westmeath | *Westmeath Examiner*, Mullingar |
| Wexford | *Free Press*, Wexford |
| Wicklow | *Wicklow People*, Wicklow |

---

## Family Tree

Assuming we are successful in locating the baptism entry of Patrick Ryan in the records of Templemore Parish we are now in a position to begin to construct a modest family tree. The pedigree or tree shown below is self-explanatory. It shows three generations of the Ryan family with dates of birth, marriage and death where the facts have been ascertained. Genealogical information so tabulated is more readily understood and as further pertinent facts come to light the tree can be extended laterally and in depth.

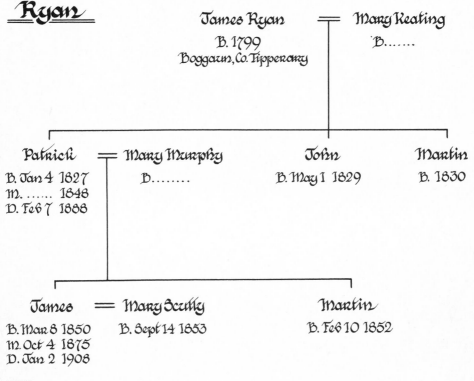

## Ryan

James Ryan
B. 1799
Boggaun, Co. Tipperary

Mary Keating
B.......

Patrick
B. Jan 4 1827
M. ...... 1848
D. Feb 7 1888

Mary Murphy
B.........

John
B. May 1 1829

Martin
B. 1830

James
B. Mar 8 1850
M. Oct 4 1875
D. Jan 2 1908

Mary Scully
B. Sept 14 1853

Martin
B. Feb 10 1852

## Wills

Our next step is to try to locate any wills made by members of the Ryan family of Boggaun. Because of their nature, wills are of outstanding value from a genealogical viewpoint in that they provide accurate and detailed information on family relationships. In Ireland up to the year 1858 the administration of wills lay in the hands of the ecclesiastical authorities. In the case of the less well-off wills were normally proved in what was known as the Diocesan Consistorial Court under the jurisdiction of the local bishop. The wills of those who possessed more in the way of material goods had to be sent for probate to the Prerogative Court of the Archbishop of Armagh. Since the Ryan family of Boggaun were evidently of small tenant stock any wills made by them would be proved in the Consistorial Court of the diocese of Cashel, within which the townland of Boggaun falls. Indexes to wills probated in many dioceses are now available in handy booklet form; unpublished indexes can be consulted in the Public Record Office. One interesting Ryan testator emerges from the list of Cashel wills, i.e. John Ryan of Gortnaskehy who had his will probated in 1791.

| Name and Place | Nature of Record | Year | Court or Registry |
|---|---|---|---|
| **O'Connor,** Hugh, Sunningdale, Donnybrook, Co. Dublin, and late of 1 Kenilworth Sq., Co. Dublin. | Probate | 1897 | P.R. |
| „ John (Rev.) ... ... | Admon. | 1812 | Prerog : |
| „ Teresa, Cole's Lane, Dublin ... | Admon. (copy) | .1920 | P.R. |
| „ William, Parkgate St., Dublin | „ „ | 1920 | „ |
| **O'Conyllan,** Teig ... ... ... | Will | d.1672 | Tuam Dio. |
| **O'Dell,** Constance, Main St., Bandon, Co. Cork. | Probate | 1861 | Cork D.R. |
| **O'Donnell,** Henry Anderson, Limerick City | „ | 1841 | Prerog : |
| „ William, Ballsbridge, Co. Dublin | Admon. (copy) | 1912 | P.R. |
| **O'Farrell,** George, Carlow ... ... | Probate | 1846 | Prerog : |
| **O'Flinn,** Andrew, Ballymoney, Co. Down ... | Admon. W.A. | 1868 | Belfast D.R. |
| **Ogden,** David, Upr. Ballycarney, Co. Wexford. | Probate | 1805 | Ferns Dio. |
| **Ogle,** Henry, Newry, Co. Armagh ... | „ | 1803 | Prerog : |
| „ Jane, Fathom, Co. Armagh ... | Admon. D.B.N. | 1813 | Newry exempt |
| „ John, Newry and Fathom ... | Probate | 1799 | Prerog : |
| **O'Grady,** Eliza, Terenure, Co. Dublin ... | Probate (copy) | 1896 | P.R. |
| „ Joseph, Rathdown Road, Dublin ... | Admon. | 1898 | „ |
| „ Julia, 27 George St., Limerick ... | Probate | 1880 | Limerick D.R |
| „ Maria de la Soledad Isabel Sofia (Hon.) | Will | 1889 | P.R. |
| „ William, Dublin ... ... ... | Admon. W.A. D.B.N. | 1848 (Orgl. Grant 1825). | Prerog : |
| **O'Hagan,** John, Newry, Co. Down ... | Probate | 1862 | P.R. |
| **O'Hara,** Charles, Lisnagarron, Co. Antrim | Grant of Admon. | 1891 | Belfast D.R. |
| „ John, Lisnagarron, Co. Antrim ... | Will and Grant | 1891 | „ |
| „ Mary, Annachmore, Collooney, Co. Sligo. | Probate | 1846 | Prerog : |
| „ Patrick, Killadoon, Celbridge, Co. Kildare. | Admon. | 1849 | „ |
| **O'Kearny,** Hatton Ronayne, Lr. Glanmire Road, Co. Cork. | „ | 1904 | Cork D.R. |
| **O'Kelly,** Patrick, Thomas St., Limerick ... | „ | 1853 | Prerog : |
| **Oliver,** Joseph, Tullymore, Co. Armagh ... | Probate | 1837 | Armagh Dio. |
| **O'Mahony,** Thaddeus (Rev.) " Holyrood " Sandymount Ave., Co. Dublin. | „ | 1903 | P.R. |
| **O'Mulrenin,** Richard J., South Circular Road, Dublin. | Probate (copy) | 1906 | „ |
| **O'Neill,** Anne, Kells, Co. Meath ... | „ | 1883 | „ |
| „ Catherine, Abbottstown, Co. Dublin | Admon. | 1862 | „ |
| „ Ellen, Carrick-on-Suir, Co. Tipperary | Probate | 1865 | Waterford D.R. |
| „ James (Rev.), Dunshaughlin, Co. Meath. | „ | 1901 | P.R. |
| „ Margaret, Meadstown, Co. Meath | „ | 1829 | Prerog : |
| „ Nicholas, Ship Street, Dublin ... | Admon. | 1817 | „ |
| **O'Reilley,** (or O'Reilly), Daniel Patrick (Rev.), St. Mary's Church, Church St., Dublin. | „ | 1895 | P.R. |
| **O'Reilly,** John, 55 Percy Place, Co. Dublin | „ | 1884 | „ |
| **Orford,** Elizabeth, Rathbride, Co. Kildare | Admon. (unad.) | 1841 | Prerog : |
| **Ormsby,** (alias Elwood), Elizabeth, Strand Hill, Cong, Co. Mayo. | „ | 1849 | „ |
| „ Thomas, Ballinamore, Co. Mayo ... | Admon. W.A. | 1836 | „ |
| **O'Rorke,** Owen, 36, 38 and 40 St. Augustine Street, Dublin. | Admon. | 1897 | P.R. |
| **Orr,** Alexander (Rev.), 10 Burlington Place, Eastbourne, Sussex. | Probate | 1897 | „ |
| „ James, Annarea, Co. Armagh ... | „ | 1842 | Armagh Dio. |
| „ James Sinclair, Ballyloughan, Co. Armagh (formerly Phibsboro', Dublin). | „ | 1863 | Armagh D.R. |

*Copy of page 59 from the fifty fifth Report of the Deputy Keeper of Public Records in Ireland, 1928 with list of testators' names.*

Gortnaskehy is sufficiently close to Boggaun to make this particular testator worthy of special note.

If the subject of our search Patrick Ryan — instead of being the son of a tenant farmer as he appears to have been — had been born into the family of a strong farmer it is likely that his father's will would be listed among the Prerogative Wills of Ireland. Genealogical abstracts in the form of chart pedigrees were made by Sir William Betham from these wills the originals of which were later destroyed in the Public Record Office fire of 1922. The abstracts covering the period 1536 to about the year 1800 are arranged in alphabetical order and run to thirty five manuscript volumes. This outstanding collection is housed in the Genealogical Office. Before consulting the actual volumes it is advisable to check first a widely available book entitled *Index to the Prerogative Wills of Ireland* by Arthur Vicars to ascertain whether the subject of one's search actually made such a will.

Also at the Genealogical Office is a second and almost equally important collection of will abstracts known as the Eustace Will Abstracts. An excellent printed index to the latter collection is available in that office.

If you are still unsuccessful in your search for that elusive last will and testament of your ancestor why not try *A Guide to Copies of Irish Wills* by Wallace Clare. This book is a substantial printed index to wills contained in such sources as learned journals, family histories and rare manuscripts. You will find copies of the book in any reasonably well stocked Irish library.

Still on the subject of wills, especially for those made in the 1700's, we can recommend the Irish Manuscripts Commission's *Registry of Deeds: Abstracts of Wills,* edited by P.B. Eustace. In the early days of the Registry's existence many wills were also apparently registered among the deeds. Genealogical abstracts have been made from these wills to form two large printed volumes covering the period 1708 to 1787. The following is an example of an abstract taken from Vol 1,page 1:

> Sullivan, Darby, Gortnecrehy, parish of Clouncagh, B. of Conelloe, Co. Limerick. 22 July 1708. Narrate, 1 1/2p., 4 Nov. 1708. Wife of Catherine Sullivan. Sons John and Thomas Sullivan. Third son Daniel, fourth son Dennis Sullivan, daughter Catherine Sullivan. John Collins, Ballynoe, parish of Clouneilty, B. Conelloe, Co. Limerick, exor.
> His real and personal estate in the Kingdom of Ireland.
> Witnesses: Teige Sullivan, Clouny, Co. Cork, Maurice Nash, Ballyhahill, Daniel O'Bryan, Curraghnageare, Richard Cantilon, Morenane, Daniel Sullivan, Gortnecrehy, John Fitzgerald, Greenhill, Timothy Sullivan, Ahadagh, Derby Sullivan and Matthew Sullivan both of the same, all of Co. Limerick.
> Memorial witnessed by: Daniel Sullivan, John Connell.
> 1, 247, 151              Thos. Sullivan (seal)
>                                a devisee

Particulars of several thousands of more wills made over the past three hundred years can be found in the Reports of the Deputy Keeper of Public

D.Grose del.          H.Brocas jc.

*The armorial altar tomb of the O'Connor family in Sligo Abbey, 1624, containing the shield and crest of the O'Connors, flanked by two figures representing St. Peter and St. Paul. In the centre compartment is a representation of Donough O'Connor and his wife Eleanor Butler kneeling in prayer. In the surrounds are numerous trophies including drum, flag, axe, shield and sword.*

Records notably the fifty fifth, fifty sixth and fifty seventh reports. Details such as the name of the testator, his place of residence and date of probate of will are set out in tabular form. You can consult copies of the reports at the National Library and, of course, at the Public Record Office itself. The actual wills themselves can be inspected at that office which, on request, will make copies available for a fee.

Wills, as we have stated, are a wonderful source of information for the pedigree hunter but not always: the following extraordinary will was made in Ireland in 1674 —

> I, John Langley, born at Wincanton, in Somersetshire, and settled in Ireland in the year 1651, now in my right mind and wits, do make my will in my own hand-writing. I do leave all my house, goods, and farm of Black Kettle of 253 acres to my son, commonly called stubborn Jack, to him and his heirs for ever, provided he marries a Protestant, but not Alice Kendrick, who called me 'Oliver's whelp'. My new buckskin breeches and my silver tobacco stopper with J.L. on the top I give to Richard Richards, my comrade who helped me off at the storming of Clonmell when I was shot through the leg. My said son Jack shall keep my body above ground six days and six nights after I am dead; and Grace Kendrick shall lay me out, who shall have for so doing Five Shillings. My body shall be put upon the oak table in the brown room, and fifty Irishmen shall be invited to my wake, and every one shall have two quarts of the best acqua vitae, and each one skein, dish and knife before him; and when the liquor is out, nail up the coffin and commit me to the earth whence I came. This is my will, witness my hand this 3rd of March 1674.
>
> John Langley

## Memorial Inscriptions

It has been said of the Irish that they are in danger of commemorating themselves to death! Be that as it may it is a happy circumstance for the person seeking his or her Irish ancestry that our forebears were generous and diligent in placing memorials over the final resting places of their dear departed. A great variety of such memorials can be seen in our country churchyards from simple iron crosses bearing only a surname to elaborate armorial altar tombs of the great Irish chieftains. Examples of some fine monuments to the families of O'Brien, McMahon, MacNamara, O'Hehir and Considine are to be seen in the Franciscan Abbey, Ennis, County Clare. Smith, in his *History of Cork* refers to the ancient tombs of the Magners, O'Callaghans, Prendergasts, Donegans, Meades, Healys and Nagles at Buttevant, County Cork. Muckross Abbey near Killarney has been for centuries the traditional resting place of the O'Donoghues, the Falveys and the MacCartheys while the chiefs of the O'Donovan, O'Hea (Hayes) and Collins septs repose in monumental splendour in Timoleague Abbey near Skibbereen, Co Cork.

The work of transcribing inscriptions from gravestones in Ireland was begun before the turn of the present century by the Association for the Preservation of the Memorials of the Dead. The published journal of the Association runs to about a dozen volumes and contains thousands of inscriptions from stones throughout the country. In addition there are numerous illustrations of tablets and monuments as well as many quaint epitaphs, rustic verses and family lore. The library of the Genealogical Office has at least one complete set of this outstanding series, the first volume of which appeared in 1888. Here are a few examples taken at random from the journal:

### Kilgefin Churchyard, Co Roscommon. (Vol.2 p.229)

Erected to the memory of the ancient family of Kilmacor by Patrick Hanly. The mothers' names for four generations were Anne Dufficy, Kate Cline, Margaret O'Farrell, Anne O'Hanley, Mabel McLoughlin, Jane O'Connor.

Also in fond memory of John Hanly 50 years, and his children James Hanly 68 years, Bridge Hanly 70, Richard 34, Jane 57, Kate 56, also his affectionate wife Ellen Hanly 64 years, Their dau. Mary 18, his uncles Martin Hanly, Rev. James Hanly P.P. Fairymount.

### Castle Caldwell, Co. Fermanagh (Vol.2 p.457)

To the
Memory
of
Denis McCabe
Fidler
who fell out of the
St. Patrick's Barge Belong
ing to Sr
James Calldwell Bart

Beware ye Fidlers of ye
Fidlers fate
Nor tempt ye deep least ye
repent too late
You ever have been deem'd to water
Foes
then shun ye lake till it with whisk'y flows
on firm land only Exercise your skill
there you may play and safely drink yr fill
D.D.D.
J.F.

### Skibbereen Abbey Churchyard, Co. Cork (Vol.6 p.246)

There is a monument in this Churchyard erected by a blacksmith, named Eugene M'Carthy of Skibbereen, to commemorate the burial place of the victims of the famine..... the following inscription appears on a marble tablet —

Precious in the sight of the Lord is the death of his Saints.

Erected to the memory of those departed ones who fell victims to the awful Famine of 1846 and 1847. Eternal Rest grant unto them O Lord and let perpetual Light shine upon them. May they rest in peace. Amen.

Owing to the absence of early parish registers in Ireland and the non-existence of burial registers gravestone inscriptions are often the only means of tracing earlier generations of many Irish families. On the occasion of a pilgrimage to the burial-place of your ancestors remember to take with you pencil and paper, a small wire brush, a pocket-knife, a piece of cloth and a large sheet of soft brown paper. You may find that you have to contend with an ivy-covered stone or one with a lightly-cut inscription that has all but vanished. If you brush and rub the stone vigorously you will be able to take an impression with the brown paper and so rescue vital details. A further generation added to your family tree should be ample reward for your patience and perseverance. There is no need to be shy in asking the advice and assistance of local people especially in regard to the location of the cemetery which, as a rule, is located at the site of the ruined old parish church or abbey.

## Religious Census 1766

Continuing our search for earlier generations of the Ryan family of Boggaun we turn our attention next to the Religious Census of 1766. This census was instituted by the Irish House of Lords and was taken up by the incumbent of each parish who listed heads of households as Catholic or Protestant. Even so the names of small cottiers and labourers rarely appeared on the census lists presumably because they were too poor to be liable for tithe assessments. Fortunately for our purpose many excellent transcripts were made by Tenison Groves, the Belfast genealogist, in the early years of the present century before the destruction of the originals in 1922.

The Tension Groves notebooks containing many thousands of names from the returns for the dioceses of Armagh, Cashel, Clogher, Cloyne, Connor, Derry, Dromore, Down, Dublin, Ferns, Kildare, Kilmore and Ossory are now in the Public Record Office, Dublin and go a long way towards offsetting the loss of the originals. The returns for Cloyne and Cashel covering the greater portion of Counties Cork and Tipperary are almost complete, and among the heads of families listed for the parish of Killavinogue are James and Thomas Ryan.

## Hearth Money Rolls 1663

Many an ancestry researcher nurtures a quiet ambition to link his forebears with one of the numerous branches of the family tree of a great Irish sept. There is of course an understandable pride in being able to display a lineage of over a thousand years of unbroken descent from an Irish chieftain to whom one owes one's name. Genealogy as we know was a strong point with the ancient Irish

## PAROCHIA DE KILLEA.

| | | Hths. | s. |
|---|---|---|---|
| Widd. Juan Boorke, Killonadag | ... | 1 | 2 |
| William White | // ... | 1 | 2 |
| Teige Morgin | // ... | 1 | 2 |
| John McLewes | // ... | 1 | 2 |
| Thomas Hackett | // ... | 1 | 2 |
| Daniell Meagher, de Parke | ... | 1 | 2 |
| James Meagher | // ... | 1 | 2 |
| William Doghin | // ... | 1 | 2 |
| Ellish Meagher | // ... | 1 | 2 |
| William Costigine | // ... | 1 | 2 |
| Connr Meagher de Garriborlinode | ... | 1 | 2 |
| Keadagh Meagher de Skahanagh | ... | 1 | 2 |
| Dermott Carroll | // ... | 1 | 2 |
| Dermott Scottye | // ... | 1 | 2 |
| Thomas Meagher | // ... | 1 | 2 |

## BARNAN AND AGHNOMEA PARISHES.

| | | | |
|---|---|---|---|
| John Ottoway, Killoskehane | ... | 2 | 4 |
| Murrogh McReger | // ... | 1 | 2 |
| Donnogh O'Doghon | // ... | 1 | 2 |
| Laghlin Fogerty | // ... | 1 | 2 |
| Roger McMurrogh | // ... | 1 | 2 |
| Roger Shannaghan | // ... | 1 | 2 |
| Laughlin Flanure | // ... | 1 | 2 |
| John McTeige | // ... | 1 | 2 |
| John Meagher Smite | // ... | 1 | 2 |
| Roger McThomas | // ... | 1 | 2 |
| John McGullerneane | // ... | 1 | 2 |
| Edmond Sweeney | // ... | 1 | 2 |
| Phillipp McCormucke | // ... | 1 | 2 |
| Josheph Loyd de Bearnane | ... | 1 | 2 |
| James Meagher | // ... | 1 | 2 |
| Darby Meagher | // ... | 1 | 2 |
| Edmond Boorke | // ... | 1 | 2 |
| Edmond Carroll | // ... | 1 | 2 |
| John Carroll | // ... | 1 | 2 |
| Murtagh Kelly | // ... | 1 | 2 |
| John Bryar | // ... | 1 | 2 |
| John Meagher | // ... | 1 | 2 |
| Keadagh Meagher | // ... | 1 | 2 |
| Thomas McKue | // ... | 1 | 2 |
| Teige Shallow | // ... | 1 | 2 |
| Edmond Quirke | // ... | 1 | 2 |
| Theobald Stapleton | // ... | 1 | 2 |
| Phillipp Russhell | // ... | 1 | 2 |
| Nicholas Russhell | // ... | 1 | 2 |
| John Meary, de Aghnemedle | ... | 1 | 2 |
| Richd. Douty | // ... | 1 | 2 |
| Thomas Shannaghan | // ... | 1 | 2 |
| Bryan Sweeny | // ... | 1 | 2 |
| Phillipp McThomas | // ... | 1 | 2 |
| Walter Vrino | // ... | 1 | 2 |
| Arthur Kenislye | // ... | 1 | 2 |
| Robt. Bruto | // ... | 1 | 2 |
| Hugh Meagher | // ... | 1 | 2 |
| Roger Shannaghan | // ... | 1 | 2 |
| Richd. Keirwan | // ... | 1 | 2 |

| | | Hths. |
|---|---|---|
| Derby Banane, de Aghnemedle | ... | 1 |
| Phillipp McRoger | // | 1 |
| Derby Shannaghan | // ... | 1 |
| John McGillfoile | // ... | 1 |

## PAROCHIA DE TEMPLEROE.

| | | |
|---|---|---|
| Bryan Sweeney, Templeroe | ... | 1 |
| Patrick Purcell | // ... | 1 |
| Edmond Meagher | // ... | 1 |
| Wm. McShane | // | 1 |
| William McGrath | // ... | 1 |
| William Gritt | // ... | 1 |

## PAROCHIA DE KILLONINOGE.

| | | |
|---|---|---|
| Bartholomew Fowkes, Clonmore | ... | 1 |
| John Ryane | // ... | 1 |
| Phillipp Carroll, Ballisorrell | ... | 1 |
| William Carroll | | 1 |
| Edmond Meagher | // | 1 |
| Derby McCnoghr | // | 1 |
| Robert Lunn, Clonbuogh | | 1 |
| William Hude | // ... | 1 |
| Daniell Headine | // ... | 1 |
| Donnogh Bergine | // | 1 |
| Therlagh Fitzpatrick, Dromard | ... | 1 |
| Roger Hamell | // | 1 |
| Derby Hogane | // ... | 1 |
| Wm. McCoreny | // | 1 |
| William Gormane | // | 1 |
| John Fighane | // | 1 |
| Murrogh Reagh | // | 1 |
| Donnogh Aghjron, Aghanoy | ... | 1 |
| Donnogh Dulchonty | // ... | 1 |
| Edmond McEvoy | // | 1 |
| Roger Quirke | // ... | 1 |
| William Buttler | // | 1 |
| Walter Buttler | // | 1 |
| Miles Cleere | // ... | 1 |
| William Troe | // ... | 1 |
| Teige Agheron | // ... | 1 |

## PAROCHIA DE CORBALLY.

| | | |
|---|---|---|
| David Welsh, Clonkrekin | ... | 1 |
| Teige Cleary | // ... | 1 |
| Teige Hynane | // ... | 1 |
| Murrogh Hinane | // | 1 |
| Phillipp Fihily | // | 1 |
| Daniell Heanin | // | 1 |
| Daniell Brimegem | // ... | 1 |
| Donogh Milline, Corbally | ... | 1 |
| William Kissine | // | 1 |
| Dermott Phichane | // ... | 1 |
| William Scully | // ... | 1 |
| Daniell McTeige | // ... | 1 |
| Dermott McWilliam | // | 1 |
| David McTeige | // ... | 1 |
| Dermott Milline | // ... | 1 |

*The Hearth Money Rolls for the parish of Killavinogue (Killaninogue), Co. Tipperary, 1665 (above) contain the name of John Ryane.*

and the main lines of the great Irish families are generally speaking well established down to the seventeenth century. Then the old gaelic order began to crumble with the consequent dispersal of families due to war, confiscation and plantation. For those whose hearts are set on long pedigrees the seventeenth century is indeed crucial to their hopes, the tracing of individuals being particularly tricky at this point in Irish history. Probably the most useful line of enquiry to pursue recordwise for the period is the Hearth Money Rolls.

Hearth Money, colloquially known as *Smoke Silver,* was a tax of two shillings on every hearth and fireplace established by act of parliament in the reign of Charles ll. The purpose of the tax was to help pay for, the wars of that penurious Stuart king. Initially the tax was payable on Lady Day and Michaelmas in equal portions; later the entire sum became payable on the tenth of January, yearly. The first collection of tax was made on Lady Day 1663 by the sheriff in each county. The persons liable to pay were entered in lists and these lists became known as the Hearth Money Rolls.

Arranged according to counties, baronies, parishes and townlands the rolls contain the names of inhabitants liable to tax, the number of hearths of which each was possessed together with the amount of tax liability. Although in later days poorer householders were exempt from the tax, no such priviledge was in force when the original rolls were compiled. Therefore it follows that a list of Hearthmoney payers is practically a list of householders. Accordingly the lists are extremely valuable for the tracing of individuals for genealogical purposes. Moreover the number of hearths with which a person is charged can be taken as an indication of his wealth and standing in the community.

For the statistically minded Sir William Petty in 1660 reckoned that a total of 300,000 hearths in Ireland represented a population of 1,300,000.

In 1788 more than a century after its introduction gross abuses in regard to the administration of the Hearthmoney tax were exposed in Grattan's Parliament by Thomas Connolly, the member from County Kildare. 'Was it not a well known fact,' said Connolly, 'that when a gentleman solicited from the minister a hearthmoney collection, that instead of its nominal value of £40 he considered it worth from £100 to £200 a year. And how did that arise but by plundering the people by taking indulgence money, and by afterwards taking their pot, their blanket and at last their door, making what return they thought fit to the public treasury'.

Bearing in mind our search for earlier generations of the Ryan family we are of course particularly interested in the Hearth Money Rolls for County Tipperary. Happily for our purpose the rolls for that county form the subject of the following book: *Tipperary Families: Hearth Money Rolls, 1665-6-7* by Thomas Laffan, Dublin 1911. On checking the returns for the parish of Killavinogue, barony of Ikerrin, we observe, among the list of taxpayers for that parish, the name of John Ryane thus enabling us to roll back the pedigree of the Ryan family to the year 1665.

## A Tipperary Sept: The O'Ryans of Owney

The Ryan family of Boggaun was clearly an offshoot of the O'Mulryans of Owney, an important sept whose descendants are today so widely distributed throughout Tipperary and adjoining counties. From time beyond recall the Ryans occupied the tract of land west of a line joining Nenagh and Newport fronting Lough Derg until war and privation forced them far beyond the confines of their ancestral lands. The story of the Ryans of Owney is told in *Records of Four Tipperary Septs* by M. Callanan, Galway, 1935, and there is no need to repeat here the wealth of detail contained in that book. As we traverse in spirit the wild country once called Owney we pause for a moment at the ruined Ryan castle of Killoscully before moving southwards over the Keeper Mountains to Foilaclug in the parish of Hollyford where according to local tradition Eamon an Chnoic or Edmond Knock Ryan, the Rapparee, is buried. Further to the west, on the Limerick-Tipperary border we enter the now ruined twelfth century cistercian monastery of Abington, in a sequestered corner of which a monument to the Ryans bore this inscription —

> The most noble William Ryan, chief of the country of Owney, the head and prince of the ancient family of the Ryans caused this monument to be erected to himself, his wife and his children.
>
> The honour of his posterity and praise of his ancestors caused William Ryan to construct this graceful work.
>
> Alas, how much nobility proved in peace and war, how much holy faith, virtue and distinguished fame are enclosed in this sepulchral monument of the Ryans. If it should be asked why that which is not destined to die should be shut up, the bones alone are covered in the earth but the other parts that know not death will enjoy perpetual day.
>
> The praise, virtue, glory and honour of the Ryan race will live for ever in this honoured name. A.D. 1632.

---

### Hearth Money Rolls

Antrim Co. 1669
Derry Co. 1663
Down Co. Subsidy Roll 1663
Tyrone Co. 1666
    Transcripts in Presbyterian Historical Society, microfilms of same in Public Record Office, Belfast.
Armagh Co.
Donegal Co.
    Transcripts in Genealogical Office.
Dublin Co. 1664
    Printed in Journal of Kildare Archaeological Society, vols. 10, 11, 1927-30.
Fermanagh Co.
    Printed in Enniskillen, Parish and Town, by W.H. Dundas, 1913.

Louth Co.
    Printed (in part) in History of Kilsaran etc., by James B. Leslie, Dundalk, 1908.
Monaghan Co.
    Printed in The History of County Monaghan etc., by D.C. Rushe, Dundalk, 1921.
Tipperary Co.
    Printed in Tipperary Families etc., edited by Thomas Laffan, Dublin, 1911.
Wicklow Co.
    Printed in Journal of Royal Society of Antiquaries of Ireland, vols.5, 6.

# CHAPTER 2

# *Records and Record Repositories*

What records of a genealogical nature exist in Ireland and where can they be found?

At the outset it should be realised that Irish records cannot match those of countries say like England or France, certainly not over the last three hundred years. The Irish were not great record keepers, partly due to historical circumstances, partly to the degree of reliance placed on oral tradition. This is best illustrated by the fact that of the hundreds of thousands of people who left Ireland during the period 1845-1855 on account of the Famine, scarcely a single record was kept at ports of embarkation such as Queenstown (Cobh), Dublin, Galway, Derry and Belfast. The destruction of the Record Tower in Dublin Castle in 1710 and later the Public Record Office in 1922 further depleted already lacking primary source materials. Despite these disasters, however, it is surprising how often Irish records can prove adequate when used to the fullest possible extent. The following is a general guide to Irish libraries, record offices and archives.

## The Genealogical Office

The Genealogical Office, 2, Kildare St. incorporates the Office of the Chief Herald and the State Heraldic Museum.

Institutional heraldry and genealogy first came to Ireland in 1552 when the country was constituted a separate heraldic jurisdiction in the reign of Edward VII. Bartholomew Butler, first king of arms and principal herald of Ireland, was styled 'Ulster' after the royal province of that name —hence the term 'Ulster's Office'. His main function was to confirm and grant coats of arms — so the office naturally became known as the Office of Arms. In 1943 the office was renamed the Genealogical Office and is now headed by a state herald with the designation of 'Chief Herald of Ireland'.

The office has functioned continuously since the year of its foundation, a fact clearly attested by its records. Four official sets of registers, which derive from its historic functions, are extant, namely, the Register of Arms, the Register of Pedigrees, the Books of Heraldic Visitation and the Funeral Entry Books of Ireland. Of these the Register of Arms and the Register of Pedigrees are current and ongoing.

Under the terms of the patent of his appointment as King of Arms, Butler was required to ratify existing coats and assign new ones to meritorious individuals through the issue of letters patent. The formal, and at times, informal recording of such ratifications and grants constitutes the single most important set of records of the Genealogical Office, namely, the Register of Arms.

Article three of his oath of office enjoined on the king of arms to have knowledge of all noblemen in his province and 'their issue truly to register'. The resulting 'Registration of Pedigree' series based on attested materials and set down in a variety of genealogical forms comes next in importance among the official collections of the Office of Arms.

A third set of records proper to the Office we may term the books of Heraldic Visitations. Broadly speaking the need for such visitations arose after the disappearance of the medieval feudal army which in the days of military heraldry provided heralds with the opportunity of armorial stock-taking, so to speak, in the course of operational forays and occasional hostings.

Warrants dated 1567 and 1607 empowered Nicholas Narbon and Daniel Molyneux, successors to Bartholomew Butler, to repair into the several parts of Ireland and enquire into the 'arms, pedigrees and genealogies ... of all noblemen'. As the record shows their heraldic enquiries rarely took them outside the Pale and were confined mainly to counties Dublin and Wexford.

A series of seventeen volumes known as 'Funeral Entries' made from funeral certificates submitted to the king of arms, mainly in the seventeenth century, accounts for the fourth set of official records appertaining to the Office of Arms. This set of records was grounded on an order of the Lord Deputy and Privy Council dated 4 Aug. 1627 'for the better preservation of the memory of the nobility and gentry of this realm, their marriages, posterity and arms. The king of arms is hereby straightly charged to make a true and fair entry of the certificates of the matches, issues, times of decease ...... of all such of the nobility and gentry of this realm as shall happen to die......'

Thus over the first one hundred and fifty years of its existence (1552-1700) the pattern of official recording in the Office of Arms was established : two of the four sets of records referred to above are current, namely the Register of Arms and Registration of Pedigrees.

The next phase (1700-1800) in the development of the Office is marked by an extension of the duties of the king of arms from the purely heraldic and genealogical into what might be termed precedence and state ceremonial — activities which centered round the court of the viceroy, the English king's representative in Ireland.

Two sets of Office records originating in the eighteenth century illustrate this development. The first of these is entitled the 'Lords Entry' volumes wherein Irish Peers were required to have their coats of arms and other family particulars entered to enable them to be placed on the 'Peerage List' of the king of arms who duly introduced them to the Irish House of Lords. The second set relates to the creation and organisation of the Order of St. Patrick, the Irish order of chivalry instituted in Dublin in 1783 and of which the king of arms was registrar.

The third distinctive phase of development in the Office of Arms took place between 1800 and 1900, a century which saw a considerable expansion in what might be termed the ancillary holdings of the Office —thanks mainly to the industry of Sir William Betham and John Burke.

Among Betham's more notable additions to the records was a thirty volume set of abstracts from Irish prerogative wills and his twenty three volume 'Red Book' series of family pedigrees grounded mainly on official documents. Much of the armorial matter in the office was, of course, published by Burke in his *General Armory,* 1884 and it was probably due to his influence that the holdings of the Office of Arms were exempted from the provisions of the 1867 Public Records Act and so saved from destruction in 1922.

One of the principal activities of the Office continues to be the design — and assignment of official heraldic achievements to individuals and corporate bodies, where these fall within its traditional jurisdiction. Such assignments are effected through the issue of letters patent over the seal of the Office and the signature of the Chief Herald under the authority of the Government of Ireland.

Due to the growing desire of ordinary people to identify at least some of their immediate forebears the Genealogical Office has become a focal point to which people of Irish descent around the world address themselves when seeking advice on such matters as surnames, family history and ancestry tracing. In addition to providing information on these and allied questions the Office offers a mail research and report service for a standard fee.

The theme of the Heraldic Museum is the heraldry of Ireland and Europe and its purpose is to demonstrate the history, development and uses of heraldry over the centuries. The museum contains a variety of heraldic exhibits including flags, seals, glass and china ware, bookplates, insignia, coins and medals, as well as an exemplification of the national, provincial, civic and municipal heraldry of Ireland.

## The Office of the Registrar-General

The office of the Registrar-General is located at 8-11, Lombard St. East, Dublin. The office is open to the public in ordinary office hours Monday to Friday. There is a public search room where one can do one's own research. The office has registers of births, marriages and deaths from 1 January, 1864. In addition Church of Ireland (Protestant) weddings are on record from 1 April 1845. Certified copies of entries in the registers are issued for a standard fee.

Of the three types of certificate issued by the Registrar-General, certificates of birth are the most desirable, so to speak, from a genealogical point of view.

Such certificates indicate place of birth — street address or townland, as the case may be — name and occupation of father and maiden name of mother. Particulars included on marriage certificates include the names of the fathers of the contracting parties and the identity of witnesses to the marriage. Certificates of death will be found to be of little value to the family historian.

### The Public Record Office

The Public Record Office is located in the Four Courts Building on Inn's Quay and despite its destruction by fire in 1922 is still a happy hunting ground for the family researcher. The Office forms part of the Ministry of Justice and the Minister is *ex officio* keeper of all records. Accordingly all correspondence should be addressed to the Deputy-Keeper. The visitor to the Office will be shown to the search room where the desired record can be consulted. Among the chief collections of the Office are Betham's notebooks containing genealogical abstracts from all prerogative wills up to the year 1800, the Tithe Composition Applotment Books for all counties of the Republic, Marriage Licence Bonds (Protestant) covering the period 1650-1845, Will and Census records not destroyed in 1922, and microfilm copies of many Church of Ireland parochial registers. Mechanical copying facilities and clerking services are available for a stipulated fee.

### The Registry of Deeds

The Registry of Deeds is located in the King's Inns, Henrietta Street off Dublin's Bolton Street. This Office has records extant from 1708, the year of its foundation. It is open to the public daily from 10.00 a.m. to 4.00 p.m. and contains a search room where one can do one's research. A great deal of information of a genealogical nature is contained in its records of deeds, leases, business transactions, marriage articles and wills. Two indexes, one surnames, the other placenames, provide the key to the source material in the Office.

### The National Library of Ireland

The National Library of Ireland, located in Kildare St., by Parliament Buildings, has extensive printed and manuscript materials relating to all aspects of Irish civilisation. The open access general reference section in the main reading room has some useful items of a topographical and genealogical nature. The call number of the book sought must first be ascertained in the indexes before a request for such a book will be serviced. The Library is open to the public daily from 10.00 a.m. to 9.00 p.m. (Friday 10.00 a.m. to 5.00 p.m.)

## The Public Record Office of Northern Ireland

The Public Record Office of Northern Ireland, Balmoral Avenue, Belfast, has a considerable corpus of genealogical material of interest to people whose antecedents came from the northern counties of Ireland. The search room is open to the public daily from 10.00 a.m. to 5.00 p.m.. There is a card index to the numerous pedigrees, family papers, wills, land records, deeds, leases, marriage settlements etc., which the Office possesses. Of special interest is the fact that the Office has microfilm copies of Church of Ireland registers for parishes in Counties Armagh, Antrim, Down, Derry, Tyrone and Fermanagh.

## Ulster Historical Foundation

The Ulster Historical Foundation, 66 Balmoral Avenue, Belfast is a non-profit making public service agency established in 1957 to provide a genealogical searching service on a fee-paying basis. Since then it has completed over 5,000 searches, mainly for overseas clients. The minimum amount of information required before a search can begin is the place (preferably townland or parish) where ancestors lived and their religion. The initial registration fee for a search is £15 sterling and this entitles clients to the benefits of membership in the Ulster Genealogical and Historical Guild for one year. The foundation has an active programme of publication in progress and a list of publications for sale will be supplied on request.

## Registrar-General's Office Northern Ireland

The Registrar-General for Northern Ireland has records of births, marriages and deaths from 1921 onwards. His office is located in Oxford House, Chichester St., Belfast.

## Trinity College

Trinity College, Dublin, the oldest higher institution of learning in Ireland, houses the Book of Kells, the celebrated illuminated manuscript and crowning glory of Ireland's golden age. The registers of the College from the year of its foundation in 1593 have been published — *Alumni Dublinenses* — containing particulars of some 35,000 students up to about 1860.

## The Royal Irish Academy

The Royal Irish Academy, 19 Dawson Street, Dublin, has a wide ranging collection of printed and manuscript material of particular interest to the Gaelic scholar. A booklet entitled *The Royal Irish Academy and its Collection* is available from the Academy.

## The State Paper Office

The State Paper Office, Dublin Castle, houses records which formerly belonged to the Chief Secretary's Office. The records include material such as convict papers, convict reference books, criminal index books, registers of convicts sentenced to penal servitude, the 1798 Rebellion papers, proceedings of the Dublin Society of United Irishmen, Fenian and Land League records, papers of the evicted tenants commission and Cabinet papers from 1922 onwards. Material from the office relating to convicts whose good conduct entitled them to apply to have their wives and children sent out to join them in New South Wales, 1828-1855 can be read in The Irish Ancestor in the 1979 and subsequent issues of that periodical.

## The Representative Church Body Library

The Representative Church Body Library, Braemor Park, Rathgar, Dublin, has a lot of material of special interest to people whose ancestors were in the Church of Ireland tradition. The library possesses extensive lists of Church of Ireland clergy, many with biographical notes attached which provide a valuable record of the clergy, their careers and their children. The library has recently acquired a number of original parochial registers of baptisms, marriages and burials from various Church of Ireland parishes around the country.

## Church Records

Church Records are of prime importance to the family researcher on account of the late commencement of state records in Ireland. Since, as a rule, people are baptised and married in their own parishes it goes without saying that parish registers are in the custody of local clergy. Catholic registers date from about 1750 for city parishes but, generally speaking, books for rural parishes commence much later. Most of the parish books have by now been recorded on film by the National Library of Ireland. A complete list of clergy and parishes will be found in the *Irish Catholic Directory* published annually in January. Protestant registers were dealt a severe blow by the destruction of the Public Record Office in 1922 when more then half the books in the entire country perished in the fire. Most of the existing books have been microfilmed by the two Public Record Offices. The Parish Register Society has printed a number of books mainly relating to Dublin city parishes. The *Irish Church Directory* gives the names and addresses of all Church of Ireland clergy in Ireland.

## Presbyterian Records

The Presbyterian tradition has always been very strong in Ireland ever since 1613 when the first Minister Edward Brice settled in Ballycarry near Larne,

County Antrim. In 1819 a Presbyterian Synod decreed — 'That every minister of this Synod shall keep, or cause to be kept, a regular registry of all marriages celebrated by him, stating the date of each marriage, the names of the parties, the congregations or parishes in which they reside and the names of at least two witnesses present at the ceremony. Each minister is enjoined to register, or cause to be registered, in a book to be kept for that purpose, the names of all the children baptised by him, the dates of their birth and baptism, the names of their parents and the places of residence'.

That is not to say that many congregations did not keep records prior to 1819. They did, — and the Presbyterian Historical Society has an impressive list of baptismal and marriage registers prior to 1820. Also among the Society's records are copies of the Religious Census of 1766 for many parishes in Ulster, lists of Protestant householders for counties Antrim, Derry and Donegal 1740 as well as a census (or what virtually amounts to one) of Presbyterians taken in the year 1775.

Another source of information are the Certificates of Transference which were given to members leaving a district to show that they were free of church censure. They took the form of brief life histories. The following from the parish of Dundonald, Co. Down will serve as an example —

> Dundonald Aprile 8th 1725 that David Cook and Margaret George his wife were orderly persons while with us and were admitted to Christian Communion.

Enquiries regarding Presbyterian Records should be directed to the Society's headquarters at Church House, Fisherwick Place, Belfast. Finally, do remember that for historical reasons records of Presbyterian births and marriages will often be found in the registers of the Established Church. So do not overlook that source if your ancestors happened to be of Irish Presbyterian stock.

### Huguenot Records

Almost three hundred years have passed since the migration to Ireland of a large number of French Protestant refugees known as Huguenots. Exiles for conscience sake, they were forced to flee France leaving all their possessions behind. But France's loss — brought about by religious persecution of Louis XIV — was Ireland's gain. Such was the contribution of the 'gentle and profitable strangers' to the culture of their adopted country that the marks of their influence are to this day clearly discernible. D'Olier Street, for example, is named after Jeremiah D'Olier, Governor of the Bank of Ireland, who was High Sheriff of Dublin in 1778. His ancestor, Isaac D'Olier, a Huguenot refugee, settled first in Amsterdam, and afterwards in Dublin.

The refugees who came to Dublin settled for the most of the part in the 'Liberties' alongside Christ Church Cathedral where they began the manufacture of tabinet, more generally known as Irish poplin. The demand for tabinet was such that in the early 1700's a number of Huguenot artisans left London for Dublin where they extended the manufacture. The Coombe and Weaver's Square became their principal quarters. Up to the beginning of the 19th century this trade was very prosperous but frequent strikes did much to ruin the industry. The manufacture was lost and the 'Liberties', instead of being the richest, became one of the poorest parts of Dublin.

Several well remembered names in Ireland, outstanding in various walks of life, are of Huguenot origin. Richard Chenevix Trench who became Archbishop of Dublin in the last century; Henry Maturin, Senior Fellow of Trinity College; Dion Boucicault, brilliant actor and author of melodramas, (who does not remember The Wicklow Wedding and The Seachraun!); Joseph Sheridan Le Fanu, the novelist — were all of Huguenot descent. The name of La Touche is inseparably linked with the establishment of banking in Ireland. David Digues La Touche, son of a noble Protestant family that possessed considerable estates near Orleans, accompanied King William to Ireland in 1688. On retiring from military service he founded a silk and poplin manufactory in Dublin. He was entrusted with the deposits of money and valuables by his fellow refugees and this suggested the formation of a bank, located near Dublin Castle. The former Munster and Leinster Bank is a lineal descendant of La Touche's concern. He died in 1745.

The Huguenot community in Dublin had a number of places of worship notably St. Mary's Chapel in St. Patrick's Cathedral. The formal opening of this Chapel is thus described in the *London Gazette* of the 21st May, 1666:

> 'The Archbishop of Dublin, with the Dean and Chapter of St. Patrick's having granted to the French Protestants of this city St. Marie's Chapel, for their Church Assembly, a place depending on this Cathedral, His Grace, the Duke of Ormond, Lord Lieutenant of Ireland, who had by his bounty contributed very largely to its reparation, was pleased to countenance their first assembly with his presence, whither he came on Sunday, April 29, his Guard and Gentlemen preceding him, with the Maces and Swords carried before him, accompanied by the Lord Primate of Ireland, the Lord Archbishop of Dublin, Lord High Chancellor of Ireland, the Council of State, and Several great Lords and Other persons of quality of Both persuasions, followed by the Lord Mayor, with the Sheriffs and Officers of the City, who had the Sword and Mace likewise carried before him.'

In 1705 a second French congregation met in the New Church of St. Mary's or Mary's Abbey or little St. Patrick's as it was variously styled. This lasted as an independent church until 1716 when it joined itself to St. Patrick's with a common set of church registers. The burial ground of these churches was at the end of Cathedral Lane off Kevin Street and was a portion of a piece of ground commonly known as the Cabbage Garden — from the plants originally grown in it. It has not been used for burials since the year 1858.

In addition to St. Patrick's and St. Mary's there were two further Huguenot congregations of note in Dublin. One of these congregations met in Wood

Street off Bride Street and was sometimes called the French Congregation of St. Brigide's. The other congregation had its chapel in Lucy Lane, which was afterwards known as Mass Street, and is now Chancery Place. This was also called the French Church by the Inns and the French Church of Golblac Lane. It was sold in the year 1773 to the Presbyterian congregation of Skinner's Row. Its burial ground was in Merrion Row, off St. Stephen's Green, where burials took place up to the early years of the present century.

The parish registers, containing records of births, marriages and deaths from 1680 to 1830, for all four Huguenot Churches in Dublin have been printed in volumes 7 and 14 of the publications of the Huguenot Society London. Dublin's Genealogical Office has copies of these volumes.

Outside the Metropolis, probably the most celebrated Huguenot settlement was at Portarlington in County Laois formerly Queen's County. The refugees, by their industry, set a good example to the local people and shortly after their settlement Portarlington became the model town of the County. The refugees, as was their practice, formed themselves into a congregation and two churches were erected for their accommodation. The old French service was read in these churches down to the year 1817, when service in English took its place, as the French language had ceased to be understood in the neighbourhood. The registers of the French Church at Portarlington are printed in volume 19 of the H.S.L. publications.

A number of smaller colonies of Huguenots were established here and there throughout Ireland where they started various branches of manufacture. A branch of the linen trade was started at Kilkenny, and at Limerick the refugees established the lace and glove trades. The woollen manufacture at Cork was begun by James Fontaine, a member of the noble family of de la Fontaine.

Finally, we might ask how much present day prosperous towns such as Waterford, Youghal, Bandon and Lisburn owe to their former Huguenot benefactors.

## Palatine Records

*In the year seventeen hundred and nine*
*In came the brass-coloured Palatine*
*From the ancient banks of the Swabian Rhine*

The traveller in the quiet countryside particularly in County Limerick may occasionally to his surprise chance upon names like Teskey, Switzer, Delmage, Fitzelle, Hartwick, Shire, Sparling, Piper, Embury, Glazier, Miller and Heck. On enquiry he would no doubt be proudly informed by bearers of these names that their forebears were of Palatine stock. Such names, of course, readily identify a large group of families who settled in Ireland, having been forced to flee the Palatine province of the Rhine because of religious persecution occasioned by the wars of the Spanish Succession.

*At the Palatine's cottage door.*

In September 1709 upwards of eight hundred German speaking Protestant refugees landed at the port of Dublin. As many more sailed directly to North America where they settled principally in Pennsylvania and North Carolina. Those who remained in Ireland were settled mainly on the Southwell (Rathkeale) and Oliver (Kilfinane) estates in County Limerick and to a lesser extent in north County Kerry. They were allowed eight acres of land for every man, woman and child at five shillings rent per acre, the Government undertaking to pay the entire amount of rent for twenty years.

In 1760 John Wesley visited the Palatine community in County Limerick: under date of July 9 we read in his journal -

> 'I rode over to Killiheen, a German settlement, nearly twenty miles south of Limerick. It rained all the way but the earnestness of the poor people made us quite forget it. In the evening I preached to another colony of Germans at Ballygarane. The third is at Court Matrass, a mile from Killiheen. I suppose three such towns are scarce to be found again in England or Ireland. There is no cursing or swearing, no Sabbath-breaking, no drunkenness, no ale-house in any of them. How will these poor foreigners rise up in the judgement against those that are round about them.'

Some twenty years later the historian Ferrar, following a visit to the same area, left us the following account of the Palatine settlement in Co. Limerick -

> 'The Palatines preserve their language, but it is declining; they sleep between two beds; they appoint a burgomaster to whom they appeal in all disputes. They are industrious men and have leases from the proprietor of the land at reasonable rents; they are consequently better fed and clothed than the generality of Irish peasants. Besides, their mode of husbandry and crops are better than those of their neighbours. They have by degrees left off their sour krout, and feed on potatoes, butter, milk, oaten and wheaten bread, some meat and fowles, of which they rear many.... The women are very industrious.... Besides their domestic employments and the care of their children, they reap the corn, plough the land and assist the men in everything. In short the Palatines have benefited the country by increasing tillage and are a laborious and independent people who are mostly employed on their small farms.'

Today their numbers are greatly reduced due to emigration and to the fact that the Government discontinued its original rent-free land scheme. Moreover, the brown-eyed dark-haired Palatine girls did not escape the attentions of the local farmers' sons if we are to judge by that well-known Munster ballad entitled *The Palatine's Daughter* –

> *As I roved out one evening through the woods of Ballyseedy,*
> *Whom should I meet on a cool retreat but a Palatine's daughter........*
> *You'll find gold and silver, oh! and land without tax or charges,*
> *And a pretty lass to wed if you choose a Palatine's daughter.*

If a desire to establish roots is about to send you in quest of your Irish-Palatine forebears you can indulge in a little preliminary armchair research by procuring a copy of *The Palatine Families of Ireland* by Hank Jones. This privately printed book is a chronicle of two hundred and six Palatine families who made their homes in places like Rathkeale, Ballingrane, Adare, Killiheen and Kilfinane. Appended to the book is a list of source material dealing with the Palatines in Ireland calculated to keep the most avid researcher busy for a long time.

### Quaker Records

People whose ancestors were in the Quaker tradition in Ireland should have little difficulty in tracing their forebears, thanks to the fact that members of the Society of Friends evidently brought to bear on record keeping the same exacting standards that govern the conduct of their everyday lives. After the visit to Ireland of George Fox, founder of the Society in 1669, regular meetings both for worship and business were established and concise and accurate accounts of the proceedings of such meetings made. A few years previously in 1654 William Edmundson, a native of Westmoreland, convened the first settled meeting in Ireland at Lurgan, Co. Armagh, attended by Richard and Anthony Jackson, John Thompson, Richard Fayle, John Edmundson and William Moon. Quickly, Meetings were established in all four provinces, the first Leinster Meeting taking place in Dublin about 1655 at the home of Richard Fowkes, a tailor, near Polegate. In Munster there were Meeting Houses in most of the major market towns including Cork, Kinsale, Limerick, Waterford, Youghal and Bandon.

Great value was attached by the Society to the preservation of records of all kinds. Records of births, marriages and deaths, in addition to giving the usual details of such events, are actually arranged in family groups with a system of page references to individuals born or married later, thus making possible the identification of the entire family group.

Records relating to the provinces of Munster, Leinster and Connaught are preserved in the Friends Meeting House in Eustace Street off Dublin's Dame Street. Here are deposited volumes of births, marriages and deaths from places as far apart as Lisburn in County Antrim to Youghal in County Cork, ranging in date from the mid-1600's to the present day. Among the records housed here are six manuscript volumes of Quaker wills, mainly 17th and 18th century, from the Meetings at Carlow, Edenderry, Mountmellick, Wexford and Dublin. Also in the Historical Library at Eustace Street are some 3,000 letters of and to Friends containing many well known signatures, a few journals, diaries and much correspondence relative to relief work, especially that done during the Famine of 1847, together with a large file of manuscript pedigrees compiled by Thomas Webb of Dublin. If for one reason or another you are unable to visit the Society's headquarters in Eustace Street, the library staff will undertake to search the records on your behalf for a fee.

Records relating to the province of Ulster are held in the Friends Meeting

House, Lisburn, Co. Antrim. In the archives here are preserved vital statistics relating to the province of Ulster and beyond, including records of the following Meetings — Antrim, Ballinderry, Ballyhagan, Ballymoney, Coleraine, Cootehill, Hillsborough, Lisburn, Lurgan, Oldcastle and Rathfryland. A most extensive account of the records at Lisburn will be found in the Report of the Deputy Keeper, Public Record Office, Belfast, 1951-53, pp. 29-309. Should you wish to know more about Quaker records the following publication will prove helpful — *Guide to Irish Quaker Records* by Olive C. Goodbody.

## Ancestry Periodicals

Once we find a record of our ancestors instinctively we begin to wonder what manner of men and women they were. What of the faces behind the names? How did the Irish in the past really live? What did they wear? What kind of homes had they? These are questions which various issues of the Irish Ancestor help to answer. This lavishly illustrated periodical is edited by Miss Rosemary ffolliott, Fethard, Co. Tipperary, Ireland to whom enquires regarding subscription rates and so forth should be addressed.

Another useful periodical is the The Irish Genealogist, journal of the Irish Genealogical Research Society. The object of this society is to promote and encourage the study of Irish genealogy and to make some contribution towards repairing the loss of records sustained in the destruction of the Public Record Office by collecting books and manuscripts relating to genealogy, heraldry and kindred subjects. Those interested in becoming members are advised to write to the Secretary of the Society.

## Availability of Records

Those who are giving some thought to tracing relatives and ancestors in Ireland will be encouraged on learning that authorities in Irish libraries, archives and record offices are liberal in regard to making available to members of the public items from their collections for research and study purposes. Short of requesting for private perusal MS.58 Trinity College Library (this happens to be the Book of Kells!) genuinely interested enquirers can expect to be given facilities to inspect almost any document that is a public record. It is hoped that readers will get a clear idea from the lists that follow of the nature and extent of the records available in the various Irish record repositories. These lists can in no sense be regarded as comprehensive but it would be fair to say that they illustrate the amount of record material still available despite the ravages of man and time.

# CHAPTER 3

# *Irish County Maps*

In 1837 Samuel Lewis, surveyor and cartographer, published *A Topographical Dictionary of Ireland,* consisting of historical and statistical descriptions, alphabetically arranged, of the several counties, cities, boroughs, towns, parishes and villages that comprise the country. In the same year Lewis published a series of elegant and austere maps to accompany his dictionary. That series, comprising thirty two finely engraved county maps, is reproduced in the section that follows.

Lewis' maps reflected the age in which he lived and were inevitably influenced by the social and economic environment of his day. His meticulously delineated roadways, for example, underline his preoccupation with means of physical communication over the landscape — all perfectly understandable against a background of rising population and modest commercial development.

Of interest to both local and family historians is the fact that the maps were clearly designed to illustrate the narrative accounts of places described in the dictionary, e.g.

> Abbeyknockmoy, a parish, in the barony of Tyaquin, county of Galway, and province of Connaught, 7 miles (S.E.) from Tuam, on the road from NEWTOWNBELLEW to GALWAY; containing 2866 inhabitants. . . .

In both the dictionary and atlas, the modern Irish counties of Laois (Leix) and Offaly will be found under their 19th century designations of Queen's County and King's County, respectively.

It should be noted that distances referred to in the dictionary are expressed in Irish miles while the maps have two scales, one expressed in English miles, the other in Irish miles.

**Key to maps**

| | |
|---|---|
| Baronies | S L I E V A R D A G H |
| Market towns | CASHEL |
| Parishes | Templederry |
| Villages | *Ballyporeen* |

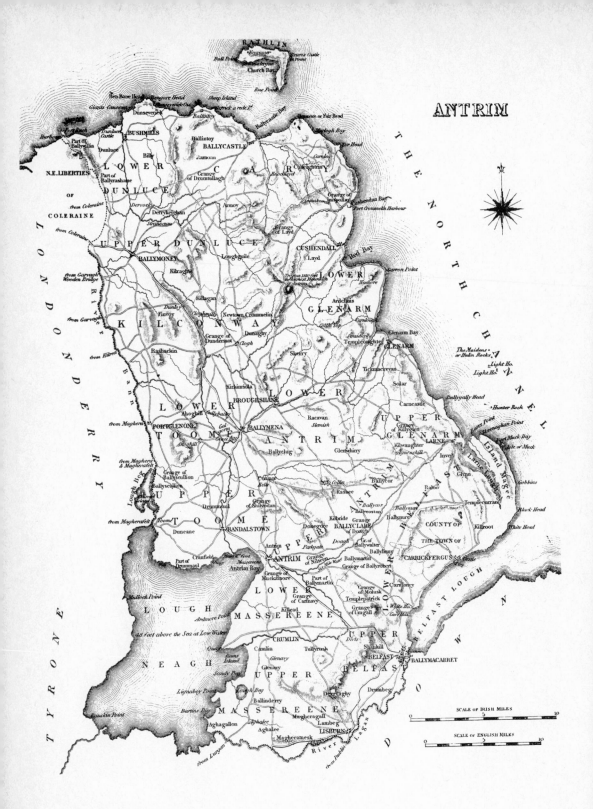

ANTRIM

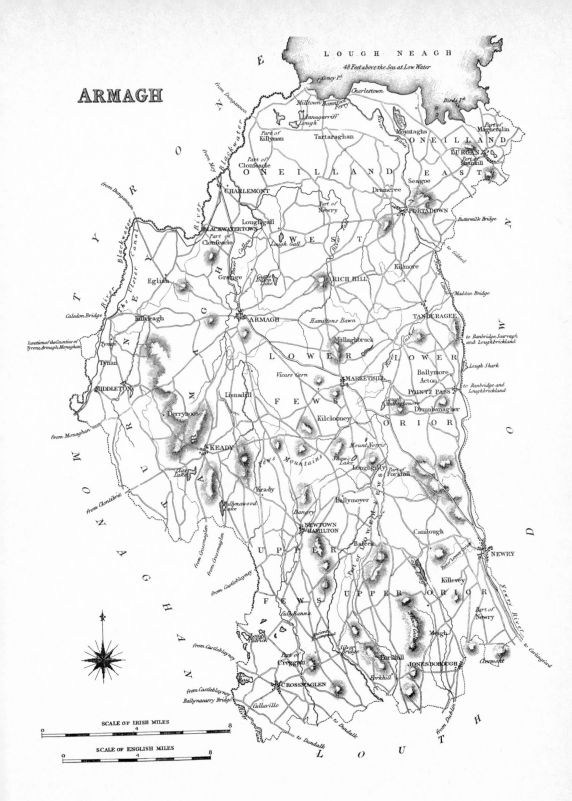

# ARMAGH

LOUGH NEAGH

48 Feet above the Sea at Low Water

CARLOW

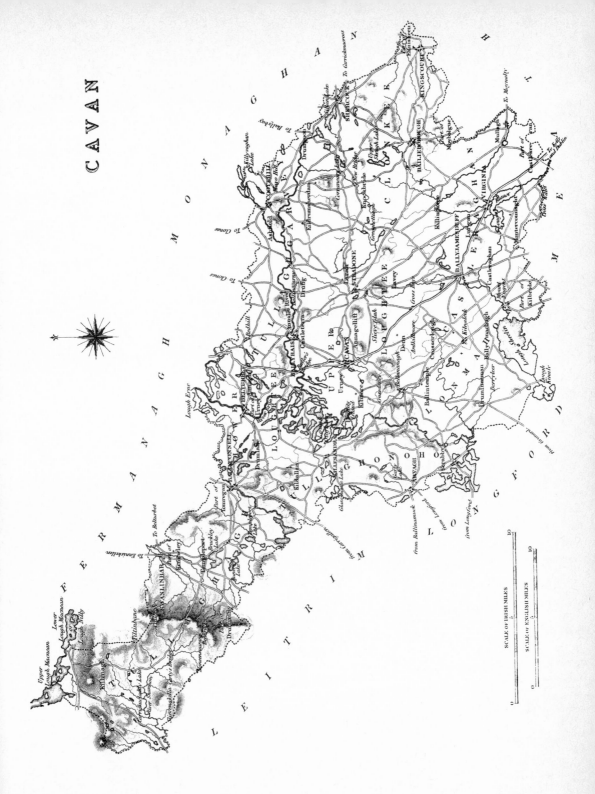

# CLARE

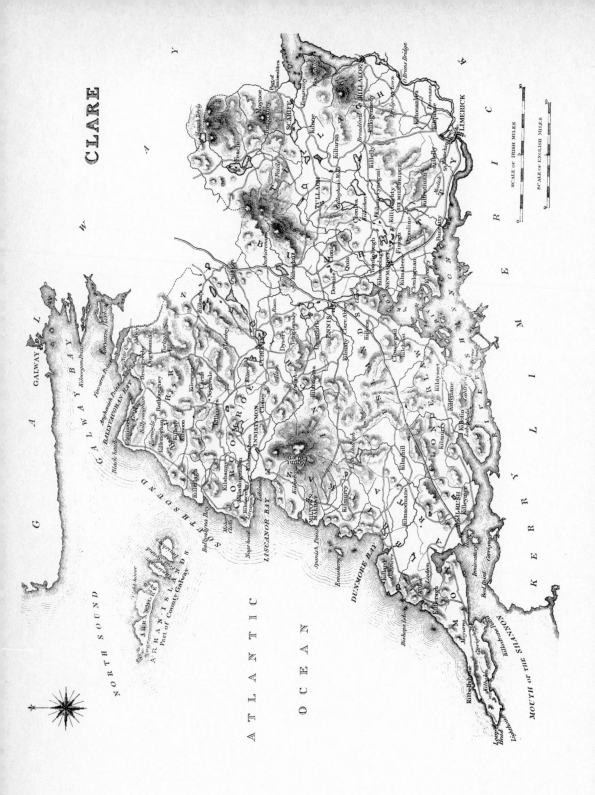

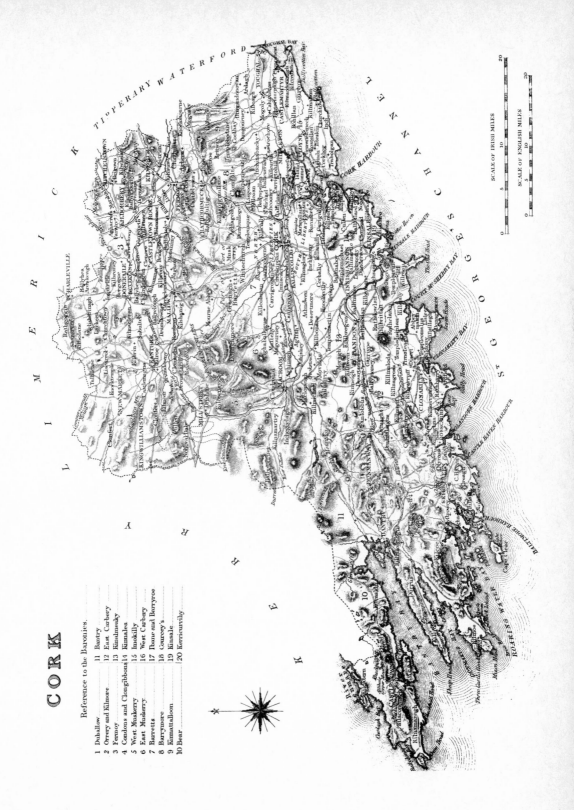

# CORK

Reference to the Baronies.

1 Duhallow
2 Orrery and Kilmore
3 Fermoy
4 Condons and Clongibbons
5 West Muskerry
6 East Muskerry
7 Barretts
8 Barymore
9 Kinnattalloon
10 Bear

11 Bantry
12 East Carbery
13 Kinnelmeaky
14 Kinnalea
15 Imokilly
16 West Carbery
17 Ibane and Barryroe
18 Courcey's
19 Kinsale
20 Kerricurrihy

SCALE OF IRISH MILES

SCALE OF ENGLISH MILES

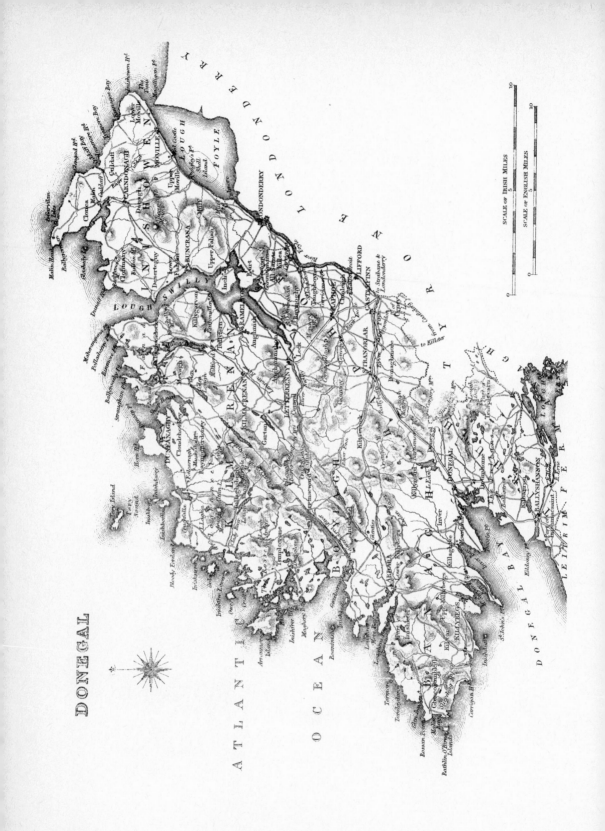

DONEGAL

SCALE OF IRISH MILES

SCALE OF ENGLISH MILES

48

# DOWN

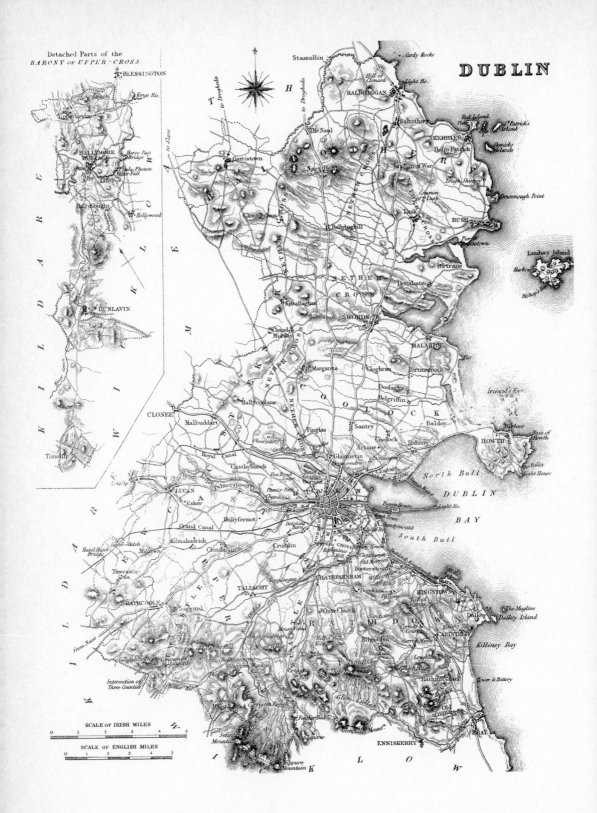

# DUBLIN

Detached Parts of the
*BARONY of UPPER-CROSS.*

BLESSINGTON

BALLYMORE
EUSTACE

DUNLAVIN

Timoth

SCALE OF IRISH MILES
0  1  2  3  4  5

SCALE OF ENGLISH MILES
0  1  2  3  4  5

Stamullin

BALBRIGGAN

Balrothery

SKERRIES

Holm Patrick

Man of War

RUSH

Lambay Island

The Naul

Garristown

Ballyboghill

Portrane

Donabate

Kilsallaghan

SWORDS

MALAHIDE

Portmarnock

St Margarets

Cloghran

Doolagh

Belgriffin

Ireland's Eye

Ballycoolane

CLONEE

Malluddart

Finglas

Santry

Coolock

Baldoyle

HOWTH

Observatory

Glasnevin

Artane

Raheny

Royal Canal

Castleknock

LUCAN

Esker

Phœnix Park

DUBLIN

DUBLIN
BAY

North Bull

South Bull

Ballyfermot

Grand Canal

Kilmahudrick

Clondalkin

Crumlin

Rathmines

Booterstown

Black Rock

RATHFARNHAM

KINGSTOWN

TALLAGHT

White Church

Dundrum

DALKEY

Dalkey Island

RATHCOOLE

Saggard

Kilgobbin

CABINTELY

Killiney Bay

Newcastle

Three Rock

Rathmichael

ENNISKERRY

BRAY

KILDARE

WICKLOW

50

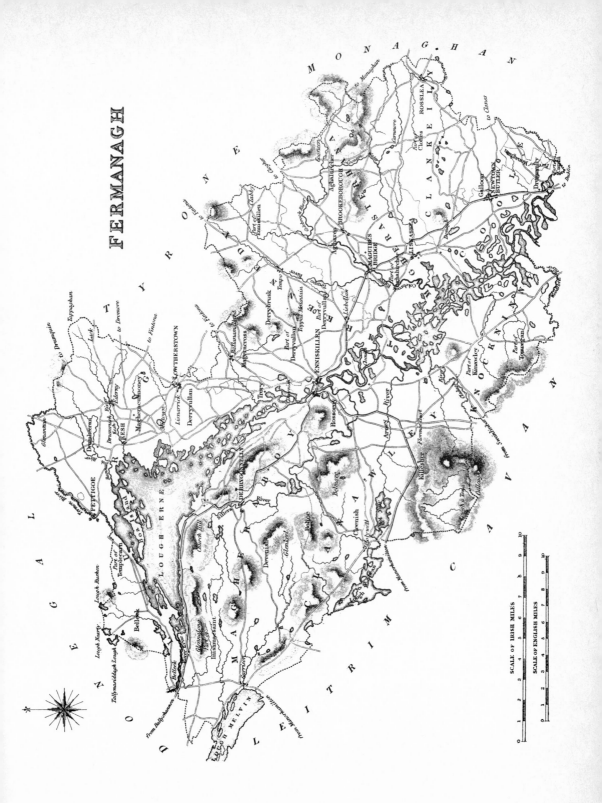

FERMANAGH

SCALE OF IRISH MILES

SCALE OF ENGLISH MILES

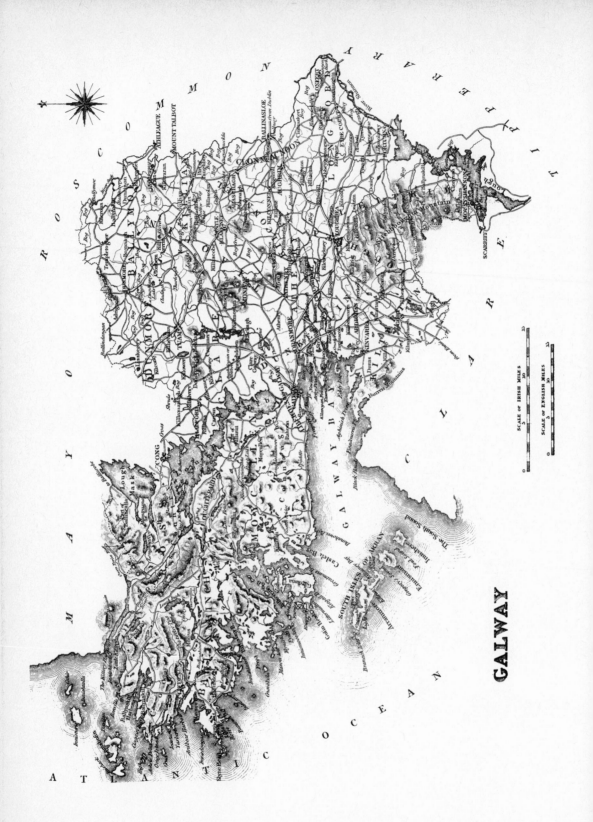

**GALWAY**

SCALE OF IRISH MILES

SCALE OF ENGLISH MILES

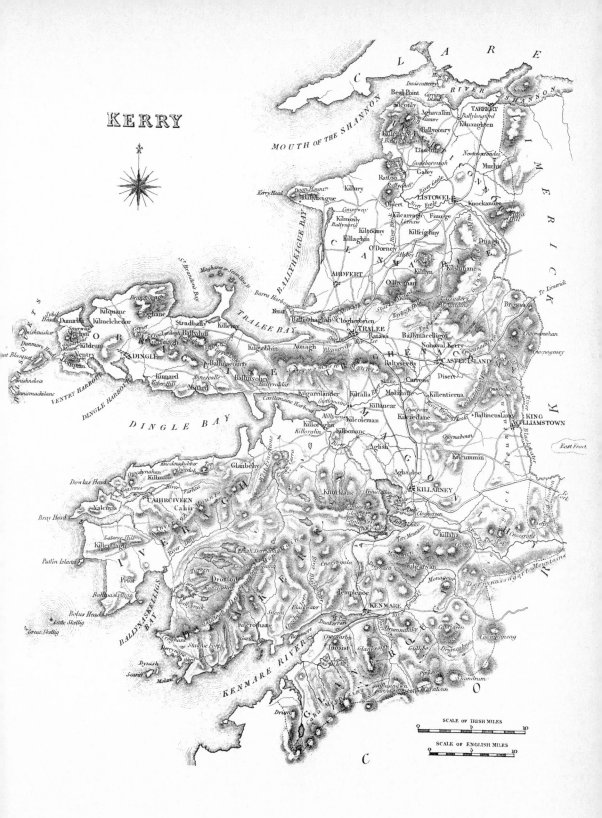

# KERRY

53

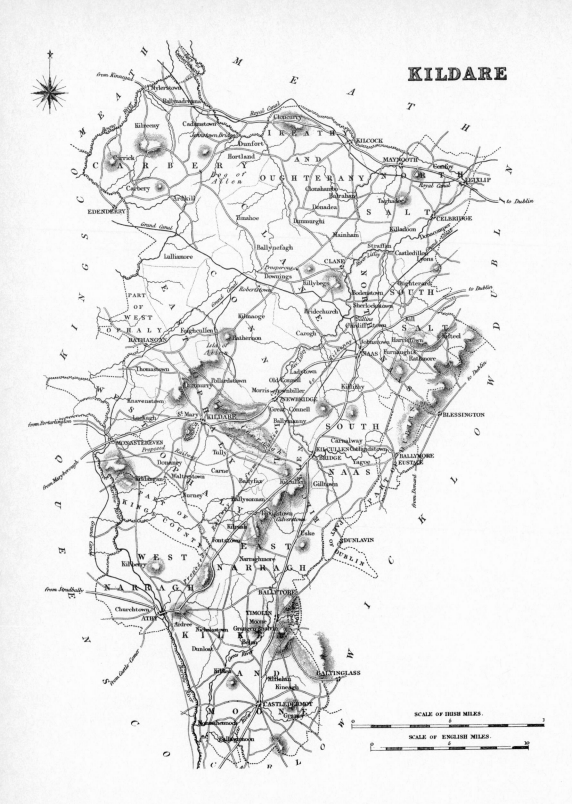

# KILDARE

SCALE OF IRISH MILES.

SCALE OF ENGLISH MILES.

54

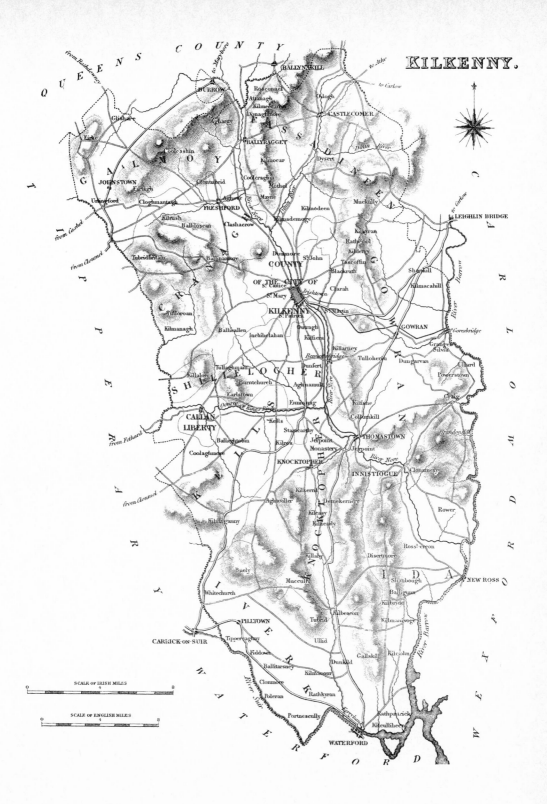

# KILKENNY.

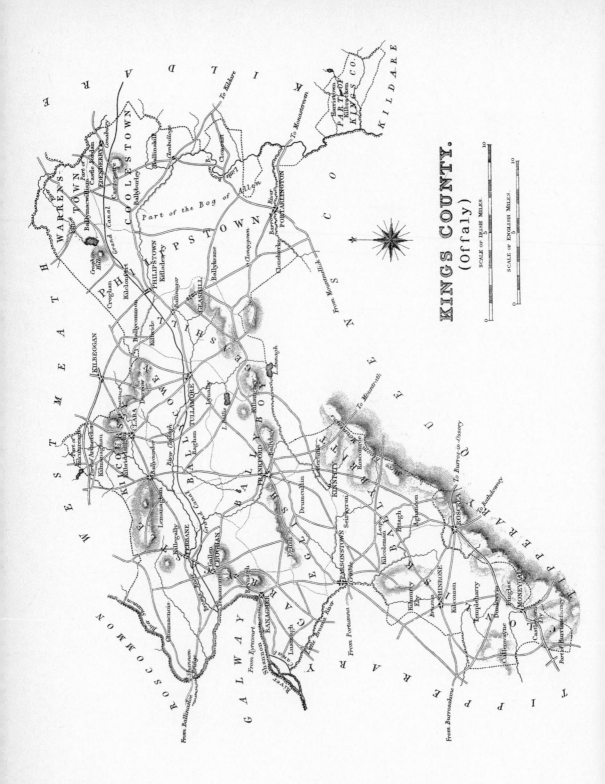

KINGS COUNTY.
(Offaly)

SCALE OF IRISH MILES.

SCALE OF ENGLISH MILES.

56

# LEITRIM

SCALE OF IRISH MILES.

SCALE OF ENGLISH MILES.

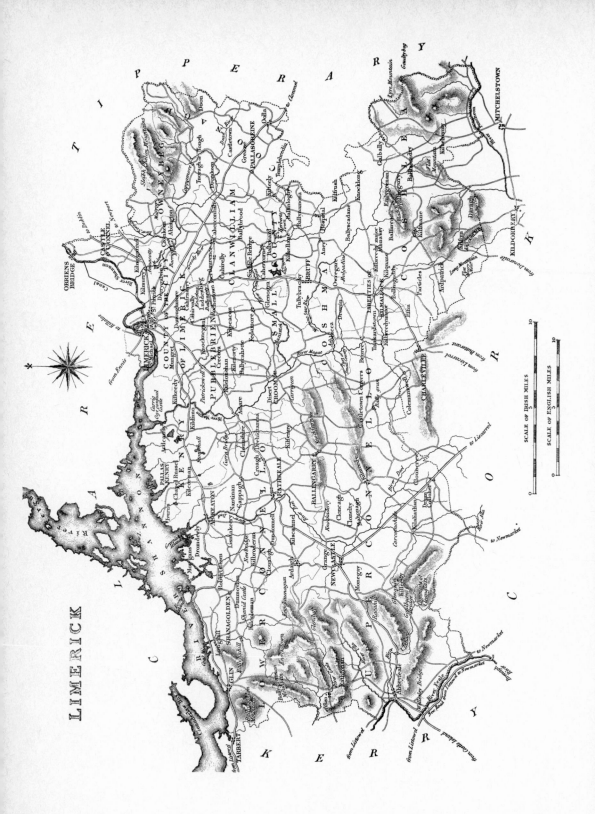

LIMERICK

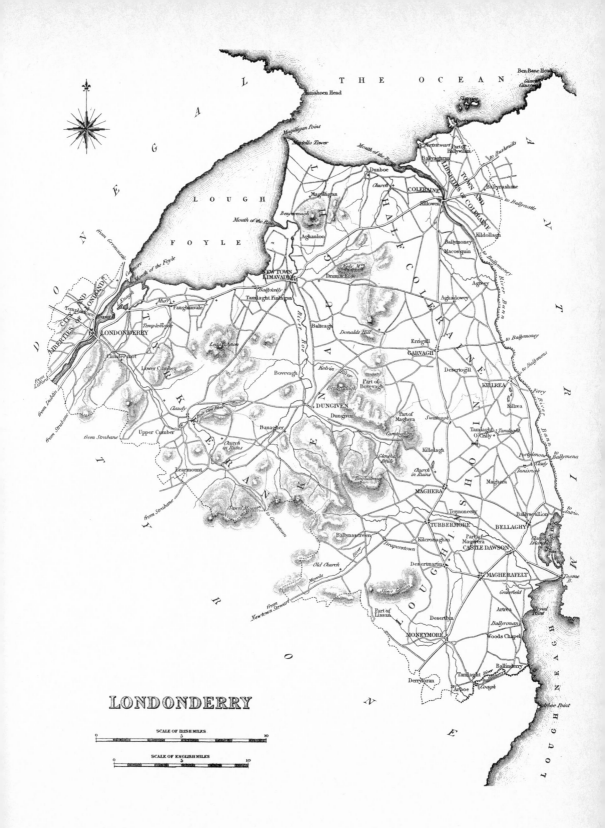

# LONDONDERRY

SCALE OF IRISH MILES

0    5    10

SCALE OF ENGLISH MILES

0    5    10

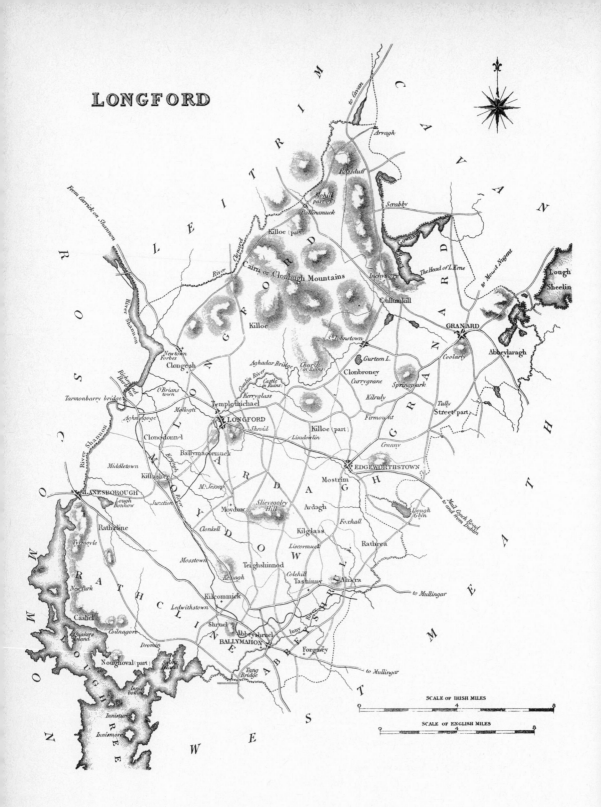

# LONGFORD

SCALE OF IRISH MILES

SCALE OF ENGLISH MILES

# LOUTH

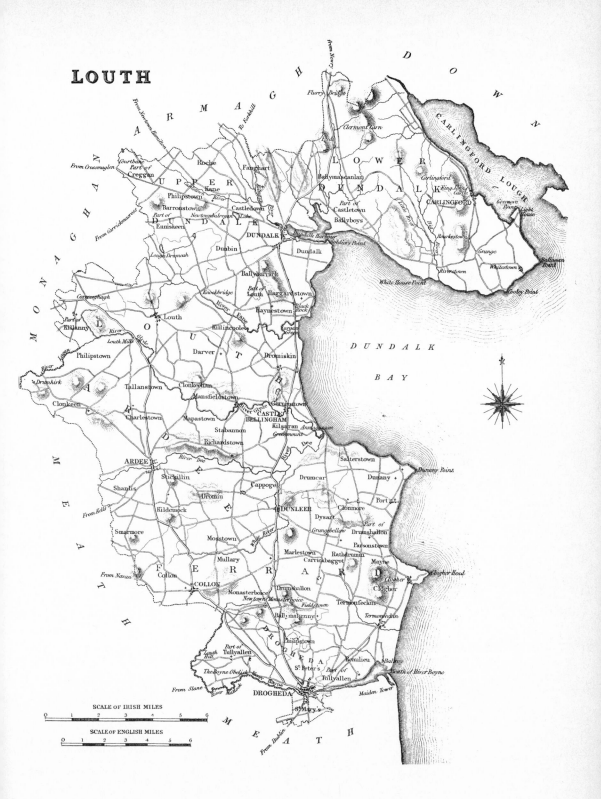

SCALE OF IRISH MILES

SCALE OF ENGLISH MILES

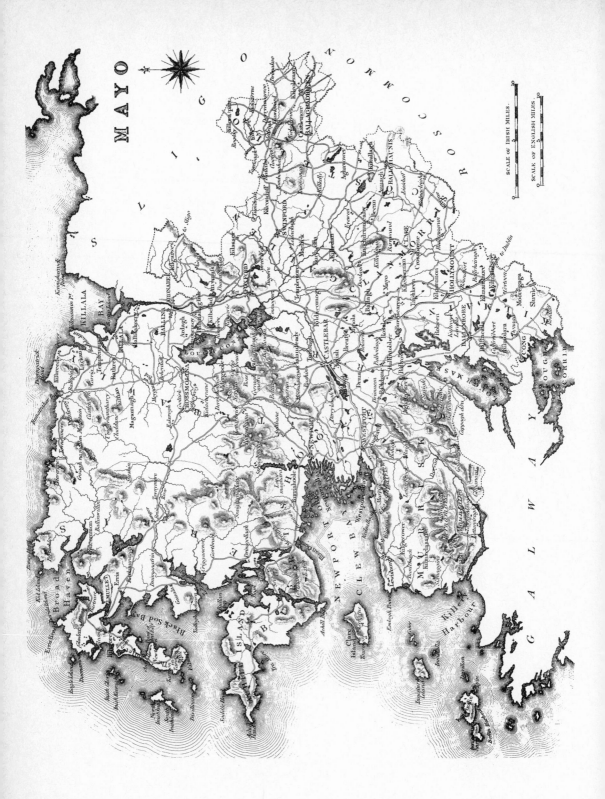

MAYO

SCALE OF IRISH MILES.

SCALE OF ENGLISH MILES.

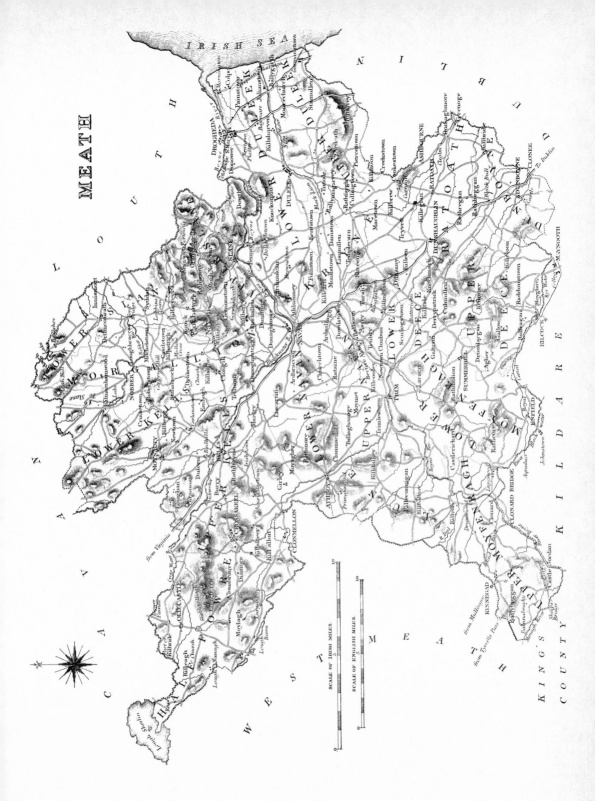

MEATH

IRISH SEA

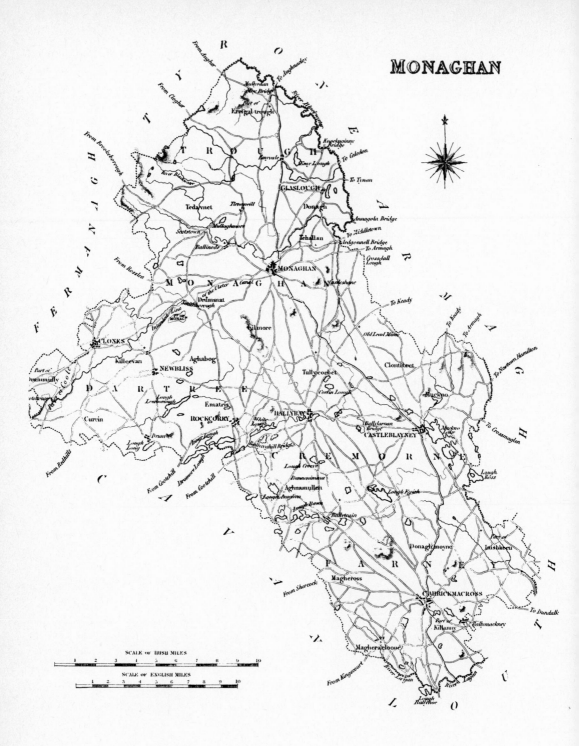

# MONAGHAN

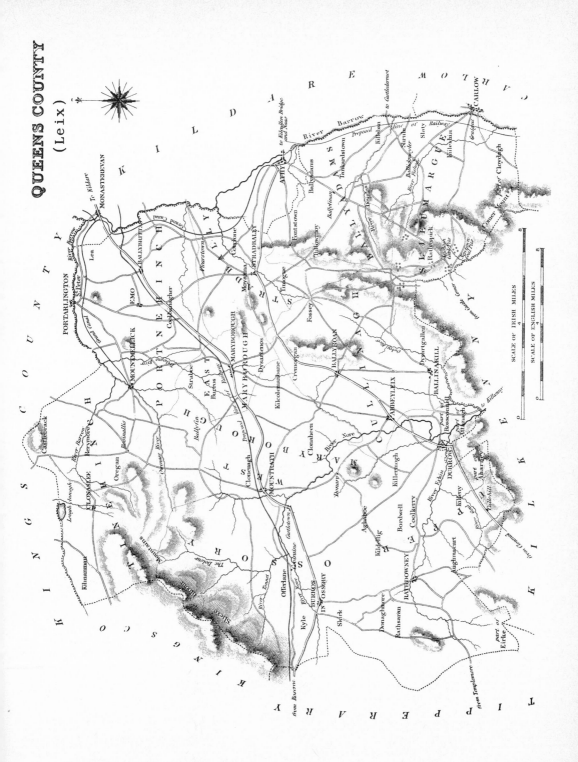

# ROSCOMMON

SLIGO

LEITRIM

MAYO

GALWAY

LONGFORD

WEST MEATH

KINGS Co.

Slieve Turragh
Lough Allen
Ballyfarnon
Killronan
READI
Drumshambo
Lough Skean
Lough Meelagh
Lough Arrow
LEITRIM
Battle Bridge
Kilbrine
Tullport
Gootchall
CARRICK
on Shannon
Lough Key
BOYLE
Ardcarney
Easterstow
Tumna
JAMES
TOWN
DRUMSNA
Part of Sligo
Lough
Kilnasan
BALLAGHADERREEN
Oughan
Killummod
Kilmore
Lough Boderig
Ballinavoher
Kilnamanagh
FRENCHPARK
Kilcola
Aughrim
Cloonaff
Lough
Bofin
Tibohine
Kilmacumse
Creeve
ROOSKEY
Belanagare
Lough Bally
ELPHIN
Kilmystan
Killglass
PART OF
Cloonagh Lough
Lough Glin
Shankhill
Drymane Lough
Lough Erie
Ballyglass
Loughglin
Kilcorkey
TOBBER
from Swineford
Lough Urbes
from Ballyhaunis
Baslick
TULSK
STROKESTOWN
Dumlin
Lough Aelun
CASTLEREA
Ogulla
Kilcodey
TARMONBARRY
from Ballinamona
Kilkeevan
Castle Plunket
Killuin
Lisonuffy
Fearbil
Erra
Ballintlough
Slievecarbyn
BALLINTOBBER
Kilbride
Tuam
Clontuskert
River Shannon
Kiltullagh
Ballintobber
HALF BALLYMOE
Ardclare
Beymore
BALLYMOE
Oran
PART OF
BALLINTOBBER
Kilgeffin
LANESBOROUGH
River Suck
ROSCOMMON
Kilteevan
Donamon
Fuerty
Hine
Gregg
Porteen
ATHLEAGUE
Kilmaine
Killenvoy
St Johns
Inchbofin
Tessaragh
Rahara
from Ballinamona
MOUNT TALBOT
Lough Funcheon
Kiltoom
Taghboy
Friars Island
Gilpenerwan Lough
Milltown Pass
Ballyforan Bridge
Dysart
Carn
Bridgewell
St Peters
ATHLONE
Lough
St Marys
River Suck
Ballyneeny
Drum
Long Island
Carrured
Taughmaconnell
Shannon
Creag
Moore
Seven Churches Ruins
from Ahascragh
Ballygill Bridge
BALLINASLOE
MOYCARNON
River Suck
SHANNON BRIDGE

SCALE OF IRISH MILES
0    5    10

SCALE OF ENGLISH MILES
0    5    10

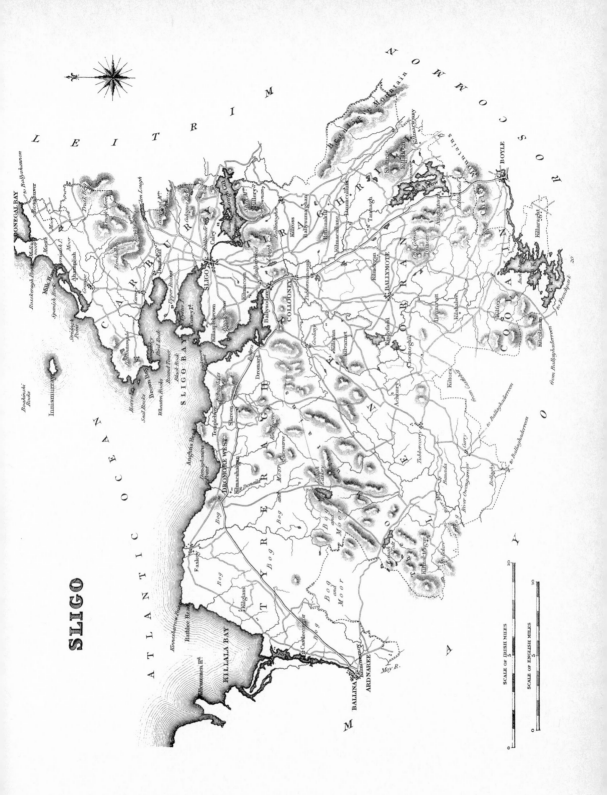

# SLIGO

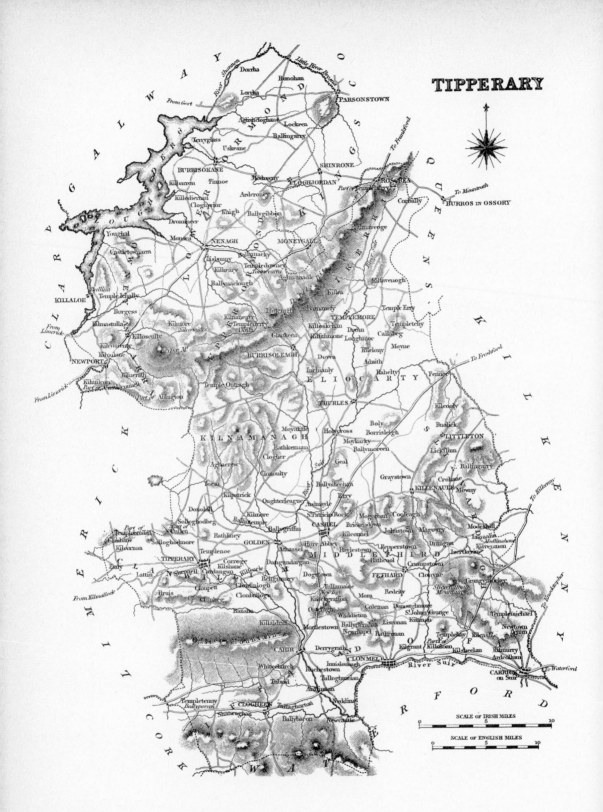

# TIPPERARY

SCALE OF IRISH MILES

SCALE OF ENGLISH MILES

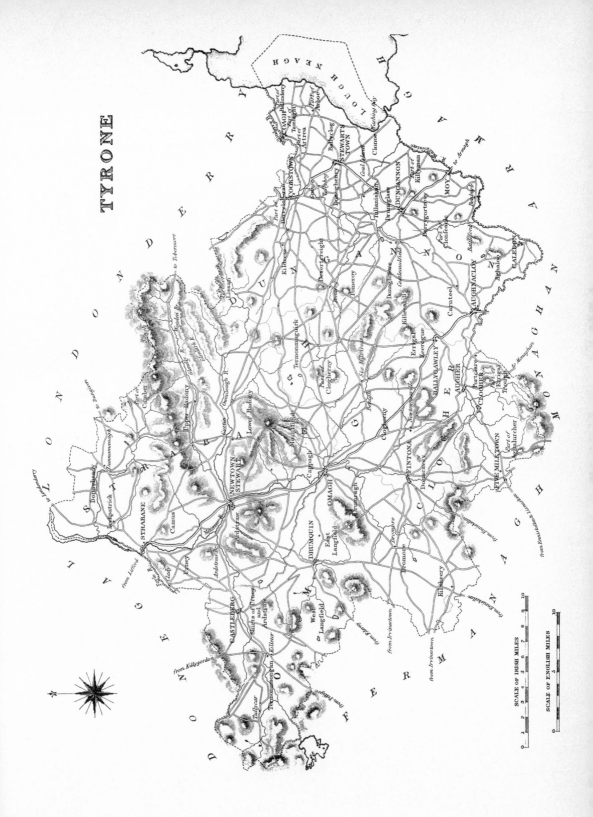

TYRONE

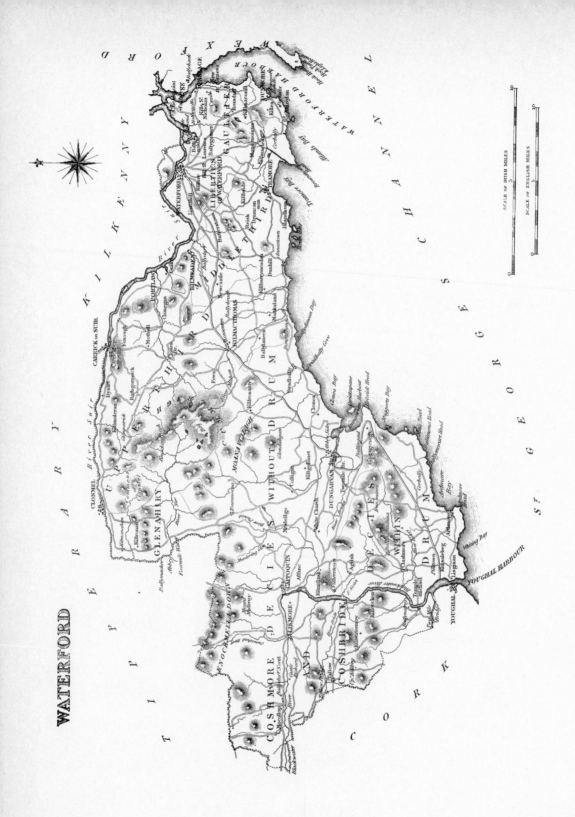

WATERFORD

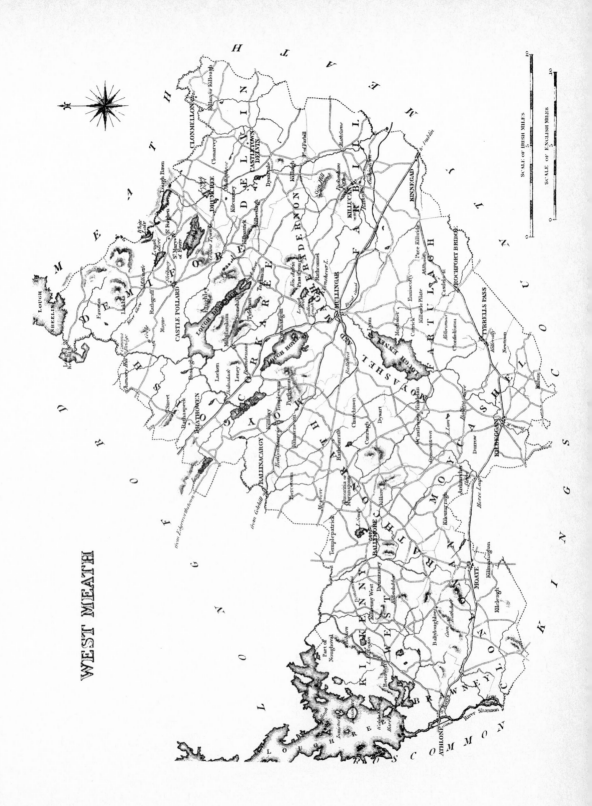

# WEST MEATH

SCALE OF IRISH MILES

SCALE OF ENGLISH MILES

# WEXFORD

SCALE OF IRISH MILES

SCALE OF ENGLISH MILES

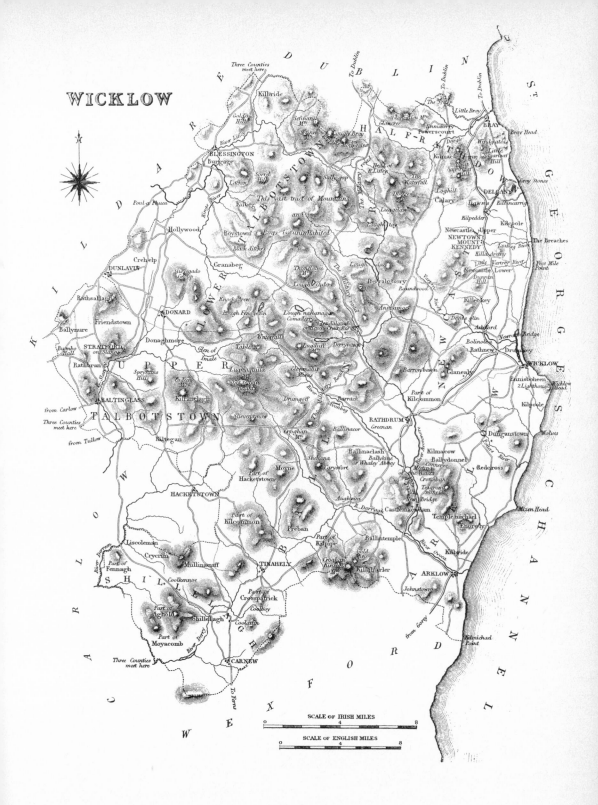

# WICKLOW

SCALE OF IRISH MILES

SCALE OF ENGLISH MILES

| 1826 | | 1826 |
|---|---|---|
| Margaretta Donoghue | Ego R. F. Mahony B. Margtam filiam legtam. Johannis Donoghue L. Johanna Leary Caths. de Coolaroonkerry | Sylvestris Donoghue Catharina Donoghue |
| Stephanus Fughroe | Idem B. Stephanum filium legtam. Johannis Fughroe L. Alang Foley Caths. de Killille — | Maria Leaffue |
| Carolus P. Brosnihan | Idem B. Carolum filium legtam. Michaeli Brosnihan L. Maria Kissane Caths. de Brentahmore — | Johannes Kissane Maria Nayle |
| Patricius Casy | Idem B. Patricium filium legtam. Maurici Casy L. Catharina Cotter Caths. de Reen | Brient Brien Margta Cotter |
| Margaretta Kerrick | Idem B. Margtam filiam legtam. Davidi Kerrick L. Maria Sullivan Caths. de L. Kissiviglen | Danielus Kerrick Margta Hannan |
| Thomas Leyne | Idem B. Thomam filium legtam. Patrici Leyne L. Honora Kissane Caths. Killarnia | Denatius Kissane Margaretta Sullivan |
| Thomas Robert | Idem B. Thomam filium legtam. Thomas Robert L. Juliana Brown Caths. de Killarnia | Robertus Robert Margta Quinn |
| Maria Connell | Ego R. C. Fullam B. Mariam filiam legtam. Gulielmi Connell L. Julia Fleming Caths. Killarnia | Cornelius Sullivan Margta Connell |

Detail showing record of baptisms from early 19th century Irish Parish Register.

# Irish Parish Registers

One of the surest ways of tracing an ancestor rooted in the ordinary stock of Ireland is through parish registers because parents invariably saw to it that their children were baptised into one or other of the christian churches. Exactly when such events began to be recorded and whether such records as were made survive to the present day are, of course, matters of considerable interest to the family historian. The age of church records will understandably vary from parish to parish but, as a general rule, registers of the relatively better off town and city parishes will be found to be appreciably older than those of rural parishes. Cities like Galway and Waterford, for example, have parish books (Roman Catholic) extending back to about the year 1680 while, on the other hand, the registers of many Mayo and Donegal parishes with entries only from the year 1850 are far too late to be of any great assistance to the family researcher. It is, however, well to remember that even in country areas where a literary tradition existed, nurtured by a bardic or classical school, local parish records will surprisingly often be extant to about 1770.

Record keeping at parish level in the eighteenth and nineteenth century in Ireland was not an easy matter for local clergy because of widespread illiteracy among congregations. Moreover, the penal laws enacted after the Treaty of Limerick in 1691 which for Catholics and Presbyterians virtually proscribed public worship were not finally removed from the statute book until the Emancipation Act of 1829. In many areas people were too poor to afford a chapel or house of worship in which circumstances the priest would journey on horseback from house to house performing baptisms, later returning to his home and entering the names of the newly baptised in his register.

A typical baptismal entry will specify the exact date of baptism, the name of the child, the names of the parents including very often the maiden name of the mother — the latter especially so in the case of catholic records — the names of the sponsors and sometimes the street or townland address of the father. A marriage entry will indicate the date of the wedding together with the names of the contracting parties and witnesses. In addition one occasionally finds in parish books items such as the names of subscribers to a chapel building fund, a list of men, horses and materials for building a chapel, parish building accounts, census of parishioners, parish history notes, minutes of famine relief committees, lists of persons receiving famine relief, lists of marriage dispensations, - not overlooking the hastily penned note to the effect that 'Fr John has gone to take the spa water at Mallow for a week'.

Even the unexpected can be met with in a parish book. Love, loyalty and the law could be said to be the ingredients of a human story underlying the following note found in a County Kilkenny parish register, illustrating religious disabilities in early nineteenth century Ireland —

> 'Rev. John Fitzpatrick told me that he married Thomas Behal and Frances Fitzgerald ... in the presence of Major Thomas Fitzgerald and Sara Fitzgerald on the 15th Nov. 1807 — but, that fearing the penalty of the law, the bride being a protestant, he had not registered the marriage in the parish book — this memorandum is therefore to supply the place of said register. November 11th, 1835. W. Hart, R.C.C.'

Established Church records, parish for parish, are much older than say Catholic or Presbyterian church records. A canon of the Irish Church in 1634 required that 'in every parish church or chapel within this realm shall be provided one parchment book at the charge of the parish wherein shall be written the day and the year of every christening and burial'. Consequently, quite a number of Irish Church books reach back in date to about the middle of the seventeenth century; for example, the registers of Christ Church, Cork begin 1643, those of Templemore (Derry) 1642, Lisburn 1639, St Michan's Dublin 1636, Harristown, Co. Kildare 1666 and St. John, Cashel 1668.

One of the side effects of Disestablishment was that parish registers of the Church of Ireland prior to 1870 were declared public records coming under the jurisdiction of the Master of the Rolls who promptly decided that country churches and rectories were not adequate to house so important a collection of records and duly commanded that the registers be sent to the Public Record Office in Dublin for safe keeping. Subsequent events were to prove him wrong for almost a thousand parish books perished in the fire that destroyed that storehouse of Irish civilisation on June 28, 1922. Fortunately, many rectors were wiser in their generation and had transcript copies made of their books before parting with the originals,thus to some extent mitigating the loss of the original registers. Many more protested that they were in a position to provide for the safety of their registers at local level and having satisfied the authorities in this regard were allowed to retain their books.

Due to the close union between church and state following the Act of Supremacy of Henry VIII in 1534, Established Church records were used much as a census might today for the information of central government, with the onus on clergy to keep records of dissenters, non-conformists and other undesirables in the eyes of the authorities. Whatever theological differences may have divided them in life, protestants, catholics, presbyterians, methodists, baptists and huguenots frequently found common ground in death in the parish graveyard and so were duly entered in the burial registers of the Established Church. Some thirty of the oldest parish books of the Established Church are of course in print thanks to the efforts of the Parish Register Society in the early years of the present century.

Presbyterian church records as a body are extant from the early years of the nineteenth century. Some forty older books, referring mainly to the eighteenth century, have been deposited in the archives of the Presbyterian Historical Society in Belfast.

The custodian of the registers of a parish is the local Parish Priest (Catholic), Rector (Church of Ireland) or Minister (Presbyterian) without whose permission in writing authorities in central archives will not allow one to inspect copies of registers they may have in their possession.

Below will be found listings of parishes and congregations, county by county, relating to the three main christian denominations in Ireland. The date appearing after each parish represents the earliest year for which baptismal registers are known to be extant for that parish. As a general rule, marriage registers will be found to be more or less coeval with baptismal registers. In addition Church of Ireland books frequently contain many excellent early burial registers. It should be stressed that the lists that follow are of a tentative nature pending the availability of a definitive statement on Irish parish registers.

Where the commencing date of a parish register is too late for the purpose of a search, it is advisable, in such circumstances, to check the records of a neighbouring parish which may have considerably older registers.

Finally, many of our parishes grew up around the sites of old monasteries and abbeys and were named after the townlands in which such foundations occurred. Accordingly, the name of an adjacent market town or post town is appended after the names of lesser known parishes for ease of location.

## Counties of Ireland and their diocesan jurisdictions

| County | Dioceses | County | Dioceses |
|--------|----------|--------|----------|
| Antrim | Connor, Derry, Down, Dromore | Limerick | Cashel, Emly, Killaloe, Limerick. |
| Armagh | Armagh, Dromore. | Longford | Armagh, Meath. |
| Carlow | Leighlin. | Louth | Armagh, Clogher. |
| Cavan | Ardagh, Meath, Kilmore. | Mayo | Killala, Achonry, Tuam. |
| Clare | Killaloe, Kilfenora, Limerick. | Meath | Armagh, Kildare, Kilmore, Meath. |
| Cork | Cork, Ross, Cloyne, Ardfert. | | |
| Derry | Armagh, Connor, Derry. | Monaghan | Clogher. |
| Donegal | Clogher, Derry, Raphoe. | Offaly (Kings) | Clonfert, Kildare, Killaloe, Meath, Ossory. |
| Down | Connor, Down, Dromore. | | |
| Dublin | Dublin. | Roscommon | Ardagh, Clonfert, Elphin, Tuam. |
| Fermanagh | Clogher, Kilmore. | | |
| Galway | Clonfert, Elphin, Killaloe, Tuam. | Sligo | Ardagh, Elphin, Killala. |
| | | Tipperary | Cashel, Killaloe, Waterford and Lismore. |
| Kerry | Ardfert. | | |
| Kildare | Dublin, Kildare. | Tyrone | Armagh, Clogher, Derry. |
| Kilkenny | Leighlin, Ossory. | Waterford | Waterford and Lismore. |
| Laois (Queens) | Dublin, Kildare, Leighlin, Ossory. | Westmeath | Ardagh, Meath. |
| | | Wexford | Dublin, Ferns. |
| Leitrim | Ardagh, Kilmore. | Wicklow | Dublin, Ferns, Leighlin. |

# Roman Catholic Church Registers

## Co. Antrim

| | |
|---|---|
| Ahoghill | 1853 |
| Antrim | 1874 |
| Armoy | 1848 |
| Ballintoy | 1872 |
| Ballyclare | 1869 |
| Ballymacarrett | 1841 |
| Ballymoney & | |
| Derrykeighan | 1853 |
| Belfast (various city parishes) | |
| St. Malachy | 1858 |
| St. Peter | 1866 |
| St. Patrick | 1875 |
| St. Mary | 1867 |
| St. Joseph | 1872 |
| Braid | |
| (Ballymena) | 1825 |
| Carnlough | 1869 |
| Carrickfergus | 1828 |
| Culfeightrin | |
| (Ballycastle) | 1825 |
| Cushendall | 1838 |
| Cushendun | 1862 |
| Derryaghy | 1855 |
| Duneane | |
| (Toomebridge) | 1834 |
| Dunloy | |
| (Cloughmills) | 1840 |
| Glenavy & | |
| Killead | 1849 |
| Glenarm | 1825 |
| Greencastle | 1854 |
| Kirkinriola | |
| (Ballymena) | 1848 |
| Larne | 1821 |
| Loughuile | 1845 |
| Portglenone | 1864 |
| Portrush | 1844 |
| Ramoan | |
| (Ballycastle) | 1838 |
| Randalstown | 1825 |
| Rasharkin | 1848 |
| Tickmacrevan | |
| (Glenarm) | 1825 |

## Co. Armagh

| | |
|---|---|
| Aghagallon & Ballinderry | |
| (Lurgan) | 1828 |
| Armagh | 1796 |
| Ballymacnab | |
| (Armagh) | 1844 |
| Ballymore & Mullaghbrac | |
| (Tandragee) | 1843 |
| Creggan | |
| (Crossmaglen) | 1796 |
| Derrynoose | |
| (Keady) | 1835 |
| Drumcree | |
| (Portadown) | 1844 |
| Forkhill | 1845 |
| Killeavy | |
| (Bessbrook) | 1835 |

| Kilmore | |
|---|---|
| (Rich Hill) | 1845 |
| Loughgall | 1835 |
| Loughgilly | 1849 |
| Seagoe | 1836 |
| Shankill | |
| (Lurgan) | 1822 |
| Tynan | 1822 |

## Co. Carlow

| | |
|---|---|
| Bagenalstown | 1820 |
| Ballon | 1785 |
| Borris | 1782 |
| Carlow | 1774 |
| Clonegall | 1833 |
| Clonmore | 1819 |
| Hacketstown | 1820 |
| Leighlinbridge | 1783 |
| Myshall | 1822 |
| St. Mullins | 1796 |
| Tinryland | 1813 |
| Tullow | 1763 |

## Co. Cavan

| | |
|---|---|
| Annagelliffe & Urney | |
| (Cavan) | 1812 |
| Annagh | |
| (Belturbet) | 1855 |
| Ballintemple | 1862 |
| Castlerahan | |
| (Ballyjamesduff) | 1752 |
| Castletera | 1862 |
| Crosserlough | 1843 |
| Denn | 1856 |
| Drumgoon | 1829 |
| Drumlane | 1836 |
| Drumlumman | |
| North | 1859 |
| Glangevlin | |
| (Swanlinbar) | 1835 |
| Kilbride & | |
| Mountnugent | 1832 |
| Killann | |
| (Bailieboro') | 1835 |
| Killinkere | |
| (Virginia) | 1766 |
| Killeshandra | 1835 |
| Kilmore | 1859 |
| Kilsherdany | |
| (Coothill) | 1803 |
| Kinawley | |
| (Swanlinbar) | 1835 |
| Kingscourt | 1838 |
| Knockbride | 1835 |
| Laragh | 1860 |
| Lavey | 1866 |
| Lurgan | |
| (Virginia) | 1755 |
| Templeport | 1836 |

## Co. Clare

| | |
|---|---|
| Ballina | 1832 |
| Ballyvaughan | 1854 |
| Broadford | 1844 |
| Carron | 1853 |
| O'Callaghan's Mills | 1835 |
| Carrigaholt | 1853 |
| Clareabbey | 1853 |
| Clondegad | 1846 |
| Clonrush | 1846 |
| Corofin | 1819 |
| Cratloe | 1802 |
| Crusheen | 1860 |
| Doonass & Trugh | 1851 |
| Doora & Kilraghtis | 1821 |
| Dysart | 1845 |
| Ennis | 1841 |
| Ennistymon | 1870 |
| Feakle Lr. | 1860 |
| Inagh | 1850 |
| Inch & Kilmaley | 1828 |
| Kilballyowen | 1878 |
| Kildysart | 1829 |
| Kilfarboy | 1831 |
| Kilfenora | 1836 |
| Kilfidane | 1868 |
| Kilkee | 1869 |
| Kilkeedy | 1833 |
| Killaloe | 1825 |
| Killanena | 1842 |
| Killard | 1855 |
| Killimer | 1859 |
| Kilmacduane | 1854 |
| Kilmihil | 1849 |
| Kilmurry-Ibrickane | 1839 |
| Kilmurry-M'Mahon | 1840 |
| Kilnoe & | |
| Tuamgraney | 1832 |
| Kilrush | 1827 |
| Liscannor | 1843 |
| Lisdoonvarna | 1854 |
| Newmarket | 1828 |
| New Quay | 1847 |
| Ogonnelloe | 1832 |
| Parteen | 1847 |
| Quin | 1816 |
| Scariff & Moynoe | 1852 |
| Sixmilebridge | 1828 |
| Tulla | 1819 |

## Co. Cork

| | |
|---|---|
| Aghabulloge | 1856 |
| Aghada | 1815 |
| Aghinagh | 1848 |
| Annakissy | 1806 |
| Ardfield & Rathbarry | 1801 |
| Aughadown | 1822 |
| Ballincollig | 1820 |
| Ballinhassig | 1821 |
| Ballyclogh | 1807 |
| Ballyhea | 1809 |
| Ballymacoda & | |
| Lady's Bridge | 1835 |
| Ballyvourney | 1825 |
| Bandon | 1794 |
| Bantry | 1819 |
| Blackrock | 1810 |
| Blarney | 1791 |
| Boherbue | 1833 |
| Bonane | 1846 |
| Barryroe | 1804 |
| Buttevant | 1814 |
| Caheragh | 1818 |
| Carrigaline | 1826 |
| Carrigtwohill | 1817 |
| Castlemagner | 1832 |
| Castlelyons | 1791 |
| Castletownroche | 1811 |
| Charleville | 1774 |
| Clondrohid | 1807 |
| Clonmeen | 1847 |
| Clonthead & | |
| Ballingeary | 1836 |
| Cloyne | 1791 |
| Cobh | 1812 |
| Conna | 1834 |
| Cork | |
| St. Finbarr | 1756 |
| St. Patrick | 1831 |
| St. Peter & Paul | 1766 |
| St. Mary | 1748 |
| Courceys | 1819 |
| Castletownbere | 1819 |
| Castlehaven | 1842 |
| Clonakilty & | |
| Darrara | 1809 |
| Donaghmore | 1803 |
| Doneraile | 1815 |
| Douglas | 1812 |
| Drimoleague | 1817 |
| Dromtariffe | 1832 |
| Dunmanway | 1818 |
| Enniskeane & | |
| Desertserges | 1813 |
| Eyeries | 1843 |
| Fermoy | 1828 |
| Freemount | 1827 |
| Glanmire | 1806 |
| Glanworth & | |
| Ballindangan | 1836 |
| Glounthane | 1829 |
| Goleen | 1827 |
| Grenagh | 1840 |
| Imogeela | 1835 |
| Inniscarra | 1814 |
| Innishannon | 1825 |
| Iveleary | 1816 |
| Kanturk | 1822 |
| Kilbehenny | 1800 |
| Kilbritain | 1811 |
| Kildorrery | 1824 |
| Killeigh | 1829 |
| Kilmichael | 1819 |
| Kilnamartyra | 1803 |
| Kilmurry | 1786 |
| Kilworth | 1829 |
| Kilmeen & | |
| Castleventry | 1821 |

## Co. Cork (Cont/d.)

| | |
|---|---|
| Kinsale | 1808 |
| Liscarrol | 1812 |
| Lisgoold | 1807 |
| Macroom | 1803 |
| Mallow | 1757 |
| Midleton | 1819 |
| Millstreet | 1853 |
| Mitchelstown | 1792 |
| Monkstown | 1795 |
| Mourne Abbey | 1829 |
| Muintervara | 1820 |
| Murragh | 1834 |
| Newmarket | 1821 |
| Ovens | 1816 |
| Passage | 1795 |
| Rath & Islands | 1818 |
| Rathcormac | 1792 |
| Rathmore | 1837 |
| Roscarberry & Lissevard | 1814 |
| Schull | 1827 |
| Shandrum | 1829 |
| Skibbereen | 1827 |
| Timoleague & Cloghagh | 1842 |
| Tracton Abbey | 1802 |
| Watergrasshill | 1836 |
| Youghal | 1803 |

## Co. Derry

| | |
|---|---|
| Ballinderry | 1826 |
| Ballynascreen | 1825 |
| Ballyscullion (Bellaghy) | 1844 |
| Banagher | 1848 |
| Coleraine | 1843 |
| Cumber Upr. (Claudy) | 1863 |
| Desertmartin | 1848 |
| Drumehose (Limavady) | 1855 |
| Dungiven | 1847 |
| Errigal | 1846 |
| Faughanvale | 1860 |
| Glendermot (Waterside, Derry) | 1864 |
| Kilrea | 1846 |
| Magilligan | 1855 |
| Maghera | 1841 |
| Magherafelt | 1834 |
| Moneymore | 1832 |
| Templemore (Derry City) | 1823 |
| Termoneeny | 1837 |

## Co. Donegal

| | |
|---|---|
| All Saints, Raymorky & Taughboyne (St. Johnston) | 1843 |
| Annagry | 1868 |
| Ardara | 1869 |
| Aughnish & Aghaninshin (Ramelton) | 1873 |
| Castlemacaward & Templecrone (Dungloe) | 1876 |
| Clonvaddog (Fanad) | 1847 |
| Clondahorky | 1877 |
| Conwal & Leck (Letterkenny) | 1853 |
| Drumhome | 1866 |
| Glencolumkille | 1880 |
| Gweedore | 1868 |
| Iniskeel (Glenties) | 1866 |
| Inver | 1861 |
| Kilcar | 1848 |
| Killybegs & Killaghtee | 1845 |
| Killygarvan & Tullyfern | 1868 |
| Killymard | 1874 |
| Kilbarron (Ballyshannon) | 1854 |
| Kilmacrenan | 1862 |
| Kilteevogue | 1855 |
| Mevagh (Carrigart) | 1871 |
| Raphoe | 1876 |
| Stranorlar | 1860 |
| Termon & Gartan | 1862 |
| Tullabegley E., Raymunterdoney & Tory | 1868 |
| Burt, Inch & Fahan | 1859 |
| Clonca (Malin) | 1856 |
| Clonleigh (Lifford) | 1773 |
| Clonmany | 1852 |
| Culdaff | 1838 |
| Desertegny & Lower Fahan (Buncrana) | 1864 |
| Donagh (Carndonagh) | 1847 |
| Donaghmore | 1857 |
| Iskaheen & Moville Upper | 1858 |
| Moville Lower | 1847 |

## Co. Down

| | |
|---|---|
| Aghaderg (Loughbrickland) | 1816 |
| Annaclone | 1834 |
| Ardkeen | 1828 |
| Ballygalget (Portaferry) | 1828 |
| Ballynahinch | 1827 |
| Banbridge | 1843 |
| Ballyphilip | 1843 |
| Bangor | 1855 |
| Bright (Ardglass) | 1856 |
| Clonallon (Warrenpoint) | 1826 |
| Clonduff (Hilltown) | 1850 |
| Donaghmore | 1835 |
| Dromara | 1844 |
| Dromore | 1823 |
| Drumaroad (Castlewellan) | 1853 |
| Drumbo | |
| Drumgath (Rathfriland) | 1841 |
| Drumgooland Upr. | 1827 |
| Drumgooland Lr. | 1832 |
| Downpatrick | 1851 |
| Dunsford | 1848 |
| Kilbroney (Rostrevor) | 1808 |
| Kilclief & Strangford | 1866 |
| Kilcoo (Rathfriland) | 1832 |
| Kilkeel | 1839 |
| Loughinisland | 1806 |
| Maghera & Bryansford (Newcastle) | 1845 |
| Magheralin | 1815 |
| Moira | 1815 |
| Mourne | 1842 |
| Newcastle | 1845 |
| Newry | 1818 |
| Newtownards, Comber & Donaghadee | 1864 |
| Saintfield (Downpatrick) | 1865 |
| Saul & Ballee | 1844 |
| Tullylish | 1833 |
| Tyrella & Dundrum | 1854 |

## Co. Dublin

| | |
|---|---|
| Balbriggan | 1816 |
| Baldoyle | 1784 |
| Balrothery | 1816 |
| Blanchardstown | 1774 |
| Booterstown | 1796 |
| Clondalkin | 1778 |
| Donabate | 1760 |

*Dublin City*

| | |
|---|---|
| St. Agatha (North William Street) | 1852 |
| St. Andrew (Westland Row) | 1741 |
| St. Audeon (High Street) | 1778 |
| St. Catherine (Meath Street) | 1740 |
| St. James (James Street) | 1752 |
| St. Lawrence O'Toole (Seville Place) | 1853 |
| St. Mary (Pro-Cathedral, Marlborough Street) | 1734 |
| St. Michael & John (Lower Exchange Street) | 1742 |
| St. Michan (Halston Street) | 1725 |
| St. Nicholas of Myra (Francis Street) | 1742 |
| St. Paul (Arran Quay) | 1731 |
| Dun Laoire | 1773 |

| | |
|---|---|
| Finglas | 1788 |
| Garristown | 1857 |
| Howth | 1784 |
| Lucan | 1818 |
| Lusk | 1757 |
| Palmerstown | 1798 |
| Rathfarnham | 1818 |
| Rolestown | 1857 |
| Saggart | 1857 |
| Sandyford | 1857 |
| Skerries | 1751 |
| Swords | 1763 |

## Co. Fermanagh

| | |
|---|---|
| Aghavea | 1862 |
| Aughalurcher (Lisnaskea) | 1835 |
| Carn (Belleek) | 1851 |
| Cleenish | 1835 |
| Culmaine | 1836 |
| Devenish | 1853 |
| Enniskillen | 1838 |
| Galloon | 1853 |
| Inishmacsaint | 1848 |
| Irvinestown | 1846 |
| Roslea | 1862 |
| Tempo | 1845 |

## Co. Galway

| | |
|---|---|
| Abbeyknockmoy | 1834 |
| Addergoole & Liskeevey | 1858 |
| Annaghdown | 1834 |
| Aran Islands | 1872 |
| Athenry | 1858 |
| Ahascragh | 1840 |
| Ardrahan | 1839 |
| Abbeygormican & Killoran | 1859 |
| Aughrim & Kilconnell | 1828 |
| Ballymacward & Clonkeenkerrill | 1841 |
| Ballinakill | 1839 |
| Bullaun, Grange & Killaan | 1827 |
| Beagh | 1855 |
| Ballinakill | 1869 |
| Boyounagh | 1838 |
| Creagh & Kilclooney (Ballinasloe) | 1820 |
| Clonfert, Donanaghta & Meelick | 1829 |
| Clontuskert | 1827 |
| Claregalway | 1849 |
| Castlegar | 1827 |
| Duniry & Kilnelahan | 1849 |
| Donaghpatrick & Kilcoona | 1844 |
| Dunmore | 1833 |
| Fahy & Kilquain | 1836 |
| Fohenagh & Kilgerrill | 1827 |
| Galway - St. Nicholas | 1690 |

## Co. Galway (Cont/d.)

| | |
|---|---|
| Kilconickny, Kilconieran & Lickerrig | 1831 |
| Kilcooley & Leitrim | 1815 |
| Killalaghten & Kilrickhill | 1853 |
| Killimorbologue & Tiranascragh | 1831 |
| Killimordaly & Kiltullagh | 1830 |
| Kilmalinoge & Lickmolassy (Portumna) | 1830 |
| Kilnadeema & Kilteskill (Loughrea) | 1836 |
| Kiltomer & Oghill | 1834 |
| Killian & Killeroran (Ballygar) | 1804 |
| Kilcummin (Oughterard) | 1809 |
| Killannin | 1875 |
| Kilcameen & Ballynacourty | 1855 |
| Kinvarra | 1831 |
| Kilbeacanty | 1854 |
| Kilchreest | 1855 |
| Kilcolgan, Dromacoo & Killeenavara | 1854 |
| Kilcornan | 1854 |
| Killora & Killogilleen | 1847 |
| Kilmacduagh & Kiltartan | 1848 |
| Kilthomas | 1854 |
| Kilkerrin & Clonberne | 1855 |
| Killascobe | 1807 |
| Killeen (Carraroe) | 1853 |
| Killererin | 1851 |
| Kilmoylan & Cummer | 1813 |
| Loughrea | 1827 |
| Lettermore | 1848 |
| Lackagh | 1842 |
| Moycullen | 1786 |
| Moylough & Mountbellew | 1848 |
| Moyrus | 1853 |
| Oranmore | 1833 |
| Omey & Ballindoon | 1838 |
| Rahoon | 1819 |
| Roundstone | 1872 |
| Salthill | 1840 |
| Spiddal | 1861 |
| Tynagh | 1809 |
| Tuam | 1790 |
| Woodford | 1821 |

## Co. Kerry

| | |
|---|---|
| Abbeydorney | 1835 |
| Annascaul | 1829 |
| Ardfert | 1819 |
| Ballybunion | 1831 |
| Ballyferriter | 1807 |
| Ballyheigue | 1840 |
| Ballylongford | 1823 |
| Ballymacelligott | 1868 |
| Boherbue | 1833 |
| Bonane & Glengarriff | 1846 |
| Brosna | 1868 |
| Cahirciveen | 1846 |
| Cahirdaniel | 1831 |
| Castlegregory | 1828 |
| Castleisland | 1823 |
| Castlemaine | 1804 |
| Causeway | 1782 |
| Dingle | 1825 |
| Dromod | 1850 |
| Duagh | 1819 |
| Firies | 1830 |
| Fossa | 1857 |
| Glenbeigh | 1834 |
| Glenflesk | 1821 |
| Kenmare | 1819 |
| Kilcummin | 1821 |
| Kilgarvan | 1818 |
| Killarney | 1792 |
| Killeentierna | 1801 |
| Killorglin | 1886 |
| Knocknagoshel | 1850 |
| Listowel | 1802 |
| Lixnaw | 1810 |
| Milltown | 1825 |
| Moyvane | 1855 |
| Prior | 1832 |
| Rathmore | 1827 |
| Sneem | 1845 |
| Spa | 1866 |
| Tarbert | 1859 |
| Tralee | 1772 |
| Tuogh | 1844 |
| Tuosist | 1844 |
| Valentia | 1825 |

## Co. Kildare

| | |
|---|---|
| Allen | 1820 |
| Athy | 1779 |
| Ballymore Eustace | 1779 |
| Balyna (Johnstown) | 1818 |
| Caragh (Downings) | 1849 |
| Carbury | 1821 |
| Castledermot | 1789 |
| Celbridge | 1857 |
| Clane | 1785 |
| Clonbullogue | 1819 |
| Kilcock | 1771 |
| Kilcullen | 1777 |
| Kildare | 1815 |
| Kill | 1840 |
| Maynooth | 1814 |
| Monasterevin | 1819 |
| Naas | 1813 |
| Narraghmore | 1827 |
| Newbridge | 1786 |
| Suncroft | 1805 |

## Co. Kilkenny

| | |
|---|---|
| Aghaviller | 1847 |
| Ballyhale | 1823 |
| Ballyregget | 1856 |
| Callan | 1821 |
| Castlecomer | 1812 |
| Clara | 1835 |
| Clough | 1858 |
| Conahy | 1832 |
| Danesfort | 1819 |
| Dunnemaggan | 1821 |
| Durrow | 1789 |
| Freshford | 1773 |
| Galmory | 1861 |
| Glenmore | 1831 |
| Gowran | 1809 |
| Graignenamanagh | 1818 |
| Inistiogue | 1810 |
| Johnstown | 1814 |
| Kilmacow | 1858 |
| Lisdowney | 1817 |
| Mooncoin | 1779 |
| Muckalee | 1801 |
| Mullinavat | 1843 |
| Paulstown | 1828 |
| Rosbercon | 1817 |
| St. Canice's (Kilkenny) | 1768 |
| St. John's (Kilkenny) | 1809 |
| St. Mary's (Kilkenny) | 1754 |
| St. Patrick's (Kilkenny) | 1800 |
| Slieverue | 1766 |
| Templeorum | 1803 |
| Thomastown | 1782 |
| Tullaherin | 1782 |
| Tulleroan | 1843 |
| Urlingford | 1805 |
| Windgap | 1822 |

## Co. Laois

| | |
|---|---|
| Abbeyleix | 1824 |
| Aghaboe | 1795 |
| Arles | 1821 |
| Ballinakill | 1794 |
| Ballyadams | 1820 |
| Ballyfin | 1824 |
| Borris-in-Ossory | 1840 |
| Camross (Mountrath) | 1816 |
| Castletown | 1772 |
| Clonaslee | 1849 |
| Durrow | 1789 |
| Mountmellick | 1814 |
| Mountrath | 1823 |
| Portarlington | 1820 |
| Portlaoise | 1826 |
| Raheen | 1819 |
| Rathdowney | 1763 |
| Rosenallis | 1765 |
| Stradbally | 1820 |

## Co. Leitrim

| | |
|---|---|
| Annaduff | 1849 |
| Aughavas | 1825 |
| Ballinamore | 1869 |
| Ballymeehan | |
| (Rossinver) | 1851 |
| Carrigallen | 1829 |
| Clooneclare (Manorhamilton) | 1853 |
| Drumlease (Dromahaire) | 1859 |
| Drumreilly | 1867 |
| Fenagh | 1825 |
| Glenade | 1867 |
| Gortletheragh | 1830 |
| Inishmagrath (Drumkeeran) | 1854 |
| Killargue | 1852 |
| Killasnet | 1852 |
| Killenummery & Killerny | 1828 |
| Kiltoghert | 1826 |
| Kiltubbrid | 1841 |
| Kinlough | 1835 |
| Mohill-Manachain | 1836 |

## Co. Limerick

| | |
|---|---|
| Abbeyfeale | 1856 |
| Adare | 1832 |
| Ardagh | 1845 |
| Ardpatrick | 1861 |
| Askeaton | 1829 |
| Athea | 1830 |
| Ballingarry | 1825 |
| Ballybricken | 1800 |
| Ballygran & Colman's well | 1841 |
| Ballylanders | 1847 |
| Banogue | 1861 |
| Bruff | 1808 |
| Bulgaden & Ballinvana | 1812 |
| Caherconlish | 1841 |
| Cappagh | 1841 |
| Cappamore | 1845 |
| Castleconnell | 1850 |
| Charleville | 1774 |
| Coolcappa | 1833 |
| Croagh | 1836 |
| Croom | 1770 |
| Donaghmore | 1830 |
| Doon | 1824 |
| Dromin | 1817 |
| Drumcollogher | 1830 |
| Effin | 1843 |
| Emly | 1810 |
| Fedamore | 1806 |
| Feenagh | 1854 |
| Freemount | 1835 |
| Galbally | 1810 |
| Glenroe | 1853 |
| Glin | 1851 |
| Hospital | 1810 |
| Kilbenny | 1824 |
| Kildimo | 1846 |
| Kilfinane | 1832 |
| Killeedy | 1840 |
| Kilmallock | 1837 |
| Kilteely | 1815 |
| Knockaderry | 1838 |
| Knockaney | 1808 |

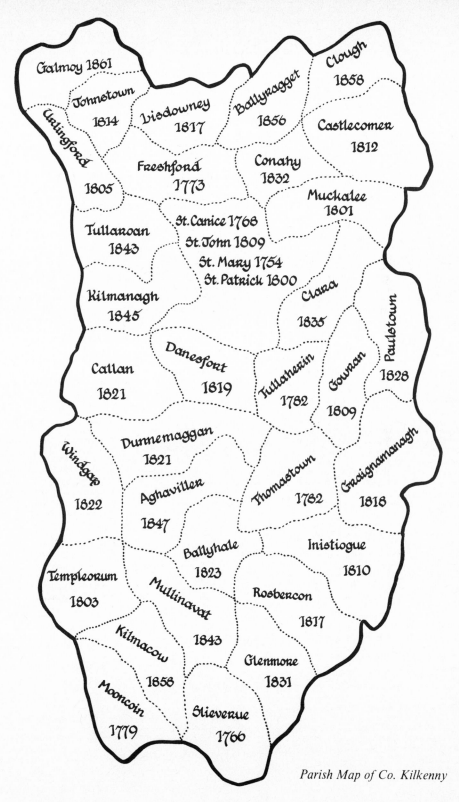

*Parish Map of Co. Kilkenny*

## Co. Limerick (Cont/d.)

| | |
|---|---|
| Knocklong | 1809 |
| Loughill | 1855 |
| Mahoonagh | 1812 |
| Manistir | 1845 |
| Monagea | 1777 |
| Mungret | 1844 |
| Murroe & Boher | 1814 |
| Newcastle West | 1815 |
| Cola & Solohead | 1809 |
| Pallesgreen | 1811 |
| Parteen | 1847 |
| Patrickswell | 1801 |
| Rathkeale | 1811 |
| Rockhill | 1842 |
| St. John's (Limerick) | 1788 |
| St. Mary's (Limerick) | 1745 |
| St. Michael's (Limerick) | 1776 |
| St. Munchin's (Limerick) | 1764 |
| St. Patrick's (Limerick) | 1812 |
| Shanagolden | 1824 |
| Stonehall | 1825 |
| Templeglantine | 1864 |
| Tournafulla | 1867 |

## Co. Longford

| | |
|---|---|
| Abbeylara | 1854 |
| Ardagh & Moydow | 1793 |
| Carrickedmond | 1825 |
| Cashel | 1850 |
| Clonbroney | 1849 |
| Clonguish | 1829 |
| Columcille (Dring) | 1845 |
| Drumlish | 1834 |
| Granard | 1779 |
| Kilcommuck | 1859 |
| Kilglass & Rathreagh | 1855 |
| Killashee | 1826 |
| Killoe (Drumlish) | 1826 |
| Mostrim | 1838 |
| Rathcline (Lanesboro') | 1850 |
| Scrabby & Columcille East (Cloonagh) | 1833 |
| Shrule (Ballymahon) | 1820 |

## Co. Louth

| | |
|---|---|
| Ardee | 1763 |
| Carlingford | 1811 |
| Clogherhead | 1744 |
| Collon | 1789 |
| Darver | 1787 |
| Dundalk | 1790 |
| Dunleer | 1772 |
| Faughart | 1851 |
| Kilkerley | 1752 |
| Kilsaran | 1809 |

| | |
|---|---|
| Lordship & Ballymascanlan | 1838 |
| Louth | 1833 |
| Mellifont | 1821 |
| Monasterboice | 1814 |
| St. Mary's (Drogheda) | 1835 |
| St. Peter's (Drogheda) | 1744 |
| Tallanstown | 1817 |
| Termonfeckin | 1823 |
| Togher | 1791 |

## Co. Mayo

| | |
|---|---|
| Attymass | 1875 |
| Addergoole | 1840 |
| Ardagh | 1870 |
| Aughaval (Westport) | 1823 |
| Achill | 1867 |
| Aghamore | 1864 |
| Aglish, Ballyheane & Breaghwy (Castlebar) | 1824 |
| Aghagower (Westport) | 1828 |
| Bohola | 1857 |
| Backs (Rathduff) | 1848 |
| Ballycastle | 1864 |
| Ballysokeary | 1843 |
| Belmullet | 1841 |
| Balla & Manulla | 1837 |
| Ballinrobe | 1843 |
| Ballyovey | 1869 |
| Bekan (Claremorris) | 1832 |
| Burriscarra & Ballintubber (Claremorris) | 1839 |
| Burrishoole (Newport) | 1870 |
| Ballyhaunis | 1851 |
| Crossmolina | 1831 |
| Clare Island | 1851 |
| Cong & Neale | 1870 |
| Crossboyne & Tagheen | 1862 |
| Clonbur | 1853 |
| Islandeady (Castlebar) | 1839 |
| Kilconduff & Meelick (Swinford) | 1850 |
| Kilgarvan (Ballina) | 1844 |
| Killasser (Swinford) | 1847 |
| Kilbeagh (Charlestown) | 1845 |
| Killedan | 1834 |
| Kilmovee | 1854 |
| Kilshalvey | 1842 |
| Kilfian | 1826 |
| Killala | 1852 |
| Kilmoremoy (Ballina) | 1823 |

| | |
|---|---|
| Kiltane (Bangor-Erris) | 1860 |
| Keelogues | 1847 |
| Kilcolman (Claremorris) | 1835 |
| Kilcommon & Robeen | 1857 |
| Kilgeever (Louisburg) | 1850 |
| Kilmaine | 1854 |
| Kilmeena | 1858 |
| Knock | 1868 |
| Kilbride | 1853 |
| Lackan | 1852 |
| Mayo & Roslee | 1841 |
| Templemore | 1872 |
| Toomore (Foxford) | 1833 |
| Turlough (Castlebar) | 1847 |

## Co. Meath

| | |
|---|---|
| Ardcath | 1795 |
| Athboy | 1794 |
| Ballinabrackey | 1826 |
| Ballivor & Kildalkey | 1837 |
| Beauparc (Yellow Furze) | 1815 |
| Blacklion | 1815 |
| Bohermeen (Navan) | 1805 |
| Carnaross | 1806 |
| Castletown (Navan) | 1805 |
| Clonmellon | 1759 |
| Curraha (Ashbourne) | 1823 |
| Drumconrath | 1811 |
| Duleek | 1852 |
| Dunboyne | 1787 |
| Dunderry | 1837 |
| Dunshaughlin | 1789 |
| Johnstown | 1839 |
| Kells | 1791 |
| Kilbride | 1802 |
| Kilmainham & Moybologue | 1869 |
| Kilcloon (Dunboyne) | 1836 |
| Kilbeg (Kells) | 1817 |
| Kilmessan & Dunsany | 1742 |
| Kilskyre (Ballinlough) | 1784 |
| Lobinstown (Navan) | 1823 |
| Longwood | 1829 |
| Moynalty | 1811 |
| Navan | 1782 |
| Nobber | 1754 |
| Oldcastle | 1789 |
| Oristown (Kells) | 1757 |
| Rathkenny | 1784 |
| Ratoath & Ashbourne | 1781 |

| | |
|---|---|
| Rosnaree & Donore | 1840 |
| Skyrne | 1841 |
| Slane | 1851 |
| Stamullen | 1831 |
| Summerhill | 1812 |
| Trim | 1829 |

## Co. Monaghan

| | |
|---|---|
| Aghabog | 1856 |
| Aughmullen | 1841 |
| Clontibret | 1861 |
| Clones | 1848 |
| Donagh (Grasslough) | 1836 |
| Donaghmoyne | 1852 |
| Drumully (Scotshouse) | 1845 |
| Drumsnat & Kilmore | 1836 |
| Ematris (Rockcorry) | 1848 |
| Errigal Trough (Emyvale) | 1835 |
| Killevan (Newbliss) | 1850 |
| Monaghan | 1835 |
| Maghaire Rois | 1836 |
| Magheracloone (Carrickmacross) | 1836 |
| Muckno (Castleblaney) | 1835 |
| Tullycorbet (Ballybay) | 1862 |
| Tydavnet | 1835 |

## Co. Offaly

| | |
|---|---|
| Birr | 1838 |
| Clara | 1821 |
| Clonmacnoise | 1826 |
| Daingean | 1795 |
| Dunkerrin | 1820 |
| Edenderry | 1820 |
| Eglish | 1809 |
| Gallen & Reynagh (Banagher) | 1811 |
| Kilcormac | 1821 |
| Killeigh (Geashill) | 1844 |
| Killina (Rahan) | 1810 |
| Kinnetty | 1833 |
| Lemanaghan (Ferbane) | 1821 |
| Lusmagh | 1850 |
| Rhode | 1829 |
| Seirkieran | 1830 |
| Shinrone | 1842 |
| Tisaran & Fuithre (Ferbane) | 1819 |
| Tullamore | 1809 |

## Co. Roscommon

| | |
|---|---|
| Ardcarne | 1843 |
| Athleague & Fuerty | 1808 |
| Aughrim & Kilmore | 1816 |
| Ballintober, Ballymoe | 1831 |

## Co. Roscommon (Cont/d.)

| | |
|---|---|
| Boyle & Kilbryan | 1793 |
| Castlemore & Kilcolman | 1851 |
| Cloontuskert, Kilgeffin | 1865 |
| Dysert & Tissara | 1850 |
| Elphin & Creeve | 1808 |
| Glinsk & Kilbegnet | 1836 |
| Kilbride | 1835 |
| Kilcorkey & Frenchpark | 1845 |
| Kilglass & Rooskey | 1865 |
| Kilkeevan (Castlerea) | 1804 |
| Killukin | 1811 |
| Kilnamanagh & Estersnow | 1853 |
| Kiltoom | 1835 |
| Kiltrustan, Lissonuffy & Cloonfinlough (Strokestown) | 1830 |
| Loughglynn | 1817 |
| Ogulla & Baslick | 1865 |
| Oran | 1845 |
| Roscommon & Kilteevan | 1820 |
| St. John's (Knockcroghery) | 1841 |
| Tibohine | 1833 |

## Co. Sligo

| | |
|---|---|
| Aghanagh (Ballinafad) | 1803 |
| Ahamlish (Cliffoney) | 1796 |
| Ballisodare & Kilvarnet | 1842 |
| Cloonacool | 1859 |
| Curry | 1867 |
| Drumcliffe | 1841 |
| Drumrat | 1843 |
| Easky | 1864 |
| Emlefad & Kilmorgan | 1824 |
| Geevagh | 1851 |
| Kilfree & Killaraght | 1844 |
| Killoran | 1846 |
| Kilmacteigue | 1845 |
| Kilshalvey, Kilturra & Cloonoghill | 1842 |
| Riverstown | 1803 |
| Skreen & Dromard | 1848 |
| Sligo, Coolera, Calry, Rosses Point & St. Mary's | 1858 |
| Templeboy | 1815 |
| Tumore | 1833 |

## Co. Tipperary

| | |
|---|---|
| Annacarty | 1821 |
| Ardfinnan | 1809 |
| Ballinahinch | 1839 |
| Ballingarry | 1814 |
| Ballylooby | 1809 |
| Ballyneale | 1839 |
| Ballyporeen | 1817 |
| Bansha & Kilmoyler | 1820 |
| Boherlahan & Dualla | 1830 |
| Borrisokane | 1821 |
| Borrisoleigh | 1814 |
| Burgess & Youghal | 1828 |
| Cahir | 1809 |
| Carrick-on-Suir | 1784 |
| Cashel | 1793 |
| Castletownarrha | 1820 |
| Clerihan | 1852 |
| Clogheen | 1778 |
| Cloghprior & Monsea | 1835 |
| Clonmel | 1790 |
| Clonoulty | 1804 |
| Cloughjordan | 1833 |
| Cappawhite | 1815 |
| Drangan | 1811 |
| Drom & Inch | 1827 |
| Dunkerrin | 1820 |
| Emly | 1810 |
| Fethard & Killusty | 1806 |
| Golden | 1833 |
| Gortnahoe | 1805 |
| Holycross | 1835 |
| Kilbarron | 1827 |
| Kilcommon | 1813 |
| Killenaule | 1743 |
| Kilsheelan | 1836 |
| Knockavilla | 1834 |
| Lattin & Cullen | 1846 |
| Loughmore | 1798 |
| Moycarky | 1793 |
| Mullinahone | 1820 |
| Nenagh | 1792 |
| Newcastle | 1846 |
| New Inn | 1820 |
| Newport | 1795 |
| Oola & Solohead | 1809 |
| Powerstown | 1808 |
| Roscrea | 1810 |
| Silvermines | 1840 |
| Templemore | 1807 |
| Templetuohy | 1809 |
| Thurles | 1795 |
| Toomevara | 1831 |
| Tipperary | 1793 |
| Upperchurch | 1829 |

## Co. Tyrone

| | |
|---|---|
| Aghaloo | 1846 |
| Ardboe | 1827 |
| Ardstraw (Cappagh) | 1846 |
| Artrea | 1832 |
| Ballinderry (Cookstown) | 1826 |
| Ballyclog | 1822 |
| Beragh | 1832 |
| Bodoney | 1850 |
| Camus (Strabane) | 1773 |
| Cappagh | 1846 |
| Clogher | 1856 |
| Clonfeacle (Moy) | 1814 |
| Clonoe (Coalisland) | 1810 |
| Desertcreat | 1827 |
| Donaghcavey (Fintona) | 1857 |
| Donaghedy | 1855 |
| Donaghenry (Coalisland) | 1822 |
| Donaghmore | 1837 |
| Dromore | 1855 |
| Drumglass (Dungannon) | 1821 |
| Drumragh (Omagh) | 1846 |
| Eglish (Dungannon) | 1862 |
| Errigal Keeran (Ballygawley) | 1847 |
| Kildress | 1835 |
| Kileeshil (Tullyallen) | 1845 |
| Kilskerry (Trillick) | 1840 |
| Leckpatrick (Strabane) | 1863 |
| Lissan (Cookstown) | 1832 |
| Longfield | 1846 |
| Pomeroy | 1837 |
| Termonamongan | 1863 |
| Termonmaguirk (Carrickmore) | 1834 |
| Urney | 1773 |

## Co. Waterford

| | |
|---|---|
| Abbeyside | 1828 |
| Aglish | 1837 |
| Ardmore | 1823 |
| Ballyduff | 1805 |
| Cappoquin | 1810 |
| Carrickbeg | 1842 |
| Clashmore | 1811 |
| Dungarvan | 1787 |
| Dunhill | 1829 |
| Kilgobnet | 1848 |
| Kill | 1831 |
| Killea | 1780 |
| Kilrossanty | 1822 |
| Kilsheelan | 1840 |
| Knockanore | 1833 |
| Lismore | 1820 |
| Modelligo | 1846 |
| Newcastle | 1846 |
| Portlaw | 1809 |
| Ring | 1813 |
| St. John's (Waterford) | 1759 |
| St. Patrick's (Waterford) | 1731 |
| St. Peter & Paul's | 1737 |
| Tallow | 1797 |
| Touraneena | 1851 |
| Tramore | 1798 |
| Trinity Within (Waterford) | 1729 |
| Trinity Without (Waterford) | 1752 |

## Co. Westmeath

| | |
|---|---|
| Ballinacargy | 1837 |
| Ballymore | 1824 |
| Castlepollard | 1763 |
| Castletown | 1829 |
| Churchtown | 1816 |
| Clara | 1821 |
| Clonmellon | 1785 |
| Collinstown | 1807 |
| Delvin | 1785 |
| Drumraney | 1834 |
| Kilbeggan | 1818 |
| Kilbride | 1832 |
| Kilkenny West | 1829 |
| Killucan | 1821 |
| Kinnegad | 1827 |
| Lemanaghan & Ballynahowen | 1821 |
| Milltown | 1781 |
| Moate & Colry | 1823 |
| Moyvore | 1831 |
| Mullingar | 1737 |
| Multyfarnham | 1824 |
| Rathaspick & Russagh | 1822 |
| Rochfortbridge | 1823 |
| St. Mary's (Athlone) | 1813 |
| Streete | 1820 |
| Taghmon | 1781 |
| Tubber | 1821 |
| Tullamore | 1801 |
| Turbotstown | 1819 |

## Co. Wexford

| | |
|---|---|
| Adamstown | 1807 |
| Ballindaggin | 1841 |
| Ballygarrett | 1828 |
| Ballyoughter | 1810 |
| Bennow | 1832 |
| Blackwater | 1815 |
| Bree | 1837 |
| Bunclody | 1834 |
| Castlebridge | 1832 |
| Clongen | 1847 |
| Cloughbawn | 1816 |
| Craanford | 1853 |
| Crossebeg | 1856 |
| Cushinstown | 1759 |
| Davidstown | 1805 |
| Enniscorthy | 1794 |
| Ferns | 1819 |
| Glynn | 1817 |
| Gorey | 1847 |
| Kilanieran | 1852 |
| Killaveny | 1800 |
| Kilmore | 1752 |
| Kilrush | 1842 |
| Lady's-Island | 1773 |
| Litter | 1789 |
| Marshallstown | 1854 |
| Mayglass | 1843 |
| Monageer | 1838 |
| New Ross | 1789 |

### Co. Wexford (Cont/d.)

| | |
|---|---|
| Oulart | 1837 |
| Oylegate | 1804 |
| Piercestown | 1839 |
| Ramsgrange | 1835 |
| Rathengan | 1803 |
| Rathnure | 1846 |
| Suttons | 1824 |

| | |
|---|---|
| Taghmon | 1801 |
| Tagoat | 1853 |
| Tintern | 1827 |
| Templetown | 1792 |
| Wexford | 1671 |

### Co. Wicklow

| | |
|---|---|
| Arklow | 1809 |
| Ashford | 1864 |
| Avoca | 1791 |
| Baltinglass | 1807 |
| Blessington | 1852 |
| Bray: | |
| Bray Town | 1800 |
| Dunlavin | 1815 |
| Enniskerry | 1825 |
| Glendalough | 1807 |
| Kilbride & | |
| Barnderrig | 1835 |
| Kilquade | 1826 |
| Rathdrum | 1795 |
| Rathvilly | 1797 |
| Valleymount | 1810 |
| Tinahealy | 1835 |
| Wicklow | 1747 |

---

# Church of Ireland Registers

### Co. Antrim

| | |
|---|---|
| Aghalee | 1782 |
| Ahoghill | |
| (Ballymena) | 1811 |
| Antrim | 1700 |
| Ballinderry | 1805 |
| Ballintoy | |
| (Ballycastle) | 1712 |
| Ballyclug | 1841 |
| Ballymacarrett | 1827 |
| Ballymena | 1815 |
| Ballymoney | 1807 |
| Ballynure | 1812 |
| Ballysillan | 1856 |
| Belfast | |
| Christ Church | 1868 |
| Mariner's | 1745 |
| St. Anne | |
| (Shankill) | 1819 |
| St. George | 1853 |
| St. John | 1853 |
| St. Mark | |
| (see Ballysillan) | |
| St. Mary | 1867 |
| St. Matthew | 1846 |
| Trinity | 1844 |
| Upper Falls | 1855 |
| Carnamoney | 1789 |
| Carrickfergus | 1740 |
| Craigs (Belfast) | 1839 |
| Derryaghey | |
| (Lisburn) | 1696 |
| Derrykeighan | 1802 |
| Drummaul | |
| (Randalstown) | 1823 |
| Dunluce | |
| (Bushmills) | 1809 |
| Dunseverick | |
| (Bushmills) | 1832 |
| Finvoy | |
| (Ballymoney) | 1811 |
| Glenarm | 1788 |
| Glenary | 1707 |
| Glynn (Larne) | 1838 |
| Inver (Larne) | 1806 |
| Lambeg | 1810 |
| Layde | |
| (Cushendall) | 1826 |

| | |
|---|---|
| Lisburn (Blaris) | 1639 |
| Magheragall | |
| (Lisburn) | 1772 |
| Muckamore | |
| (Antrim) | 1847 |
| Skerry | 1805 |
| Stoneyford | 1845 |
| Templecorran | 1848 |
| Templepatrick | 1827 |
| Whitehouse | |
| (Belfast) | 1840 |

### Co. Armagh

| | |
|---|---|
| Aghavilly (Armagh) | 1844 |
| Annaghmore | |
| (Loughgall) | 1856 |
| Ardmore | 1822 |
| Armagh | 1750 |
| Ballymore | |
| (Tandragee) | 1783 |
| Ballymoyer | |
| (Whitecross) | 1820 |
| Camlough (Newry) | 1832 |
| Creggan | |
| (Crossmaglen) | 1808 |
| Derrynoose | |
| (Armagh) | 1710 |
| Drumbanagher | |
| (Newry) | 1838 |
| Drumcree | |
| (Portadown) | 1780 |
| Eglish (Moy) | 1803 |
| Grange (Armagh) | 1780 |
| Keady | 1780 |
| Kilcluney | |
| (Markethill) | 1832 |
| Killylea | 1845 |
| Loughgall | 1706 |
| Loughgilly | |
| (Markethill) | 1804 |
| Milltown | |
| (Magheramoy) | 1840 |
| Mullavilly | |
| (Tandragee) | 1821 |
| Newtownhamilton | 1823 |
| Sankill | 1681 |
| Tartaraghan | |
| (Loughgall) | 1824 |
| Tynan | 1686 |

### Co. Carlow

| | |
|---|---|
| Aghade (Carlow) | 1740 |
| Aghold | 1700 |
| Barragh | |
| (Enniscorthy) | 1831 |
| Carlow | 1744 |
| Dunleckney | 1791 |
| Fenagh (Carlow) | 1809 |
| Hacketstown | – |
| Killeshir (Carlow) | 1824 |
| Kiltennell | |
| (New Ross) | 1837 |
| Myshall | 1814 |
| Painestown (Carlow) | 1833 |
| Rathvilly | 1826 |
| Tullow | 1696 |
| Urglin (Carlow) | 1710 |

### Co. Cavan

| | |
|---|---|
| Annagelliffe (Cavan) | 1804 |
| Annagh (Belturbet) | 1801 |
| Ashfield (Cootehill) | 1821 |
| Bailieborough | 1744 |
| Ballymachugh | 1816 |
| Billis (Virginia) | 1840 |
| Castleterra | |
| (Ballyhaise) | 1800 |
| Cavan | 1842 |
| Cloverhill | 1861 |
| Drumgoon | |
| (Cootehill) | 1802 |
| Drung | 1785 |
| Kildallon | |
| (Ballyconnell) | 1856 |
| Kildrumferton | |
| (Kilnelack) | 1801 |
| Killeshandra | 1735 |
| Killsherdaney | |
| (Cootehill) | 1810 |
| Killoughter | |
| (Redhills) | 1827 |
| Kilmore (Cavan) | 1702 |
| Knockbride | |
| (Bailieborough) | 1825 |
| Lurgan (Virginia) | 1831 |
| Quivy (Belturbet) | 1854 |
| Swanlinbar | 1798 |
| Tomregan | |

| | |
|---|---|
| (Ballyconnell) | 1797 |

### Co. Clare

| | |
|---|---|
| Ennis | 1805 |
| Killaloe | 1679 |
| Kilnasoolagh | |
| (Newmarket) | 1731 |
| Kilrush | 1773 |
| Ogonnilloe | |
| (Scariff) | 1807 |

### Co. Cork

| | |
|---|---|
| Abbeymahon | |
| (Timoleague) | 1827 |
| Abbeystrewry | |
| (Skibbereen) | 1778 |
| Aghabullog | |
| (Coachford) | 1808 |
| Aghada (Cloyne) | 1815 |
| Ardfield | |
| (Clonakilty) | 1835 |
| Ballyclough | |
| (Mallow) | 1795 |
| Ballydehob (Skull) | 1826 |
| Ballyhay | |
| (Charleville) | 1728 |
| Ballyhooly | |
| (Mallow) | 1788 |
| Ballymartyl | |
| (Ballinhassig) | 1785 |
| Ballymodan | |
| (Bandon) | 1695 |
| Ballymoney | |
| (Ballineen) | 1805 |
| Berehaven | 1787 |
| Blackrock | |
| (st. Michael) | 1828 |
| Brigown | |
| (Mitchelstown) | 1775 |
| Buttevant | 1757 |
| Carrigaline | 1723 |
| Carrigamleary | |
| (Mallow) | 1779 |
| Carrig Park | 1779 |
| Carrigtwohill | 1779 |
| Castlemagner | 1810 |
| Castletownroche | 1728 |
| Churchtown | |
| (Mallow) | 1806 |

**Co. Cork (Cont/d.)**

| | |
|---|---|
| Clenore (Mallow) | 1813 |
| Clonfert | |
| (Newmarket) | 1771 |
| Clonmeen (Mallow) | 1764 |
| Cloyne | 1708 |
| Cork | |
| Christ Church | 1643 |
| St. Luke | 1837 |
| St. Nicholas | 1721 |
| St. Anne | 1772 |
| St. Finbarr | 1752 |
| Corbeg | 1836 |
| Desertserges | |
| (Bandon) | 1837 |
| Doneraile | 1730 |
| Douglas (Cork) | 1792 |
| Drishane | 1792 |
| Dromdaleague | 1812 |
| Dromtariff | |
| (Millstreet) | 1825 |
| Fanlobbus | |
| (Dunmanway) | 1855 |
| Farrihy | |
| (Kildorrery) | 1765 |
| Fermoy | 1801 |
| Garrane | |
| (Middleton) | 1856 |
| Glanworth | 1805 |
| Inniscarra (Cork) | 1820 |
| Innishannon | 1693 |
| Kanturk | 1818 |
| Kilbolane | |
| (Kanturk) | 1779 |
| Kilbrogan (Bandon) | 1752 |
| Kilcummer | |
| (Fermoy) | 1856 |
| Killanully | |
| (Carrigaline) | 1831 |
| Killowen (Bandon) | 1833 |
| Kilmeen | |
| (Clonakilty) | 1806 |
| Kilworth | 1766 |
| Knocavilly | |
| (Bandon) | 1837 |
| Liscarrol | 1805 |
| Lisgould | |
| (Middleton) | 1847 |
| Lislee (Bandon) | 1809 |
| Litter (Fermoy) | 1811 |
| Macroom | 1727 |
| Magourney | |
| (Coachford) | 1757 |
| Mallow | 1776 |
| Marmulland | |
| (Passage West) | 1801 |
| Middleton | 1810 |
| Monanimy | |
| (Mallow) | 1812 |
| Monkstown | 1842 |
| Mourne Abbey | |
| (Mallow) | 1807 |
| Murragh (Bandon) | 1754 |
| Nathlash | |
| (Kildorrery) | 1844 |

| | |
|---|---|
| Nohoval | |
| (Kinsale) | 1785 |
| Queenstown | |
| (Cobh) | 1761 |
| Rahan (Mallow) | 1773 |
| Rathcooney | |
| (Glanmire) | 1749 |
| Rincurran | |
| (Kinsale) | 1793 |
| Rushbrook | 1806 |
| Templemartin | |
| (Bandon) | 1806 |
| Timoleague | 1823 |
| Tullylease | 1850 |
| Wallstown | |
| (Doneraile) | 1829 |
| Youghal | 1665 |

**Co. Derry**

| | |
|---|---|
| Ballinderry | |
| (Moneymore) | 1802 |
| Ballyeglish | |
| (Moneymore) | 1868 |
| Ballynascreen | 1808 |
| Banagher (Derry) | 1839 |
| Castledawson | 1744 |
| Clooney | 1867 |
| Coleraine | 1769 |
| Cumber (Clady) | 1804 |
| Desartlyn | |
| (Moneymore) | 1797 |
| Desartmartin | 1797 |
| Drumachose | |
| (Limavady) | 1728 |
| Dungiven | 1778 |
| Glendermot | 1810 |
| Kilcronaghan | |
| (Tubbermore) | 1749 |
| Killowen | |
| (Coleraine) | 1824 |
| Kilrea | 1801 |
| Learmount | |
| (Derry) | 1832 |
| Londonderry | 1642 |
| Maghera | 1785 |
| Magherafelt | 1718 |
| Tamlaght | |
| (Portglenone) | 1858 |
| Tamlaghard | |
| (Magilligan) | 1747 |
| Tamlaghfinlagan | 1796 |
| Termoneeny | |
| (Castledawson) | 1821 |
| Woods Chapel | 1800 |

**Co. Donegal**

| | |
|---|---|
| Ardara | 1829 |
| Burt | 1802 |
| Clondevaddock | |
| (Ramelton) | 1794 |
| Donegal | 1803 |
| Drumholm | |
| (Ballintra) | 1691 |
| Fahan (Buncrana) | 1761 |
| Finner | 1815 |
| Glencolumbkille | 1827 |

| | |
|---|---|
| Inniskeel (Ardara) | 1826 |
| Inver | 1805 |
| Kilbarrow | |
| (Ballyshannon) | 1785 |
| Kilcar | |
| (Killybegs) | 1819 |
| Killaghtee | |
| (Glenties) | 1810 |
| Killybegs | 1789 |
| Kilteevogue | |
| (Stranorlar) | 1818 |
| Moville | 1814 |
| Muff | 1803 |
| Raphoe | 1831 |
| Stranorlar | 1821 |
| Taughboyne | |
| (Derry) | 1819 |
| Templecarn | 1825 |
| Tullyaughnish | |
| (Ramelton) | 1798 |

**Co. Down**

| | |
|---|---|
| Aghaderg | |
| (Loughbrickland) | 1814 |
| Annalong | |
| (Castlewellan) | 1842 |
| Ardkeen | 1746 |
| Ballee | |
| (Downpatrick) | 1792 |
| Ballyculter | |
| (Strangford) | 1777 |
| Ballyhalbert | |
| (Kircubbin) | 1852 |
| Ballyphilip | |
| (Portaferry) | 1745 |
| Ballywalter | |
| (Newtownards) | 1844 |
| Bangor | 1803 |
| Clonduff | |
| (Hilltown) | 1782 |
| Comber | 1683 |
| Donaghadee | 1778 |
| Donaghcloney | 1834 |
| Downpatrick | 1750 |
| Drumballyroney | |
| (Rathfriland) | 1831 |
| Drumbeg (Lisburn) | 1823 |
| Drumbo (Lisburn) | 1791 |
| Drumgooland | 1779 |
| Dundonald | |
| (Belfast) | 1811 |
| Gilford | 1869 |
| Hillsborough | 1777 |
| Holywood | 1806 |
| Inch | |
| (Downpatrick) | 1767 |
| Innishargy | 1783 |
| Kilbroney | |
| (Rostrevor) | 1814 |
| Kilcoo | 1786 |
| Killaney | 1858 |
| Killinchy | 1819 |
| Kilmood | |
| (Killinchy) | 1822 |
| Kilmore | 1820 |
| Knockbreda (Belfast) | 1784 |

| | |
|---|---|
| Knocknamuckley | |
| (Gilford) | 1838 |
| Loughlin Island | |
| (Clough) | 1760 |
| Magheralin | 1692 |
| Moira | 1845 |
| Moyntags | |
| (Lurgan) | 1822 |
| Newcastle | 1823 |
| Newry | 1822 |
| Saintfield | 1724 |
| Seagoe | 1672 |
| Seapatrick | |
| (Banbridge) | 1802 |
| Tullylish | |
| (Banbridge) | 1820 |
| Tyrella (Clough) | 1839 |
| Warrenpoint | 1825 |

**Co. Dublin**

| | |
|---|---|
| Balbriggan | 1838 |
| Blackrock | 1855 |
| Castleknock | 1709 |
| Chapelizod | 1812 |
| Clondalkin | 1728 |
| Clonsilla | 1830 |
| Donabate | 1811 |
| Donnybrook | 1712 |
| Holmpatrick | 1779 |
| Howth | 1804 |
| Irishtown | |
| (Sandymount) | 1812 |
| Killesk | 1829 |
| Kilmainham | 1857 |
| Kilsallaghan | 1818 |
| Kilternan | 1817 |
| Kingstown | |
| (Dun Laoghaire) | 1843 |
| Lusk | 1809 |
| Malahide | 1822 |
| Monkstown | 1680 |
| Newcastle | 1773 |
| Santry | 1753 |
| Swords | 1705 |
| Taney (Dundrum) | 1835 |
| Whitechurch | |
| (Terenure) | 1825 |

*For Dublin City parishes see page 88.*

**Co. Fermanagh**

| | |
|---|---|
| Aghadrumsee | |
| (Clones) | 1821 |
| Aghalurcher | |
| (Lisnaskea) | 1788 |
| Aghaveagh | |
| (Lisnaskea) | 1815 |
| Belleek | 1822 |
| Bohoe | |
| (Enniskillen) | 1840 |
| Clabby | |
| (Fivemiletown) | 1862 |
| Coolaghty (Kesh) | 1835 |
| Derryvullan | |
| (Enniskillen) | 1803 |

## Co. Fermanagh (Cont/d.)

| | |
|---|---|
| Devenish | |
| (Ballyshannon) | 1800 |
| Drumkeeran (Kesh) | 1801 |
| Galloon | 1798 |
| Innishmacsaint | 1813 |
| Killesher | |
| (Enniskillen) | 1798 |
| Kinawley | 1761 |
| Lisnaskea | 1804 |
| Mullaghafad | |
| (Scotstown) | 1836 |
| Magheracross | 1800 |
| Magheraculmoney | |
| (Kesh) | 1767 |
| Maguiresbridge | 1840 |
| Tempo | 1836 |
| Trory | |
| (Enniskillen) | 1779 |

## Co. Galway

| | |
|---|---|
| Ahascragh | 1775 |
| Ardrahan | 1804 |
| Aughrim | 1814 |
| Ballinacourty | |
| (Oranmore) | 1838 |
| Ballinakill | |
| (Clifden) | 1852 |
| Ballinakill | |
| (Portumna) | 1766 |
| Creagh | |
| (Ballinasloe) | 1823 |
| Galway | |
| St. Nicholas | 1782 |
| Inniscaltra | |
| (Mountshannon) | 1851 |
| Kilcolgan | 1847 |
| Kilcummin | |
| (Oughterard) | 1812 |
| Killannin | |
| (Headford) | 1844 |
| Loughrea | 1747 |
| Moylough | |
| (Mountbellew) | 1821 |
| Moyrus | |
| (Roundstone) | 1841 |
| Omey (Clifden) | 1831 |
| Tuam | 1808 |

## Co. Kerry

| | |
|---|---|
| Aghadoe | |
| (Killarney) | 1842 |
| Ballymacelligot | 1817 |
| Ballynacourty | |
| (Kilflynn) | 1803 |
| Ballyseedy | |
| (Tralee) | 1830 |
| Castleisland | 1835 |
| Dingle | 1707 |
| Dromod (Prior) | 1827 |
| Kenmare | 1799 |
| Kilcolman | |
| (Killorglin) | 1802 |
| Kilgarvan | 1811 |
| Kilnaughton (Tarbert) | 1793 |

| | |
|---|---|
| Liselton | 1840 |
| Listowel | 1790 |
| Tralee | 1771 |
| Valentia | 1826 |

## Co. Kildare

| | |
|---|---|
| Athy | 1669 |
| Ballymore-Eustace | 1838 |
| Ballysax | 1830 |
| Carbery | 1814 |
| Celbridge | 1777 |
| Clane | 1802 |
| Clonsast | |
| (Celbridge) | 1805 |
| Harristown | |
| (Athy) | 1666 |
| Kilcullen | 1778 |
| Kildare | |
| St. Bridget | 1801 |
| Kill | 1814 |
| Lackagh | |
| (Monastereven) | 1830 |
| Naas | 1679 |
| Straffan (Naas) | 1838 |
| Timolin | |
| (Baltinglass) | 1812 |

## Co. Kilkenny

| | |
|---|---|
| Blackrath | |
| (Kilkenny) | 1810 |
| Castlecomer | 1799 |
| Clonmore | 1817 |
| Fertagh | |
| (Johnstown) | 1797 |
| Fiddown | |
| (Pilltown) | 1686 |
| Gallskill | |
| (Pilltown) | 1753 |
| Graig | 1827 |
| Grangesylvae | |
| (Gowran) | 1850 |
| Innistiogue | 1797 |
| Kilbeacon | |
| (Pilltown) | 1813 |
| Kilcollum | 1817 |
| Kilkenny | |
| St. Canice | 1789 |
| St. Mary | 1729 |
| Kilmacow | 1792 |
| Kilmanagh (Callan) | 1784 |
| Kilmoganny | |
| (Knocktopher) | 1782 |
| Macully (Pilltown) | 1817 |

## Co. Leitrim

| | |
|---|---|
| Drumlease | |
| (Dromahaire) | 1828 |
| Kiltoghert | |
| (Carrick-on- | |
| Shannon) | 1810 |
| Manorhamilton | 1816 |
| Outragh (Ballinamore) | 1833 |

## Co. Leix (Queen's)

| | |
|---|---|
| Abbeyleix | 1781 |
| Ballyfin | 1821 |
| Castletown | 1802 |
| Clonenagh | |
| (Mountrath) | 1749 |
| Coolbanagher | 1802 |
| Durrow | 1731 |
| Killeban | 1802 |
| Lea | |
| (Portarlington) | 1801 |
| Maryborough | |
| (Portlaoise) | 1793 |
| Mountmellick | 1840 |
| Offerlane | |
| (Borris-in-Ossory) | 1807 |
| Oregan | |
| (Rosenallis) | 1801 |
| Portarlington | 1694 |
| Rathdowney | 1756 |
| Rathsaran | |
| (Rathdowney) | 1810 |
| Stradbally | 1772 |
| Timahoe | 1845 |

## Co. Limerick

| | |
|---|---|
| Abington | 1811 |
| Adare | 1804 |
| Ardcanny | |
| (Pallaskenry) | 1802 |
| Ballingarry | 1785 |
| Bruff | 1850 |
| Cahernarry | |
| (Nr. Limerick) | 1857 |
| Cappamore | 1858 |
| Doon | 1804 |
| Fedamore | 1840 |
| Kildimo | 1809 |
| Kilfergus (Foynes) | 1812 |
| Kilfinane | 1804 |
| Kilflyn | |
| (Ardpatrick) | 1813 |
| Kilkeedy | |
| (Mungret) | 1799 |
| Kilmoylan | 1812 |
| Limerick | |
| St. John | 1697 |
| St. Mary | 1726 |
| St. Michael | 1801 |
| St. Munchin | 1700 |
| Rathkeale | 1746 |
| Rathronan (Ardagh) | 1818 |
| Shanagolden | 1803 |
| Tullybrackey (Bruff) | 1820 |

## Co. Longford

| | |
|---|---|
| Ardagh | 1811 |
| Clonbroney | 1821 |
| Clongesh | 1820 |
| Forgney | |
| (Ballymahon) | 1803 |
| Granard | 1820 |
| Kilcommick | |
| (Ballymahon) | 1795 |
| Killashee (Lanesboro') | 1771 |

| | |
|---|---|
| Mostrim | |
| (Edgeworthstown) | 1801 |
| Moydow | 1794 |
| Street | 1801 |
| Shrule | 1821 |
| Templemichael | |
| (Longford) | 1795 |

## Co. Louth

| | |
|---|---|
| Ardee | 1735 |
| Charlestown | 1822 |
| Collon | 1790 |
| Drogheda | |
| St. Peter | 1654 |
| St. Mary | 1811 |
| Dundalk | 1729 |
| Jonesborough | 1812 |
| Mellifont | 1812 |
| Tullyallen | 1812 |

## Co. Mayo

| | |
|---|---|
| Achill | 1854 |
| Aghagower | |
| (Westport) | 1825 |
| Ballincholla | |
| (The Neale) | 1831 |
| Ballysakeery | |
| (Ballina) | 1802 |
| Cong | 1811 |
| Crossmolina | 1768 |
| Dugort | 1838 |
| Killala | 1757 |
| Kilmainemore | |
| (Ballinrobe) | 1744 |
| Kilmoremoy | |
| (Ballinahaglish) | 1801 |
| Knappagh | |
| (Westport) | 1855 |
| Turlough | |
| (Castlebar) | 1821 |
| Westport | 1801 |

## Co. Meath

| | |
|---|---|
| Athboy | 1736 |
| Ballymaglasson | |
| (Dunshaughlin) | 1800 |
| Clonard | 1792 |
| Drumconrath | 1785 |
| Dunshaughlin | 1800 |
| Kells | 1773 |
| Killochonagan | |
| (Trim) | 1853 |
| Kilmore | |
| (Kilcock) | 1800 |
| Knockmark | |
| (Dunshaughlin) | 1825 |
| Nobber | 1828 |
| Oldcastle | 1814 |
| Rathbeggan | |
| (Dunboyne) | 1821 |
| Rathcore | |
| (Enfield) | 1810 |
| Syddan (Navan) | 1720 |
| Trim | 1836 |

## Co. Monaghan

| | |
|---|---|
| Ballybay | 1813 |
| Carrickmacross | 1796 |
| Castleblaney | 1810 |
| Clones | 1682 |
| Currin | |
| (Rockcorry) | 1810 |
| Donagh | |
| (Glasslough) | 1796 |
| Emyvale (Trough) | 1809 |
| Killarney | |
| (Carrickmacross) | 1825 |
| Killeevan (Clones) | 1811 |
| Kilmore | 1796 |
| Magheracloone | 1806 |
| Monaghan | 1802 |
| Newbliss | 1841 |
| Tedavnet | |
| (Scotstown) | 1822 |
| Tyholland | |
| (Monaghan) | 1806 |

## Co. Offaly (King's)

| | |
|---|---|
| Ballyboy | |
| (Frankford) | 1796 |
| Birr | 1772 |
| Castlejordan | |
| (Edenderry) | 1823 |
| Cloneyhork | |
| (Portarlington) | 1824 |
| Clonmacnoise | 1824 |
| Durrow | 1816 |
| Ettagh (Roscrea) | 1825 |
| Ferbane | 1819 |
| Gallen (Cloghan) | 1842 |
| Geashill | 1713 |
| Kilbride | |
| (Tullamore) | 1811 |
| Killeigh | |
| (Tullamore) | 1808 |
| Kinnitty | 1800 |
| Monasteroris | |
| (Edenderry) | 1698 |
| Shinrone | 1741 |
| Templeharry | |
| (Shinrone) | 1800 |

## Co. Roscommon

| | |
|---|---|
| Ardcarna (Boyle) | 1820 |
| Boyle | 1793 |
| Bumlin | |
| (Strokestown) | 1811 |
| Croghan | |
| (Boyle) | 1862 |
| Estersrow | |
| (Boyle) | 1800 |
| Kilbryan | |
| (Boyle) | 1852 |
| Kilglass | |
| (Rooskey) | 1823 |
| Kilkeevan | |
| (Castlerea) | 1748 |
| Kiltoom | |
| (Athlone) | 1797 |
| Kiltullagh | |
| (Castlerea) | 1822 |

## Co. Sligo

| | |
|---|---|
| Ballysumaghan | |
| (Collooney) | 1828 |
| Drumcliff | 1805 |
| Easkey | 1822 |
| Emlafad | |
| (Ballymote) | 1831 |
| Kilmactranny | |
| (Boyle) | 1816 |
| Knocknarea | |
| (Sligo) | 1842 |
| Lissadell | 1836 |
| Sligo | |
| St. John | 1802 |

## Co. Tipperary

| | |
|---|---|
| Aghnameadle | |
| (Moneygall) | 1834 |
| Ballingarry | |
| (Cashel) | 1816 |
| Ballintemple | |
| (Golden) | 1805 |
| Borrisnafarney | |
| (Roscrea) | 1827 |
| Cahir | 1801 |
| Carrick-on-Suir | 1803 |
| Cashel | 1668 |
| Clonmel | 1766 |
| Clonoulty | |
| (Cashel) | 1817 |
| Cloughjordan | 1827 |
| Cullen | |
| (Tipperary) | 1770 |
| Dunkerrin | 1800 |
| Fethard | 1804 |
| Holycross | 1784 |
| Innislonagh | |
| (Clonmel) | 1801 |
| Mealiffe | |
| (Thurles) | 1791 |
| Modreeny | 1827 |
| Newport | 1782 |
| Shanrahan | |
| (Clogheen) | 1793 |
| Templemichael | |
| (Carrick-on-Suir) | 1791 |
| Terry Glass | |
| (Borrisokane) | 1809 |
| Tipperary | 1779 |
| Toem (Cashel) | 1802 |
| Tullamelan | |
| (Clonmel) | 1823 |

## Co. Tyrone

| | |
|---|---|
| Arboe | |
| (Cookstown) | 1773 |
| Ardtrea | |
| (Cookstown) | 1811 |
| Badoney (Gortin) | 1818 |
| Ballyclog | |
| (Stewartstown) | 1818 |
| Brackaville | 1836 |
| Caledon | 1791 |
| Camus | 1803 |
| Cappagh | 1758 |
| Carnteel | |
| (Aughnacloy) | 1805 |

| | |
|---|---|
| Clonfeacle | |
| (Dungannon) | 1763 |
| Derg (Castlederg) | 1807 |
| Derrylorgan | |
| (Cookstown) | 1796 |
| Desertcreat | |
| (Cookstown) | 1812 |
| Donagheady | |
| (Strabane) | 1754 |
| Donaghenry | |
| (Dungannon) | 1734 |
| Donaghmore | |
| (Castlefin) | 1748 |
| Drumglass | |
| (Dungannon) | 1664 |
| Drumrath | |
| (Omagh) | 1800 |
| Edenderry | |
| (Omagh) | 1841 |
| Errigal | |
| (Garvagh) | 1812 |
| Findonagh | |
| (Donacavey) | 1777 |
| Fivemiletown | 1804 |
| Kildress | |
| (Cookstown) | 1749 |
| Killyman | |
| (Dungannon) | 1741 |
| Kilskerry | |
| (Enniskillen) | 1772 |
| Lissan | |
| (Cookstown) | 1753 |
| Sixmilecross | 1836 |
| Termonmongan | |
| (Castlederg) | 1812 |
| Tullyniskin | |
| (Dungannon) | 1794 |
| Urney (Strabane) | 1813 |

## Co. Waterford

| | |
|---|---|
| Cappoquin | 1844 |
| Dungarvan | 1741 |
| Innislonagh | 1800 |
| Killea | |
| (Dunmore) | 1816 |
| Kilmeadon | 1683 |
| Killrosantry | 1838 |
| Kilwatermoy | 1860 |
| Kill (Passage) | 1730 |
| Lismore | 1693 |
| Macully | 1817 |
| Portlaw | 1741 |
| Tallow | 1772 |
| Templemichael | 1801 |
| Waterford | |
| St. Olave's | 1658 |
| St. Patrick's | 1723 |

## Co. Westmeath

| | |
|---|---|
| Abbeyshrule | 1821 |
| Athlone | |
| St. Mary | 1746 |
| Delvin | 1817 |
| Kilbixy | |
| (Ballinacargy) | 1843 |
| Kilkenny | |
| (Ballymore) | 1783 |

| | |
|---|---|
| Killucan | 1700 |
| Mayne | |
| (Castlepollard) | 1808 |
| Willbrooke | |
| (Athlone) | 1756 |

## Co. Wexford

| | |
|---|---|
| Ardamine | |
| (Gorey) | 1807 |
| Ballycanew | 1733 |
| Ballycarney | |
| (Ferns) | 1835 |
| Carnew | 1749 |
| Clonegal | 1792 |
| Clonmore | 1828 |
| Enniscorthy | 1798 |
| Ferns | 1775 |
| Gorey | 1801 |
| Inch (New Ross) | 1726 |
| Killanne | 1771 |
| Killegney | |
| (Enniscorthy) | 1800 |
| Killeney | 1788 |
| Killinick | |
| (Wexford) | 1804 |
| Killurin | 1816 |
| Kilmallog | |
| (Wexford) | 1813 |
| Kilnehue | |
| (Gorey) | 1817 |
| Kilpipe (Arklow) | 1828 |
| Kiltennell | |
| (Gorey) | 1806 |
| Leskinfere | |
| (Gorey) | 1802 |
| Mulrankin | 1768 |
| Newtownbarry | |
| (Bunclody) | 1779 |
| Owenduff | |
| (Taghmon) | 1752 |
| Rathaspick | 1844 |
| Rossdroit | |
| (Enniscorthy) | 1802 |
| Tacumshane | |
| (Rosslare) | 1832 |
| Templescobin | |
| (Enniscorthy) | 1802 |
| Tomhaggard | |
| (Rosslare) | 1809 |
| Toombe (Ferns) | 1770 |
| Wexford | 1674 |

## Co. Wicklow

| | |
|---|---|
| Ballinaclash | |
| (Rathdrum) | 1839 |
| Ballintemple | |
| (Arklow) | 1823 |
| Ballynure | |
| (Dunlavin) | 1807 |
| Blessington | 1695 |
| Bray | 1666 |
| Castlemacadam | |
| (Ovoca) | 1720 |
| Crosspatrick | |
| (Tinahely) | 1830 |
| Delgany | 1666 |
| Dunlavin | 1697 |

## Co. Wicklow (Cont/d)

| | |
|---|---|
| Glenealy | 1825 |
| Kilcommon (Hacketstown) | 1814 |
| Killiskey (Ashford) | 1818 |
| Mullinacuff (Tinahely) | 1838 |
| Newcastle | 1698 |
| Ovoca | 1720 |
| Powerscourt | 1677 |
| Preban (Tinahely) | 1827 |
| Rathdrum | 1706 |
| Shillelagh | 1833 |
| Stratford (Baltinglass) | 1812 |
| Wicklow | 1655 |

## Church of Ireland : Published Parish Registers

Published·Dublin Parish Registers in publications of Irish Memorials Association / Dublin Parish Register Society.

St. John, marr., bapt., bur., 1619-1699, vol.1.

St. Patrick, marr., bapt., bur., 1677-1800 vol.2.

St. Peter and St. Kevin, bapt., marr., bur., 1699-1761, vol.9.

St. Michan, bapt., marr., bur., 1636-1685; 1666-1700, vols.7, 3.

St. Catherine, bapt., marr., bur., 1630-1715, vol.5.

Parish of Monkstown, bapt., marr., bur., 1699-1786, vol.6.

St. Nicholas without, bapt., marr., bur., 1694-1739, vol.10.

St. Bride, bapt., marr., bur., 1632-1800, vol.11.

St. Mary, Donnybrook, marr., 1712-1800, vol.11.

St. Nicholas within, marr., 1671-1800, vol.11.

Parish of Finglas, burials, 1664-1729, vol.11.

St. Michael, marr., 1656-1800, vol.11.

St. Michan, marr., 1700-1800, vol.11.

St. John, marr., 1700-1800, vol.11.

St. Nicholas within burials, 1671-1825, vol.11.

St. Audeon, burials, 1672-1692, vol 12.

St. Mary, Crumlin, marr. and bapt. 1740-1830, vol.12.

St. Andrew, marr., 1801-1819, vol.12.

St. Catherine, marr., 1715-1800.

St. Ann, Dawson St., marr., 1719-1800.

St. Luke, marr., 1716-1800.

St. Werburg, marr., 1704-1800.

St. Mary, marr., 1697-1800.

# Presbyterian Registers

†*In Presbyterian Historical Society's Archives, Belfast.*

## Co. Antrim

| | |
|---|---|
| † Antrim | 1674 |
| Armoy | 1842 |
| Ballycarny | 1832 |
| Ballycastle | 1829 |
| Ballyeaston (Ballyclare) | 1821 |
| Ballylinney (Ballyclare) | 1837 |
| Ballymena | 1825 |
| Ballymoney | 1817 |
| Ballynure | 1819 |
| Ballywillan (Portrush) | 1816 |
| Ballymacarrett (Belfast) | 1837 |
| Ballysillan | 1839 |
| Belfast | |
| Fisherwick Place | 1810 |
| † Rosemary St. | 1722 |
| Broadmills (Lisburn) | 1824 |
| Broughshane | 1830 |
| Buckal | 1841 |
| †Carnmoney | 1708 |
| Carrickfergus | 1823 |
| Castlereagh | 1807 |
| +Cliftonville | 1825 |
| Cloughwater | 1852 |
| Connor (Ballymena) | 1819 |

| | |
|---|---|
| Crumlin | 1839 |
| Cullybackey | 1812 |
| †Dongore (Templepatrick) | 1806 |
| †Drumbo (Lisburn) | 1764 |
| †Dundonald (Belfast) | 1678 |
| Dundron (Belfast) | 1829 |
| Finvoy (Ballymoney) | 1843 |
| Gilnahurk (Belfast) | 1797 |
| Glenarn | 1850 |
| Glenwherry (Ballymena) | 1845 |
| Grange (Toomebridge) | 1824 |
| Kilraught (Ballymorey) | 1836 |
| Larne | 1824 |
| Loughmourne | 1848 |
| †Lylehill (Templepatrick) | 1832 |
| Masside | 1843 |
| Portrush | 1843 |
| Raloo (Larne) | 1840 |
| Randalstown | 1837 |
| Rasharkin | 1834 |
| Templepatrick | 1831 |
| Tobberleigh | 1831 |

## Co. Armagh

| | |
|---|---|
| Ahorey (Loughgall) | 1838 |
| † Armagh | 1707 |
| Bessbrook | 1854 |
| Cladymore | 1848 |
| Clare (Tandragee) | 1838 |
| Cremore | 1831 |
| Donacloney (Lurgan) | 1798 |
| Gilford | 1843 |
| Keady | 1819 |
| Kingsmills (Whitecross) | 1842 |
| Knappagh | 1842 |
| Lislooney | 1836 |
| Loughgall | 1842 |
| Lurgan | 1746 |
| Markethill | 1821 |
| †Mountnorris | 1804 |
| Newmills (Portadown) | 1838 |
| Newtownhamilton | 1823 |
| Portadown | 1822 |
| Poyntzpass | 1850 |
| Richhill | 1856 |
| Tandragee | 1835 |
| Tullyallen | 1795 |
| Vinecash (Portadown) | 1838 |

## Co. Cavan

| | |
|---|---|
| Bailieborough | 1852 |
| Ballyjamesduff | 1845 |
| Bellasis | 1845 |
| Cavan | 1851 |
| Cootehill | 1828 |
| † Killeshandra | 1743 |

## Co. Cork

| | |
|---|---|
| Bandon | 1842 |
| Cork | 1832 |
| Cobh (Queenstown) | 1847 |

## Co. Derry

| | |
|---|---|
| †Ballykelly | 1699 |
| Banagher (Derry) | 1834 |
| Boveedy (Kilrea) | 1841 |
| Castledawson | 1835 |
| †Coleraine | 1842 |
| Crossgar (Coleraine) | 1839 |
| †Cumber (Claudy) | 1827 |
| Derrymore (Limavady) | 1825 |
| Derry | 1815 |
| Draperstown | 1837 |
| Drumachose (Limavady) | 1838 |
| Dunboe (Coleraine) | 1843 |

**Co. Derry (Cont/d)**

| | |
|---|---|
| Dungiven | 1835 |
| †Faughanvale | |
| (Eglinton) | 1819 |
| Garvagh | 1795 |
| Gortnassy (Derry) | 1839 |
| †Killaigh | |
| (Coleraine) | 1805 |
| Kilrea | 1825 |
| Lecompher | |
| (Moneymore) | 1825 |
| Limavady | 1832 |
| Maghera | 1843 |
| †Magherafelt | 1703 |
| Magilligan | 1814 |
| Moneymore | 1827 |
| Portstewart | 1829 |

**Co. Donegal**

| | |
|---|---|
| Ballindrait | 1819 |
| Ballyshannon | 1836 |
| Buncrana | 1836 |
| Burt | 1834 |
| Carnone (Raphoe) | 1834 |
| †Carrigart | 1844 |
| Convoy | 1822 |
| Donegal | 1825 |
| Donoughmore | |
| (Castlefin) | 1844 |
| Knowhead (Muff) | 1826 |
| Letterkenny | 1841 |
| Monreagh | |
| (Derry) | 1845 |
| Moville | 1834 |
| Newtowncunning- | 1830 |
| ham | |
| Ramelton | 1808 |
| Raphoe | 1829 |
| St. Johnston | 1838 |
| Trentagh | |
| (Kilmacrennan) | 1836 |

**Co. Down**

| | |
|---|---|
| Anaghlone | |
| (Banbridge) | 1839 |
| Anahilt | |
| (Hillsborough) | 1780 |
| Annalong | 1840 |
| Ardaragh (Newry) | 1804 |
| Balltdown | |
| (Banbridge) | 1809 |
| Ballygilbert | 1841 |
| Ballygraney | |
| (Bangor) | 1838 |
| Ballynahinch | 1841 |
| Ballyroney | |
| (Banbridge) | 1831 |
| Ballywalter | 1824 |
| †Banbridge | 1756 |
| Bangor | 1833 |
| Carrowdore | |
| (Greyabbey) | 1843 |

| | |
|---|---|
| Clarkesbridge | |
| (Newry) | 1833 |
| Clonduff | |
| (Banbridge) | 1842 |
| Clough | |
| (Downpatrick) | 1836 |
| Cloughey | 1844 |
| Comber | 1847 |
| Conligh | |
| (Newtownards) | 1845 |
| Donaghadee | 1822 |
| Downpatrick | 1827 |
| Dromara | 1823 |
| Dromore | 1834 |
| Drumbanagher | |
| (Derry) | 1832 |
| Drumgooland | 1833 |
| Drumlee | |
| (Banbridge) | 1826 |
| Edengrove | |
| (Ballynahinch) | 1829 |
| Glastry | 1728 |
| Groomsport | 1841 |
| Hillsborough | 1832 |
| Kilkeel | 1842 |
| Killinchy | 1835 |
| †Killyleagh | 1693 |
| Kilmore (Crossgar) | 1833 |
| †Kirkcubbin | 1785 |
| Leitrim | |
| (Banbridge) | 1837 |
| Lissera (Crossgar) | 1809 |
| Loughagherry | |
| (Hillsborough) | 1801 |
| Loughbrickland | 1842 |
| Magherally | |
| (Banbridge) | 1837 |
| Millisle | 1773 |
| Mourne (Kilkeel) | 1840 |
| Newry | 1829 |
| Newtownards | 1833 |
| †Portaferry | 1699 |
| Raffrey (Crossgar) | 1843 |
| Rathfriland | 1804 |
| Rostrevor | 1851 |
| Saintfield | 1831 |
| †Scarva | 1807 |
| Seaforde | 1826 |
| Strangford | 1846 |
| Tullylish | |
| (Gilford) | 1813 |
| Warrenpoint | 1832 |

**Co. Dublin**

| | |
|---|---|
| Abbey | |
| (Abbey St.) | 1777 |
| Ormond Quay | 1787 |
| Clontarf | 1836 |

**Co. Fermanagh**

| | |
|---|---|
| Enniskillen | 1837 |
| Lisbellaw | 1849 |
| Pettigo | 1844 |

**Co. Galway**

| | |
|---|---|
| Galway | 1831 |

**Co. Kerry**

| | |
|---|---|
| Tralee | 1840 |

**Co. Laois (Queens)**

| | |
|---|---|
| †Mountmellick | 1849 |

**Co. Leitrim**

| | |
|---|---|
| Carrigallen | 1844 |

**Co. Limerick**

| | |
|---|---|
| Limerick | 1829 |

**Co. Longford**

| | |
|---|---|
| Tully | |
| (Edgeworthstown) | 1844 |

**Co. Louth**

| | |
|---|---|
| Corvally | |
| (Dundalk) | 1840 |
| Dundalk | 1819 |

**Co. Mayo**

| | |
|---|---|
| Dromore | |
| (Ballina) | 1849 |

**Co. Monaghan**

| | |
|---|---|
| Ballyalbany | 1802 |
| Ballybay | 1833 |
| Ballyhobridge | |
| (Clones) | 1846 |
| Broomfield | |
| (Castleblaney) | 1841 |
| †Cahans | |
| (Ballybay) | 1752 |
| Castleblaney | 1832 |
| Clones | 1856 |
| Clontibret | 1825 |
| Corlea | 1835 |
| Derryvalley | |
| (Ballybay) | 1816 |
| Drumkeen | |
| (Newbliss) | 1856 |
| †Frankford | |
| (Castleblaney) | 1820 |
| †Glennan | |
| (Glasslough) | 1805 |
| Middletown | |
| (Glasslough) | 1829 |
| Monaghan | 1824 |
| Newbliss | 1856 |
| Scotstown | 1856 |
| Stonebridge | |
| (Newbliss) | 1821 |

**Co. Tyrone**

| | |
|---|---|
| Albany | |
| (Stewartstown) | 1838 |

| | |
|---|---|
| Ardstraw | 1837 |
| Aughataire | |
| (Fivemiletown) | 1836 |
| Aughnacloy | 1843 |
| Ballygawley | 1843 |
| Ballygorey | |
| (Cookstown) | 1834 |
| Ballynahatty | |
| (Omagh) | 1843 |
| Ballyreagh | |
| (Ballygawley) | 1843 |
| Brigh | |
| (Stewartstown) | 1836 |
| Carland | |
| (Castlecaulfield) | 1759 |
| Castlederg | 1823 |
| Cleggan | |
| (Cookstown) | 1848 |
| Clenanees | |
| (Castlecaulfield) | 1840 |
| Clogher | 1819 |
| Coagh | 1839 |
| Cookstown | 1836 |
| Donaghheady | |
| (Strabane) | 1838 |
| Drumguin | 1845 |
| Dungannon | 1790 |
| Edenderry | |
| (Omagh) | 1845 |
| Eglish | |
| (Dungannon) | 1839 |
| Fintona | 1836 |
| Gillygooly (Omagh) | 1848 |
| Gortin | 1843 |
| Leckpatrick | |
| (Strabane) | 1838 |
| Minterburn | |
| (Caledon) | 1829 |
| Moy | 1851 |
| Newmills | |
| (Dungannon) | 1850 |
| Omagh | 1821 |
| Orritor | |
| (Cookstown) | 1831 |
| Pomeroy | 1841 |
| Sandholey | |
| (Cookstown) | 1844 |
| Strabane | 1828 |
| Urney | |
| (Sion Mills) | 1837 |

**Co. Waterford**

| | |
|---|---|
| Waterford | 1770 |

**Co. Wexford**

| | |
|---|---|
| Wexford | 1844 |

**Co. Wicklow**

| | |
|---|---|
| Bray | 1836 |

# CHAPTER 5

# Preliminary Research in Home Country

It frequently happens that people of Irish descent seeking ancestors and relatives in Ireland lack the essential information necessary for commencing a search in Ireland. There is little use, for example, in attempting to trace 'John Gallagher who left Ireland about 1850 for America' since a hundred persons could be found to fit such a set of circumstances.

Except in the case of exceedingly rare Irish surnames the minimum requirement for commencing a worthwhile search in Ireland would be a knowledge of the county of origin of the ancestor sought.

Much time and expense can be saved during an Irish tour and the chances of success greatly enhanced if an effort is made beforehand to ascertain as much as possible about the family connections in one's own country, with special reference to the original ancestor. Failure to check such personal records as early nostalgic letters from the homeland, old diaries and the family bible may mean overlooking precious original information not elsewhere available. Sometimes the gravestone of the original settler gives specific though not always accurate information. Since a vast number of Irish emigrants settled in the United States, Australia, Canada and England, a word on the official genealogical records of these countries may prove helpful.

## American Records

For the average American enquirer the most critical factor in bridging the gap between the United States and Ireland is the date and place of arrival in America and the exact part of Ireland from which the original ancestor came. Due to a breakdown in family tradition it often becomes necessary to consult American immigration entry forms, census returns, passenger lists, etc. These records are housed in the U.S. National Archives in Washington.

### Passenger Lists

The Archives has incomplete series of customs passenger lists of ships arriving at the Atlantic and Gulf of Mexico ports. The following table shows the dates of passenger lists and related indexes in the Archives —

| Port | Customs lists | Immigration lists | Indexes |
|---|---|---|---|
| Baltimore | 1820-92 | 1891-1909 | 1820-1952 |
| Boston | 1820-74 & 1883-91 | 1891-1943 | 1848 & 1902-20 |
| New Orleans | 1820-1902 | 1903-45 | 1853-1952 |
| New York | 1820-97 | 1897-1942 | 1820-46 & 1897-1943 |
| Philadelphia | 1800-82 | 1883-1945 | 1800-1948 |
| Certain Minor Ports | 1820-73 | 1893-1945 | 1890-1924 |

Supplementing the indexes listed above is a general index to quarterly reports of arrivals at most ports except New York, 1820-74.

A customs passenger list normally contains the following information for each passenger: his name, age, sex, and occupation, the country from which he came, and the country to which he was going, and, if he died in passage, the date and circumstances of his death. The immigration passenger lists that are more than 50 years old (those less than 50 years old are not available for reference purposes) vary in information content but usually show the place of birth and last place of residence in addition to the information found in the customs passenger lists. Some of the immigration passenger lists include the name and address of a relative in the country from which the passenger came.

The Archives will search the customs passenger lists if, in addition to the name of the passenger and the name of the port of entry, an enquirer can supply the following information — the name of the vessel and the approximate date of its arrival or the name of the port of embarkation and the exact date of arrival. It will also search the immigration passenger lists over 50 years old if an enquirer can give the full name and age of the passenger and names and ages of accompanying passengers, the name of the port of entry, the name of the vessel, and the exact date of arrival. The Archives will also consult such indexes as it has to the names on the customs and immigration passenger lists provided an enquirer can supply the name of the port of entry and the supposed year of arrival.

Positive microfilm copies of passenger lists more than 50 years old are available for use in the Archives microfilm reading room by researchers or their agents.

## Census Returns

A census of the population has been taken every 10 years since 1790. The Archives has the 1790-1870 returns, a microfilm copy of the 1880 returns, and the surviving fragment of the 1890 returns. The 1790-1840 returns show the names of the heads of the households only; other family members are tallied unnamed in age and sex groups. The 1850-90 returns include the name, age and State, Territory or Country of birth of each person in a household. Additional information is included with each succeeding census.

The available returns for the 1790 census were published by the Federal Government in the early 1900's. The published census returns for 1790 are for Connecticut, Maine, Maryland, Massachusetts, New Hampshire, New York, North Carolina, Pennsylvania, Rhode Island, South Carolina and Vermont. Returns for the remaining States — Delaware, Georgia, Kentucky, New Jersey, Tenessee and Virginia — were burned during the War of 1812.

The Archives staff will, free of charge, search for a specific name in any index it has. For returns not indexed, the staff can make a very limited search for a particular name in a given year's returns if provided with the State and County in which the person lived. If the county had a large population, particularly after 1850, the specific town or township is needed. If the residence was in one of the larger cities, the street address or ward is also needed. This information can be found in city directories and ward maps normally available in city and State libraries, historical societies, and archives. When the requested entry is found, the fee for a photocopy of the census page on which it appears will be given. If the search is too extensive for the Archives staff to undertake, the fee for a microfilm copy of the related census will be given.

### Military Service Records

Registers of enlistments in the U.S. Army, 1798-1914, and compiled military service records of volunteers, 1775-1903, including records of service in the Army of the Confederate States of America, are in the Archives. The registers relate to service performed in both peacetime and wartime. They usually show for each recruit his name, age, place of enlistment, regiment or company and date and cause of discharge, or, where applicable, date of death or date of desertion and of apprehension after desertion. The compiled military service records normally show the soldier's rank, military organization and term of service. Occasionally they also show his age, the place of his enlistment and the place of his birth.

### Naturalization Records

The Archives has naturalization proceedings of the District of Columbia courts, 1802-1926. These records show, for each person who petitioned for naturalization, his age or date of birth, his nationality and whether citizenship was granted. The Archives also has photocopies and indexes of naturalization documents, 1787-1906, filed by courts in Maine, Massachusetts, New Hampshire and Rhode Island. These records were copied and indexed by the Work Projects Administration in the late 1930's. The Archives staff will search these records for information about naturalizations that occurred before September 17, 1906, if given the full name of the petitioner and the approximate date of naturalization.

### Land Records

The land records in the Archives (dated chiefly 1800-1950) include donation land entry files, homestead application files and private land claim files relating to the entry of individual settlers on land in the public land States. Land records for Maine, Vermont, West Virginia, Kentucky, Tenessee, Texas, and Hawaii are maintained in the State capitals. The donation land entry files and homestead application files show, in addition to the name of the applicant, the location of the land and the date he acquired it, his residence or post office address, his age or date and place of birth, his marital status, and if applicable, the given name of his wife or the size of his family. If an applicant for homestead land was of foreign birth, his application file contains evidence of his naturalization or of his intention to become a citizen. Supporting documents show the immigrant's country of birth and sometimes the date and port of arrival. Genealogical information in records relating to private land claims varies from the mention of the claimant's name and location of the land to such additional information as the claimant's place of residence when he made the claim and the name of his relatives, both living and dead.

## Australian Records

Australians of Irish descent recall with pride names such as Charles McMahon, speaker of the Assembly, Victoria; Robert Burke-O'Hara, celebrated explorer; Paddy Hannon, first man to ride into Kalgoorlie and after whom Hannon Lake in that district is today named; Charles O'Connor, Coolgardie water-works engineer; Daniel Mannix, Archbishop of Melbourne, not forgetting, of course, Ned Kelly, Jack Duggan and a host of other 'wild colonial boys'

When the story of the Irish contribution to the development of Australia is fully chronicled, that contribution will be found to be more pronounced in New South Wales and Victoria, with Queensland not far behind. By comparison, the Irish presence in the other States, South Australia and Western Australia, for example, will be found to be more muted.

Many an Australian family tree, if shaken hard enough, will be found to contain an Irish ancestor. More than likely, such an ancestor will have arrived in Australia in the 19th century either as a free settler or as a convict. In the course of that century an estimated 300,000 Irishmen and women headed for the southern continent of their own free will. They were joined by 40,000 of their fellow countrymen who were shipped out there, mainly through the ports of Dublin and Cork, whether they liked it or not.

Of the tranches of local records which allow an Australian family historian to identify an ancestor as Irish, three are of prime importance — first, those generated by convict transportation; secondly, those associated with assisted immigration; thirdly, records of births, marriages and deaths.

## Convict Transportation Records

It is a matter of general knowledge that the penal colonies of New South Wales (1788 — 1841) and Van Dieman's Land also known as Tasmania (1803 — 1853) received the bulk of convicts despatched from Ireland. The following is one of thousands of similar items to be found in the Archives Office of Tasmania in Hobart —

> 'A convict named ..... was transported per 'Duke of Richmond' arriving Hobart Town on 2nd January 1844. He was tried in Tipperary on the 2nd August, 1843, and was sentenced to fourteen years transportation for 'assaulting a habitation'. He was well conducted in prison and was never convicted before. His occupation was a quarryman aged twenty five years ..... was single when transported, his native place was.....'

It is scarcely necessary to point up the genealogical value of such a record in any search for further particulars about our unnamed convict. For one thing, the fact that the exact date and place of his trial are known opens up the possibility of locating a report of the trial in a contemporary provincial newspaper such as the *Tipperary Free Press* or the *Tipperary Constitution.*

Records of convict ships and their cargoes putting into Sydney Cove are deposited in the New South Wales State Archives in Sydney. A comprehensive account of these records will be found in *Guide to the Convict Records in the Archives Office, N.S.W.* available from that office, 2 Globe St., The Rocks, Sydney.

Convict ancestry in Australia is not now thought of as something to hide. Aside from the fact that the offences of transportees were frequently of a trivial and obscure nature transportation to Australia eventually lost much of its deterrent effect. Faced with the dire circumstances of life in 19th century Ireland, one girl, who had returned to Dublin after completing a seven year sentence in Australia, deliberately committed a crime which she knew carried a sentence of transportation. When, at her trial, the judge duly obliged her, she threw her bonnet in the air and cried 'Hurrah for old Sydney and the sky over it'.

## Assisted Immigration Records

Throughout the 19th century most of the Australian colonies provided assisted passages from the United Kingdom and Ireland to encourage tradesmen and labourers to settle in Australia. The colony of N.S.W. was foremost in the promotion of such schemes. On virtually every assisted immigrant disembarking at Sydney the authorities recorded the following details — name, age, occupation, religious denomination, place of origin, level of literacy, parents' names as well as a number of other particulars. The relevant records on which these details appear are the Agents' Immigrant Lists 1838 — 1896, the Board's Immigrant Lists 1848 -1891 and the Entitlement Certificates of persons on Bounty ships 1832 — 1845. These papers are in the N.S.W. State Archives where the enquirer is referred to *Guide to Shipping and Free Passenger Records.*

## Records of Births, Marriages & Deaths

In Australia civil registration of births, marriages and deaths is a matter for the Registrar-General in each of the several states that comprise that country. Starting dates for compulsory registration vary from one state to another: civil registration began in South Australia in 1842, in Victoria in 1853 and in New South Wales in 1856.

It is worthy of note that Queensland, Victoria and N.S.W. death certificates frequently give the place of origin of the deceased. Such certificates, in the case of Australians of Irish descent, offer the possibility of linking the emigrant ancestor with his home place in Ireland.

Microfiche copies of the indexes to births, deaths and marriages for New South Wales covering the period 1788 — 1899 can be read in the Search Room at the Archives Office of N.S.W. in Sydney. Details of this facility are contained in Leaflet No.33 prepared by that office.

The Public Record Office of Victoria — City Reference Office, Melbourne, has several leaflets outlining its holdings and the procedure for consulting such holdings. In the catalogue of shipping there are two card indexes, one to assisted arrivals, the other to unassisted arrivals, in Victoria and South Australia. These indexes are arranged in alphabetical order under the names of passengers. The date range covered by the indexes is — Assisted, 1839 to 1871 and Unassisted, 1852 to 1875. The office appears to have a variety of other source materials including probate, naturalization and inquest papers available for consultation by the public in microfilm form.

It has to be realised that little in the way of documentary record survives (if such indeed were ever made) for many early Irish settlers in Australia. Perhaps the only record of such settlers is to be found on their gravestones — '..... here lies John Grady, a native of Co. Tipperary.'

Those seeking further advice on all aspects of Australian genealogical records and family history should write, enclosing a stamped addressed envelope and international reply coupon with small donation to cover expenses to — The Society of Australian Genealogists, Richmond Villa, 120 Kent Street, Sydney 2000, N.S.W. Australia.

## Canadian Records

On the 4th of August 1831 a Nova Scotia newspaper carried a report on the brig 'Duncan' bound from Dublin to St. John, New Brunswick with 250 emigrants on board. On the 25th July, forty days out from Dublin her passengers apparently complained to a passing ship that the captain had for several days been in a state of intoxication and did not know where the vessel was, and they intended next day to put her in charge of the mate and make for the first port. On the first of August the 'Duncan' was found east of Halifax almost empty, most of her passengers having already leaped to the safety of *terra firma.*

Many an Irish famine emigrant caught his first glimpse of the New World as his ship approached the general area now represented by the maritime provinces of Nova Scotia, New Brunswick and Prince Edward Island. Recent estimates suggest that up to twenty per cent of the present population of Canada is composed of Irish stock.

In recent years searches by Canadian archivists hoping to uncover the manifests of ships plying between Ireland and Canada have not proved positive — if indeed such ever existed. While in many instances the names of ships entering the maritime ports of Canada in the last century are known, as indeed are the aggregates of their human cargoes, surviving nominal passenger lists for the period appear to be very rare indeed.

In the absence of such lists the marriage of the newly arrived immigrant offers the best hope of linking him to his place of origin in Ireland. It is evident from the registers of waterfront churches in the maritime provinces that thousands of freshly arrived hopefuls from Ireland married shortly after their arrival in Canada. (see The Irish Ancestor, Vol.1,1976). The marriage entries frequently include the native counties of the parties, and occasionally, their exact place of origin —

> 18 Dec. 1832.
> Matthew Nolan, Old Ross, Co. Wexford, widower of Eleanor Power of Waterford, to Honora Burke (of Richard and Barbara Kean, Co. Mayo). Parish of St. Peter, Halifax, Nova Scotia.

While on the subject of church records it is worth noting that the Public. Archives of Canada, Ottawa, holds some original parish registers, as well as transcripts and microfilm copies of others. This collection is by no means comprehensive, even for a region. The published *Checklist of Parish Registers* lists all the registers that are available on microfilm (including originals and transcripts) with notation of the dates covered and the micro reel numbers.

More parish registers are located in the state provincial archives as well as in the archives maintained by the various christian denominations. More still remain in clerical hands in local parish and mission districts.

In Canada as in other countries, records of births, marriages and deaths constitute a key source for genealogical information. However, civil registration of vital statistics did not become the general practice in Canada until undertaken by the various provincial governments in the later decades of the 19th century. A list of civil registration offices with addresses and details of holdings will be found in a booklet entitled *Tracing your Ancestors in Canada* published by the Public Archives of Canada.

The booklet also contains a list of census returns (some quite early) available on microfilm at the Public Archives of Canada. Copies are available in the state provincial archives.

Canada : Addresses of principal archives

> Public Archives of Canada, Wellington Street, Ottawa, Ontario.
> Provincial Archives of Newfoundland & Labrador, Military Road, St.John's, Nfld.
> Public Archives of Nova Scotia, University Ave., Halifax, N.S.
> Public Archives of Prince Edward Island, Charlottetown, P.E.I.
> Provincial Archives of New Brunswick, Fredericton, N.B.
> Archives Nationales du Quebec, Sainte-foy, Que.
> Archives of Ontario, Grenville Street, Queen's Park, Toronto.
> Provincial Archives of Manitoba, Vaughan Street, Winnipeg, Man.
> Provincial Archives of Alberta, Edmonton, Alba.
> Provincial Archives of British Columbia, Belleville Street, Victoria, B.C.

## English Records

A short account of genealogical research facilities in England is included here for two reasons: first, a large number of people of Irish descent are now resident there due to the proximity of the two islands, and secondly, because many records of Irish interest, e.g. Crown books, police, army and navy enlistments etc. were transferred to London on the establishment of Irish Free State in 1922.

London, as the seat of government, has the outstanding record repositories such as the Public Record Office, the National Central Library, the British Library and the General Register Office.

The General Register Office is located in St. Catherine's House, Kingsway, London and the Registrar has the following records —

> 1. Records of Births, Marriages and Deaths, registered in England and Wales from 1st July 1837.

2. Marine Register Book — records of Births and Deaths at sea since 1st July 1837.
3. Non-Parochial Registers, mainly prior to 1837. These are mostly registers kept by nonconformist bodies and in some cases go back as far as 1761.
4. Army Returns — Births, Marriages and Deaths in the Army Registers extending as far back as 1761.
5. Consular Returns — vital statistics of British subjects in foreign countries since July 1849.

Parish registers, as in Ireland, are kept in parish churches throughout the country, the custodian being the incumbent, who is legally entitled to charge a small fee for searching the records. Books begin at various dates, many reach back to 1750, a few are considerably older.

The Public Record Office, Chancery Lane, London and Ruskin House, Kew Gardens, Surrey has many linear miles of documents and papers relating to the actions of the central government and the courts of law of England and Wales from the eleventh century, of Great Britain from 1707, and of the United Kingdom from 1801 to the present day. It will be recalled that Ireland was part of the United Kingdom until 1921.

Of particular interest from an Irish point of view are the census returns for England and Wales taken 30 March 1851 which give, among other details, an indication of the county of origin of members of the households. While the Public Record Office does not itself engage in genealogical research it will, on request, supply a list of agents who are competent to undertake work in that office.

The standard guide to the holdings of the English P.R.O. is entitled *Guide to the Contents of the Public Record Office,* 3 Vols., H.M.S.O., London.

# CHAPTER 6

# Emigrant Passenger Lists to America

Compulsory emigration from Ireland due to poverty rose sharply following the Act of Union in 1800. The truth of this is evinced by the sharply increased numbers leaving the modestly industrial province of Ulster in the opening decades of the nineteenth century. The loss of native parliament exposed weak home industry to excessive competition from English factories resulting in thousands having to seek a fresh livelihood in the New World. Worse was to follow. The failure, due to blight, of the potatoe crop in successive years in the forties deprived the masses of their staple food and resulted in the population being cut from eight millions to four by starvation and emigration.

> *With my bundle on my shoulder*
> *Sure there's no man could be bolder*
> *I'm leaving dear old Ireland without warning,*
> *For I've lately took the notion*
> *To cross the briny ocean*
> *I'm bound for Philadelphia in the morning.*

Once the decision to emigrate had been taken — and frequently there was little choice — a sailing ticket was procured from the local agent of the shipping line, usually a small shopkeeper in the nearest market town. Then came the long trek to the port of embarkation. Here delays of several weeks were not unusual while the would-be passenger sought a place on a ship. The cost of a steerage passage from Ireland to America for a family of eight in 1855 amounted to £24. Under the Emigration and Passenger Acts the master of each ship was required to provide certain daily rations of food and water but mess utensils and bedding had to be provided by the passenger. Voyages usually took from fifty to eighty days depending on weather conditions.

Not only individuals but also whole families and even groups of people from the same district made the perilous voyage together. In 1850 owing to the aftermath of the famine a Wexford priest took the greater part of his parishioners to New Orleans. He was Fr. Thomas Hore of the united parishes of Annacurra and Kilaveney in north County Wexford. In November 1850 Fr. Hore together with 462 of his flock sailed from Liverpool on the ship *Ticonderoga.* The passenger list of that ship, headed by the name Thomas Hore, is preserved in the Louisiana State Library at Baton Rouge.

The pressing problems of over population and poverty in 19th century Ireland caused the Government to initiate a number of state-aided emigration schemes. One of the better known of these was the Peter Robinson emigration scheme. Robinson, a Canadian, while on a visit to Ireland, was struck by the number of persons who had no prospect of obtaining useful employment in their native land. Forthwith he arranged for the transport of several hundred families mainly from the Blackwater area of County Cork to Upper Canada where they were given grants of land by the Government. The names of the ships involved, which sailed from Queenstown (Cobh) at various dates between 1823 and 1825, were as follows — the *Star, Fortitude, Regulus, Resolution, Elizabeth, Brunswick, Hebe* and *Stakesby.* The passenger lists of those ships, discovered in an old locker about a hundred years later, revealed that 415 families (over 2,000 persons) sailed to Upper Canada from County Cork in the mid 1825's. The ships' papers containing the original lists of emigrants' names are now preserved in the library of Peterboro, Ontario.

While no official register of passengers leaving Irish ports in the last century was kept shipping lines appear to have made carefully compiled lists of persons using their ships. The whereabouts of many of these lists is now a matter of conjecture but it is known that the Cunard Line records dating from 1840 were destroyed by the British Board of Trade in 1900. Some of the lists made their way to the British Museum in London and it is on a manuscript in that institution that many of the lists below are based. Quite a number of lists have been abstracted from records in the National Archives, Washington and from early U.S. papers and periodicals. The frequency with which passengers describe themselves as 'labourers' and 'farmers' is accounted for by the fact that there was a ban in force at the time against the emigration of skilled labour so desperately needed to power Britain's industrial revolution.

A List of Passengers who have sailed on board the Mars for America from Dublin, 29 March, 1803. Age given in most cases after the name.

Wm. Ford          gent
John Morris       servant
Wm. Sherlock      merchant
Hugh Jackson        "
Robert Gibson     American merchant
----- Teeling     clerk
James Murphy      labourer
John Hobleton       "

A List of Passengers on the Ship Portland for Charlestown, 29 March, 1803. Age given after the name.

Charles Adams 48, farmer of Limerick
Margt.Adams his wife 39,    "
Ric O'Carroll 22, farmer of Bolinbroke
Danl. O'Carroll 20,  "
Thos. Egan 29, writing clerk Limerick
Martin Corry 58, labourer    "
John Connery 29, labourer    "
Mary Egan 60,                "
Eliza Corry 33,              "
Mary Connory 24,             "
Mary Egan junior, 27,        "
Betty Fitzpatrick 26,        "
Michl. Quillan 48, gent      "
Mary Quinlan 46,             "
Mary Quinlan junior, 13,     "
Thos. O'Duyer 22, gent       "
Michl. O'Donnovan 26, gent   "
John Mullins 26, labourer    "
James Meehan 26,  "   Clare
Patk. Kernan 24,  "        "
Terence Murray 18,  "      "
Patrick Magrath 21,  "     "
Andrew Lee 26,    "   Caperas
Ric Ennery 19, writing clerk Limerick
Hugh Morgan 22, labourer     "
James Kerly 37, farmer   Ballyhoben
John Walsh 27, labourer  Limerick
Ann Considen 22,              "
John Cummins 21,  "  Claraline Co. Tipperary
Wm. O'Brien 26,   "   Thomas Town
Margaret Fehilly 24,     Limerick
Margt. Hayes 18,             "
Mary Callaghan 14,           "
Joseph Fihilly 7,            "
Michl. Fihilly 5,            "
John Fihilly 3,              "
Mary Fihilly 2,              "

A List of Passengers on the Ship Eagle for New York, 29 March, 1803.

Alex Radcliffe 23, farmer    Ballyroney
John Menter 28, labourer     Belfast
Wm. Calvert 33,   "          Killeagh
Ann Calvert 24, spinster       "
James Bryson 27, farmer      Kilrock
Peter Leonard 28,  "         Hillsboro
Wm. Logan 36, labourer       Dromore
Thos. Bain 18, farmer        Dounpatrick
Joseph Webb 25, labourer     Cockslem
Wm. Wilson 22,   "           Derrylea
Margt. Wilson 20, spinster     "
Wm. Kineard 52, farmer         "
Robt. Kineard 18, labourer     "
Wm. Hancock 19,   "            "
Thos. Wilson 23,   "         Armagh
James Diennen 19,   "        Dovehill
John English 40,   "         Tynan
Isabella English 32,  "        "
Wm. Kerr 18,   "               "
James Lister 20,   "           "
George Lister 25,   "          "
John Graham 24,   "            "
Thos. Spratt 50, farmer      Clough
John Browne 24, farmer       Saintfield
Saml. Campbell 18, labourer  Banbridge
Charles Martin 20, farmer    Ballymoney
Robert Halridge 16, clerk      "
Robt. Eakin 38, farmer       Coleraine
Wm. Rafield 23, farmer       Ballymena
Wm. Woods 27, labourer       Sea Patrick
Neha. Kidd 20,   "           Keady
John Shields 20, farmer        "
John Cully 24,    "            "
David Clement 22,   "          "

Andrew Clement 20, farmer    Keady
Wm. McAlister 20,    "       Ballycaste

A List of Passengers on the Ship SUSAN for New York from Dublin, 5 April, 1803.

John Dornan 43,  bookseller   Dublin
Mrs. Mary Dornan 40,            "
Three small children
Mrs. Annie Russel 38,         Louth
Three small children
Mrs. Frances Russel 40, grocer Dublin
John Midleton 29, merchant    Louth
James Erwin 28, physician       "
Wm. Erwin 26,    "              "
Chas. Rivington 25, merchant  New York
Robert Noble 60,    "           "
Mrs. Nelly Welch 31, spinster Wexford
Miss Mary Ann Finly 21, spinster  Meath
James Truer 22, farmer       County Meath
Thomas Fitzgerald 23, farmer County Wexford
James Byrne 19, farmer       County Meath
John Byrne 21,   "              "
Wm. Finly 18,    "           County Wexford
James Kelly 24,  "             "    "
John Riley 31,   "             "    "
James Kelly 25,  "             "    "

A List of Passengers to go on board the American Brig NEPTUNE, Seth Stevens,Master, for Newcastle and Philadelphia, burthen per admeasurement 117 tons, at Warren Point, Newry, 29 March, 1803.

John Grimes 28, labourer
Agnes Grimes his wife, 26
James Crummy 45, farmer
Agnes Crummy his wife 30
Mary    " their daughter 15
Sarah   "    ditto     12
James   " their son 6
David        ditto
Susan Dene 18, spinster
David Gallon 40, farmer
John Henry 40,    "
Hanna Henry his wife 30
Nancy   " their daughter 13
James   " their son 11
William Countes 21, labourer
Mary Countes his wife 21

List of Passengers to proceed by the American Ship RACHEL, Benjamin Hale, Master, to New York from Sligo, 15 April, 1803.

Robert Ormsby  clerk     Owen McGowen labourer
James Gillan farmer      Fredk. Corry    "
John Read  clerk         Pat Gilmartin   "
James Henderson clerk    Pat Gilan       "
Peter McGowan schoolmaster Pat Foley     "
Chas. Armstrong clerk    Pat Feeny
Lauee. Christian labourer Michl. Horan
Patt Christian    "      John Farrel
James Donald      "      John Commins
Wm. Corry         "      Danl. Gilmartin
Danl. McGowan     "

List of passengers on board the Ship MARGARET, Thomas Marsh, Master, bound for New York, from Newry, 18 April, 1803.

Eliz Brothers 44
Mary    "  19
Saml.   "  12, labourer
James   "  10
William "  7
M Ann Anderson 30
Matu. Doubly 12
James Farrell 3
James Harkness 40, labourer
Jane    " his wife 36
Thos.   " his son 12
Margt.  " his daughter 10
Sarah   "    "    "   10
Abigal  "    "    "   8
Robt.   " his son 6
James   "    "  "  4
Eliz Story 47

Ben Story 18, farmer
Ann Story 16
Hugh Alexander 29, labourer
Jane    "  his wife 22
Jane    " his daughter 3
Sarah   " • "    "  2
Robert Goocy 20, farmer
Samuel Douglas 18,  "
Thomas Haxten 19, labourer
John Rolston 27,    "
Ann Beard 24
Ann Beard 2
James McClean 60, farmer
Eliz McClean 60
David McClean 24, labourer
John        "       "
George      "       "
William Riddle 19,  "
Samuel Magil 21,    "
Samuel Magil 39,    "
Biddy Enery 35

List of passengers intending to go from Belfast to Philadelphia in the Ship EDWARD, from Belfast, 19 April 1803.

James Greg 46, farmer
Thomas Greg 18,   "
John Greg 19,     "
Thomas Fleming 19, labourer
Hugh Porter 24,    "
John Martin 21,    "
Alexr. McMeekin 21,  "
Adm. Dunn 30, farmer
Thomas Monks 60, farmer
Robert Monks 22,   "
Joseph Monks 20,   "
Thomas Monks 17    "
John Smith 20,  labourer
Hu. McBride 26,    "
W.    "  25,       "
W. Dawson 28,      "
Jno. Craven 25,    "
James Fox 40,      "
Ja. Mooney 16,     "
James Towel 22,    "
James Burns 20,    "
Robt. Labody 32, gent
Hers McCullough 27, farmer
Wm. Scott 22,      "
James Kirkman 40,  "
Wm. Bingham 14,    "
John Norris 16,  labourer
Hugh Murphy 18,    "
Edwd. Wilson 18,  gent
Ardsal Hanlay 22, labourer
James Read 23,     "
Jos. Haddock 27,   "

A List of Passengers who intend going to Newcastle, Wilmington and Philadelphia in the Ship PENNSYLVANIA, Elhana Bray, Master, from Londonderry, 16 April, 1803.

Patrick Lealer 50, labourer of Shabane
Robert Donaldson 46,  "      "
Bell Donaldson 36, spinster  "
Mary      "  24,     "       "
Jane      "  25,     "       "
Mary      "  20,     "    Clanely
Nancy Maxwell 30,    "       "
Robert    "  10, labourer    "
Nash Donald 26,    "         "
Patrick Donal 50,  "         "
Margaret Steel 26, spinster  "
Peter Derin 56, labourer     "
James McGonagal 26,  "    Tulerman
Charles Canney 28,   "       "
Richard Dougherty 36,  "     "
Margaret Heaton 28, spinster "
Patrick McCallen 33, labourer "
Hugh Breeson 40,   "         "
Mary O'Donnell 25, spinster Strabane
Samuel Gilmour 30,   "    Sr. Johnston
Ann Gilmour 15,  spinster    "
Jas. Elgin 10,  labourer     "
James Boyd 26,     "         "
William Oliver 26,   "    Sr. Johnstown

Thomas Wilson 25, labourer  Sr. Johnstown
Nancy Wilson 26, spinster       "
Jas. Wilson   20, labourer  Muff
Nancy Wilson junr. 24, spinster Sr. Johnstown
John Wilson   56, labourer      Muff
Saml.  "      45,   "
Eleanor "     36, spinster Newton Limavady
John Moore    22, farmer        "    "
Bridget Dever 55, spinster      "    "
John Lewis    33, labourer      "    "
Fanny Lewis   70, spinster      "    "
Fanny Lewis junr., 15, spinster "    "
Andw. Lewis   20, labourer      "    "
Susan  "      36, spinster      "    "
George "      33, labourer      "    "
James Stewart 25,   "     Dungiven
Jas. King     45,   "           "
Willm. McBride 50,  "           "
Will. Parker  50,   "           "
Alexr. Houston 45,  "           "
Francis "     20,   "           "
John Brigham  26, farmer        "
Jane Brigham  25, spinster Ballyshannon
Eliz Brigham  26,   "           "
Ezekl. Brigham 25, labourer     "
David Brigham 22,   "           "
Wm. White     18,   "           "
Jas. Mitchell 22,   "     Derry
Fras. Dormet  20,   "           "
Wm. Montgomery 22,  "           "
May    "      41, spinster      "
Saml.  "      12, labourer      "
Rebecca "     10, spinster Ballendreat
Robert Little 26, labourer      "
John Little   24,   "           "
Mathw. Armstrong 23, "          "
Jas. Todd     20,   "           "

A List of Passengers who intend going to
New York in the Ship CORNELIA of Portland,
sworn at Londonderry, 15 April, 1803.

Andrew Little 35, labourer
Jane   "      26, spinster
John   "      12, labourer
Margaret "     9, spinster
William "      6, a child
Eliza  "       4,   "
Jane   "       2,   "
Hugh McAvery  24, farmer
Jane McAvery  30, spinster
Jane McAvery   1, a child
Simon Neilson 25, labourer
Mary   "      25, spinster
Archibald Armstrong 18, farmer
James Neilson  3, a child
Catherine Rodgers 30, spinster
Wm. Brown     20, labourer
James McCann  25,   "
David Henderson 20, "
Cons. Dougherty 20, "
Thos. McDonagh 50, farmer
Catherine "   50, spinster
Catherine "   50,   "
James  "      15, farmer
Hugh McDonagh 13,   "
Richard "     11,   "
Thomas "       2, a child
Hugh Donnelly 32, labourer
Mary   "      28, spinster
Hugh Kennen   51, labourer
Catherine Donnelly 4, a child
Hugh Kennen    3, a child
James Tracy   30, farmer
Rose Tracy    32, spinster
Margaret Tracy 2, a child
James McCarron 29, farmer
Jane McCarron 29, spinster
John McCarron  5, labourer
Fanny McCarron 3, a child
John McQuoid  20, labourer
Robert Leonard 22,  "
Jane   "      20, spinster
John Kelly    24, labourer
Eliz Bruce    26, spinster
Robert Harper 30, farmer
Jane Harper   29, spinster
Charles Harper 35, farmer
John Forster  24, labourer

Jane Little   21, spinster
James Harper   7, labourer
Anthony O'Donnell 19, labourer
Manus Brown   19,    "
Edwd. Brown   20,    "
Patrick Collin 22,   "
John Gallougher 22,  "
Chas. Dougherty 23,  "
Rebecca Beatty 21,  spinster
James Muldoon 24, labourer
James King    25,  farmer
John Lenox    30,  farmer
William Coldhoune 30, labourer
Patrick Caldwell 25, "
Jane   "      20,  spinster
Thomas McKennen 3, a child
John Beatty   28,  farmer
Isabella Beatty 22, spinster
Stephen "      2, a child
Mary McIver   17,  spinster
Judith "      19,    "
Shane  "      25,  farmer

A List of Passengers who intend going to
New York on the Ship AMERICAN, 340 Tons burthen,
Alexander Thompson, Master, sworn at Londonderry,
9 April, 1803.

David Kerr    28, farmer      Donegal
Hannah Kerr   25, spinster       "
Robert Virtue 22, farmer         "
Ann Virtue    25, spinster       "
Alexander Thompson 21, farmer Fermanagh
L. Jenkin     labourer           "
Andw. Brander   "                "
L. Miller       "                "
James McCafferty "               "
John Ward       "                "
Robert Fitzpatrick "             "
Robert Stinson   "               "
William Taylor   "          Sligo
Elinor  "    spinster            "
Mary    "       "                "
John Longhead labourer     Donegal
R. Longhead   spinster           "
Robt. Longhead labourer          "
John Longhead   "                "
John Whiteside  "                "
Ann    "    spinster             "
Arthur Johnston farmer           "
Mary   "    spinster             "
Thomas Longhead labourer         "
Thomas "      28,  "             "
James McCrea  20,  "       Ballantra
John   "      25   "             "
Barbara Spence 24, spinster      "
Catherine "   23,  "             "
John Coulter  23   labourer Petigo
Dennis Carr   22,  "             "
Catherine Carr 21, spinster      "
James Tremble 26,  farmer   Donegal
Patk. McGeragh 22, farmer        "
Alex McKee    27,  farmer        "
Fanny McKee   26,  spinster      "
Patrick McMullen 29, labourer    "
Hugh Devarney 26,  labourer Monaghan
Bryan Devine  28,    "           "
Ann    "      25,  spinster      "
Mary McGinn   22,    "      Cavan
Thos. McGinn  27,  labourer      "
James Murphy  27,    "           "
Thomas Murphy 23,    "           "
Thomas McSurgan 26,  "           "
Mary   "      23,  spinster      "
Mark O'Neill  25,  labourer Drunguin
Jane   "      23,  spinster      "
Henry  "      17,  labourer      "

A List of Persons who intend going to Philadelphia
in the Ship MOHAWK of and for Philadelphia, burthen
500 tons, John Barry, Master, sworn at Londonderry,
23 April, 1803.

Neal Callaghan 19, labourer  Ardmalin
Darby Dougherty 25,  "           "
John Thompson 35,    "           "
Charles Hethrington 40, labourer Dungannon
Christy Hethrington 36, labourer "

Susna. Hethrington 40,       Dungannon
Josh.   "      14,            "
Eliza   "      16,           "
George  "      10,           "
James Walker 32, house servant Enniskillen
Ann Walker   30,             "
Ralph  "     36, labourer    "
Anne   "     32,   "         "
Alexr. Wood  26, labourer  Lisnaska
Mary   "     20,   "         "
Wm. Alexander 32,  "       Donagheady
Jane   "     30,             "
James  "     11,             "
Martha "     10,             "
William Bacon 28, labourer  Taughbone
Elizabeth "  27,             "
William "    12,             "
John McGrenan 18, house servant "
Pat McGafferty 19, labourer "
Tho. Donan   23,   "         "
Anne Martin  20,   "       Enniskillen
Thomas Drum  36,   "         "
Nathl. Drum  34,   "         "
Francis Smyth 29,  "         "
William Drum 20,   "         "
Mary Drum    16,   "         "
Pat Lunny    20,   "         "
John Bates   21,   "       Donamanagh
James Murray 20,   "         "
Richd. Jones 24, house servant Strabane
Barry McAna  24, labourer    "
William Glin 25,   "       Letterkenny
Owen McDade  28,   "       Carne
Robert Hopkins 21, "       Bolea
Robert Graham 20,  "         "
Abraham Philips 35, "      Urney
Robert McCrea 30, house servant Strabane
Pat Diven    28,   "    "      "
Henry Forrester 24, labourer Clonis
Saml. Faggart 30,  "         "
Margt.  "    28,   "         "
Elizth. Niely 21, stewart  Newton
John McCoy   20, labourer  Clougher
John Hastings 21,  "       Stewartstown
John Simpson 25,   "         "
George Walker 20,  "         "
Samuel Thompson 28, "      Dungannon
Anna   "     30,             "
Andw.  "     25,   "         "
James  "      6,             "
Sarah  "     22,             "
James Campbell 28, "         "
Mary   "     20,             "
Patk. Brodley 19, house servant Londonderry
Alexr. "     28, labourer  Newtonstewart
Archd. Anderson 19, "      Armagh
James Tait   36,   "         "
James McGonegall 25, "     Buncrana
Ferrol McAward 21, "         "
Patk. McDonell 20, "         "
Denis Lynchakin 20, "        "
Neal Dougherty 20, "         "
William Kelly 23,  "         "
John Carton  35,   "       Claggen
David McConaghy 10, "      Ballyarton
Robert McQuistin 26, "     Dungiven

List of Persons who have engaged their
Passage on board the ship Ardent, Burthen 350
tons, Richard Williams, Master, bound for
Baltimore, sworn at Londonderry, 23 Apl., 1803.

Thomas Ramsey 28, farmer   Nr. Muff Co. Done-
                                 gal.
Hugh Elliott 40,   "       Rancel
Mrs.   "     54,             "   "
James  "     20,   "         "   "
Hugh   "     14,             "   "
Jean Elliott 18,             "   "
James Richey 58,   "       Donan
Mrs.   "     52,             "   "
Wm.    "     18,   "         "   "
Cath.  "     16,             "   "
Ann    "     14,             "   "
John   "     20,             "   "
Andw.  "     12,             "   "
Ellen  "     10,             "   "
Andw. McKee  38,   "         "   "
Mrs.   "     34,             "   "
Eliza Richey  9,             "   "

Nancy McKee 16,         Donan Co. Donegal
Pat   "  14,         "
Eliz Finlay 57,         "      "
John  "  22, farmer  "      "
James  "  17,    "       "      "
Pat Cunigan 60, drover Killaughter  "
James Manilus 26,  "     Kilcar    "
Hugh Clark 30, farmer  Donan     "
Mrs. Clark, Snr. 28,     "      "
James  "  17, farmer  "     "
Wm.  "  26,  "      "     "
Mrs. Clark Junr. 22,     "     "
Alexr.  "  8,      "     "
Mrs. Richey 38,      "     "
George  "  9,      "     "
Charles  "  44,  "     "     "
Andw. McCullough 40, farmer  "    "
Mrs. McCullough 34,      "     "
Andw.  "  16,      "     "
Jean  "  14,      "     "
George  "  12,     "     "
Alexr.  "  10,      "     "
John Montgomery 24, gentleman Killybegs  "
John Jones 20,    "      "     "
Wm. Graham 22, farmer  Tyrough  "
Francis Graham 22,  "     "     "
James Cunningham 17,  "   Glenery  "
John Crawford 28,  "  Ballybofey  "
John Erwin 56,   "     "     "
George Crawford 32,  "  Doren  "
Ann Boyle  14,    "  Mt. Charles  "
David Graham 48,   " Dergbridge Co. Tyrone
Sarah  "  41,      "     "

---

List of Passengers who intend to proceed on
board the American Ship JEFFERSON to New York
from Sligo, James Adams, Master, sworn at
Sligo, 16 April, 1803.

Peter Gonagle labourer    Pat Nelis  labourer
James Clenten  "      Edmd. Gilfeader "
Edmd. Leyonard  "     Thomas Reily  "
Pat. Waterson  "      James McKey  "
John McGan       James Curry  "
Thos. Wymbs  dealer    Danl. Gilmartin "
Michl. Wymbs  "      Thos. Farrel  "
Pat Hangdon  labourer  John Higgins  "
John Harken  "      William Kalens "
Frans. Kelly  "

---

The following duplicate of the foregoing, sworn
28 April, 1803, by James Adams, the Master,
gives fuller information.

Peter Nangle 40,  labourer     Sligo
James Clenton 26,   "  Clurbagh "
Edmd. Leynerk 20,   "    "    "
Pat Waterson 55,   "    "    "
John McGan 32,   "  Carns  "
Thos. Wymbs 36,  dealer   "    "
Michl.  "  30,   "    "    "
Pat Haregdon 41,  labourer  Moneygold "
John Harken 26,   "  Grange  "
Fras. Kelly 29,   "  Bunduff  "
Pat Nelis 27,   "  Creery  "
Edmd. Gilfeader 23,  "  Mt. Temple"
Thos. Reilly 29,   "    "    "
Jas. McKey 36,   "    "    "
Jas. Curry 28,   "    "    "
Danl. Gilmartin 29,  "    "    "
Thos Farrell 23,   "    "    "
Jno. Higgins 37,   "  Clurbagh "
Wm. Kalens 42,   "    "    "

---

A List of Passengers who intend going to
Baltimore in the Ship SERPENT of Baltimore,
Archd. McCockell, Master, sworn at Londonderry,
30 April, 1803.

Joseph Neilson 26, farmer   Strabane
Margt.  "  24,        "
Jane  "  14, spinster    "
Elizabeth  "  12,  "      "
John  "  10,        "
James  "  10,        "

---

Saml. McCarthy 25, labourer  Omagh
Davd. Falls 25,  "      "
Saml. Turner 30,  "   Strabane
Jno. Neilson 27,  "      "
Pat Mounigle 28,     Rosquill
Neal McPeak 30,       "
Michl. McCann 40, farmer   "
Phelix McCann 35, farmer   "
Patk.  "  28,  "     "
Peter  "  18,  "     "
Nelly  "  37,      "
Susan  "  40       "
Hannah  "  16  spinster  "
Mary  "  14,      "
James McBride 25, farmer  "
Catherine McBride 24,     "
Peter Corbitt 25,     Rathmullen
Isabella Corbitt 23,     "
John Mundell 40,     Gortgarn
Margaret Mundell 39,     "
Sameul  "  46,     "
Wm. Jno.  "  25,     "
Isabella  "  20, spinster  "
Jane  "  16,      "
Mary  "  14,      "
Elizh.  "  12,      "
Margt. Craig 36,      "
Geo. Laird 25, farmer  "
Saml.  "  22,      "
Mary  "  24,      "
Rachl.  "  25, spinster  "
Peter Kenedy 27, farmer  "
Margaret Kenedy 25,     "
Emelia  "  6,      "
James Reed 40, farmer  Maghera
Agnes Reed 37,      "
Sally  "  15, spinster  "
Mary McCool 45,      "
James  "  24 farmer  "
Jn.  "  20,  "     "
Nelly Ross 35,      "
James Rolls 18,  labourer  "

---

Passengers List of the Ship STRAFFORD for
Philadelphia, sworn at Londonderry, 14 May, 1803.

John McGan 34,  farmer  Coagh
Elizabeth McGan 30, spinster  "
Sarah  "  2,      "
Elinor  "  infant    "
Wm. Walker 30, farmer  "
Mary Anne Walker 20, spinster  "
Eliz  "  18,      "
Wm. Mitchel 20, farmer  Cumber
Thos. Conigham 18,  "  Ballymony
Alexr. Stewart 20, labourer Ketreights
John Moore 19,  "  Loughgin
James Hamilton 23,  "    "
Wm. Smily 23,  "  Ketreights
Edw. Clarke 40, farmer  Enniskillen
John Miley 45,  "    "
Wm. Loughridge 30,   Cookstown
Mg.  "  24,      "
Jane  "  7,      "
James  "  5,      "
Eliza  "  2,      "
Nancy Harkin 30, seamstress Birdstown
Nelly  "  4,      "
Wm.  "  6,      "
John Chamber 20, farmer  Co. Tyrone
Wm. Gray 24,  "    "    "
James Ralston 45,  "   "    "
Mary  "  40,     "    "
James  "  15,     "    "
Mary  "  12,     "    "
Davd.  "  9,      "    "
Josh.  "  5,      "    "
Anne  "  34, seamstress "    "
Anne  "  2,      "    "
Robt.  "  19, labourer  "    "
Davd.  "  15,  "    "    "
John  "  11,     "    "
Jane  "  8,      "    "
Anne  "  5,      "    "
Josh.  "  2,      "    "
John  "  40, farmer  "    "
Sarah  "  40, seamstress "    "
Davd.  "  9,      "    "
Andw.  "  7,      "    "
Wm.  "  3,      "    "

---

James Ralston 5,     Co. Tyrone
Elinor Shean 60,    Co. Down
Mary Anderson 24,    "   "
Mary  "  2,     "   "
John Wilson 22, farmer  "
Wm. Carr 20,  "      "
James Moore 19,    Ballykelly

---

A List of Passengers to go on board the Ship
PATTY, sworn at Newry, 5 May, 1803.

Wm. Griffis 34, labourer  Down
Andrew Hurs 30,  "     "
John Kenedy 41,  "     "
Saml. McBride 28,  "  Tyrone
John Gibson 50, farmer  "
Patk. Lynch 27, labourer  "
David Hunter 28,  "     "
Edward  "  34,  "     "
George  "  14,  "     "
Alexr. Armstrong 29,  "  Armagh
Mary Harvey 45, spinster  "
Eliza  "  23,  "     "
Robt.  "  48, farmer  "
Biddy Brown 38, spinster  Down
Henry Williams 28, gentleman Armagh
Saml. Patton 32, labourer  Down
Joseph  "  36,  "     "
George Tilforde 28,  "    "
John Blair 29,  "     "
John McDale 36,  "     "
Walter Potts 25,  "     "
William Roncy 19,  "     "
James Eakin 46, farmer  "
Samuel  "  50,  "     "
James Fitspatrick 37,  "    "
Mary  "  32, spinster  "
Edward Maugher 26, labourer Queens County
John Fleming 24,  "     "
Thomas Dick 32, farmer  Down
James Nelson 28,  "     "
John Armstrong 29,  "    "

---

List of Passengers on board the PRUDENCE,
of Philadelphia, Sworn at Dublin, 9 March,
1804.

Thos. Maitland 22,    Baltinglass
Ann  "  56,      "
and child  7,      "
Mary Ann Maitland 19,    "
James Barry 25, Apothecary, Dublin
John McDermott 26, Clerk  "
James McCarty 26,  "    "
John Gitten 30,  "    "
and child  8,      "
Jane Hines 22, Glasnevin  "

Additional List of Passengers taken on
board since the above was sworn to:

John Nixon 26, farmer Manor Hamilton, Leitrim
John Trevin 27,  "    "    "    "
James Gore 24, clerk,  Dublin

---

List of Passengers in the EAGLE, for New York,
sworn at Belfast, 10 March, 1804.

Josiah Kerr 28, height 5-8 clerk, Loughbickyard.
    Thin faced and pretty fair
Joseph  "  21, 5-10 farmer, Hillsborough.
    Smooth and fair faced
Hamilton  "  17, 5-0 farmer, Hillsborough.
    Smooth and fair faced
John McMurdy 30, 5-7 farmer, Banbridge. Pitted
    with the small-pox
James McMullen 28, 5-6 farmer, Loughbrickland.
    Red haired, smooth faced, and
    lame of a knee
Robert Cavert 36, 5-2 labourer, Rathfyland.
    Smooth and fair faced
Jas. Fulton 22, 5-8 labourer, Maghrolin.
Arthur Walker 27, 5-9 labourer, Drumore.
    Yellow and smooth faced
Thos. Gordon 28, 5-5 labourer, Drumore. Yellow
    and pitted with small-pox

Robert Whany 28, height 5-7 farmer, Drumore.
Ruddy, a little pitted
Robt. Smith 21, 5-6 labourer, Hillsborough.
Sallow thin and smooth faced
Hu. Hanison 13, 5-11 farmer, Drumore. Ruddy
Complexion and black eyed.
Paul Rogan 30, 5-8 labourer, Loughbuckland.
Spare faced
Wm. McKee 26, 5-10 labourer, Mt. Stewart.
Thin faced and ruddy
Archd. Williams 21, 5-8 farmer, Castle Dawson.
Smooth faced, fair haired
John Benson 19, 5-3 labourer, Near Drumore.
Little pitted, black hair
Robert Patterson 24, 5-4 farmer, Ballindeny.
Black hair and ruddy
Adam Patterson 20 5-6 farmer, Ballindeny. Fair
haired, a little pitted
John Dickson 33, 5-7 farmer, Banbridge. Smooth
face, black hair
James Black 34, 5-11 linnen draper, Banbridge.
Smooth faced, black hair
James Moones 21, 5-7 farmer, Ballendeny. Little
pitted, fair hair
Anthy. McMordy 44, 6-0 farmer, Banbridge. Ruddy
complexion
Eliz Kerr 49, 5-4 spinster, Loughbickland.
Brown complexion
Eliz Kerr 30, 5-6 spinster, Hillsborough.
Brown and smooth faced
Sarah Kerr 49, 5-4 spinster, Hillsborough. A
little pitted with the small-
Marg Cavart pox
Marg. Cavart 28, 5-0 spinster, Rathpiland. Fair
and smooth faced
Eliza Walker 24, 5-3 spinster, Dromon. Fair, a
little pitted
Margaret Gordon 21, 5-4 spinster, Dromon. Fair
and smooth faced
Margaret Walker 25, 6-0 spinster, Hillsboro'.
Yellow and a little pitted
Jane Whany 35, 4-0 Dromon. Tender eyed and
fair
Nancy Williams 23, 5-6 spinster, Castle Dawson.
Black haired, a little pitted
Jane Dickson 21, 5-3 spinster, Banbridge. Smooth
and fair faced
Hamilton Brown 35, 5-4 farmer, Killnechy. Pale
faced and pitted
Jane " 35, 5-4 spinster, Killnechy.
Pale faced and pitted
Wm. Whaly a child 7.

List of Passengers to go on board the American
Ship MARIA, of Wilmington, bound for Philadelphia,
sworn at Londonderry, 10 March 1804.

| | | |
|---|---|---|
| Nancy McKeever | 45 | spinster |
| Robert Fulton | 43 | labourer |
| John Rice | 38 | " |
| Mary Ann Hammond | 27 | spinster |
| Nancy Fulton | 31 | " |
| Robert Millar | 26 | labourer |
| Arthur Murphy | 49 | " |
| James Dougherty | 33 | " |
| Jas. McKinley | 23 | " |
| Sarah Murphy | 21 | spinster |
| Mary McGomery | 17 | " |
| Margt. Pearson | 52 | " |
| Frans. Scott | 47 | labourer |
| James Dogherty | 51 | " |
| Saml. McKinley | 33 | " |
| Patt Karlin | 42 | " |
| John McConway | 28 | " |
| Mary McConway | 26 | spinster |
| Hugh Smith | 44 | labourer |
| Humphry Graham | 50 | " |
| Thos. Graham | 36 | " |
| Barny McCanna | 43 | " |
| Robert Leonard | 21 | " |
| Henry Rankin | 17 | " |
| Wm. Anderson | 53 | " |
| Wm. Edmond | 41 | " |
| John Anderson | 28 | " |
| Heny. Anderson | 46 | " |
| Wm. Harkin | 25 | " |
| Jos. Arskine | 56 | " |
| Jas. Waker | 40 | " |
| Saml. Bellman | 33 | " |

| | | |
|---|---|---|
| John Bellman | 35 | labourer |
| Saml. Anderson | 46 | " |
| Margt. Anderson | 36 | spinster |
| Ann Walker | 24 | " |

List of Passengers to New York on the CHARLES
and HARRIOTT, sworn at Sligo, 29 March, 1804.

| | | |
|---|---|---|
| Martin Carney | labourer | Mogherow |
| Peter Carroll | " | " |
| Wm. Curry | " | Conought |
| Fras. McGowan | clerk | Mogherow |
| Roger Gill | labourer | Co. Fermanagh |
| Bryan McManus | " | |
| Philip Rogers | " | Sligo |
| Robert Muns | " | Drumclief |
| Alexr. Rutledge | " | Tyrecagh |
| Hugh Murray | clerk | Sligo |
| Wm. Moreton | labourer | Co. Fermanagh |
| Thos. McIntire | clerk | Sligo |
| Bryan Collen | labourer | Brenduff |
| John Flynn | " | Drumcliff |
| Michael Golden | " | " |
| John Elliott | " | Mulloghmore |
| Michl. Dunn | " | " |
| Peter McGarry | " | Colooney |
| Michl. O'Hara | " | Co. Sligo |
| James | " | " " |
| Edwd. | " | " " |
| Payton Farrell | " | Boyle |
| Patt Fox | " | Boyle |
| Mark McGowan | " | Carney |
| Thos. | " | " |
| Con. Hart | " | Co. Fermanagh |
| James McMorrow | " | Sligo |
| Alexr. Martin | " | Sligo |
| Wm. Chambers | " | Leitrim |
| Edwd. Chambers | " | " |

A List of passengers from Londonderry to New York,
on the ship AMERICAN, sworn at Londonderry,
31 March, 1804.

| | | |
|---|---|---|
| Patk. McKay | 40, farmer | Moghera |
| Alexr. " | 21, " | " |
| Nancy " | 40, | " |
| Thomas Bradley | 20, " | Ballyarlin |
| John Dougherty | 20, " | Rushbank |
| James Parks | 28, gentleman | Londonderry |
| Thomas McGomeray | 19, clerk | New York |
| Captain Sterling | 25, mariner | Londonderry |
| James Bond | 18, clerk | Rushbank |
| John Clyde | 13, servant | Coningham |
| Geo. Crawford | 19, farmer | Nn. Cumber |
| Robert Johnston | 20, farmer | Ballyauret |
| Thos. Ramsey | 21, " | Nn. Stewart |
| Gerard Twine | 23, " | Cumber |
| Owen McGlenhy | 34, labourer | Cumber |
| Mary McGlenhy | 32 | Ennishowin |
| John Donaghy | 41, labourer | Nn. Limavady |
| James Dougherty | 39, " | " " |
| Elenor Dougherty | 38, | Desartmarten |
| James Patterson | 25, farmer | Moneymore |
| Alexr. McDonald | 19, labourer | " |
| Hugh Ramsay | 29, " | " |
| Alexr. Ramsay | 23, " | " |
| James Dougherty | 29, tanner | " |
| William Donaghy | 48, farmer | " |
| John " | 19, farmer | " |
| Alex. " | 24, " | Cain |
| Sarah " | 39, | " |
| William McLaughlin | 50, farmer | " |
| John McLoughlin | 28, farmer | " |
| Alexr. " | 25, " | " |
| Mary " | 48, " | Nn. Limavady |
| James Buchannon | 35, labourer | Magilligan |
| William Miller | 28, servant | |
| Alex Dougherty | 35, labourer | |

A List of Passengers intending to go by the
British Brig ALEXIS, of Greenock, to Wilmington,
North Carolina, sworn 29 March, 1804.

| | | |
|---|---|---|
| Hu. McNight | 40, farmer | Near Belfast |
| Jas. " | 54, " | " " |
| Batty " | 36, " | " " |
| Margt. age uncertain | | " " |
| John McNight child | | |

| | | |
|---|---|---|
| Batty McNight junr. child | | Near Belfast |
| Eliza " | | " |
| James Flanagan age uncertain, | | labourer, Dundalk |
| James Gordon " | " | farmer |
| Hu. Wilson age uncertain | " | " |
| Thos. Gormen " | labourer | Creggans |
| Wm. Greyson " | " | " |
| Oliver Plunket " | " | " |
| Michael Mackay " | " | Cullaville |
| Terence Murphy " | " | Carrickmacross |
| Willm. Vance " | " | " |
| Patrick Fenor " | | |
| Indorsed from Newry. | | |

A List of Passengers from Sligo to New York,
sworn 29 March, 1804.

| | | |
|---|---|---|
| Wm. Jeffers | farmer | Loghadill |
| Alex Griffith | " | " |
| John Hodman | " | " |
| Geo. Taylor | labourer | " |
| Robt. Griffith | " | " |
| Jno. Low | " | Moghean |
| Robt. Elliott | " | " |
| Archd. " | " | " |
| David Ellis | farmer | Tilton |
| Thos. Armstrong | " | " |
| Andw. Taylor | labourer | " |
| Geo. Young | " | " |
| Michl. Farrill | " | " |
| Jno. McMorrow | " | Cloghfin |
| Peter Brady | " | " |
| Jno. Carty | " | Ardnaston |
| Patt McDonogh | " | Ardnastran |
| Andw. McNossen | clerk | " |
| McDonogher | labourer | " |
| James McDonogher | " | " |
| " " junr. | " | " |
| Robt. Cracy | " | Loghfin |
| Edwd. Crawford | " | " |
| Edwd. Crawford | " | " |
| Ben Caffry | " | " |
| Jas. Caffuny | " | " |
| Wm. Vaugh | clerk | " |
| Henry Dowler | " | Barton |
| Jno. Duffy | labourer | " |
| Hugh Crawford | " | " |
| Thos. Pattinson | " | " |
| Hugh Davis | " | " |

List of Passengers of the Ship SUSAN, of and for
New York, sworn at Dublin, 28 March, 1804.

| | |
|---|---|
| Patrick Glenning | 22, fair, labourer, Monasterevan, Kildare |
| Mary " | 24, fair, spinster, Monasterevan, Kildare |
| Michael Cawlin | 23, Dark, labourer, Nober, Meath |
| Mary Kenny | 36, " married, Dublin |
| Edward Donagan | 21, fair, labourer, Connotwood, Queens County |
| Michael Branghill | 30, Sallow, ·labourer, Bala Braughin, Kings County |
| Eliza Fullard | 26, fair, spinster, Edenderry, Kings County |
| Frances Fullard | 11, fair, spinster " Kings County |
| Jane Fullard | 10, fair, spinster " Kings County |
| Nicholas Caffrey | 21, light, farmer, Monasterevan, Kildare |
| Patrick Wogan | 20, fair, gentleman, Dublin |
| Good Rhind | 23, light, " " |
| Keeron Carrill | 23, " servant " |
| Thomas Durm | 28, Dark, labourer, Bala Braughan, Kings County |
| Michael Taylor | 38, sandy, labourer, Dublin |
| Thomas Matland | 21, light, labourer, Dunlavin, Wicklow |
| Anne Matland | 56, dark, married, " Wicklow |
| Mary Ann Matland | 20, fair, spinster " Wicklow |
| James Barry | 23, fair, gentleman, Dublin |
| Edward McDermott | 30, dark, " " |
| Robert Dyas | 19, light, " Kings Court, Cavan |

James Gore   26, sandy, gentleman, Dublin
James Yates 34,  "   "   Newry
Joseph Dempsey 18, fair, servant, Upper Wood, Queens County
Judith Campbell 25, brown, married, Knockmack, Meath
Jane Hyres   30, brown, married, Drogheda
Mark Kelly   30,  "   farmer, Monasterevan, Kildare
Mary Kelly   30, brown, married,   "   Kildare
John Foran   35, sandy, labourer,   Kildare
Simon Donnolly 22, dark,   "   Naas
Luke Toole   28, fair, clerk, Donnybrook, Dublin
William Christian 25, fair, labourer, Dublin
Nicholas Hobart 30, dark,   "   Mullingar, Meath
Michael Murthe   25, labourer, Lurganlyseen, South

---

A List of Passengers to Philadelphia on board the BROTHERS of Philadelphia, sworn at Londonderry, 14 April, 1804.

Margaret Osburn 27, spinster, Omagh, Tyrone
Thom Thompson 23, farmer, Castlefin, Donegal
Ann Hearney   35, spinster, Dungiven, Derry
Patk.   "   12, child   "   "
John   "   9,   "   "   "
Biddy   "   7,   "   "   "
Nanny   "   4,   "   "   "
Noble Young   22, farmer, Pethgow, Fermanagh
Jas.   "   21, labourer   "   "
Sarah   "   50, spinster   "   "
J. Hibran   30, labourer, Castlefin, Donegal
Jos.   "   22,   "   "   "
Jane Himton   35, spinster   "   "
Jas. Boyd   26, farmer, Pettigo, Fermanagh
Margt. Wishart 21, spinster   "   "
Jas.   "   51, labourer, Dungannon, Tyrone
Chas. Kelly   21,   "   Drunmore,   "
Hugh   "   22,   "   Dunmore   "
Margt. Osburne 27, spinster, Omagh   "
Jane   "   6, child   "   "
Jas.   "   4,   "   "   "
Chas. Flanigan 34, labourer, Ballyshannon, Donegal
Mary   "   28, spinster   "   Donegal
Jno.   "   6, child   "   "
Hu. Kelly   30, labourer   "   "
Jas. Boyle   40,   "   "   "
Wm. Robinson   32,   "   Coleraine, Derry
Ann   "   22, spinster, Innishannon, Donegal
John Doherty   30, labourer,   "   Donegal
Mary   "   26, spinster   "   "
Pat McLoughlin 32, labourer,   "   "
R. McLoughlin 24,   "   "   "
Wm. Doherty   23,   "   "   "
Jas.   "   28, farmer, Beet,   "
Jas. Dunn   24,   "   "   "
Mary   "   19, spinster   "   "
Jas. Porter   35, farmer

---

List of Persons who wish to go to Baltimore, sworn 14 April, 1804.

Robert Gibson   28, farmer   Dromon, Down
Sarah   "   27,
Mary   "   60,   Hillsborough, Down
John   "   30,   "   "
David   "   28,   "   "
Ann   "   20,   "   "
Elizabeth "   18,   "   "
Jane Taggart   40,   Dromon,
Ann   "   14,   "   "
Jane   "   12,   "   "
Wm. Cotter   28, labourer, Ballymona, Antrim
Ann Cotter   26,
Felix Divine   38, dealer, Philadelphia, America
Robert Nesbit   40,   "   Killinchy, Down
James McCausland 30, farmer, Cookstown, Tyrone
Susanna   "   28,
Alexander Richardson 28, dealer, Baltimore, America
Mary Ann   "   26,   "   "
William Greer   25, dealer   "   "

James Cleland   24, dealer, Ballymillon, Down
George   "   21, farmer   "   "
William Lindley 20,   "   "   "
Robert Lowry   55, dealer, Killinchwood,   "
Mary Lowry   55,   "   "   "
Robert   "   26, farmer   "   "
James   "   24, labourer   "   "
Wm.   "   20,   "   "   "
Jane   "   18,   "   "   "
George Hutton   21, farmer   "   "
Francis Delap   50,   "   Comber   "
Alexander   "   22,   "   Comber   "
Jane   "   50,   "   "   "
Jane   "   20,   "   "   "
Christian   "   18,   "   "   "
Andrew Morrow   40, labourer, Ballyargin   "
Jane   "   30,   "   "   "
Mary Boyd   31,   Dromon   "
Daniel Boyd   34, farmer   "   "

---

A List of Passengers who intend going to New York in the American Ship WILLIAM AND JANE from Belfast, sworn at Belfast, 14 April, 1804.

John Eaton   30, farmer,   Tanlagh, Derry
Jas.   "   28,   "   "   "
Saml.   "   29,   "   "   "
Mary   "   25, spinster   "   "
Matw. Maxwell   25, gentleman, Ballooly, Rathfryland, Down
Robt. Loughran 23, labourer, Near Cookstown, Tyrone
Brizbr.   "   25, spinster   "   Tyrone
Wm. Henderson   21, farmer, Raloe near Larne, Antrim
John Lundy   34, farmer, Near Tandragee, Armagh
Philp. McKevy   25, farmer, Raloe near Larne, Antrim
Alexr. Robb   24, labourer, Broadisland, Antrim
Wm. Alexander   20, labourer,   " Antrim
Widow Brown   60, spinster, Kelleleagh, Down
Margt.   "   25,   "   "   "
Barbara   "   18,   "   Killilegh   "
John McCulloh   21, labourer, Drumbo   "
Margt. Withers 25, spinster   "   "
John Robinson   28, labourer, Near Porlavo Archin, Down
John Steen   13, labourer, Near Coan, Antrim
John Burns   30,   "   Drumgolan near Rt. Fayland, Down
Denis Doyle   34, labourer, Drumgolden nr. Rt. Fayland, Down
Margt.   "   34, spinster, Drumgolden nr. Rt. Fayland, Down
Michl.   "   27, labourer, Drumgolden, nr. Rt. Fayland, Down
Eliza   "   27, spinster, Drumgolden nr. Rt. Fayland, Down
Arthur O'Neal   23, farmer, near Castlereagh, Down
Saml. Morrison 27,   "   Killinchy   "
Mary   "   25, spinster   "   "
James Rusk   23, farmer, Derriaghy near Lisburne
George McCray   20,   "   Donerisk nr. Cookstown, Tyrone

---

A List of Passengers in the American Ship JANE of New Bedford for New York, sworn at Dublin, 17 April, 1804.

James Normidge   26, dark, surgeon, Britan Street,
Mary   " his wife 19, dark, Britan Street, cabin
George Nalleran 34, dark, clerk, Britan Street,"
Jane   " his wife, 26, dark, Britan Street,
Edward Dartnell 27, fair, clerk, Britan Street, single, cabin
Catherine Corish 32, married, James Street, cabin
Miss Corish   8,   "   "   "
Michael Smith   24, dark, farmer, single, Clighen, Cavan, steerage
John Mullahy   22, dark, farmer, single, Callan, Kilkenny, steerage
John Shilly   35, dark, farmer, single, Callan, Kilkenny, steerage
Denis Finning   25, fair, steerage

Thomas Mahir   24, dark, farmer, married, Callan, Kilkenny, steerage
Mary   " his wife, 22, married, Callan, Kilkenny, steerage
infant child
Patrick Cormack 17, dark, farmer, single, Callan, Kilkenny, steerage
William Carty   17, dark, farmer, married, Barton, A.N. steerage
Alice White   50, dark single, Callan, Kilkenny, steerage
May White   20, dark, single, Callan, Kilkenny, steerage
Catherine White 22, dark, single, Callan, Kilkenny, steerage
Eleanor White   18, dark, single, Callan, Kilkenny, steerage
Margt. Cormick 20, dark, single, Callan, Kilkenny, steerage
John Rossiter   22, dark, farmer, single, Wexford, steerage
Thomas Bahan   26, dark, clerk, single, Bride Street, steerage

---

List of Passengers of the American Ship MARY of New Bedford to Philadelphia, sworn at Dublin, 17 April, 1804.

Richard Fell   50, dark, merchant, married, Philadelphia, cabin
Patrick Kenney 39, dark, clergyman, single, Lusk, Dublin, cabin
James R. Bainbridge 20, fair, clerk, single, Bride Street, cabin
Lawrence Cafsidy 25, dark, clerk, single, Coombe, cabin
Oliver W. Stone 22, fair, clerk, single, Largan, Armagh, cabin
Elizabeth Hudson 22, fair, single, Grafton Street, cabin
Ann Mullhollan 17, fair, single, Ballycumber, Kings County, cabin
Miss Gordon   17, fair, single, Philadelphia, cabin
William Coogan 40, dark, farmer, married, Pensylvania, steerage
James Fagan   30, dark, farmer, single, Mountrath, Queens County, steerage
James McCarty   25, dark, farmer, single, Wexford, steerage
Henry Byrne   30, dark, farmer, single,   " steerage
Owen Garter   26, dark, farmer, single, Mountrath, steerage
William Power   28, dark, farmer, single, Fitthind, Tipperary, steerage
Mathew Daily   25, dark, farmer, single, Kilkullen, Kildare, steerage
Thomas Daily   23, dark, farmer, single, Kilkullen, Kildare, steerage
Edward Gumen   35, dark, farmer, single, Ruihale, Queens County, steerage
Mathew Boyn   30, dark, labourer, single, Kildare, steerage
Catherine Daily 22, dark, single, Kilkullen, steerage
William Gathan 10, child, Dublin, steerage
Mary Fagan   25, married, Mountrath, steerage
Robert Dickinson 30, dark, farmer, married, Wickton, steerage
Rose Dickinson nis wife 25, Wickton
Patrick Kogan   30, dark, farmer, single, Barris in Opary, steerage
Anthony Hagdon 25, dark, single, Barris in Opary, steerage
Ann Field Porter 20, dark, single, Barris in Opary, steerage

---

A List of Passengers on the American Ship PRESIDENT of New Bedford from Newry for New Castle in America, sworn 21 April, 1804.

Edward Lynch   22, labourer, Armagh
Robt. Frances   30, farmer,   Cavan
Jane Frances   28,   "
Mary   "   2,   "
Margt. Farley   20,   "

Wm. Gilmore 50, labourer Cavan
Jane " 50, "
Frances Gilmore 21, "
James " 19, labourer "
Rose Gilmore 17, "
Joulan " 16, "
Bartley Hart 17, "
Andw. McQuillan 40, farmer "
Margt. McMullen 41, "
John McMullen 20, farmer "
Saml. " 13, "
Wm. Wright 40, labourer "
David Ferguson 54, " Armagh
Robt. " 25, farmer Down
Wm. " 21, " "
Hugh " 19, " "
Jas. " 16, " "
Eliza " 14, " "
Jas. McBride 37, " "
Wm. McBride 22, " "
Sarah " 10, " "
Jas. Lard 30, " Armagh
Margt. " 31, "
Jane " 8, "
Sarah " 2, "
Jas. Murphy 36, " "
Mary " 30, "
James " 5, "

A List of the Passengers for Philadelphia on
the American Ship COMMERCE, sworn 28 April,
1804.

Hugh Jelly 35, labourer, Loughinisland, Down
Hugh Thomson 36, " Kilmore "
Joseph Lindsey 33, " Sea Patrick "
James Beck 30, farmer, Ashegarg "
John " 25, " "
Margt. " 24, spinster " "
Thomas Kilpatrick 37, farmer, Kellead, Antrim
Patt Cunningham 30, " Loughinisland, Down
Sarah Mitchell 25, spinster " "
Wm. McGowan 35, farmer Dunmurray, Antrim
John Gordon 36, " Keddy, "
Willm. Dinwiddie 40, " Dunaghy, "
Geo. Logan 30, labourer Killinchy, Down
Geo. " 25, " "
Robt. McCaughty 25, farmer, Cammoney, Antrim
Jane " 20, spinster " "
Isaac Dickey 20, farmer, Magheragill, Down
Anne Stewart 18, spinster, Belfast, Antrim
Thos. Stevenson 21, farmer, Dunaghy, "
John Douglass 38, " Seaford, Down
Mary " 38, spinster " "
Agniss McAfee 20, " Belfast, Antrim
Geo. Martin 35 farmer, Blaris, Down
John Shery 34, " " "
Patrick McCarroll 26, farmer, Augher, Tyrone
John Duross 21, farmer, Dublin
Francis O'Neill 27, labourer "
Emelia O'Neill 22, spinster "
Richd. Courtney 25, farmer, Clough, "
Margt. " 24, spinster " "
Mathew Bailie 48, farmer " "
Eliza " 46, spinster " "
Stewart " 20, farmer " "
Matty " 18, spinster " "
William Ferris 25, farmer Ballymena, Antrim
Ann " his wife 32, " "

A List of Passengers in the American Ship DILIGENCE
of New Bedford for New York, sworn at Dublin,
30 April, 1804.

Richard Despard 25, married, fair, merchant, New
     New York, an American, cabin
Mary his wife 28, fair, cabin
James McAnnally 47, married, fair, cabin
Thomas Taylor 25, single, light, farmer, Bally-
     water, Wexford, steerage
William Berford 19, single, dark, farmer, Bally-
     water, Wexford, steerage
Thomas Price 24, married, fair, labourer,
     Dublin, steerage
Hanoia his wife 17, married yellow, Dublin
Mary Doland 26, Single, dark, servant to

Mrs. Despard, Mountrath
Geo. Reynolds 50, married, fair, farmer, St. Mar-
     garet, Dublin, steerage
Mary his wife 40, dark, steerage
Jonathan son 8, fair, steerage
Thomas son 7, fair, steerage
Eliza their daughter 5, steerage
William Davison 28, married, sandy, farmer,
     Laiterbeag, Cavan, steerage
Mary his wife 28, brown, Laiterbeag, Cavan,
     steerage
William their son 5, fair, steerage
Edward " 4, "
Easter Brown 20, single, fair, servant to
     Mr. Davison
Betsy McMullin 60, widow, dark, Caverhalman,
     Cavan, steerage
Jane her daughter 28, single, dark, Caverhalman,
     Cavan, steerage
Fany McMullin 18, single, fair, "
     Cavan, steerage
Henry Shields 30, married, dark, farmer, Kings
     Court, Cavan, steerage
Ann his wife 29, married, dark, Kings Court,
     Cavan, steerage
James Higgins 27, single, dark, farmer, Caver-
     halman, steerage
John Brady 27, single dark, farmer, Caver-
     halman, steerage
John McMullin 50, married, fair, farmer, Pattle,
     Cavan, steerage
Mary his wife 50, fair, steerage
Jonathan their son 20, single, fair, Pattle, Cavan,
     steerage
William " son, 18, single, fair, "
     steerage
Thomas " 16, single, fair, " "
     steerage
Andrew " 13, fair " "
     steerage
Easter their daughter 9, fair, " "
Alexandrew McMullin 22, married, fair, farmer,
     Pattle, Cavan, steerage
Barbara his wife, 22, fair, Pattle, Cavan, steerage
Patrick Redmond 47, married, dark, farmer, Baley,
     Wexford
Bridget his wife 35, dark, Baley, Wexford
Jonathan their son 12, fair " "
Nicholas " 10, " "
Eliz. daughter 7, " " "
Bridget " 5, " " "

Passengers on the Brig GEORGE of New Bedford,
bound for New York, in addition to the list
before the Privy Council, sworn at Dublin, 29 August,
1803, Jacob Taber, Master.

Peter Roe 30, merchant Ross
Stephen French 45, " Carrick-on-Suir
Hugh Madden 30, Clerk Dublin
Mats. Joyce 18, " "

Passengers engaged to sail on board the Brig GEORGE
of New Bedford, Jacob Taber, Master, for New York,
sworn at Dublin, 29 August, 1803.

John O'Brien 28, clerk Dublin
Michl. Bannon 23, farmer Mayo
John Lyons 30, " Tullamore
Mark Evans 30, " Queens County
Ann Evans his wife
James Hennessy 25, labourer Dublin
Patrick Doyle 20, farmer Mayo
Bernard Fitzpatrick 36, farmer Tullamore
His wife & child "
Heny. O'Hara 23, farmer Clare
Peter Roe 30, merchant Ross
Shephard French 45, merchant Carrick-on-Suir
Mats. Joyce 18, clerk Dublin

Passengers of the American Ship SUSAN, John O'Connor,
Master, from Dublin to New York, sworn 6 Sept., 1803.

Abraham Bell 28, merchant, cabin, New York
Robert Bleakly 26, linen merchant, cabin, Armagh
Davd. " 24, " " " "

Mrs. Mathew 45, cabin, Londonderry
Simon Felix Gallagher, 45, Catholic pastor,
     cabin, Londonderry
John Carbery 36, merchant, cabin, Danish
     Island
John Watters 27, clerk, steerage, Navan
James Hornidge 25, surveyor, steerage, New
     York
John Curtis 28, super cargo, steerage, Dublin
Thomas Roberts 25, farmer, steerage, England
John North 36, gentleman, steerage, America
Laurence Toole 22, labourer, steerage, Dublin
Walter Fleming 21, clerk, " New York
Hugh Maddin 23, " Dublin
Roger Morris 28, " " "
William Sedgwick 36, " " "
Arthur Fulham 12, " Edenderry
Jane Hughes 22, " Down
Mary Kelly 40, " Dublin
Mary Mathews 12, " " "
Mary O'Brien 9, " " "
Ann " 8, " " "
Eliza Langley 22, " Kilkenny
Margaret Nowlan 22, " "
Biddy O'Connor 14, " Wexford
Mary Larkin 16, " " "
Mary Ann Reilly 22, " Dublin

List of Passengers on the FORTITUDE of New
York, Hezekia Pinkham, Master, bound for
New York, sworn at Cork, 1 September, 1803.

John Sullivan Scully 35, merchant Cork
Mary " his wife 28, "
James Ryan 34, farmer Bantry
Mary " his wife 30, "
James Long 22, shop keeper, Bantry
Denis Sullivan 21, " " "
Corn " 17, farmer "
John Barry 25, " "
Mary Harte 40, sailors wife Cobh
Mary Hart her daughter 10, "
John Harte her son 5, "
Thos. Johnson 30, clerk Cork
Mary Stewart 55, "
Wm. Devayne 60 gentleman Exeter Devon
Harriott Devayne her daughter 24, "
Charlotte " " 22, " "
James Hughes 30, gentleman Richmond,
     America
Mary " his wife 28, Richmond, America

A List of Passengers of the ship AMERICAN of
New York, from Londonderry to New York, sworn
at Londonderry, 10 September, 1803.

John Patton 34, merchant New York
Robert Boreland 20, farmer Strabane
Mary " 19, spinster "
Hannah McGhee 45, " "
Edward McGowan 25, labourer Tamlaght,
     Derry
William Dunn 25, farmer, Gellygordon
Thomas Buchannon 22, " "
John Donahy 21, labourer Limavady
John Patterson 30, farmer Moneymore
Mathew " 27, " "
George " 26, " "
Eliza " 20, "
James Dougherty 23, labourer Ramullen
James Cormick 28, clerk Strabane
Rebecca " 20, spinster "
Alexander McKinley 23, farmer "
John Torbet 18, labourer Tyrone
Thomas Miller 28, farmer Coagh
David " 24, " "
Marth. " 50, "
Elizh. " 23, spinster "
Robert Foster 22, farmer "
Martha Foster 22, spinster "
William Browne 34, farmer "
Margaret Browne 26, spinster "
Philip McGowan 34, farmer Gleek Tam-
     laght
Grace " 27, spinster Gleek
     Tamlaght

Philip McGowan junr. 12, Gleek Tamlaght
John McKenney 38, merchant New York
David Birket 30, farmer Castlefin
William Beatty 25, trader New York
George Lindsey 32, farmer Pettigo
William Cook 26, "
Isaac Cockran 27, merchant New York
James McFarland 24, farmer Tyrone
Alex McIntire 29, farmer, Waterside, London-
derry
Edward McClary 21, farmer, Tamlaght, Derry
Mary McGhee 38, spinster Cookstown

---

Additional list of Passengers intending to
proceed to New York on board the American Ship
SUSAN, from Dublin, sworn 13 September, 1803.

John Price 35, surgeon, New York, cabin
Thomas Dawdal 25, labourer, Dublin, steerage
John Gavan 30, attorney " "
Thos. Flood 20, clerk " "
Andrew Flynn 23, " " "
Patrick Synnott 25, farmer Wexford "
Francis Murphy 50, " America "
Owen " 25, " Monaghan "
Andrew Connor 45, merchant Dublin "

Names of persons who wish to go to Philadelphia
in the Snow GEORGE of Philadelphia, indorsed
from Belfast, sworn 22 September, 1803.

Ephriam Lee 26, farmer, Killeshandra,
Co. Cavan
Edwd. Lee 23, farmer, Killeshandra,
Co. Cavan
Hugh Gably 18, labourer, Killinchy, Down
Robt. Walsh 22, dealer, Downpatrick, "
Alexr. Fulton 34, farmer, Loughsill "
Thos. Kelly 36, " Grange, "
Edwd. Donnelly 27, " Lessan Tyrone
Will. Lowry 29, labourer, Killinchy Down
Thos. Service 18, labourer Brochan Antrim
Sarah Dawson 17, Connor "
Marcus Toole 39, servant Belfast
Jane Toole 28, " " "
John Dodds 30, farmer Dromal "
Henry Wilson 24, schoolmaster Belfast "
John Thompson 28, dealer Ballymony "
Patrick Mullan 21, " Tynan Armagh
James Strachan 20, farmer Connor Antrim
John Johnson 19, " " "
Nathl. Byst 30, dealer Gencany "
Jane Develin 32, " Ballymow Armagh
Roger " 35, farmer " "
Patrick McKey 38, " Drumgoland Down
Alexr. Stewart 21, " Tullylisk "
James Ganet 30, dealer Annalult "
Mathew Timoly 28, labourer Ballymasaw "
Thos. Armstrong 31, farmer Clonfeech Armagh
Mary " 27, " " "
Thos. Mathews 27, dealer Belfast Antrim
Eliza " 25, " Belfast Antrim
Joseph Wilson 22, dealer " "
John Pumphy 29, farmer " "

A List of Passengers on board the BETSY for New York,
sworn at Newry, 22 September, 1803.

James Kilheath 25, farmer Kilkeel
Jane " 26, "
Pat Murray 28, labourer Hillsborough
Sarah Murray 26, "
Robert Smith 28, farmer Clough
Jenny " 26, "
James Conwell 28, " Armagh
Catherine Conwell 27, "
Anthony " 26, " "
Bernard " 25, " "
Jeremiah " 24, " "
Mick Burns 25, labourer "
George Tedford 28, " Down
Eliza " 28, "
Rachael Weston 20, Charlestown, America
Pat McCullough 26, farmer Armagh
Sally McCullough 27, "
Pat Cassidy 17, " "

John Humphry 32, merchant Lisburn
Owen McUraney 22, labourer Carrickadrummond
James Moore 45, " Cranfield
Nelly Small 30, Down
Saml. Patterson 21, " Grange

---

A List of Passengers who have engaged to go
in the Brig LADY WASHINGTON, John Luscombe,
Master, from Belfast to Charleston, sworn
22 September, 1803.

Jane McCance 54, Blackumigo, So. Carolina
William Craig 54, farmer, Mageradroll, Co. Down
Agnes Craig his wife, child and servant boy
Hugh McCance 55, farmer Magerdroll
Elizh. " his wife 57,
Hugh " his son 19,
Samul. " " " 22,
Jane " his daughter 19,
John Blackwood 15, farmer Clough
David Bell 26, merchant Belfast, Antrim
Saml. Carson 36, " " " "
Arthur O'Neill 24, farmer Drumarra, Down
Saml. Leslie 22 " Kilmore "
Willm. " 20, " " "
John Wilson and wife 43, 35, Ballycam
William Hoey 18, farmer Ballykill, Antrim
John Young 22, labourer, Glenary "
John Sherlock 23 " "
Saml. Rabb 23, farmer, Ballinahurch Antrim
Thomas Caldwell 20, labourer, Broad Island
William Caldwell 18, " " "
Widow Lamont Charleston, So. Carolina
John Lowry 35, farmer Garvagh, Down

---

A List of Passengers of the Ship INDEPENDANCE
who have contracted to take their Passage to
New York in the said ship being of the burthen
of 300 Tons and upwards, Mathias Fleming,
Master, sworn at Londonderry, 31 Oct., 1803.

Edward McKelvy 35, farmer Letterkenny
Mrs. McKelvy his wife 35, "
Three children to the above
Luke Creyon 20, labourer Sligo
Roger " 18, " "
John C. Steward 24, farmer "
Francis Wood 26, labourer Letterkenny
Isabella " his wife and infant child
Thomas Leary 28, farmer Raphoe
Michael " 20, " "
Rose Caffry 18, spinster "
Thomas Laughlin 18, farmer "
Thomas Caffry 20, labourer "
John Hopkins 24, " Letterkenny
John Fisher 26, " "
Wm. Latemore 30, " "
Mary " 28, "
James Ward 25, " "
Henry Tory 28, " "
Joseph Robinson 20, " "
Margt. Miller 20, spinster Derry
Mathew McDole 36, labourer Carrickfergus
T. McDole 20, spinster "

List of Passengers intending to go to Norfolk
in America with the Ship VENUS, Resolve Waldron,
Master, Burthen 246 Tons, sworn at Dublin,
14 November, 1803.

John Sherman 18, merchant, 13 Little Britten
Street, Dublin
Edward Rooney 30, merchant, 45 Smithfield
George McEntire physican, 17 Crampton Court
Mrs. McEntire 22, " " " "
Edward Dempsy 22, farmer Kilmbullock, Kings Co.
Thos. " 18, " " " "
Mary " 50, " " " "
Esther " 20, " " " "
Judy " 19, " " " "
Catherine " 16, " " " "
Thos. Best 17, gentleman Smithfield

List of Passengers on board the FORTITUDE
bound to New York, sworn at Cork, 18 February,
1804.

Margaret Mahony 30, Dunmanaway
Anne " 9, her daughter "
Goody Burke 30, Kilkenny
Ellen " 12, " " "
Edward " 9, " son "
Biddy " 7, " daughter "
Denis " 5, " son "
John Buen 55, farmer Co. Waterford
Pierce Corbett 22, " " "
Saml. Grace 19, " Cork
Thos. Mackay 30, " "
Ellen " 25, his wife "
Ellen " 2, their daughter "
Thos. Brien 23, farmer Cork
Thos. Brook 36, gentleman "
Denis Flanigan 28, farmer Limerick

List of Passengers going to New York on the
GEORGE of New Bedford, sworn at Belfast,
25 February, 1804.

Andrew Smith 24, farmer Down
James Sprowl 30, " "
Alexr. Cochran 36, " "
Agnes " 28, wife and four children
from 1 to 8 years old
Elenor Martin 70, spinster Down
Margt. Fleming 20, "
Wm. Hinger 20, gentleman Drumara
Peter O'Hamill 27, labourer Antrim
Thomas Duncan 18, " "
John Johnston 50 farmer "
John Crothers 44, " "
Wm. " 34, " "
Rt. " 30, wife and four children from
1 to 8 years old
Thos. Gray 30, farmer Antrim
Jane " 27, spinster "
Hans Wilson 24, farmer Bangor
Edw. Templeton 20, " Coleraine
Jane " 18, spinster "
John Dawson 18, farmer Antrim
David Rea 24, " Down

List of Passengers who have contracted to
take their passage to Baltimore on board the
Ship SERPENT of Baltimore, burthen 280 tons,
Archd. McCorkell, Master, sworn at the
Custom House, Londonderry, 5 May, 1804.

Charles Cochran 24, farmer Fermanagh
Elizh. " 24, spinster "
Henry " 3, child
John Irvin 21, farmer Drunhing
Charlotte Irvin 45, spinster "
Andrew McGee 21, farmer, Killygordon
William Brandon 21, labourer Crumlin
Henry " 20, " "
Gerard " 18, " "
James " 16, farmer "
John " 14 labourer "
Mary " 18, spinster "
Edward " 15, labourer "
Isabella " 10, spinster "
Christopher" 8, child "
Mary " 40, spinster "
Thomas " her son 4 "
Jane " her daughter 6 "
Oliver McCausland 22, farmer Omagh
Thomas Harvey 22, " "
James Davis 26, " Dungannon
Margt. " 25, spinster Dungannon
Samuel Scott 60, farmer Cosquin
Ann Scott 69, spinster "
Rebecca Scott 30, " "
Francis " 22, " "
Jane Carter 30, spinster "
John Carter 35, farmer "
Ann Scott 20, spinster "
Samuel Scott 28, farmer "
John Johnston 22, " Ardshaw
James McColley 19, labourer Linamore
Stephen Johnston 21, " Adderny

| | | |
|---|---|---|
| John Ball | 36, farmer | Higham |
| John Dogerty | 21, farmer | Clonmany |
| Prudence Ball | 30, spinster | Higham |
| Edward Ball | 14, labourer | " |
| John Ball | 12, " | " |
| George Doherty | 21, farmer | Clonmany |

A muster foll of Passengers to go on board the Brigantine SALLY, Timothy Clifton, Master, for New York, Burthen 156 tons, Port of Newry, sworn 9 May, 1804.

| | | |
|---|---|---|
| Wm. McBerney | 35, farmer | Diamary, Down |
| Alice McBerney | 32 | " " |
| Three children under 5 | | |
| David Kelly | 36, farmer | " " |
| Mary " | | |
| Six children under 10 | | |
| Eliza Martin | 30, | Killevey, Armagh |
| James McCrum | 30, | Tynan " |
| Sarah " | 30, | " " |
| Two children under 4 | | |
| Richard Stewart | labourer " | " |
| John Famister | 30, farmer | " |
| Ann " | 22, | " |
| Jane " | 25, | " |
| Robt. Kinmar | 25, labourer | Keady, Armagh |

Roll of Passengers by the Brig. JEFFERSON of Newberry Port in the U.S.A. Barthen 138 tons, bound from Ballyshannon to New Castle and Philadelphia, Daniel Knight, Master, sworn 10 May, 1804.

| | | |
|---|---|---|
| Francis Maquire | 38, sandy, labourer, Barony of Lurg, Fermanagh | |
| Bridget " | 36, dark | " " " |
| Edward Thompson | 34, fair, labourer | " " " |
| John " | 24, dark | " " " |
| Mary " | 22, fair | " " " |
| Edward " junr. | 8, " | " " " |
| Patt Conolly | 33, dark | " Resinuer, Leitrim |
| Rose " | 31, " | " |
| Charles Stephenson | 29, farmer | Firehugh, Donegal |
| John Stephenson | 27, " | " " |
| Margt. " | 22, fair | " " |
| Thomas Diver | 25, " Chapman, cabin " | |
| Robert Johnson | 15, fair, clerk | Donegal |
| John Connor | dark, labourer, Drumcliffe, Sligo | |
| Will. Stephenson | 20, fair, farmer, | Donegal |
| Francis Cullin | 16, sallow, labourer, Resinuer, Leitrim | |
| Hugh McPartlan | 23, dark, " | Ballyshannon |
| Mary " | 22, fair, " | " |
| Daniel Tiffany | 24, " " | Resinuer, Leitrim |

List of Passengers in the WILLIAM AND MARY of New York, burthen 420 tons, to sail from Londonderry to New York, sworn at Londonderry, 18 May, 1804.

| | | |
|---|---|---|
| James Crawford | 45, farmer | Kinnaty |
| John Robinson | 40, " | Omagh |
| Jane " | 36, | " |
| Robt. " | 20, " | " |
| Joseph " | 18, labourer | " |
| James " | 11, " | " |
| John Robinson | 16, farmer | " |
| Mary " | 7, spinster | " |
| Barbera " | 5, " | " |
| Ann " | 3, " | " |
| Henry Mills | 35, farmer | Ballyogrey |
| James Fulton | 30, farmer | Omagh |
| Patrick McNamee | 25, labourer | Augher |
| Joseph Gray | 40, farmer | " |
| Hugh Doherty, senr. | 38, labourer | " |
| Hugh " junr. | 16, " | " |
| John " | 14, labourer | " |
| Unity " | 32, spinster | " |
| Elinor Doherty | 19, " | " |
| John Caldwell | 30, farmer | " |
| Elizh. " | 29, spinster | " |
| James " | 9, farmer | " |
| Elizh. " | 7, spinster | " |
| Jane " | 17, " | " |
| Thomas " | 30, farmer | " |
| John Crawford | 28, " | " |
| Elizh. Caldwell | 29, spinster | " |

| | | |
|---|---|---|
| Isabella Caldwell | 13, spinster | Augher |
| Joseph " | 11, farmer | " |
| Joseph " | 9, " | " |
| Isabella " | 7, spinster | " |
| Alexr. " | 10, farmer | " |
| Jane " | 7, spinster | " |
| Joseph Watt | 30, farmer | " |
| Patrick McCann | 24, labourer | " |
| Joseph Lowther | 24, " | " |
| Thomas Quin | 25, " | Hollyhill |
| Edwd. Divin | 24, " | " |
| James Hargan | 25, " | " |
| John Mulheron | 26, " | " |
| Sarah Gray | 30, spinster | Strabane |
| Boshale Gray | 28, labourer | N. Town Stewart |
| Neal Crosby | 24, labourer | " |
| John Rodgers | 21, " | " " |
| Robert Rodgers | 23, " | " " |
| James McDivitt | 24, " | " " |
| William Trevine | 27, " | " " |
| Saml. McMellan | 24, " | " " |
| Robert Wilson | 24, " | " " |
| Robert McCay | 24, " | " " |
| John Read | 25, " | Bollindret |
| Alexr. Hunter | 21, " | " |
| Robt. " | 19, " | " |
| John Ross | 26, " | New York |
| John King | 32, " | " " |
| Susanna Armstrong | 38, spinster | Carns |
| Mary " | 23, " | " |
| John " | 18 labourer | " |
| James McGuire | 30, " | " |
| John Getty | 50, " | Loughinwale |
| Abigail Getty | 45, spinster | " |
| James " | 26, labourer | " |
| Robert Adams | 45, " | " |
| Elizh. " | 45, spinster | " |
| John Adams | 15, labourer | " |
| Archebald Adams | 12, " | " |
| Mary " | 10, spinster | " |
| Elizh. " | 8, " | " |
| Martha " | 6, " | " |

Roll of Passengers to be received on board the Ship CATHERINE of Dublin, 170 tons burthen as per Register, George Thomas, Master, now in the Port of Killybegs and bound for New Castle and Philadelphia. Sworn at Ballyshannon 9 June, 1804.

| | | |
|---|---|---|
| John Conyngham | 55, dark, farmer, Monargin in Killybegs, Donegal, hold | |
| Isabella " | 49, dark, Monargin in Killybegs, Donegal, hold | |
| William Conyngham, | 26, fair, Monargin " Donegal, hold | |
| Isabella " | 23, dark, " " Donegal, hold | |
| Alexr. " | 21, fair, labourer Donegal, hold | |
| Jas. " | 18, fair, labourer, Donegal, hold | |
| John " | 15, fair, labourer Donegal, hold | |
| Catherine " | 12, fair, Donegal, hold | |
| George " | 49, dark, schoolmaster, " Donegal, hold | |
| Andrew " | 34, dark, farmer, Lochris in Mishue, Donegal | |
| Elitia " | 34, fair, " " Mishue, Donegal, hold | |
| John " | 12, fair, Lochris in Mishue, hold | |
| Andrew " | 6, fair, " " " | |
| Robt. Johnston | 15, fair, Donegal, cabin | |
| Robt. Henderson | 45, dark, farmer, Lochris in Mishue, Donegal, hold | |
| Elenor " | 44, dark, Lochris in Mishue, Donegal, hold | |
| Elenor " | 18, dark, " " " Donegal, hold | |
| Jane Henderson | 15, dark " " " | |
| Prudence " | 13, dark, Lochris in Mishue, hold | |
| George " | 11, dark " " " " | |
| Ann " | 8, fair " " " " | |
| Alexr. " | 6, fair " " " " | |
| Arthur Fawcet | 19, fair, labourer " " " | |
| John Porter | 43, dark, farmer " " " | |
| Elitia " | 44, " " " " | |
| Catherine Porter | 22, " " " " | |

| | | |
|---|---|---|
| William Porter, | 20, fair, Lochris in Mishue, Donegal, hold | |
| Alexr. " | 18, fair " " " | |
| William Harran | black, 37, Carrick East, Drumhome, Donegal, hold | |
| Elizh. " | 37, dark, Carrick East, Drumhome, Donegal, hold | |
| Ann Harran, | 15, dark, Carrick East, Drumhome, hold | |
| Jane " | 13, dark " " " hold | |
| John " | 10, dark " " " hold | |
| Alexr. " | 7, fair " " " hold | |
| Matthew Brown | 18, dark, labourer, Carrick East, Drumhome, hold | |
| William Harran | 37, farmer, Carrick Breeny, Drumhome, hold | |
| Jane " | 32, fair, Carrick Breeny, Drumhome, hold | |
| Barbera " | 11, fair, Carrick Breeny, Drumhome, hold | |
| Jane Harran | 8, fair, Carrick Breeny, Drumhome, hold | |
| Thos. Grier | 30, dark, Big Park, Drumhome, hold | |
| Jane " | 23, fair, Big Park, Drumhome, hold | |
| John McCrea | 24, black, labourer, Lignanornan, Drumhome, hold | |
| Cath. Fawcett | 21, dark, Mt. Charles Inver, Drumhome, hold | |
| Elinor Devenny | 27, fair, Benro in Killartie, Donegal, hold | |
| Archd. Scott | 26, black, farmer, Tullymore in Misheel, Donegal, hold | |
| Elinor Scott | 20, dark, Tullymore in Misheel, hold | |
| Wm. " | 20, dark, labourer, Ardara in Killybegs, Donegal, hold | |
| Jas. McDade | 22, fair, labourer, Killarhel, in Misheel, Donegal, hold | |
| Andw. Lamon | 18, black, Ardegat in Misheel, hold | |
| Patt Kennedy | 52, dark, farmer, Meenhallu in Killymard, Donegal, hold | |
| Susan " | 52, dark, Meenhallu, hold | |
| Edward " | 24, dark, " " | |
| John " | 19, dark, labourer, Meenhallu, hold | |
| James " | 13, fair, labourer " hold | |
| Patrick " | 16, " " | |
| Charles " | 11, " " " | |
| Biddy McCafferty | 20, dark, " | |
| Danl. Sheerin | 24, dark, Ardara in Killybegs, Donegal, hold | |
| Michl. Carlain | 26, dark, Killybegs, Donegal, hold | |
| Geo. Maxwell | 24, dark, Raferty in Killartie, hold | |
| Jas. Syms | 45, dark, farmer, Bractcla in Killartie, hold | |
| Mary " | 40, fair, Bractcla in Killartie, hold | |
| Samuel " | 6, fair, " " " hold | |
| Elizh. " | 4, " " " " | |
| Tera Allis | 30, " Drimahy in Done, Donegal, hold | |
| James Allis | 14, fair, labourer, Drimahy in Done, hold | |
| Owen McGloghlin | 29, dark, farmer, Glen, Donegal, hold | |
| Nelly McGloghlin | 30, dark, Glen, Donegal, hold | |
| ---- McGloghlin | 5, dark, " " hold | |
| Patt Gillespy | 35, fair, " " " | |
| Pegy " | 24, " " " " | |
| John McClosky, | 25, fair, Drimreny in Inver, Donegal, labourer, hold | |
| Rose McClosky | 19, fair, Drimreny in Inver, hold | |
| John Syms | 30, fair, Glen, Donegal, hold | |
| Cath. " | 21, fair, " " " | |

Passengers engaged to Sail on board the American Brig. ATLANTIC, Robert Askins, Master, burden 196 tons, for Boston. Sworn at Dublin 19, June, 1804.

Sydenham Davis, 20, height 5-2, dark, farmer, Summerhill, Kilkenny

Ralph Morgan    20, height 5-11, sallow, labourer,
                Raheen, Kilkenny
Michl. Ryan     22, 5-7, fair, labourer, Thomas-
                town, Kilkenny
John O'Hara     31, 5-3, dark, labourer, Kil-
                murray, Kilkenny
Hugh Heffernan  22, 5-6, dark, labourer, Clonsart,
                Kings County
Walter Madigan  35, 6 ft. fair,   "  Thomastown,
                Kilkenny
Cath.    " his wife 28,             "
Andw. Shortell  21, 5 ft. dark, labourer "
                Kilkenny
Danl. Nowlan    21, 5-10, dark, clerk, Tullow,
                Carlow
John Bolger     36, 5-5,   "  labourer, Dublin
Cath.  " his wife 36,               "
Saml. Duke      21, 5-5, dark, labourer, Thomas-
                town, Kilkenny
Martin Switzer  28, 5-10, fair, labourer, Navan,
                Meath
James Maxwell   20, 5-8, dark,   "  Dublin
William Gorman  32, 5-10,  "  clerk,   "

---

Additional Passengers engaged to sail on board
the Brig. ATLANTIC, Robert Askins, Master, for
Boston. Sworn 26 June, 1804.

Wm. O'Brien     20, 5-6, dark, clerk,   Dublin
Michl. Kane     25, 5-6, fair,   "      "
Michl. Mallon   33, 5-6, dark, brewer, Dungannon,
                Tyrone
Henry Bowerman  40, 5-8, fair, Lieut. Novascotia
                Infantry
Anthony Kearns  23, 5-7, dark, labourer, Dunleer,
                Louth
Andrew Melvin   25, 5-9, dark, clerk, Bray, Wicklow
Thomas Reynolds 22, 5-6, fair   "  Klena, Longford

---

List of Passengers for New York on the ship EAGLE,
Charles Thompson, Master, sworn at Belfast,
4 August, 1804.

Wm. Biggem farmer, Bushmills. His name was sent
in by the High Sheriff, who does not know his age
Alex. Beggs    30, 5-9, pale faced, farmer,
               Ballyroban
Margt.  " his wife 30, 5-9, fair faced, Bally-
               roban
Thos. Clyde    21, 5-9, fair faced, farmer,
               Ballyroban
Wm. McQueen    39, 5-8, pockpitted, farmer,
               Bangor
Jane    " his wife dark colored, 36, 5-2, Bangor
Jane Robinson 26, 5-5, fair faced, Belfast
John Searight  30, 5-9, fair faced, farmer,
               Banbridge
Jane    " 30, 5-5, fair faced, spinster,
               Banbridge
John Henry     18, 5-6, fair faced, farmer,
               Banbridge
Jas. Anderson  28, 5-6, fair faced,   "
               Banbridge
Tho. Norris    58, 5-10, sallow, farmer,
               Belfast
Jas. Warden    21, 5-9, brown, labourer,
               Randalstown
Robt. McCroy   30, 5-7, fair, labourer,
               Randalstown
Hu. Liddy      20, 5-6, brown,   "
               Randalstown
David Bell     47, 5-7, brown, farmer,
               Banbridge
Patience Bell 45, 5-5, his wife and their child
George    " 16, 5-3, brown  Banbridge
               their son
Thos. Bell 14, 5-0, brown, their son  "
Alexr. Ellis 36, 5-8, farmer, pitted, Ballymena
Margt.  " his wife 30, 5-6, fair faced  "
Jno. Crothers 44, 5-8, brown, farmer, Randalstown
Laifanny Crothers 32, 5-4, his wife, fair,
               Randalstown
Jenny Crothers 68, Randalstown
Nanny Acheson 21, 5-4, spinster, fair, Randalstown
Jane Wilson 30, 5-5, spinster, brown, servant to
               Lafanny Crothers, Randalstown
Joseph Warden 26, 5-8, farmer, brown, Randalstown

---

James Warden 22, 5-8, brown, farmer,
             Randalstown
Robt. Carrothers,35, 5-8, brown, farmer,
             Randalstown
Willm.  "    29, 5-7, farmer, brown,
             Randalstown
Eliza Carrol, 22, 5-4, spinster, brown, servant
             to Jenny Crothers, Randalstown
Isiah Young 28, 5-6, farmer, fair, Monaghan
Henry Hose  25, 5-7, merchant, a citizen of the
             United States of America

---

A Report of Passengers on board the American
Ship ACTIVE, whereof Robert McKown is Master,
burden 138 tons, bound for Philadelphia, sworn
at Newry, 6 May, 1803.

James Moore 21, clerk      Martha Parnell 18
James Rendles 40, labourer Robert Mills 40, labourer
John      " 38,  "         Eliza Barnett 16
Eliza     " 16,  "         Jane   " 12
Thomas    " 12,  "         Wm. Stewart 50, labourer
John Barnett 38, "         Margt. " 38
Margt.    " 34,  "         Ann    " 24
Eliza Laverty 20 "         Agnes  " 20
Andrew Barnett 24 "        Susannah " 18
Annabella  " 20

---

A Report of Passengers on board the American Ship
DIANA of New Bedford, burden 223 tons, whereof Henry
Hurter is Master, bound for New York, sworn at
Newry, 18 May, 1803.

Isabella Allen 32,         Market-hill
John Collins   36, labourer  "    "
Patk. Crowley  39,   "      "    "
Mary           " 39         "    "
Richd. Burden  28,   "      Fentona
James Farrel   40,   "      Stewartstown
Patrick Philips 24,  "      Strabane
Thomas Rooney  40,   "      Banbridge
Mary Martin    20,          "
Charlotte Brothers 26       "
Isaac Collins  30,   "      Monaghan
John Martin    36,   "      "
John Brothers  30,   "      "
Thomas Lewis   30,   "      "
John Michael   30,   "      Dundalk
Wm. Sleith     23,   "      "
Henry Ellis    30,   "      Newry
Thos. Fure     39,   "      "
Thos. Smith    37,   "      Bathfriland
Rebecca Brothers 45,        Newry
Benjamin Philips 30,        Dundalk
Hanna Mytrood  25,          Newry
James Downs    30,   "      Cootehill
Samuel Crawley 35,   "      "
John Burden    32,   "      Ballybery
Sarah Barder   31,          "
Rebecca Deblois 24,         Ballyconnell
Eliza Whithom  23,          Killyshandon
Mary Cahoone   22,          Cavan
Mary Overing   25,          "

---

A List of Passengers intended to go from this
Port by the Ship HOPEWELL of and for New York,
burden 125 tons, sworn at Newry, 6 June, 1803.

Peter Downey    22, labourer
William Thornbury 40,  "
Wm. Daly        30,    "
Geo. Ferrigan   32,    "
Wm. Martin      36,    "
Sam Smyley      35,    "
John McCeaverell 35,   "
Pat Cullager    20     "
David Humphries 52,    "
Joseph     " 26,       "
Robert     " 40,       "
Moses      " 17,       "
James Couser 18        "
Robt. Humphries 19,    "
James Reed   20,       "
Thos. McLeherry 21,    "
John Anderson 25,      "

---

A List of Passengers intending to go from
Belfast to New York in the Ship WILMINGTON,
Thomas Woodward, Master, 360 tons, sworn
9 July, 1803.

John Houston 30, farmer
Mrs.    "    27
---- Houston 5, children
       "     7,    "
       "     2,    "
Robert Stewart 27, farmer
Mrs.      "  24
----      "  2, child
James Galway 18, farmer
Thomas Allen 25, farmer
Willm. Erskin 32,   "
Isabella Dick 16,
John Cross   35,
Wm. Crozier  26,   "
Henry McHenry 40, gentleman
Hen. Read    30,   "
Jane Curry   36,
Mary    "    14,
Eliza   "    12,
John Curry   9,
Robt. Warwick 30, gentleman
Hen. Garrett 33, farmer
S. Ann  "    27,
Mary Maucally 23,
John Browne  45, gentleman
Robt. Jackson 30,   "
John Murphy  28,    "
John Thompson 26,   "
Thos. McCrellos 34, farmer
Thos. McConaghy 27,  "
John Cameron 39,    "
Lavinia  "   20
Agnes    "   17
Martha   "   14
Elinor   "   8
Saml. Chestnut 30, gentleman
Mary Cameron 36

---

List of Passengers engaged to sail on
board the American Ship MARGARET, Wm. M.
Boyd, Master, for Wiscasset in the United
States, sworn (indorsed from Dublin)
12 July, 1803.

Edwd. Irwin   50, labourer  Wexford
Geo. Phillips 30,   "        "
Thos. Maguire 32,   "        "
Patrick Irwin 31,   "        "
Jos. Cavanagh 34,   "        "
Tho. Best     22,   "        "
Mary Irwin    40             "
Ann     "     9              "

---

A List of Passengers intending to go in
the Brig. SALLY, Timy. Clifton, Master,
for New York, burden 147 tons, now lying
in the Harbour of Dublin, sworn 5 August,
1803.

Alice Flood    22, spinster    Dublin
Margt. Kelly   15,    "         "
Elizh. Flood   24     "         "
Alice Purfield 18,    "         "
Ann Eagle      10,    "         "
George Eagle   9               "
Mary Bennett   30,             "
Nich. Campbell 24, labourer    "
Nancy Fallis   20, spinster    "
James Grant    17, Scotch labourer  ----
Hugh Kelly     24, labourer    Dublin
Bernard Fitzpatrick 38, farmer Tullamore
Ellen Fitzpatrick 28, his wife  "
Mary     "  their daughter     "
John Lyons     30, farmer      "
& infant

---

A List of Passengers engaged to sail on
board the Brig. GEORGE of New Bedford,
burden 172 tons, Jacob Taber, Master, for
New York, sworn 16 August, 1803.
John O'Brien    28, clerk    Dublin

Michael Brannon 23, farmer Mayo
John Lyons 30, farmer Tullamore
Mark Evans 30, " Queens Co.
Mary " his wife
James Henney 25, farmer Dublin County
Patk. Doyle 20, " Mayo
Bernd. Fitzpatrick 36, " Tullamore
his wife & child
Henry O'Hara 23, " Clare

---

A List of persons who have engaged their passage in the Ship EAGLE, Andrew Riker, Master, of and for New York, sworn 27 August, 1803.

Robert Small 27, height 5-5 labourer, Ballymony
Wm. Conroy 40, 5-10, farmer, Pensylvania
Alexr. McKeown 18, 5-5, labourer, Belfast
Wm. Williamson 25, 6-1, " Killinchy
Owen Miskelly 25, 5-10 "
Killy " spinster "
Wm. Magill 23, 5-11, labourer "
Roger Welsh 24, 6-1, " "
James Reid 22, 5-7, " Saintfield
Thomas Armstrong 31, 5-9, farmer Clonfeakle
Mary ------- spinster "
John Treanor 25, 5-9, farmer Killinchy
John Murphy 24, 5-9 labourer "
Alexr. Orr 21, 5-9, gentleman Ballymony
Jas. Boyd 30, 5-9, merchant, Nr. Ballameane
Saml. B. Wiley 30, 5-10, clergyman, Philadelphia
John Moorhead 24, 5-7½ merchant Antrim
Marcus Heyland 22, 5-3, " Coleraine
Wm. Freeland 20, 5-8, farmer Co. Armagh
Wm. Deyrman 25, 5-10, labourer Drumbo
Jas. Mild 25, 5-10, farmer Aughaloo
Jos. Caldwell 22, 5-8, merchant Ballymony
Mrs. Orr Tobermore
John Breen 15, 5-7, farmer Killenely
Saml. McNeill 20, 5-8, grocer Ballymena
Jas. Campbell 30, 5-5, labourer Carmoney
Saml. Miniss 21, 5-7 " Saintfield
James Macauley 22, 5-11 " "
Wm. Dixon 22, 5-7 " "
Saml. Moore 18, 6 ft. gentleman Portglenone
Alexr. Graham 34, 5-8, M.D. last residence Glasgow
Thos. Neilson 24, 5-5 merchant Ballinderry
Saml. " 11, 5-8 "
Robt. " 28, 5-7, " "
James Grant 28, 5-7 " Armahilt

---

List of Passengers on board the American Ship MECHANIC of Baltimore, Peter Thorn, Master, from Dublin to Baltimore, Navigated with ten men, 203 tons burden, sworn 28 May, 1804.

Benjamin Clegg 22, single, fair, gent. Stradbally, Queens County, cabin
George Clegg 26, single, dark, gent. Stradbally, Queens County, cabin
Rev. Matthew Ryan 60, single, fair, clergyman, Dublin, steerage
James Carney 55, married, dark, farmer, Athy, Co. Kildare, steerage
Mary " 50, married, fair, Athy, steerage
Thomas " 30, single " farmer, Athy, steerage
John " 20, single, fair, farmer, Athy, steerage
Nicholas Carney 19, single, fair, farmer, Athy, steerage
Martin Carney 11, single, fair, farmer, " steerage
Ellen Dobbyn 20, single, " " Queens Co., steerage
William Rogers 30, single, brown, gent. St. Margarets, Dublin, steerage
John Hay, 23, single, fair, gent., Newry, Down, steerage
George Reynolds 42, married, brown, gent. St. Margarets, steerage
Mary " --- married, fair, St. Margarets, steerage
Matthew Christian 22, single, brown, labourer, Borris, Queens County, steerage

---

List of Passengers who have contracted to take their passage on board the ship DUNCAN of Whitehaven, burden 238 tons, Abraham Sebson, Master, for New York, sworn at Londonderry, 26 May, 1804.

George Cuthbert 35, labourer, Coleraine
James Alcorn 40, " Glenvenogh, Donegal
Michl. " 16, " " "
John " 17, " " "
Mary Gallagher 35, spinster " "
Ann Cuthbert 13, " " "
Fanny " 12, " " "
John Coyle 20, farmer " "
James McCaran 20, " " "
Edward McCaran 22, " " "
James Todd 19, labourer, Largilly
John Gibson 19, " Ballycloy
Thomas Paul 20, " County Down
George Elliot 24, farmer "
James Gamble 25, " Donaghady, Co. Tyrone
Samuel Patterson 26, labourer "
George Watson 29, " "
William Sanderson 35, " Langfield
Margt. " 18, spinster "
Sidney " 28, farmer "
James Davitt 24, farmer Astraw "
Patrick McGawly 26, labourer, Urney "
John Ginn 28, " Drumceeran "
Margt. " 26, spinster "
Jane " 20, " " "
Anne " 50, " " "
Matthew Gibson 38, farmer "
Eliza " 28, spinster "
Fanny " 18, " " "
Charles Johnston 38, labourer Co. Fermanagh
Ann Johnston 26, spinster "
Thomas Keys 24, farmer Magheranny
Eliza Keys 20, spinster "
Francis Crow 22, labourer "
Richard Guthrie 34, " "
James Crozier 22, " Dromash
James Brisland 26, farmer Co. Tyrone
Margaret Woods 28, spinster, Lissenderry

---

A List of Passengers intending to go by the American Brig. Ceres of New York, Herbert Forrester, Master, from Newry for New York, sworn 31 May, 1804.

Robert Tronson 17, gentleman Newtown, Hamilton
Thomas Hanlon 26, farmer Armagh
Judith " 26, "
Joseph Love 23, labourer "
Rose Love 18, "
John Pebbes 43, gentleman Hamiltonsbawn
Ann " 37, "
Margt. " 14, "
Sarah 9, "
Annebella Pebbes 5, "
Mary Jane " infant "
Ann Murray 26, Fivemiletown
Betsy " 23, "
Mary Patterson 34, Lisdromore
Patt McConell 24, labourer Moy
Kitty 22, Moy

---

A List of Passengers intended to be taken on board the Ship LIVE OAK of Scarboro, Christopher Dyer, Master, burden 400 tons, bound to New York in America, sworn at Londonderry, 23 June, 1804.

Henry Wilson 24, farmer Dungannon
Jane " 20, his wife "
Mary " 2 month old child "
Mark McQuillan 21, farmer Nughnacloy
William Pedin 22, labourer Nughadown, Derry
William Davidson 20, " " "
Susan Greer 40, married Cookstown
Sarah " 20, spinster "
Susan " 15, " "
Mary " 14, " "
Hannah " 12, " "
Anna " 7, " "
Joseph " 4, " "
Sarah Dougal 20, servant girl "
John Webb 50, farmer "
John Webb 19, " "
Susan Webb 16, spinster Cookstown
Janet " 44, married "
Thomas " 15, farmer "
Maria " 10, spinster "
Jane " 5, "
Alice " 8, "
William Hannah 22, labourer Armagh
John " 20, " Newtown
Stewart
William Patrick 19, farmer " "
Samuel Steel 16, " " "
Jane Patrick 18, spinster " "
Nancy " 4 month old child " "
Alexr. McKeever 21, labourer, Gortin, N. Stewart
David Anderson 20, " " "
Alex. Irvine 21, " " "
James Russell 22, " Dunnamany
Elizh. " 22, married "
Isabella " 5 month old child "
James Sands 26, labourer, Cranah, Moneymore
Mary " 26, married "
Robert " 7, child "
John " 5, " "
Ellen " 1, " "
Mary " 22, spinster "
Jo. Hunter 45, farmer Gortmurry, Moneymore
William McKeon 23, " Lisabany, "
Ann " 24, spinster "
William Blair 20, farmer N. Limavady
John Murdock 20, " Glass Lough, Monaghan
Patrick Gallagher 21, labourer, Furmeny, Omagh
John " 22, " "
John McQuin 15, " Cookstown
Ann " 17, spinster "
Ostin Allen 19, farmer "
James Crooks 60, " "
Jane Crooks 50, married "
Mary Crooks 20, spinster "
Margt. " 18, " "
Saml. " 17, farmer "
John " 16, " "
Sarah " 14, spinster "
James " 12, farmer "
Benjam " 11, " "
James " 6, child "
Alexr. McKeon 20, labourer, Lisabany, Ternamenter, Tyrone
John McCue 20, " "
James Walker 54, " Dromagalagh
Wm. Dick 30, " Kilane Ceepeyt, Near Ballymena
Samuel Gault 30, " Kilane "
Samuel Reed 30, farmer, Castledaunt, nr. N. Stewart
Alex. " 28, farmer, Castledaunt "
Wm. " 23, " "

---

The following extracts are from 'The Shamrock'; or 'Hibernian Chronicle', a weekly newspaper published in New York, 1810-1817.
(From the issue of December 29th, 1810)
A List of Passengers by the ship ERIN, Murphy, from Dublin:

Miss W. Larkin Co. Wexford
Miss F. Walsh " "
John Barry Co. Louth
Edward Furlong Co. Wexford
Michael Butler " "
Mary Butler " "
Bridget Rigan " "
Bridget Byrnes Co. Louth
John Byrnes " "
Nicholas Byrnes " "
C. Byrnes, junior " "
Francis Duffy Co. Monaghan
Fargus Duffy " "
Mary Walsh Co. Galway
John Walsh (child) " "
William Ray Co. Cavan
Mrs. H. Bowles Co. Sligo
James McNally Co. Meath
Patrick Ryan Co. Wexford

William Malvin, wife, 5 sons & 4 daughters,
    Co. Cavan
Owen Duffy    Co. Monaghan
Ann Weapher    Rathfarnham
James Murphy    Co. Louth
John Giles    Bailieborough
Andrew Waters    Co. Wexford
William Stewart    Belfast
John Bishop and wife    Co. Dublin
Patrick McCabe    " "
James O'Brien    Co. Meath
Terence Farley    Co. Cavan
Isabella Plaus    Co. Longford
Joseph Manly    New York
Emanuel Toole    Dublin
William Bleakly    "
John Fitzgerald    "
John Roberts    "
Darby Kelly    Co. Meath
Mathew Neall, and wife    " "
Edw. McGuinness    " "
Patrick Keally    Dublin
John Thomas    Ballyhayes
Thomas Hales    Glasstown
Francis Leonard    "
James West    "
John McBrien    "
Simon Horan    Mullicash
Thomas Hearn    New York
J. Cunningham    Sligo
Christian Wogan    Co. Dublin
James Diffy    Co. Cavan
Wm. Floughsby    Dublin
Mart Ryan    New Ross, Co. Wexford

(Issue of Jan. 12, 1811)
List of Passengers per THE HARVEY HIDE, from
Belfast

| Name | Parish | County |
|---|---|---|
| William Simpson | Lochgall | Armagh |
| Mrs. John Speirs | Donegoare | Antrim |
| William Davis | Blairis | Down |
| Robert Harvey | " | " |
| Mrs. R. Harvey | " | " |
| Leonard Dobbin | Killeman | " |
| Mrs. Dobbin | " | " |
| Isaac Jenkinson | Lochgall | Armagh |
| Mrs. Jenkinson | " | " |
| James " | " | " |
| Elizh. " | " | " |
| Isaac " | " | " |
| Ann " | " | " |
| Mrs. Wm. Miller | Ahahill | Antrim |
| William Davis | Hillsboro | Down |
| James Coal | Drumboa | " |
| Alley Coal | " | " |
| J. Montgomery | Counmoney | Antrim |
| Mrs. J. Kennedy | Douaghmore | Tyrone |
| William Law | Kalmchie | Down |
| John Aslein | Belfast | Antrim |
| James Couples | Aughderg | Down |
| Elizh. Couples | " | " |
| Alex. McMurray | Kelmore | Armagh |
| Hannah McMurray | " | " |
| James Spiers | Donegoare | Antrim |
| James McCance | Newtonards | Down |
| Samuel Anderson | " | " |
| John Welsh | " | " |
| Louisa Welsh | " | " |
| John McKenzie | " | " |
| H. Mubrea | " | " |
| James Moore | Donaghmore | Tyrone |
| John Brown | Lochgall | Antrim |
| Francis Brown | Kelbroghts | " |
| David Bell | Lochgall | Armagh |
| John Davidson | " | " |
| Mrs. W. Campbell | Blairis | Down |
| Wm. Frances | Drumall | Antrim |
| Martha Frances | " | " |
| James Auld | Grange | " |
| Mary " | " | " |
| Robert Grendle | Kellmore | Armagh |
| Sarah Grendle | " | " |
| William Coil | Daryluren | Tyrone |
| Peter Coil | " | " |
| Sarah Coil | " | " |
| Rosa Coil | " | " |
| John McLanna | " | " |
| Thomas Lictson | Larne | Antrim |

| Mary Lictson | Larne | Antrim |
|---|---|---|
| Mary Harrison | Aughdary | Down |
| John " | " | " |
| John Liston | Kellmore | Armagh |
| Eliza " | " | " |
| T. Anderson | Newtonards | Down |
| George Anderson | " | " |
| Jennet " | " | " |
| Alex. McKenzie | Lochgall | Armagh |
| Philip " | " | " |
| Ralph " | " | " |

List of Passengers by the ship RADIUS, Clark,
from Cork.
As published in "The Shamrock", New York,
May 11, 1811.

| Hugh Parker | Cork |
|---|---|
| Hugh Sadler | " |
| Frances " | " |
| Samuel Freeman | Waterford |
| David McKardy | Dungannon |
| John Bull | Kilkenny |
| Jane Hannah | London |
| Mary Connor | Cork |
| Jeremiah Connor | " |
| Eliza Kirby | " |
| Cornelius Kirby | " |
| Mary Ann " | " |
| Margt. Keane | " |
| Richard Carey | " |
| Thomas Rice | " |
| Thomas Fowey | Castlelions |
| Timothy Murphy | " |
| Robin Pigott | Castlehyde |
| James Barry | Youghal |
| Thomas McKey | Fermoy |
| Ellen McKey | " |
| Henry Bullen | Clonakilty |
| Mary " | " |
| John Leaky | Glanmire |
| James Sanders | " |
| John Ranihan | Cork |
| James Barry | Watergrasshill |
| Jerry Maloney | Aglis |
| John " | " |
| Edmund Murray | " |
| Margt. Maloney | " |
| John Gunn | Castlereagh |
| Stephen Cronin | Castlemartyr |
| James Fogarty | Dungarvin |
| Bridget Gallivan | Cappaquin |
| John Cunningham | " |
| Frances " | " |
| Michael Cavanagh | " |
| Peter Slattery | " |
| Margt. " | " |
| John Slattery | Lismore |
| William Devine | Tallow |
| Redmond Kent | Lismore |
| John Kearceay | " |
| Margt. " | " |
| Patrick Foley | " |
| John Callihan | Tallow |
| Luke Linnen | Cappaquin |
| Henry O'Brien | Clonmel |
| Massy Hassett | Borris O'Kane |
| Richard " | " |
| Michael Kearney | " |
| Thomas Rian | " |
| James Guess | " |
| Thomas Dunnahough | Narragh |
| John Lane | Clonmel |
| Mary Lane | " |
| Catherine Buckley | " |
| Ellen Lane | " |
| John Blake | Emily |
| John Casey | " |
| Francis Kearney | Birr |

'We were led into error by the daily papers
stating that the HANIBAL was last from Cork;
she never touched at Cork after leaving Belfast,
on the 2nd January - we now annex a list of her
passengers, furnished us by one of themselves"

| Napshall Fendlay | Lesburn |
|---|---|
| Joseph Knox | Balleybay |
| Peter Hughes | " |

| Robt. McElwrath, wife and one child | |
|---|---|
| | Hollowood |
| Nathaniel Alsop and wife | Sanfield |
| Geo. Brown, wife and seven children | |
| | Banbridge |
| John Carr | Hellsborro |
| Henry Cochrane | Co. Mayo |
| Wm. " | " " |
| Robt. " | " " |
| Henry Drain | Co. Antrim |
| John " | " " |
| John McFall | Portglenone |
| Owen McPeak | Portglenone |
| Jas. Hughes | Dublin |
| James Connor | Lisburn |
| Patrick Garvin | " |
| Charles Davis | Armagh |
| Charles Ferris | " |
| Patrick Mollin, wife and four | |
| children | " |
| Robert English | Scotland |
| Wm. Ross, wife and four children | Verners- |
| | bridge |

List of Passengers per the PERSEVERANCE,
Capt. Crawford, from Belfast to New York,
6 April, 1811.

| Andrew Stewart, wife and one child | |
|---|---|
| | Stewartstown |
| George Wallace | Town of Antrim |
| Hugh McMullan | Co. Down |
| Moses Montgomery, wife and three | |
| children | Killele |
| Alexander White | Dromore |
| Elizh. Nielson and one child | " |
| James Martin | Bangor |
| Alex. Ritchie | " |
| Stephen Stewart | England |
| Stephen " | " |
| Thomas Donaldson, Cooper in Fife, Scotland | |
| Henry Scott | " " |
| Daniel Aiken | Glasgow |
| William Donnelly | Belfast |
| John Danwoody | " |
| Wm. Danwoody | " |
| David Park | " |
| Mathew McMurrey | " |
| William Stewart | Dunsmurry |
| Alexan. " | " |
| Jane " sen. | " |
| Jane " junr. | " |
| Andrew Kenmaer | Broom-Hedy |
| Samuel Piper | Menneyre |
| Robert Wilson, wife and three | |
| children | Dunmuny |
| Elizabeth Wilson | " |

Amongst those passengers, are 10 weavers,
1 miller, 1 bricklayer, 1 saddler, 1 hosier,
1 cooper, and 1 gardener. Three of the
first are Cotton Weavers.

List of passengers by the ship PROTECTION,
Bearns, from Belfast to New York 27 April,
1811.

| Patrick McCartney | Banbridge |
|---|---|
| Eliza McCartney | " |
| Ellen " | " |
| Catherine Parker | " |
| Mary Sinclaire | " |
| James Ferris | " |
| William Gordon | " |
| Easter " | " |
| Sarah Bryans | Moy |
| John Gamble | Ballybay |
| Eliza " | " |
| James " | " |
| Wm. " | " |
| Joseph " | " |
| George " | " |
| Bell " | " |
| John Morron | " |
| Wm. Clement | " |
| John Smyth | Downpatrick |
| James Glass | Belfast |
| Nevin See | Ballybay |
| Owen Maron | Ballytrea |
| Christopher Banecan | " |

| | |
|---|---|
| Samuel Magell | Banbridge |
| Ellen " | " |
| John " | " |
| Robert Forsyth | " |
| Valentine Forsyth | " |
| Mary " | " |
| Robert " | " |
| John " | " |
| Sarah " | " |
| George Irwine | Waringstown |
| George " | " |
| Rachael " | " |
| Robert McCracken | Ballymacaret |
| John Henry | Rathfreland |
| Wm. Carse | Killinchy |
| Robert Hamilton | Cumber |
| James Taylor | Armagh |
| James Bell | Lisburn |
| Louisa Taylor | Armagh |
| Jane McWherter | Newry |
| David Bell | Lisburn |
| Mgt. " | " |
| Henry Brown | " |
| Rachael " | " |
| James Ross | Killinchy |
| Thomas McKee | Newtownards |
| Margt. " | " |
| Robert " | " |
| Samuel McCartney | Banbridge |
| Hannah " | " |
| John Sinclaire | " |
| Anne " | " |
| Eliza McMullen | Larne |
| Patrick McKee | Armagh |
| Easter Teas | Belfast |
| Margt. Watt | Banbridge |
| Henry McComb | Keady |
| Ann " | " |
| Margt. " | " |
| Thomas " | " |
| John McWhatey | Armagh |
| Jane " | " |
| Alexander McKenny | Bangor |
| James Pinkerton | Killinchy |
| Thomas Hamilton | Antrim |
| John Conaghy | " |
| Robert Douglas | Ballymena |
| Ann Bunham | Newry |
| Wm. Patterson | Bangor |
| Eliza. " | " |
| John Andrews | Combers |
| Hugh McCawley | Crumlin |
| Mathew McCully | |
| Robert Sterling | Doagh |
| James " | |
| James Watt | Lisburn |

Of the above passengers there are
2 between 5 and 10 years old
16 " 10 " 20 inclusive
43 " 20 " 30 "
12 " 30 " 40 "
— " 40 " 50 none
3 " 50 " 60 inclusive
1 of 70
1 of 72
79, chiefly farmers, and some with considerable property in guineas."

Passengers per THE ALGERNON, Clark, from Belfast to New York, 18 May, 1811.

| | |
|---|---|
| Robert Lowry and family | Charlemont |
| Alex. Beally " " | Hillsborough |
| Wm. and Eliza Armstrong | Co. Down |
| John Neilson and family | " " |
| James Tate | Maze |
| Robert Hasby | Maze |
| James Kennedy | Halls Mill |
| John and Mary Hamilton | Hillsborough |
| James Amberson | Halls Mill |
| John Gurley and family | Co. Down |
| Hamilton McCullough | Co. Tyrone |
| Edward Pepper and family | Moyallon |
| James and Sarah McConnell | Hill Hall |
| Richard Hinds and family | Dromore |
| Wm. Copeland and family | Co. Down |
| James Morrison and family | Armagh |
| Ellen Tetterton | Banford |
| Robert Tetterton and family | " |

| | |
|---|---|
| John Bonnel | Queen's County |
| John Morrow | Banford |
| Edward Dail and family | Rathfreland |
| Robert and Rachel Kennedy | Banford |
| Wm. Orr and family | Hill Hall$ |
| John Orr " " | " " |
| Mary Nixon, George Nixon and family | Kill Warlin |
| Ann Coin and children | Belfast |
| Hobert Hall and family | " |
| Wm. Cobora " " | Kill Warlin |
| Henry McCurry | Hillsborough |
| Mary Curry | " |
| A Carlton | " |
| John Wall and family, Easter Wall, Banbridge | |
| Samuel Gelison and family | Co. Down |
| Samuel Burns | Halls Mills |
| Mary Sinton and family | Moyallon |
| James Gamble | Ballynahinch |
| James Deek | " |
| Agnus Deek | " |
| John Smith | " |
| Susan Smith | " |
| George Thompson | Belfast |
| John Maguinis | Co. Down |
| Isabella " | " |
| John Morrison | Magheragel |
| Sally Green | Lurgan |
| John Lamb | Maze |
| James Maharg | Co. Down |
| Sarah McMahon | Dromore |
| Joseph Mark | " |

Of these passengers there are
42 under 10 years of age
38 between 10 and 20 years of age
36 " 20 " 30 " " "
19 " 30 " 40 " " "
8 " 40 " 50 " " "
5 " 50 " 60 " " "
___
148"

Passengers per the WESTPOINT, from Londonderry to New York 25 May, 1811.

| | |
|---|---|
| John Lambert | John Hamilton |
| Henry Lenon | Benjamin McLary |
| John Dougherty | Samuel Gilmer |
| Edward Rice | John Madden |
| Margt. Christie | Margt. Hanlan |
| and her child | and family |
| John O'Neill | James Grey |
| Philip McLaughlin | Catherine Kerr and family |
| Ann McLaughlin | Benj. McLaughlin |
| Martha Sloane | Conell Curry |
| Robt. Thompson | Geo. McCaughall |
| Thomas Russell | Corn. McGinley |
| James Russel | W. Marshall and family |
| Joseph Marshall | Thos. McMenamy |
| Eliza Marshall | Jos. McMenamy |
| George " | Robt. McElkeney |
| John McCready | James Brown |
| Nath. McCaghy and family | Mgt. McMenamy |
| James Steel | Wm. " |
| Michael Hamard | Michael Denvant |
| Math. Kirpatrick | James Ward |
| John McKinlay | Connel Sweeny |
| George McKinlay | Peter Lyons |
| Edw. Hamilton | Cornelius Lyons |
| Jane Donnell | Isaac Vance |
| Dennis Hanagan | William Brown |
| James Dougherty | D. Vance |
| James Piden | Charles Logan |
| Thomas Freeborn and family | Rebecca Crawford |
| Patrick Kearny | Hugh Strong |
| James Carrigan | Chr. Strong |
| Wm. " | Cath. Graham and family |
| Henry Scott | John Smiley |
| Alexander Scott | Wm. Thompson |
| Andrew Funston | Susan McCafferty |
| Ar. Donaghy | William Porter |
| Roger McGuire | John Hutton |
| Patterson Jolly | John Campbell |
| John Hamill | A. Witherington |
| Mary McGohey | Elizabeth Miligan |

Passengers per the JUPITER, William H. Hutchins, Master, from Belfast to New York, 1 June, 1811.

| | |
|---|---|
| Hugh Johnson | Hillsborough |
| Elizabeth Johnson | " |
| Matthew Murdough | Moirà |
| William Harshaw | Down |
| John McCoskery | " |
| John Boyd | " |
| John McKee | Magradill |
| Jane " | " |
| Hugh Perry | Cullsallag |
| Margt. " | " |
| David Evart | " |
| Arthur Deolin | " |
| Joseph Camble | Dungannon |
| John Turkenton | " |
| James " | " |
| Jane " | " |
| Thomas Dixon | " |
| Joanna " | " |
| John Clark | Lurgan |
| Thomas McDowl | Saintclaire |
| John " | " |
| Alexander McDowl | " |
| Elizabeth " | " |
| Rachael " | " |
| Mary Ann " | " |
| Thomas Fair | " |
| Ann " | " |
| James " | " |
| Patrick Sweeny | Ballinahinch |
| William " | " |
| Prudence " | " |
| Edward Patton | Grable |
| John Glass | " |
| John Johnson | Antrim |
| Elnor " | " |
| David " | " |
| Elizh. " | " |
| Wm. Chaley | " |
| James McAlpin | Molany |
| Jane " | " |
| Hugh " | " |
| Conway Hamilton | " |
| Margt. " | " |
| Elizh. " | " |
| James Gallery | Moreyrea |
| Eliza " | " |
| Wm. McKelery | " |
| Jane " | " |
| John Ewart | " |
| James Kearns | Aghadie |
| Elizh. " | " |
| Andrew George | Killead |
| Wm. " | " |
| Martha " | " |
| Mark McAtter | Blares |
| Betty " | " |
| Alexander Mention | " |
| Agnes " | " |
| William Reid | Cumber |
| James Gelston | " |
| Thomas Stephans | " |
| Elnor " | " |
| David McMagan | Banbridge |
| Sarah " | " |
| Agnes " | " |
| William Anderson | " |
| Cath. " | " |
| Samuel Jamison | Killinchie |
| Agnes " | " |
| Bernard Conaghy | Banbridge |
| John McKee | Ballinahinch |
| Charles McCarton | " |
| James McCalton | " |
| Samuel Gamble | " |
| Robert Patrick | Belfast |
| Daniel Deolin | Banbridge |
| Geroge Best | " |
| Seragh " | " |
| Alexander McDowl | Llandery |
| Ezibella " | " |
| Thomas Harrison | Cairn |
| Jane " | " |
| James McAttur | Killead |
| Ann " | " |
| John Mitchon | " |
| Seragh Rhea | " |
| David Rhea | " |
| Samuel Stephenson | " |

| | |
|---|---|
| Thomas McKey | Dunleery |
| Samuel Cleland | " |
| Henry Cook | Armagh |
| John Stephanson | " |
| Thomas Phillips | Glenary |
| Eliza " | " |
| James McMullen | Tyrone |
| Eliza " | " |
| Robert " | " |

Passengers by the Brig. ORLANDO, Josiah Cromwell, Master, arrived in New York, 19 May, 18111.

| | |
|---|---|
| John Davison and family | James Thompson |
| Thomas Kennedy | Margt. " |
| James Frasier | Henry Johnston |
| | and family |
| Robert " | Felix McAllisted |
| Mary Russell | James " |
| Jas. Morrow | John Quin |
| and family | and family |
| Wm. Maxwell | Henry McMahon |
| Ann Patterson | James Ker. |
| Mary Logan | Thomas Sherran |
| James Little | James Henderson |
| | and family |
| Henry Drake | James Anderson |
| Thos. W. Ray | John Cannon |
| Richard Hughes | James Brady |
| and family | and family |
| William Burns | Elizabeth Burns |
| Robert McCane | John Owens |
| Thomas Stark | James Johnson |
| William Munn | Martha Little |
| and family | Jane Morrow |
| Rachael Hun | Anah Dreison |

Passengers by the Ship AFRICA, John E. Scott, Master, from Belfast to New York, arrived 9 June, 1811.

| | |
|---|---|
| George Roberts | Armagh |
| Samuel McCammar | " |
| William Murphy | Monagher |
| Mary " | " |
| John Hawthorn | Bellikiel |
| Agnes " | " |
| David Scott | " |
| Margt. " | " |
| John Logan | " |
| Jacob Pierson | Armagh |
| Jane " | " |
| Margt. Moffit | " |
| James Rock | " |
| Mary " | " |
| Joseph Bridget and family | Belleck |
| JohnMcCullaugh " " | Carmery |
| William Heson | " |
| William Spratt | " |
| Mary " | " |
| William Shaw | Billamegary |
| Margt. " | " |
| John Porter | " |
| Eliz Fullan | Lisburn |
| Sealton Fullan | " |
| Andrew Martin | Kilmore |
| Jane Morrow | Monaghan |
| Ellen " | " |
| Jane " | " |
| John Finlay | " |
| James Cowser | " |
| William McCaird | " |
| Sophia Cowser | Armagh |
| Eliza " | " |
| Jane Clagher | " |
| Hugh O'Ray | Belfast |
| John Gruir and family | " |
| Robert Moore | Dungannon |
| Eliza " | " |
| Thomas Moore and family | Rathfriland |
| Thomas Calvin | " |
| William Forcade and family | Belfast |
| Henry Moore | Rathfriland |
| Mary " | " |
| John Patterson | Belly Keell |
| Arthur Shee | Rathfriland |
| William Willis | Dungannon |
| Felix Farren | " |
| Margt. Willis | " |

| | |
|---|---|
| Sally Farren | Dungannon |
| James " | " |
| Thomas Kelly | " |
| Molly " | " |
| Hugh Cunningham | Rathfriland |
| Michael McAnorney | " |
| Patrick Maney | " |
| Jane McFade | Hillsborough |
| John Buchanon | Carrickfergus |
| Samuel Irvine and family | Dungannon |
| William Gatt | " |
| John McCartney | Loughbrickland |
| Nancy " | " |
| James Bodd | " |
| James McCurtney | " |
| Martha Heran | " |
| James Herker | Belfast |
| William Quail and family | Downpatrick |
| William Stockdale | " |
| Jane " | " |
| Jane Warren | Belfast |
| Hugh " | " |
| Ann Aiken | Dromore |
| Jane Aiken | " |
| John Cleland | Lisburn |
| Wm. Armstrong | Down |
| Arabella Armstrong | " |
| Wm. " | " |
| Eleanor Blany | " |
| Joseph Patterson | " |
| David " and family | " |
| Mary " | " |
| Wm. Willis | " |
| James White | " |
| Robert Burke | " |
| Edward Hazleton | " |
| James Morgan and family | " |
| George Patterson | " |
| Eliza Thompson | " |
| Maria " | " |
| Sarah " | " |
| John " | " |
| James " | " |
| George " | " |
| Joseph " | " |
| John Hodgsdon | " |
| John Lockat | " |
| John Fulton | Lisburn |

Passengers by the Ship AEOLUS, from Newry, Charles Henry, Master, arrived in New York,23 May, 1811.

| | |
|---|---|
| John Fulton and family | Abraham Keating |
| Moore McDonald | Thomas Seeman |
| Samuel Hunter | Luke Morgan |
| and family | John Hunter |
| William Clark | Peter Grabbin |
| John Seave | Edward De Hart |
| and family | Samuel McMurray |
| Joseph Fleman | and family |
| William Boyd | John Harshaw |
| and family | and family |
| Francis Henrietta | Frances Henrietta |
| John Kell | John Hughes |
| Betsey Fleman | James Copeland |
| Jane Sleeman | Thomas Copeland |
| James McCabe | John Sewere |
| Betsey McCabe | Francis Devan |
| John Walker | Eliza Lister |
| and family | and child |
| F. McLaughlin | John McGurrah |
| and family | and family |
| George Lemman | James Bell |
| Mary Lemman | Joseph Douglass |
| John Thompson | Elizabeth Smith |
| and family | and family |
| Betsey Hetherton | William Ballah |
| James Moore | James McSleeve |
| Samuel Crary | Isaac Armstrong |
| Margt. Armstrong | Margaret Moore |
| and child | |

Passengers by the GOLCONDA, from Londonderry to New York.
(Published by 'The Shamrock', 15 June, 1811.)

| | |
|---|---|
| Robert Philson | John McFaden |

| | |
|---|---|
| John Fletcher | John McConley |
| John Duffey | Danl. McGinness |
| Alex. Smiley | William Crone |
| James " | Michael Donald |
| Daniel Kirr | Eleanor " |
| James Shawkling | Mary Atkins |
| Dudly Dougherty | John Mollony |
| Dennis Boyle | Darby Burns |
| John Cannon | Peter Haughey |
| John Caldwell | John Burns |
| and family | and family |
| Dan. Cunningham | John Rodgers |
| Margt. Alexander | Alex. Glass |
| Isabella Glass | David Stewart |
| Francis Minetes | William Henry |
| Biddy Minetes | Jacob Giller |
| Mary Haggerty | John Kerr |
| Barney Donald | Benjamin Haughey |
| James Burns | John McColley |
| Murphy Burns | Henry Burns |
| John White | John Fanan |
| Thomas Burns | Catherine Burns |
| Thomas Faren | James Burns |
| Coudy Cunningham | Margt. McGrave |
| Mary Rodgers | William Pollock |
| Patrick Barney | Samuel Pollock |
| Michael Manely | John McMannyman |
| Henry Manely | Philip Carling |
| William Hickings | Edward McGanty |
| Patrick " | Samuel Johnson |
| Michael Hagerty | Dominick Golley |
| Daniel " | Thomas Scott |
| John Burns | C. Cunningham |
| and family | J. Cunningham |
| Timothy Timons | Issabelly Timons |
| Jeremiah Starr | Robert Lyons |
| Ralph Waddel | Bany Traner |
| Rodger Murray | Thomas Burns |
| John Hazelton | and family |
| John Rudder | Jacob Bell |
| Patrick Rudder | Mary Bell |
| John McGreedy | John Fanen |
| Edw. McConway | James Taylor |

List of Passengers by the Ship MARY, Wallington, from Londonderry, arrived at Philadelphia, 17 June, 1811.

| | |
|---|---|
| Thos. McGrath | Adam Woods |
| Margt. McGrath | David Harvey |
| James McGrath | Thos. Dougherty |
| Martha Smith | Abigal " |
| Wm. Key | Patrick Flanagan |
| Wm. Craig | William Ross |
| Elizabeth Morrison | Andrew Gibson |
| Martha " | Barnard Davis |
| John Moorhead (drowned) | Joseph Magis |
| Samuel Wallace | Sarah Wishat |
| Wm. Ceyrin | Mary " |
| Wm. Williams | Ruth " |
| John Cummings | Sarah " |
| Z. Bennett | Margaret Duncan |
| Nathan Rogers | George Williams |
| Wm. Beatty | Charles Hamilton |
| Jane " | Daniel " |
| George " | Robert Wishat |
| William Clark | David McKnight |
| Ann Clark | Mary " |
| Eleanor Ross | Andrew " |
| Joseph " | Jane " |
| David Clark | Thomas " |
| Wm. Hamilton | Daniel " |
| James Edmondon | Francis Monegan |
| James Gillaspie | Jane McBrine |
| Terrence McLorten | Ann Brown |
| Cather. McLorten | Patrick Connelly |
| Harvey Rculstone | Pat. McGellaghan |
| Martha " | Alex. Larkie |
| James " | Mary " |
| Archer Wason | Robert Norris |
| Jane " | Mary " |
| Sarah Curragan | Cornelius Crossen |
| James Fife | Catherine Doyle |
| Joseph Douglass | Abrm. McIntire |
| Laurin Folhall | John Rein |
| Mary Genagal | John Clary |
| William McCurdy | John Thorne |
| Morgan " | Arch. Raulstone |
| James Hunter | James Fee |
| Wm. Hunter | Antho. Campbell |

*Departure of the Nimrod and Athlone steamers with emigrants on board from Queenstown, Co. Cork.*

| | |
|---|---|
| Eleanor Hunter | Gabriel Andrews |
| Samuel Glen | Andrew Mills |
| James Thompson | Francis Maze |
| Patrick Crosson | Patrick Fee |
| James Woods | Anthony Mulden |
| Joseph Tagart | James Laverty |
| Patrick McLeon | Jane Lurkie |

Passengers by the BELISARIUS, from Dublin to New York, 6 July, 1811.

| | |
|---|---|
| Richard King | William Turner |
| Jane King | William Morgan |
| James " | Lawrence Current |
| Mary " | Peter Courtney |
| Jane King and | Michael McHolland |
| five children | Thomas Bird |
| Benjamin Tuckerbury | Richard Langer |
| and family | Mary Bird |
| Peter Folly | Valient Needham |
| William Phelan | Catherine Needham |
| Patrick " | Eliza " |
| James Graham | Mathew Murphy |
| Bartlett Turner | Joseph Gilbert |
| John Gilbert | Ann " |
| Mary Ann Gilbert | Ally Burton |
| John Birk | Patrick Pierce |
| Eliza " | Michael Murphy |
| Thomas Walsh | and family |
| Thomas Newan | William Sutton |
| James Costagan | Edward Lacy |
| Edward Dove | John Dunn |
| James Charowell | Martin Baimbrick |
| Rev. Mr. Ryan | and family |
| Denis Menieur | William McDonald |
| Robert Hughes | Stephen Mathews |
| and family | and wife |
| Wm. Nailor | Henry Stanhope |
| and family | and wife |
| Jane Connor | William Harding |
| and family | and wife |

Passengers by the Ship HUNTRESS, Thomas Ronson, Master, from Dublin to New York, arrived 24 June, 1811.

| | |
|---|---|
| John Field | Dublin |
| Peter Kenney | " |
| Cath. " | " |
| Jos. Craig and family | " |
| Chas. " " " | " |
| John " | " |
| George Echard | " |
| Peter Toole | " |
| John Armitage | Tipperary |
| John Horan | Kings County |
| John " | Tipperary |
| T. Kinch and family | Wexford |
| James Kinch | " |
| John Stout | " |
| John Keating | Dublin |
| Mary " | " |
| M. Gregory and family | Meath |
| John Gregory | Co. Louth |
| Bridget Harman | " " |
| Thomas Branigan | " " |
| Michael Devine | " " |
| Susan Gunea | Dublin |
| James Byrne | Wicklow |
| Patrick Meeghan | Tipperary |
| M. Flanery and family | " |
| N. Carden " " | " |
| Margaret Phelan | " |
| John Cullin | Kilkenny |
| Patrick Cancannon | " |
| Patrick Lawler | Wexford |
| John Doyle | " |
| John Murphy | " |
| Michael Doyle | " |
| Patrick Finney | " |
| Matthew Finney | " |
| John Dealy | " |
| Thomas McCormick | Longford |
| George Lanigan | " |
| Patrick Forley | Cavan |
| William Ryan | Tipperary |
| Thomas Davis | Wicklow |
| Edward Clark | Cavan |

| | |
|---|---|
| Owen Gerighaty | Meath |
| Martin Justin | Queen's County |
| Henry Sutliff | " " |
| Edward " | " " |
| Betsey Lucus | " " |

Passengers by the Ship SHAMROCK, McKeon, from Dublin to New York, 6 July, 1811.

| | |
|---|---|
| Edward Caffray | Queen's County |
| Morris Fitzgerald | Dublin |
| Mark Pigott | Carlow |
| Matthew Ketly | Kilkenny |
| William Walsh | " |
| John Scully | " |
| Timothy Murphy | Borris a Kane |
| John Stockdale | King's County |
| Miles Byrne and family | Dublin |
| Matthew Murphy | " |
| Wm. Fitzpatrick | Queen's County |
| G. Edwards and family | Dublin |
| John Laplin | Kilkenny |
| James Ryan | Queen's County |
| J. Shinluig and family | Antrim |
| Richard Hallugan | Co. Louth |
| Henry Colin | " " |
| Andrew Daye | Queen's County |
| James Trenar | " " |
| Patrick " | " " |
| James Durham | Dublin |
| Margaret Durham | " |
| Henry Stephenson | " |
| T. Fitzpatrick and family | Cavan |
| Thomas Phelan | Kilkenny |
| John Platt | Youghal |
| Thomas Ryan | Tipperary |
| David Ryan | " |
| Thomas Delany | Wexford |
| Nicholas Sinnot | Wicklow |
| James McKey | Tipperary |
| Wm. Reynolds | King's County |
| John Carrall | Tipperary |
| Thomas Murtagh | Drogheda |
| Michael Kelly | " |
| Brian Reilly | Castle Pollard |
| William Ryan | Dublin |
| M. Erraty and family | Kilkenn? |
| John McEvory | Dublin |
| Benjamin Wilson | New York, U.S.A. |
| Wm. Thompson | Philadelphia U.S.A. |
| Mary McClane | Cavan |
| John Bradley | Tipperary |
| Henry Withers | Dublin |
| Michael Alchorn | Philadelphia U.S.A. |
| Patrick Rorke | Tipperary |
| Patrick Sherlock | Dublin |
| John Wright | " |
| Elize Wright | " |
| James Kerwan | Castle Pollard |
| Wm. McGrath | Drogheda |
| Thomas Corcoran | Dublin |
| Wm. Corcoran | " |
| Michael Leary | Castle Pollard |
| John McClane | Co. Cavan |
| Mary " | " " |
| Peter Philar | Queen's County |
| James Ryan | Dublin |
| Catherine Wright | Cavan |
| Wm. Stanley and family | Dublin |

List of Passengers on board the Ship MARGARET, of which Thomas Marsh is Master, burden 300 tons, bound for New York, 18 April, 1803.

| | | | |
|---|---|---|---|
| Eliz. Brothers | 44 | Hugh Alexander | 29 |
| Mary " | 19 | Jane " | 22 |
| Samuel " | 12 | Jane " | 3 |
| James " | 10 | Sarah " | 2 |
| William " | 7 | Robert Gooey | 20 |
| M. Ann Anderson | 30 | Saml. Douglas | 18 |
| Mathew Doubly | 12 | Thomas Harten | 19 |
| James Farrell | 30 | John Rolston | 27 |
| Eliz. " | 22 | Ann Beard | 24 |
| Wm. " | 3 | Ann Beard | 2 |
| James Harkness | 40 | James McClean | 60 |
| Jane " | 36 | Eliz. " | 60 |
| Thos. " | 12 | David " | 24 |
| Margt. " | 10 | John " | 22 |

| | | | |
|---|---|---|---|
| Abigail Harkness | 8 | George McClean | 28 |
| Sarah " | 10 | Wm. Riddle | 19 |
| Robt " | 6 | Samuel Magil | 21 |
| James " | 4 | Samuel " | 39 |
| Eliz. Story | 47 | Biddy Enery | 35 |
| Ben " | 18 | | |
| Ann " | 16 | | |

List of Passengers intending to go from Belfast to Philadelphia in the Ship EDWARD, burden 231-86/95 tons per Register.

| | | | |
|---|---|---|---|
| James Greg | 46 | James Fox | 40 |
| Thomas " | 18 | Patk. Mooney | 16 |
| John " | 19 | James Tower | 22 |
| Thomas Fleming | 19 | James Burns | 20 |
| Hugh Porter | 24 | Robert Labedy | 32 |
| John Martin | 21 | Hers. McCullough | 27 |
| Alex. McMeikin | 21 | Wm. Scott | 22 |
| Wm. Dunn | 30 | James Kirkman | 40 |
| Thos. Monks | 60 | Wm. Bingham | 40 |
| Robt. " | 22 | James " | 14 |
| Joseph " | 20 | John Norris | 16 |
| Thomas " | 17 | Hugh Murphy | 18 |
| John Smith | 20 | Edwd. Wilson | 18 |
| Hu. McBride | 26 | Ardsal Hanlay | 24 |
| W. " | 25 | James Read | 23 |
| W. Dawson | 28 | Jos. Haddock | 27 |
| Jn. Craven | 25 | | |

List of Passengers who intend going to Newcastle and Philadelphia on board the ship BRUTUS of Philadelphia, George Craig, Master, burden 500 tons, 19 April, 1805.

| | | |
|---|---|---|
| Thomas Kennan | 25 | Stewartstown |
| Patrick Curley | 20 | " |
| Bennet Boles | 22 | " |
| John Wilkinson | 23 | Nn. Stewart |
| Michael Kelley | 25 | Omagh |
| Thomas Callaughan | 23 | Strabane |
| John Wilson | 19 | Nn. Conningham |
| James Clendining | 18 | " |
| Patrick Cue | 22 | Aughnacloy |
| James Wilson | 20 | Nn. Conningham |
| Wm. Stewart | 25 | Coleraine |
| Alexr. Eakin | 28 | " |
| James Thompson | 25 | Donegal |
| Isaac Cochran | 27 | Ballynoconey |
| James Ferrier | 24 | Bushmills |
| George Morrow | 28 | " |
| John MacCad | 29 | " |
| James Peoples | 23 | Letterkenny |
| Darby Bayle | 24 | " |
| Alexander Thompson | 30 | " |
| Stephen Alley | 24 | Derry |
| John Ewing | 20 | " |
| James Smily | 27 | " |
| Thomas Murphy | 26 | " |
| Patrick " | 30 | " |
| John Hasson | 24 | Cumber |
| Jean Bayle | 21 | " |
| John Johnston | 23 | " |
| David King | 29 | " |

A List of Passengers who intend going to New York on Board the Ship Rover of New York, George Bray, Master, burden 287 65/95 tons.

| | | | |
|---|---|---|---|
| Michael Muldoon | 27 | gentleman | Co. Meath |
| Mrs. Muldoon | 24 | | " " |
| John Jamison | 21 | merchant | Dublin |
| Robt. Greer | 38 | chapman | Dungannon |
| Fras. Ennis | 24 | gentleman | Queen's Co. |
| Henry Herron | 28 | merchant | Dublin |
| Elinor Neilson | 22 | spinster | Clones |
| Francis Evatt | 21 | labourer | Co. Cavan |
| Jno. MacNeill | 19 | " | " |
| Mich. Connor | 21 | " | Wexford |
| Ben. Hood | 30 | " | King's Co. |
| Morris MacNeill | 19 | " | " " " |
| Hugh Brady | 18 | clerk | Dublin |
| Stephen Flynn | 24 | " | " |
| Pat. Cranning | 30 | " | Drogheda |
| Wm. Armstrong | 22 | apothecary | Co. Meath |

Peter Donnolly 18 clerk Dublin  
David Jones 29 clerk "  
Margt. Hawthorne 34 spinster, Britain St., Dublin  
Jas. " 8 "  
Kitty " 5 "  
Sally (servant girl) 19 "  
Patt Fegan 30 labourer Co. Kildare  
James Heeran 32 clerk " "  
James Wyland 20 " King's Co.  
Patk. Lansdown 21 farmer Co. Meath  
Thos. Fitzgerald 35 farmer Co. Dublin  
Patt MacNaughly 27 labourer Co. Longford  
Matt. Mickson 20 clerk Dublin  
Peter Smith 12 " Co. Cavan  
Andrew Murphy 21 labourer Co. Cavan  

---

List of Passengers on board the Ship AKIN ALEXANDER, Captain Howland, from Londonderry to New York, 14 September, 1811.

| | |
|---|---|
| William Crow | John & Margt. Vale |
| Jane " | James Eakins |
| Margt. " | Rosannah Eakins |
| Mathew Orr | Margt. " |
| Alex. Armstrong | Margt. " junr. |
| Jane Campbell | Sarah Eakins |
| John Grey | Rebecca McMahin |
| H. Welch | John McFarland |
| P. Kirk | wife & family |
| John Jackson | Margt. Farland |
| William Orr | William Buchanan |
| John Johnston | George Wason |
| Margt. Wason | Arm. Armstrong |
| 14 children | |

---

List of Passengers per Ship FAME, Captain, William Pollock, arrived at Philadelphia, from Derry, 31 August, 1811, in 63 days.

| | |
|---|---|
| Samuel Torrers | George Crocket |
| John Rutherford | Samuel " |
| Mary " | Moses Hunter |
| Sarah " | John Kerr |
| George Crockett | Robert Hector |
| John " | James Grimes |
| Robt. " | Robert McArthur |
| George Smyth | John " |
| Arch. McElroy | Mrs. McTogart |
| and family | and family |
| James Alcorn | Joseph Alcorn |
| John Alcorn | Elizabeth Cross |
| and family | Francis Alcorn |
| Jane Simon | and wife |
| Martha Martin | Charles Quin |
| Rose Carolan | Samuel Dickey |
| Martha Quigley | Nathaniel Dickey |
| H. McLaughlin | John Wilson |
| James Reed | Matthew Kerr |
| James Arthur | James Dickey |
| Samuel Martin | John George |
| James Martin | Esther Bailey |
| Robert Orr | James McCloskey |
| James Neilson | Ruth Torrers |
| James Anderson | Samuel " |
| James McConnell | Ann " |
| Hugh McKinley | Samuel Rodgers |
| George Culbert | Joshua Orr |

---

List of Passengers per the Ship MARIA DUPLEX, from Belfast to New York, 21 September, 1811.

James Gray Antrim  
James Bennett Armagh  
Dennis Carroll Tyronw  
James McBride  
wife and family Down  
Andrew Morran and wife Down  
John Walsh " " Dublin  
Mrs. Bryson Belfast  
John Barr and family Ballinahinch  
Miss Mary Rodgers Belfast  
Miss Susanna Bowen Belfast  
William Quale Downpatrick  
Patrick Kelly Dublin  

---

List of Passengers per the Ship PROTECTION to New York, 28 September, 1811.

William Boyd Killybegs  
Robert Campbell Killinchy  
Henry Atkinson Dromore  
Eliza Atkinson "  
James " "  
Henry " "  
Jane " "  
Samuel Blair Cullybackey  
Eliza " "  
William Gray Armagh  
Jane " "  
Walter " "  
George " "  
Samuel " "  
John " "  
Elizabeth Gray "  
Jane " "  
Thomas Davis "  
Thomas Preston "  
John Wattsher Tyrone  
Anna Martin Antrim  
Nancy Martin "  
James Luke "  
Jane Martin Charlemont  
Isaac Cubbert Armagh  
John Syllyman Kellywaller  
Billy " "  
John P. Barron New York  
Effy Tweedy Dromore  
John Robinson Willsborough  
Jane " "  
Thomas " "  
Mary " "  
Hugh Neil Crumlin  
John Wallace Bangor  
Thomas Harris Banbridge  
Mary Ann Willis Stewartstown  
Thomas Knox Brougshane  
William " "  
Jane " "  
Henry Williamson Saintfield  
Elizh. " "  
Jane " "  
Robert McDonald Portoferry  
Jane Knox Broughshane  
Mathew Willis Stewartstown  
Joseph Verty Penreth  
Joseph " "  
Anthony Clothard Kellenchy  
Thomas Hamilton Connors  
Thomas McClure Saintfield  
Robert J. Walker Galway  
Robert McGaw Stewartstown  
Thomas " "  
Anthony Bridge Bedford, State of Pennsylvania  
Mary Campbell Belfast  
Jeremiah Campbell "  
Samuel Boony Greencastle  
Sarah " "  
Harriet " "  
John Quin Antrim  
Margt. " "  
Jane " "  
Henry " "  
James Thomson Lisburn  
Jane " "  
John Hughes Bangor  
Jane Sloan Doagh  
Jane Watt Castlewilliam  
Hugh Laverty Newtownards  
Jane "  

---

Passengers by the WHITE OAK, from Dublin to New York, 5 October, 1811.

| | |
|---|---|
| James Hannah and family | ---- coe and sister |
| John Bacon " " | Dennis O'Brien |
| ---- Martin " " | James Mulony |
| ---- Moran " " | Mary McManus |
| ---- Cannon " " | John Burke |
| William Kennedy | near Mullingar |
| and Wife | Edward Smith |
| | near Drogheda |

---

Passengers by the Ship MARINER, from Londonderry, arrived at New-London, 21 Dec., 1811, in 48 days.

| | |
|---|---|
| James Mulloy and family | James Corrins |
| Wm. McFarland " " | John McColgin |
| David Virtue " " | John Moffit |
| Archibald Elliott | William West |
| and family | David West |
| Edw. Dever and family | Dennis Dogherty |
| Thomas Long " " | Bernard Arenner |
| Charles Kane " " | John Boyle |
| Robert McKnott | James Knox |
| and family | and family |
| John Scanlon | Wm. Reynolds |
| Widow McPharland | Hugh Atcheson |
| and 2 children | and wife |
| James Bryan | M. Murphy |
| and wife | and wife |
| Anne Bryan | Mary Ross |
| S. Henderson | John Rafferty |
| Alexander Carr | Edward Timmony |
| John Henderson | Henry Williams |
| William Scott | Alexander Hall |
| James " | Robert " |
| Richard Crozier | John McEwen |
| Elizh. " | Hugh Reed |
| P. McPharland | John Boyd |
| Oliver Beatty | Patrick Mathew |
| Aily Rice | Patrick McGrath |
| Maurice Ferry | David Lindsay |
| John Alges | James " |
| John McAskin | Torry Monaghan |
| Thomas Hunter | |

---

List of Passengers per Ship HARMONY, Capt. Hobkirk, from Londonderry, arrived at Philadelphia, 31 October, 1811, in 70 days.

| | |
|---|---|
| Edward Loughead | Eliza Blair |
| Cath. Loughead | James Blair |
| Robert Rankin | Hugh Gallen |
| Manus McFaddin | Mary Gallen |
| Eleanor " | Margt. " |
| Mathew Nanson | Owen " |
| Hugh Anderson | Sally " |
| Ann " | Biddy " |
| James " | Mary " |
| Mary Bull | James " |
| Thomas McShane | Cath. " |
| Michael McCue | John Colvin |
| Daniel McCue | John Hamill |
| John Gordon | Robert Thompson |
| Robert Hamilton | Roger McNeal |
| Andrew Irvine | Mary Norris |
| John Irvine | John Coyle |
| Bernard Size | Daniel Loughy |
| Hannah " | James Logue |
| William Moore | Thomas Devilt |
| Adam George | James Cullen |
| John Rea | Mary Logan |
| John Young | Philip McGowan |
| Mary " | Fran. McLaughlin |
| John Manson | Biddy McLaughlin |
| Wm. Kirpatrick | James Blair |
| John " | John Devilt |
| Joseph Steel | Allen Kerr |
| Elizabeth Steel | Patrick Browne |
| Sally Steel | Bridget Browne |
| Samuel Patterson | Charles McKay |
| Wm. Knox | Mary Browne |
| Gerard Hunter | Wm. Logue |
| Martha " | Samuel Boyd |
| John " | Ellen " |
| Mary " | Mary Ann " |
| John Smiley | John Gilmour |
| Henry Dougherty | John Cochran |
| Cath. Dougherty | James Kavanagh |
| Anthy. " | Elea. McLaughlin |
| Thomas Stirling | Rose Griffeth |
| Martha " | Biddy " |
| Edw. McCafferty | Wm. McFarland |
| George Blair | Mary Logue |
| Jane " | Biddy " |
| Cath. " | Michael Rodder |
| Wm. " | Chas. Gallagher |
| Mary Gallagher | Charles McCoun |
| Cath. " | Bryan Cooney |
| Patk. " | Samuel Chestnut |

Michl. Gallagher    John Hanlan
Hugh      "         Jane Colvin

---

List of Passengers per the Ship WESTPOINT... 

List of Passengers per the Ship ERIN from Dublin to New York, 16 November, 1811.

| | |
|---|---|
| Mr. Thomas and Mrs. Robinson | Queens County |
| Mr. Cornelius Smith | Manoch, County -------- |
| John Lynch | Navan |
| John Androhan | Wexford |
| William Gibbons | of Ohio |
| Thomas Neil | Dublin |
| James Harrold | " |
| David and Dennis Doyle | " |
| Mrs. Cooper | " |
| Mrs. Riley | Co. Wexford |

---

Passengers by the Ship WESTPOINT, T. Holden, Master, from Londonderry to New York, 23 November, 1811.

| | |
|---|---|
| Robert Hunter | New York |
| James White | N. Limavady |
| Bernard McCosker | Omagh |
| John Hemphill and family | Dugh Budge |
| John Wawb | Castlefin |
| David Doak | Fannit |
| Susana McDermot and family | Derry |
| Francis Gillespie | Ballyshannon |
| Daw Griffin | Fannit |
| William Rafferty | Gawagh |
| Patrick McVeagh | Campsey |
| William Thompson | Carrick |
| Robert Henry | Coleraine |
| James Martin | N. Limavady |
| John      " | |
| Patrick Cartau and family | Claudy |
| Alex. Thompson   " | Leuck |
| Alex. Brown   "   " | Aughanwerry |
| Robert O'Neill   "   " | Co. Antrim |
| John Crampsier | Magilligar |
| Donaldson Black   " | Co. Tyrone |
| Elinor McCready | Gortward |
| Wm.    " | |
| John Graham | Kilrea |
| Thomas Hutchinson | " |
| Joseph Douglas | " |
| Thomas Martin | " |
| Daw. Kelley | Ballintrea |
| Ann Coulter | Co. Derry |
| Sarah Coulter | " |
| Patrick Divin | Ballyshannon |
| Hugh Coulter | Pettigo |
| Hugh Stevenson | Donegal |
| Mr. Cochran | Ballymoney |
| Joseph McCoy and family | Florinscourt |
| Cath. Kelley | Fannit |
| Edward McMennomy | Ballybofey |
| John Kelley | " |
| John Hilton | Gawagh |
| Edward Dogherty | Cauakeel |
| Robert Johnston | Pettigo |
| Francis Johnston | " |
| Alex. McAlvin and family | Co. Antrim |
| Samuel Moorhead | " |
| John Jack | "   " |
| James O'Donnell | Rushey |
| Ann Donaghey | Roeman |
| John      " | Rushey |
| Patrick Froster | Straban |
| George Kirk | Mountcharles |
| George McKee | " |
| James Love | Donagheda |
| Robert Love | " |
| George McEliver | " |
| Nancey Wason | Ray |
| David Hunter | Omagh |
| James C. Sproul | Stranorla |
| Eliza Paul | Omagh |
| John Hunter | N. Limavady |
| Farguis McGaughrin | Donegal |
| John Cummings | Ballymoney |
| Paul Boggs | New York |
| Luke Flyn | Co. Cavan |
| John O'Neill | " |
| Ann Masterson | " |
| Elizh. Wardlaw | " |
| Edward Masterson | " |

---

| | |
|---|---|
| Elizabeth Hasting | Co. Cavan |
| Edward McMinimin | Castlefin |
| Nancy McKagh | " |
| Hugh McElvin | Dromore |
| Hugh Catherwood | Coleraine |
| Neal Janga | Castlefin |

---

Passengers by the Ship HIBERNIA, Graham, from Belfast to New York, 30 November, 1811.

| | |
|---|---|
| David McClean and family | Wm. Stewart |
| Mary Willikin    " | Eliz. Armstrong |
| Cath. Goal      " | Luke Jackson |
| Edward McKever  " | Wm. Thompson |
| Thomas Mathews  " | Mary Reilly |
| Polly Connolly  " | Margt. Auld |
| L. Barklie      " | James Getty |
| Richard Blair, Ann Blair | Alex. McCullough |
| H. Stewart | Bernard Doorish |
| P. Quin | Ann Wright |
| Nicholas Lapsy | Wm. Freeland |
| John McGaw and family | R. Armstrong |
| James Leman | Margt. Leman |
| John McNeilly | James Gaffin |
| James Shephard | George Roberts |
| Robert Peadon | Thomas Reilly |
| Daniel Quin | John Jones |
| Hugh Quin | Benj. Stewart |

---

Passengers by the Ship AEOLUS, from Newry to New York, 14 December, 1811.

| | |
|---|---|
| John Brown and family | John Murphy |
| Robert McIndoo and wife | James Harpur |
| Wm. Burns and family | Lucy Fuller |
| John Davidson and family | John McConnell |
| Margt. Ferris and family | Samuel Evans |
| Daniel McKey    " | Alice McKenney |
| John George     " | John Moore |
| John Class      " | George Black |
| John McMullen   " | James Kerr |
| Robert Cunningham " | Mary Orr |
| George Grady and niece | Wm. Bell |
| David Hawthorn and family | Mary Roark |
| James Ryers and wife | Edward McQuaid |
| Henry Holland and family | John Flanigan |
| Hannah Couden and family | Patrick    " |
| John Triven and wife | Peter Casey |
| Samuel Kirk and family | George Wilkins |
| John Jeffrys    "    " | Hugh Crothers |

---

Passengers by the Ship ALEXANDER, Captain Fanning, from Londonderry to New York, 21 December, 1811.

| | |
|---|---|
| James Wright and wife | Eliz. Ritchie |
| William Rea and family | Joseph Caldwell |
| Tully Sieven    "    " | Francis Bradley |
| Thomas Rogers and family | Thomas Swan |
| Francis McManus and wife | Hugh Wallace |
| Patrick Campbell "    " | Percival Kain |
| James Buden and family | John Thompson |
| Alexander Child | Dean Knox |
| Anne McClure | Wm. McMalin |
| Wm. Maitland | Eliza McKinney |
| John Givun | Anne Miller |
| Wm. Thompson | Cath. Bradley |
| George McKinney | Phillip Kelley |
| Robert Moore | James Collins |
| P. McDevill | Sally Devlin |

---

List of Emigrants from the Parish of Magilligan for the years 1833-1834. Particulars given in the following order: Name, Age, Religion, Townland and Destination.

| Name | Age | Religion | Townland | Destination |
|---|---|---|---|---|
| John Quinn | 19 | R.C. | Ballymagolane | Quebec |
| James Melon | 23 | " | Oughtymore | Phila. |
| Nancy Melon | 25 | " | " | Quebec |
| Jane Doherty | 18 | " | " | N. York |
| Wm. Kelly | 20 | E.C. | Ballyscullion | Phila. |
| Wm. Doherty | 22 | R.C. | " | " |
| Edw. " | 25 | R.C. | " | " |

---

| Name | Age | Religion | Townland | Destination |
|---|---|---|---|---|
| Michael Doherty | 24 | R.C. | Ballyscullion | Phila. |
| Cath. McLaughlin | 20 | " | Ballycarton | Quebec |
| Pat. McCormick | 25 | " | Duncrun | Phila |
| Wm. McCormick | 23 | " | " | " |
| Jas. Kennedy | 20 | " | " | N. York |
| John Doherty | 22 | " | " | Quebec |
| Wm. Rudden | 24 | " | Ballycarton | " |
| Cath. McLaughlin | 26 | " | " | " |
| Abraham Kilmary | 30 | " | " | " |
| Hugh Lane | 23 | " | Claggan | Phila. |
| Robt. Smith | 23 | " | Ballyscullion | " |
| Mark McLaughlin | 30 | " | Ballyleighery | Quebec |
| Wm. Ferson | 24 | P | Ballymultimber | Phila |
| Wm. Doherty | 24 | " | " | " |
| Mary A. Snell | 28 | E.C. | Servant at Bellarena | Quebec |
| John Bleakley | | | | |
| Samuel Tate | 28 | P. | Woodtown | Quebec |
| Thos. Tate | 20 | " | " | " |
| Thos. Paterson | 35 | E.C. | " | " |
| Jas. McNally | 30 | R.C. | Aughill | " |
| Margt. McNally | 21 | " | " | " |
| Geo. Redgate | 25 | " | " | N. York |
| Wm. McFeely | 24 | " | " | " |
| Jas. Farren | 25 | " | " | Quebec |
| Ellen Doherty | 20 | " | Tirreeven | " |
| Wm. Gilchrist | 40 | " | Ballymaclary | " |
| Sara " | 41 | " | " | " |
| John " | 10 | " | " | " |
| Wm. " junr. | 8 | " | " | " |
| Patrick " | 12 | " | " | " |
| Holland O'Brien | 25 | " | " | " |
| Margt. " | 35 | " | " | " |
| Margt. Tonner | 7 | " | " | " |
| Margt. McCague | 24 | " | Clooney | " |
| Ellen O'Kane | 20 | " | " | St. Johns |
| Margt. " | 18 | " | " | " |
| Margt. " | 18 | " | " | " |
| Margt. " | 18 | " | " | " |
| Nancy McCague | 22 | " | " | " |
| Geo. Doherty | 26 | " | Upr. Drumons | N. York |
| Nancy " | 22 | " | " | Phila |
| Hugh McTyre | 22 | " | " | Quebec |
| Betty McTyre | 23 | " | " | " |
| Robert Smith | 24 | " | " | Phila |
| John Bleakley | | | | |

---

Emigrants from Aghadowey in the year 1834.

| Name | Age | Religion | Townland | Destination |
|---|---|---|---|---|
| Margt. Wallace | 22 | P. | Bough | Quebec |
| James Orr | 30 | " | Cullycapple | Phila. |
| Jane " | 32 | " | " | " |
| Margt. " | 11 | " | " | " |
| Elizh. " | 9 | " | " | " |
| Elizh. " | 9 | " | " | " |
| Ann " | 5 | " | " | " |
| Isabella Orr | 7 | " | " | " |
| Hannah " | 3 | " | " | " |
| Thomas Mullen | 25 | R.C. | Mullaghmore | " |
| John " | 30 | " | " | " |
| Bernard " | 23 | " | " | " |
| Cath. " | 22 | " | " | " |
| John " | 20 | " | Glassgort | " |
| John McFetridge | 24 | P. | Lands Agivey | Phila. |
| Margt. McGonigle | 5 | " | " | " |
| John " | 3 | " | " | " |
| Jonathan Tracey | 20 | R.C. | Cahery | Quebec |
| Margt. " | 21 | P. | " | " |
| Mary Canning | 30 | " | " | " |
| Soba Mairs | 40 | " | Ballylough | Phila. |
| Margt. Mairs | 18 | " | " | " |
| Ann " | 43 | " | " | " |
| Sara " | 12 | " | " | " |
| Jane " | 10 | " | " | " |
| Matilda Mairs | 3 | " | " | " |
| John Moon | 25 | " | Clarkhill | " |
| Jonathan Moon | 24 | " | " | " |
| Edward " | 20 | " | " | " |
| Daniel Thompson | 20 | " | Ballywillan | N. York |
| William Young | 25 | " | Shanloughead | Phila. |
| John Smith | 20 | " | Moneycarris | " |
| Jane Jamison | 19 | " | Aghadowey | " |
| Andrew McAlister | 40 | " | Keely | Quebec |
| Ann " | 16 | " | " | " |
| Ann " | 38 | " | " | " |
| Thos. McAlister | 14 | " | " | " |
| James " | 12 | " | " | " |
| Margt. " | 10 | " | " | " |
| Robert " | 8 | " | " | " |

| Name | Age | | Townland | Destination |
|---|---|---|---|---|
| Susan McAlister | 6 | P. | Keely | Quebec |
| Mary | " 4 | " | " | " |
| Andrew | " 2 | " | " | " |
| Michael McAfee | 24 | R.C. | " | " |
| Martha | " 22 | " | " | " |
| Martha McAlister | 50 | P. | Dirnagrove | " |
| Rebecca | " 18 | " | " | " |
| Olive | " 14 | " | " | " |
| James Neil | 20 | P. | Drumacrow | N. York |
| John Fleming | 21 | " | " | " |
| James Moore | 22 | " | Ballincallymore | " |
| Isabella Moore | 21 | " | " | " |
| Wm. Workman | 70 | " | Mullan | Quebec |
| Mary | " 60 | " | " | " |
| John | " 20 | " | " | " |
| Richard | " 16 | " | " | " |
| Margt. | " 18 | " | " | " |
| James McKeemins | 25 | " | " | " |
| Edward Quinn | 20 | R.C. | Mullaghinch | N. York |
| Mary Gillon | 45 | " | Meanougher | Quebec |
| Patrick Logue | 16 | " | " | " |
| Ann Logue | 14 | " | " | " |
| Sam. Patterson | 33 | P. | Clintagh | Phila |
| Elizh. Patterson | 25 | " | " | " |
| Joseph | " 62 | " | " | " |
| Richard | " 43 | " | " | " |
| Mary | " 26 | " | " | " |
| Margt. Stewart | 30 | " | " | " |
| James Morrison | 20 | " | Crossmakeever | Quebec |
| Hugh Kennedy | 20 | " | " | " |
| John Adams | 28 | " | Carnroe | " |
| Elizh. McClurg | 40 | E.C. | Lisnamuck | N. York |
| Jane | " 16 | " | " | " |
| Arch. | " 14 | " | " | " |
| Jackson | " 10 | " | " | " |
| Hugh Hemphill | 27 | P. | Ballybritain | Phila. |
| Robt. Henery | 22 | " | Lisboy | " |
| Jas. McFarrell | 30 | " | Ballymacallaghan | Quebec |
| John Boyd | 20 | " | " | N. York |
| Mary Jane Fream | 18 | " | " | " |
| William Hill | 25 | " | Bovagh | " |
| Cath. Boyd | 25 | " | Ballymacallaghan | " |
| Hanah Doherty | 25 | " | Bovagh | Quebec |
| Eliz. Adams | 22 | R.C. | Mullaghmore | " |
| Michael McAlice | 24 | " | " | " |
| Elizh. | " 22 | " | " | " |
| Jas. Jameson | 40 | E.C. | " | " |
| Jane | " 30 | " | " | " |
| Robert Reid | 60 | P. | Margagher | Phila. |
| Ann | " 55 | " | " | " |
| John | " 21 | " | " | " |
| Miss | " 16 | " | " | " |
| Esther | " 10 | " | " | " |
| Sarah | " 52 | " | " | " |
| Levy | " 16 | " | " | " |
| Jas. Anderson | 30 | " | Margoher | " |
| Sam. Fulton | 44 | " | Ballinclough | " |
| Mary Ann Fulton | 42 | " | " | " |
| Robert | " 20 | " | " | " |
| Thos. Boyd | 23 | " | Ballygauley | " |
| Esther | " 20 | " | " | " |
| Robert McNeil | 24 | " | Aghadowey | " |
| Andrew Harkin | 18 | " | " | " |
| Robert Blair | 50 | " | " | " |
| Rosey | " 48 | " | " | " |
| Joseph | " 20 | " | " | " |
| James | " 18 | " | " | " |
| Robert Riddells | 64 | " | Lisnamuck | Phila. |
| Mary Ann | " 60 | " | " | " |
| Mary Ann | " 12 | " | " | " |
| Charles | " 20 | " | " | " |
| Elizh. | " 41 | " | " | " |
| Matty | " 22 | " | " | " |
| Charles | " 40 | " | " | " |
| William | " 12 | " | " | " |
| Matilda | " 10 | " | " | " |
| Samuel | " 8 | " | " | " |
| Margt. | " 6 | " | " | " |
| Robert | " 4 | " | " | " |
| Hugh | " 2 | " | " | " |
| James Boyes | 40 | " | " | " |
| Ann | " 38 | " | " | " |
| John | " 18 | " | " | " |
| James | " 16 | " | " | " |
| David | " 12 | " | " | " |
| Leslie | " 10 | " | " | " |
| Ann Creiten | 22 | " | " | " |
| Fanny | " 24 | " | " | " |
| John Rosburg | 17 | " | " | " |
| Margt. Fulton | 18 | " | Ballyclough | " |
| Samuel | " 14 | " | " | " |
| James Fulton | 12 | P. | Ballyclough | Phila. |
| Mary Ann | " 10 | " | " | " |
| Thomas | " 8 | " | " | " |
| James Fisher | 17 | " | " | " |
| Samuel | " 19 | " | " | " |
| Jas. Stewart | 19 | " | Crevolea | " |
| David Torrens | 20 | " | " | Quebec |
| Robert McEntire | 28 | " | Collins | Phila. |
| Wm. McFetridge | 22 | " | " | " |
| David Canning | 24 | " | " | " |
| Thomas Sanderson | 22 | " | " | " |
| Andrew Cochrane | 24 | " | Ballinlees | " |
| Samuel Barr | 28 | " | Leggury | St. John |
| Francis Burke | 40 | R.C. | Cornamuckla | Phila. |
| Mary | " 30 | " | " | " |

---

List of Emigrants from the Parish of Balteagh to New York for the years 1833-1834.

| Name | Age | | Townland | Destination |
|---|---|---|---|---|
| Alex. George | 21 | P. | Terrydremond | Phila |
| Sally Thompson | 30 | " | " | " |
| Alex. Eakin | 26 | " | " | " |
| Mary McManus | 20 | " | " | " |
| Mary | " 22 | " | " | " |
| Cath. | " 18 | " | " | " |
| Mary A. Diamond | 6 | " | " | " |
| John | " 4 | " | " | " |
| Joseph McCool | 21 | " | " | " |
| Henry McGowen | 22 | R.C. | Ballyquin | St. John |
| Thos. Lafferty | 18 | " | " | " |
| Joseph Smith | 18 | P. | Carnet | N. York |
| Ann Lynn | 16 | " | " | " |
| Jane Lynn    twins | 16 | " | Derry Little | " |
| James Scullion | 18 | R.C. | Ardmore | Quebec |
| Wm. McNamara | 20 | E.C. | " | " |
| James Ceahy | 20 | P. | " | Phila. |
| Margt. Adams | 23 | " | Edenmore | N. York |
| Eleanor Boyle | 30 | R.C. | Ballymulty | " |
| Sally | " 1 | " | " | " |
| Susanna | " 1 | " | " | " |
| (twins) | | | | |
| Mary Ann | " 4 | " | " | " |
| John | " 7 | " | " | " |
| Joseph | " 5 | " | " | " |
| John Woods | 20 | E.C. | Drumagosker | Quebec |
| Robt. Hutcheson | 22 | P. | Lislane | Phila. |
| David Ross | 24 | " | " | " |
| Jane | " 26 | " | " | N. York |
| Jas. Cunningham | 19 | " | " | " |
| Michael O'Kane | 50 | R.C. | " | " |
| Robert McCauley | 30 | P. | Ballyleighery, | Phila. |
| Jane O'Kane | 48 | R.C. | Lislane | N. York |
| Thos. Colwell | 30 | P. | Cloghan | Quebec |
| Eliza Colwell | 32 | " | " | " |
| John McCloskey | 25 | " | " | " |
| Eliza | " 25 | R.C. | " | " |
| Ann Bradley | 22 | " | " | " |
| Mary | " 18 | " | " | " |
| Patrick McDaid | 30 | " | " | " |
| Edward Mullen | 25 | P. | Maine | " |
| Mary Lagan | 20 | R.C. | Drumsurn | " |
| John Long | 18 | P. | " | " |
| David Ross | 24 | " | Gortnarny | Phila. |
| John Scott | 30 | " | Aghansillagh | " |
| Robert Scott | 32 | " | " | " |
| John Clyne | 21 | " | Terrydoo Clyde | " |
| John Doons | 22 | " | Terrydoo Walker | N. York |
| Robt. McCausland | 20 | " | " | " |
| Joseph Kennedy | 30 | " | Ballyvelin | Phila. |
| Bell Ollover | 18 | " | Drumgesh | " |
| Eliza Ollover | 20 | " | " | " |
| Mary Logan | 20 | R.C. | Killoyle | St. John |
| Bernard Log | 15 | " | " | Phila. |
| John Logue | 18 | " | " | " |

---

List of Emigrants from the Parish of Bovevagh to New York for the Years 1833-1834.

| Name | Age | | Townland | Destination |
|---|---|---|---|---|
| Wm. McClenaghan | 17 | R.C. | Drumadreen | N. York |
| Alex. Smith | 18 | P. | " | " |
| William Dale | 40 | " | " | " |
| Eliza | " 38 | " | " | " |
| John | " 5 | " | " | " |
| James Lowden | 40 | " | Drumneechy | Phila. |
| Jane | " 36 | " | " | " |
| Mary | " 3 | " | " | " |
| John Lowden | 1 | P. | Drumneechy | Phila. |
| Neil Begley | 20 | R.C. | " | " |
| Jane Sterling | 50 | P | Gorticlare | N. York |
| Ann | " 25 | " | " | " |
| Sally | " 20 | " | " | " |
| Joseph Hamilton | 40 | " | " | " |
| Ann | " 38 | " | " | " |
| Daniel Haran | 20 | R.C. | Inisconagher | Quebec |
| James McBeath | 25 | " | Camnish | " |
| Marcus Dogherty | 18 | " | " | " |
| John Boyle | 24 | E.C. | Dirnaflaw | N. York |
| John Ferguson | 23 | P. | " | " |
| Patrick McCloskey | 18 | R.C. | " | Quebec |
| Andrew McCully | 50 | P. | " | Phila. |
| Cath. | " 48 | " | " | " |
| Letitia Guy | 30 | P. | Leeke | N. York |
| Samuel Hamilton | 20 | P. | " | Quebec |
| Mary Ann Guy | 20 | " | " | " |
| Mary Devlin | 40 | R.C. | " | " |
| Margt. | " 35 | " | " | " |
| Eliza Connor | 48 | E.C. | " | " |
| Alex. McEntin | 18 | P. | " | " |
| Margt. Connor | 20 | E.C. | " | " |
| Dennis Devlin | 40 | R.C. | " | " |
| Peter | " 42 | " | " | " |
| James | " 40 | " | " | " |
| Dennis | " 26 | " | " | " |
| Ann | " 28 | " | " | " |
| Molly | " 64 | " | " | " |
| John Moore | 20 | P. | Killybleught | Phila |
| Samuel McFadden | 22 | " | Bovevagh | Quebec |
| Robert Taylor | 20 | " | " | " |
| Wm. O'Kane | 24 | " | " | " |
| Margt. | " 22 | " | " | " |
| Kyle Quigley | 20 | E.C. | " | " |
| Gordon Meehan | 20 | " | " | " |
| Jas. McManamin | 30 | R.C. | " | " |
| Bryan O'Kane | 28 | " | Ardanarn | " |
| Eleanor McCloskey | 22 | R.C. | " | " |
| Mary A. | " 20 | " | " | " |
| James Craford | 18 | P. | " | N. York |
| James Douglis | 18 | " | " | " |
| Robt. Stewart | 20 | " | Templemoyle | " |
| Thos. Forrest | 25 | " | " | Quebec |
| John Forrest | 46 | " | Carnet | N. York |
| John Mullen | 30 | R.C. | Formal | " |
| Alex. Anderson | 26 | P. | Ballymoney | " |
| Patrick Farrell | 23 | R.C. | " | " |
| Jas. McCloskey | 25 | R.C. | Farkland | " |
| Eliza | " 18 | P. | " | " |
| Bernd. McLaughlin | 30 | R.C. | Muldony | " |
| Michael Deehan | 24 | R.C. | " | " |
| Pat Brawley | 32 | " | " | " |
| Neill Deehan | 24 | " | " | " |
| Henry Hasson | 24 | " | " | " |
| Ann | " 22 | " | " | " |
| Mary Deehan | 20 | " | " | " |
| Ann Dogherty | 20 | " | " | " |
| Jas. McFeely | 35 | " | " | " |
| Bernd. | " 20 | " | " | " |
| Jas. | " 40 | " | " | " |
| Mgt. McCloskey | 14 | R.C. | Drum | " |
| James Hutton | 32 | P. | Ballyharigan | St. John |
| John Stinson | 20 | " | Glenconway | Phila. |
| John Rea | 20 | " | " | " |
| Alex. Nutt | 18 | " | " | " |
| Grace McCloskey | 25 | R.C. | Gortnahey Beg | Quebec |
| Jas. O'Neill | 18 | " | Derryland | St. John |
| Ann Coughlin | 26 | " | " | " |
| Bell Boyle | 20 | P. | " | " |
| Wm. Donaldson | 20 | " | Flanders | N. York |
| Ann Heaney | 22 | R.C. | Derryard | Quebec |
| John McEntee | 20 | " | " | " |
| Jane | " 6 | " | " | " |
| Mary McCay | 20 | E.C. | " | " |
| Ann | " 18 | " | " | " |

---

List of Emigrants from Drumachose and Limavady in 1833 and 1834 to New York.

| Name | Age | | Townland | Destination |
|---|---|---|---|---|
| Jas. McCloud | 30 | P. | Drummond | St. John |
| Pat. Gallaher | 22 | R.C. | " | " |
| David Lynn | 20 | P. | " | " |
| Ollover Martin | 40 | " | " | " |
| Jas. Hagerty | 28 | " | " | " |
| Wm. McConaghy | 16 | " | " | " |
| Jas. Cook | 40 | " | " | " |
| Jane | " 38 | " | " | " |
| Dan. | " 20 | " | " | " |
| Ann | " 18 | " | " | " |

| Name | Age | Religion | Place | Destination |
|---|---|---|---|---|
| Jane Cook | 14 | P. | Drummond | St. John |
| Kitty Ann Cook | 8 | " | " | " |
| Bell Cook | 10 | " | " | " |
| Jas. Cook | 6 | " | " | " |
| Molly Mullen | 30 | R.C. | " | " |
| Marcus " | 10 | " | " | " |
| Edward " | 6 | " | " | " |
| Patrick " | 4 | " | " | " |
| Robert " | 2 | " | " | " |
| John " | 8 | " | " | " |
| Elenor Grey | 30 | " | " | " |
| Mary McCay | 26 | " | " | " |
| John Brawley | 24 | " | " | " |
| John McMackin | 22 | " | " | " |
| Jas. Dogherty | 17 | " | " | Phila. |
| Docia Mullen | 22 | " | " | St. John |
| Wm. Conway | 10 | " | " | " |
| Hugh Right | 64 | P. | Bovalley | " |
| Wm. Connor | 24 | R.C. | Ardgarvin | " |
| Wm. Brown | 30 | P. | Limavady | Phila. |
| Hugh McClary | 22 | E.C. | " | N. York |
| Robert McAllister | 18 | E.C. | " | " |
| John Taggart | 16 | E.C. | " | " |
| Jas. Scott | 24 | " | " | Quebec |
| Wm. Creer | 24 | " | " | St. John |
| Jas. Flanigan | 28 | " | " | Quebec |
| Eliza " | 26 | " | " | " |
| Alice " | 4 | " | " | " |
| Mary A. Miller | 18 | P. | " | " |
| Daniel McFaull | 23 | E.C. | " | St. John |
| Pat. McLaughlin | 26 | R.C. | " | " |
| Mary A. " | 24 | " | " | " |
| John McElvan | 19 | " | " | " |
| Wm. McLaughlin | 18 | " | " | " |
| Daniel Lynn | 19 | " | " | " |
| Wm. Hunter | 23 | P. | " | Quebec |
| Jos. Callaghan | 20 | " | " | Van Dia. Land |
| Jas. " | 20 | " | " | N.S.Wales |
| Matw. Nodwell | 30 | " | Glenkeen | St. John |
| Cath. " | 28 | " | " | " |
| Mary Ann " | 5 | " | " | " |
| Eliza " | 3 | " | " | " |
| Thos. Rankin | 30 | " | Termaquin | N. York |
| John Johnston | 18 | " | " | Phila. |
| Molly Heney | 40 | " | " | " |
| Rachel Kennedy | 50 | " | Ballyavelin | " |
| Joseph " | 30 | " | " | " |
| Jane " | 28 | " | " | " |
| Mary " | 7 | " | " | " |
| Geo. " | 5 | " | " | " |
| Fullerton" | 3 | " | " | " |
| Kennedy (male) | 1 | " | " | " |
| Pat. Garven | 20 | R.C. | Drumramer | St. John |
| Arch. McSparran | 40 | P. | " | Phila. |
| M.H.McSparran | 35 | " | " | " |
| Jas. Richey | 50 | " | Ballycrum | St. John |
| Molly " | 48 | " | " | " |
| Samuel " | 20 | " | " | " |
| Jas. " | 18 | " | " | " |
| Geo. Douglass | 20 | " | Leck | " |
| Matthew Douglass | 21 | P. | Largyreagh | Phila. |
| John Canning | 20 | P. | " | " |
| Marcus " | 18 | " | " | " |
| Annyan " | 11 | " | " | " |
| Matilda Sterling | 22 | " | " | " |
| John Conn | 25 | " | Gortgarn | N. York |
| Jas. Flanagan | 1 | E.C. | " | " |
| Mary A. " | 3 | " | Limavady | Quebec |
| Conoly Dogherty | 18 | R.C. | " | N. York |
| Wm. Hunter | 30 | " | " | " |
| Jas. McLaughlin | 24 | R.C. | " | " |
| Cath. " | 18 | " | " | " |
| Elenor Murray | 35 | " | " | " |
| Mary Ann " | 15 | " | " | " |
| Edward " | 46 | " | " | " |
| Daniel " | 18 | " | " | " |
| Edward " | 17 | " | " | " |
| Wm. Hunter " | 24 | P. | " | |
| Edward Mullan | 17 | " | Derrybeg | " |
| Sara Linsey | 20 | " | Derrymore | Phila. |
| Eliza " | 18 | " | " | " |
| Jas. " | 20 | " | " | " |
| Jas. McCloskey | 26 | " | Bolea | " |
| Samuel Smith | 20 | " | " | " |
| Wm. Campbell | 20 | " | " | " |
| Jane McCloskey | 28 | " | " | " |
| Martin Wisely | 18 | " | " | " |
| Margt. " | 45 | " | " | " |
| Chas. Mullen | 24 | R.C. | Dunbeg | " |
| Wm. Wisely | 16 | P. | Bolea | " |
| Geo. Allen | 26 | " | Ballyriskmore | " |
| Robert McFetridge | 28 | P. | Ballyriskmore | Phila. |
| Michael Langey | 26 | R.C. | Collessan | Quebec |
| Mary Eaton | 22 | P. | " | " |

List of Emigrants from Tamlaghtfinlagan in 1833 and 1834.

| Name | Age | Religion | Place | Destination |
|---|---|---|---|---|
| Sally McClane | 22 | P. | Ballymore | N. York |
| David Wark | 20 | " | " | " |
| Jas. Baird | 58 | " | " | Phila. |
| Wm. " | 28 | " | " | " |
| James Baird jr. | 23 | " | " | " |
| Robt. " | 18 | " | " | " |
| John " | 9 | " | " | " |
| Ann " | 30 | " | " | " |
| Elenor " | 17 | " | " | " |
| Mary Ann Baird | 14 | " | " | " |
| Martha Baird | 7 | " | " | " |
| John McCanlis | 25 | " | " | " |
| John Stewart | 40 | " | " | " |
| Jane " | 40 | " | " | " |
| Wm. " | 16 | " | " | " |
| John " | 14 | " | " | " |
| Robt. " | 12 | " | " | " |
| Hugh " | 1 | " | " | " |
| Elizh. " | 8 | " | " | " |
| Mary Ann Stewart | 6 | " | " | " |
| Andrew Morrison | 22 | " | Moy | " |
| Joseph McCracken | 21 | " | " | Quebec |
| James Neilly | 25 | " | " | " |
| Joseph Neilly | 23 | " | " | Phila. |
| Robert Busby | 52 | " | Ballynary | N. York |
| Robert " jr. | 24 | " | " | Phila. |
| Elizh. " | 50 | " | " | N. York |
| Ann " | 18 | " | " | " |
| Rachel " | 16 | " | " | " |
| David " | 12 | " | " | " |
| William Neely | 55 | " | " | Phila. |
| Jane " | 40 | " | " | " |
| James " | 20 | " | " | " |
| William " | 15 | " | " | " |
| John " | 25 | " | " | " |
| Mary Ann " | 22 | " | " | " |
| Andrew Alcorn | 20 | " | " | " |
| Martha " | 20 | " | " | " |
| Joseph Getty | 20 | " | Largy | " |
| John McCash | 60 | " | " | " |
| Jane " | 56 | " | " | " |
| William " | 30 | " | " | " |
| Joseph " | 24 | " | " | " |
| Hugh " | 22 | " | " | " |
| Eacy Neily | 20 | " | " | " |
| James Beer | 22 | " | " | Quebec |
| Elizh. " | 24 | " | " | " |
| Samuel " | 26 | " | " | " |
| Jane " | 20 | " | " | " |
| Mary Jackson | 20 | " | " | " |
| John Campbell | 46 | " | Maghermore | St. Johns |
| Mary " | 44 | " | " | " |
| Mary A. " | 9 | " | " | " |
| Wm. Gilderson | 40 | R.C. | " | " |
| Thos. " | 8 | " | " | " |
| Wm. " | 4 | " | " | " |
| John " | 2 | " | " | " |
| Mary " | 6 | " | " | " |
| John Lowry | 32 | P. | " | Phila. |
| Mary " | 30 | " | " | " |
| Jas. Mullen | 40 | R.C. | Drumreighlin | " |
| Sarah " | 40 | " | " | " |
| Ann Mullen | 10 | " | " | " |
| Margt. Mullen | 8 | " | " | " |
| Jane " | 6 | " | " | " |
| Sally " | 4 | " | " | " |
| Jas. McDonnell | 35 | P. | " | Quebec |
| Andrew " | 30 | " | " | " |
| William " | 24 | " | " | " |
| Eliza " | 32 | " | " | " |
| Edward McLaughlin | 24 | R.C. | " | St. Johns |
| William Pedin | 19 | E.C. | Tamlaght | N. York |
| Mary Pedin | 16 | " | " | " |
| John Keer | 22 | P. | " | Phila. |
| James McCook | 22 | " | " | " |
| John " | 20 | " | " | " |
| John Hutchenson | 20 | " | " | N. York |
| James " | 23 | " | " | " |
| Patrick McCay | 30 | R.C. | " | " |
| John Thompson | 30 | P. | Drumcarney | " |
| Henry " | 26 | " | " | " |
| Scott Hunter | 26 | " | Tarnakelly | Phila. |
| Mary Ann Cartin | 28 | R.C. | Tarnakelly | Phila. |
| Michael " | 28 | " | " | " |
| John O'Kane | 26 | " | " | St. Johns |
| T. White Morrison | 20 | P. | Drummore | Phila. |
| J. " | 18 | " | " | " |
| John Stewart | 18 | " | " | " |
| Sam. Caskey | 50 | " | " | " |
| Ann " | 47 | " | " | " |
| John " | 22 | " | " | " |
| Mary " | 24 | " | " | " |
| Eliza " | 22 | " | " | " |
| Ann " | 20 | " | " | " |
| Milly " | 18 | " | " | " |
| Margt. Jane Caskey | 16 | " | " | " |
| Jos. Crawford | 26 | " | Culmore | " |
| John Wilson | 20 | " | Clagan | " |
| John Devine | 30 | R.C. | Glack | " |
| John Craig | 20 | " | Sistrokeel | " |
| Mary " | 18 | P. | Glasvenagh | St.Johns |
| Robt. McCauly | 30 | " | " | " |
| George Gordon | 18 | " | " | " |
| Neil Healy | 28 | R.C. | Ballyking | " |
| Margt. " | 26 | " | " | " |
| Mary Ann Healy | 4 | " | " | " |
| Eliza Healy | 2 | " | " | " |
| John Healy infant | | " | " | " |
| John White | 19 | P. | " | " |
| Jas. McCauly | 30 | " | " | " |
| Ann " | 28 | " | " | " |
| Girl, name forgotten | 4 | P. | " | " |
| Girl, name forgotten | 2 | " | " | " |
| Margt. Entiney | 18 | P. | Drummond | " |
| Ann Littlewood | 24 | R.C. | " | " |
| Chris. Stewart | 24 | E.C. | Ballykelly | N. York |
| James Campbell | 28 | P. | " | " |
| John Diamond | 28 | P. | " | " |
| Daniel " | 26 | " | " | " |
| Thos. Meine | 22 | " | " | Quebec |
| Matilda Connor | 22 | E.C. | " | St. John |
| Andrew Dearmott | 40 | P. | " | Quebec |
| Ann " | 25 | " | " | " |
| Sara Ann " | 7 | " | " | " |
| Fanny " | 3 | " | " | " |
| Girl, name forgotten | 1, | P. | " | " |
| Owen McCloskey | 30 | R.C. | " | " |
| Patrick " | 28 | " | " | " |
| John McLaughlin | 50 | P. | " | St. John |
| Ann " | 50 | " | " | " |
| Martha " | 22 | " | " | " |
| Cath. " | 24 | " | " | " |
| Ann McGarry | 50 | R.C. | " | " |
| Margt. McGee | 45 | E.C. | " | " |
| Eliza " | 1 | " | " | " |
| Matty " | 32 | " | " | " |
| A. McMilne | 18 | P. | Walworth | " |
| Margt. " | 18 | E.C. | Finlagan | " |
| John Latten | 20 | " | Drumdonaghy | N. York |
| Solomon Mitchell | 35 | R.C. | " | " |
| Susanna " | 36 | " | " | " |
| Thos. " | 12 | " | " | " |
| John " | 10 | " | " | " |
| Joseph " | 8 | " | " | " |
| Mary Ann " | 6 | " | " | " |
| Rosey " | 4 | " | " | " |
| Susanna " | O.L. | | " | " |
| Daniel Martin | 22 | P. | Ardnargle | Phila. |
| Wm. Piper | 22 | " | Corndale | " |
| Wm. Lagan | 22 | " | Burnally | " |
| Mary O'Kane | 22 | R.C. | Lomond | Quebec |
| Wm. " | 20 | " | " | " |
| Thos. Stewart | 50 | P. | " | " |
| Jane " | 46 | " | " | " |
| John " | 22 | " | " | " |
| James " | 17 | " | " | " |
| Thomas " | 15 | " | " | " |
| Alex. " | 13 | " | " | " |
| Barton " | 11 | " | " | " |
| Jane " | 9 | " | " | " |
| Robert Main | 20 | " | Culmore | " |
| Alex. Peery | 22 | " | " | N. York |
| Ann Smith | 50 | " | " | " |
| John " | 24 | " | " | " |
| Eliza " | 18 | " | " | " |
| Sam. Crother | 24 | " | Carrymuddle | " |
| Mat " | 20 | " | " | " |
| Eliza " | 3 | " | " | " |
| Jane " | 14 | " | " | " |
| Mary Ann Crother | 1 | " | " | " |
| Wm. Kinney | 60 | " | " | " |
| Jane " | 34 | " | " | " |
| Joseph Miller | 25 | " | " | " |

Cath. Miller 24 P. Carrymuddle N. York
Elenor " 2 " " "
Wm. Gault 18 E.C. Broglasgow "
Robert McLaughlin 24 P. " St. Johns
Wm. Sloan 20 " " "
David " 24 " " "
Wm. Wark 18 " Broheris N. York
Mary Jane Wark 20 " " "
Mary Torrens 26 " Carnreagh "
Mgt. J. McLaughlin 20 P. Carrowclare "
Sam Wark 20 P. Farlow "
Jacob Wark 18 " " "
John Simpson 24 " " "
Eliza " 22 " " "
Wm. Dogherty 30 R.C. " "
Margt. " 28 " " "
John " 7 " " "
Robt. " 5 " " "
Saly " 3 " " "
Ann " 1 " " "
John Moore 28 P. Moneyhanna Quebec
Margt. McMine 26 " " "
Mary A. " 20 " " "
Joseph White 22 " " "
John Johnston 22 R.C. " "
Wm. " 20 " " "

List of Emigrants from Coleraine to New York in the years 1833-1834. Particulars given in the following order: Name, Age, Religion, Townland, and Destination.

John McClean 5 P. North Brook Quebec
Ann " 2 " " "
Sam Ramsay 38 " New Row St. John
Jane " 22 " " "
Cath. " 7 " " "
Eliza " one month " " "
John " 5 " " "
Sam " 3 " " "
Thos. Duffy 21 R.C. " Quebec
John McCrotty 21 " " "
John Dunlop 24 E.C. Blindgate St. "
Mary Hurley 19 R.C. Ferryquay St. Phila.
Wm. Taylor 24 E.C. Millbrook St. Quebec
Mary " 20 " " "
Wm. " 18 months" " "
Andrew Douglas 22 " " "
John Miller 21 P. Church St. Phila.
Mgt. McCauley 20 " " N. York
Dorothea Linigam 23 " Diamond Quebec
Sibby Black 45 Sec. Blindgate St. St. John
James " 17 " " "
Mary A. " 4 " " "
Mathy " 1½ " " "
Eliza " 3 " " "
Stewart " 14 " " "
Joseph " 10 " " "
Robert " 3 " " "
Archibald Hill 30 P. Long Commons "
Margt. " 31 " " "
John Hughes 25 " Gaol Lane N. York
Thomas McLaughlin 21 R.C. " "
John Cassidy 24 " " Quebec
Henry McLaughlin 27 " " N. York
Thos. Sheils 24 " Ferryquay St. "
John Hughes 22 " " "
Wm. McLaughlin 35 " New Row Van De L.
Hester " 20 " " "
Chas. " 20 " " "
Thos. Bell 36 P. Long Common Liverpool
Chas. McLaughlin 10 R.C. Bellhouse lane, Van De L.
John McIntyre 10 " " "
Wm. Baxter 28 E.C. Meeting Lane Quebec
Jas. Rodgers 23 " " "
John Hinds 40 P. Society S. Ho. London
Hariot " 40 " " "
John " jr. 12 " " "
Hariot " 10 " " "
Mary Hinds 9 " " "
Wm. " 8 " " "
Frederick Hinds 6 " " "
Chas. Hinds 5 " " "
Jas. " 4 " " "
Arthur " 2 " " "
John McIntyre 50 Sec. Shamble St. Quebec
Wm. Creighton 25 P. Society St. N. York
Elizh. " 30 " " "
Chas. Williamson 25 " Rampart Quebec
Margt. " 30 " " "

Jane Williamson 1 P. Rampart Quebec
Hugh Rankin 16 " Blagh Phila.
Wm. " 18 " " "
John McAtyre 25 " Ballysally St. John
Wm. McKee 19 " " "
Ann " 23 " " "
John McClane 25 " " Quebec
Jane " 25 " " "
Wm. Kennedy 18 " Cross Glebe "
Martha Hannah 52 " Dundooan N. York
John " 29 " " "
Eliza " 24 " " "
Martha " 22 " " "
Lydia " 20 " " "
Robt. " 18 " " "
Mary " 16 " " "
Henry " 14 " " "
Alex. Dunlop 22 " Spittle Hill Quebec
Jas. Dunlop 17 " " "
John McClelland 50 " Loguestown "
Neal " 46 " " "
Susan " 45 " " "
Rachel " 19 " " "
Mary A. " 21 " " "
Neal " 17 " " "
John " 14 " " "
James " 9 " " "
Hugh " 14 " " "
Wm. " 3 " " "
Susan " 5 " " "
John " infant 1, P. " "
Jas. Reilly 21 P. Millburn "
Wm. Little 74 E.C. " Scotland
Mary Ann Little 35 " " "
Andrew " 19 " " "
George " 17 " " "
John " 15 " " "
Wm. Little Jr. 4 " " "
Hendrick Little 9 " " "
Mary Ann " 6 " " "
Jas. Parkhill Servt. 14 E.C. Millburn Scotland
Wm. Reilly 30 E.C. Tullans Quebec
Hester Wilson 35 P. " N. York
John Westley 24 " " Phila.
John Parke 35 " " Quebec
Hannah " 28 " " "
Geo. McCann 21 R.C. " "
Wm. Steel 25 P. " "
Henry Boyd 40 " " Phila.
John Miller 21 " " "
Margt. " 18 " " "
Thos. Shiel 30 " " "
Hugh Brian 28 " " "
Mary Steel 24 " " Quebec
John Brook 24 " Windy Hall "
Alex. McKee 38 " Knockanturn "
Jane " 30 " " "
Wm. " 12 " " "
James " 10 " " "
Margt. Jane McKee 8, P. " "
Alex. McKee Junr. 5 " " "
John Usher 20 P. " "
John Lyons 25 " " "
Hugh McAlister 26 " Boghill Phila.
Jas. Wright 24 " " "

Returned in 1834
Robert Girvin 20 E.C. Spittlehill N. York
Thos. Hegerty 21 P. Danes Hill "
Henry Caulfield 16 " Bridge Street, New Orlean
Sam McCay 16 " " "
Jas. Gilmour 19 Sec. " N. York

Returned in 1835
Wm. Orr 20 " " Quebec
John Kane 35 P. Diamond "
John Streen 50 E.C. Nth. Brook St. N. York
Isabella " 48 " " "
Wm. Steen 18 " " "
Saml. " 7 " " "
Anne " 20 " " "
Isabella Steen Jun. 9 E.C. " "
Patrick Gannon 17 P. " Quebec
Anne McClean 35 " " "
James " 7 " " "

Emigrants from Dunboe - 1833
Nancy Donaghy 25 Pres. Articlave St. John
Francis McGawney 30 E.C. " "

James McGawney 22 E.C. Articlave St. John
Mary Smith 22 Pres. " Quebec
Robert " 4 mths. " St. John
Cochran Colman 18 E.C. " "
Mary Colman 30 " " "
Stephen Thorpe 18 " " "
William Paul 50 Pres. " "
Sarah " 16 " " "
Elizh. " 45 " " "
Alex. Proctor 40 " Knocknober Phila.
Cochran Sterling 28 " Knockmult St. John
Gilbert Smith 22 " Benarees Quebec
Elizh. " 22 " " "
Robert Fulgrave 22 " Fermoyle St. John
Allen Black 22 " " Quebec
George Lestly 30 " Beatwell Phila.
John Clarke 21 " " Quebec
Nancy " 30 " " "
Jane " 2 " " "
Mary Ross 22 " Sconce "
Thomas " 36 " " "
Jane " 24 " " "
Robert " Jnr. 6 " " "
Thomas " 4 " " "
George McLaughlin 33 R.C. Mullanhead "
William Smith 22 Pres. Fermullen St. John
Wm. Devenny 20 R.C. Farnlester Quebec
John Smith 22 Pres. Ballyhacket "
  Glenahoy
Ellen " 32 " " "
John McLaughlin 1 " " "
James Blair, Sen. 26 " Ballywildrick Phila.
Mary " 20 " " "
John Clarke 20 " Glebe "
Thomas Brosters 20 " " "
Mary " 18 " " "
Jane " 20 " " "
Isaac McMillan 20 " Ardina "
Charles Hazlett 35 " Bogtown "

Emigrants 1834

Hugh Evans 20 Pres. Articlave St. John
John Beatty 28 " " N. York
Robert Ray 18 " Knocknogher Penn.
Margt. Hindman 22 " Killyveaty Quebec
Chas. Wilson 25 " Pottagh Phila.
John Bond 32 " Bratwell "
Anne " 27 " " "
Mary " 5 " " "
Margt. " 2½ " " "
Barbara Bond 2 " " "
John McLaughlin 25 R.C. Bellany "
Jane Dunlop 23 Pres. Drumgully N. York
Thos. Johnston 26 " " St. John
Robt. McClement 19 " " "
Wm. McLaughlin 29 " Ballyhacket Quebec
  Glenaboy
Mary McLaughlin 25 " " "
James Blair 22 " Ballywildrick Phila.
Isaac Wark 20 " Ballywoodstock "
John Alexander 20 " " "
Jas. Williams 18 " Articlave N. York

List of Passengers
on Ship TORONTO
from London to
New York,
21 July, 1845.

William Moore
Tim McCarty
John Whaling

---

List of Passengers
on Ship WARSAW
from Glasgow to
New York,
1 August, 1845.

Joseph Donnelly
Peter Diven
James Dortherky
Nancy       "
Jane        "
Ruth Caldwell
George Ballantine
Elizabeth Grogan
John Hamilton

---

List of Passengers
on Ship STEPHEN
WHITNEY from
Liverpool to New
York, 1 August,
1845.

Margaret O'Connor
Mary Beaty
Rebecca Church
Mary Gleeson
Elias Dudley
Mary Shaw
Francis Shaw
Agnes Gilmore
Sarah       "
Philip Conlin
Susan Falkner
James Campbell
Catherine Wilson
Isabella    "
Hugh Hays
John McLoughlin
Edward Evans
Thomas Develin
Alexander McMullin
Margaret    "
Elisha      "
Mary        "
Daniel      "
Alexander   "
John Murphy
Mary Murphy
Mary Brady
James Allen
Margaret Rourke
Mary McBride
John        "
Elizabeth Allen
William     "
Mary Quinlan
Michael Crawford
Sally McQuade
John Fullerton
Ellen       "
James Whiteford

---

Passengers on Ship
CLYDE from
Liverpool to New
York, 2 August,
1845.

James Cassidy
Mary Hunt
Francis McNulty
Timothy Daly
Anne        "
Patrick     "
Margaret Keeffe

---

James Keady
Maria       "
Michael Rochford
Catherine Hackett
Thomas Bourke
Mary Walker
Pat         "
Ann         "
Eliza       "
Michael     "
James Kelly
William Kelly
Mary Kelly
Patrick Smith
Andrew      "
William     "
Mary        "
Jane        "
Francis     "

---

Passengers on Ship
ST. GEORGE from
Liverpool to New
York, 29 September,
1845.

John Russell
Michael Russell
Marsella Russell
Thomas McManus
Jane Young
Susan Young
John McNally
Ann         "
Biddy       "
Mary        "
Margaret    "
Eliza       "
Ann         "
Patrick     "
Daniel      "
Hugh        "
Arthur O'Neil
James Hare
Sally Dougherty
Thomas Clancy
Mary Clancy
Ellen Wall
Eliza Drennan
John        "
William     "
Sarah       "
William Barrington
Margaret        "
Francis Shaw
Mary Shaw
John Mallon
William Black
Catherine Dougherty
Samuel Wallace
George Abrahm
Fredrick McGee
John Boylan
Eliza Wallace
Ellenor Martin
Mary E. Divine
Isabella Gascoyne
Margaret Patterson

---

Passengers on Ship
OHIO from Liverpool
to New York,
29 September, 1845.

John Richie
Margrate Richie
Francis Pollard
Joseph McCoy
John        "
Fanny       "
Joseph      "
Ann Kinney
Bridget Gibney
Elizabeth McCan
Ellen McCan
Sarah Linch
Rose Galloway
Rose Beaty

---

Mary Hurst
Bridget Hacket
Margrate    "
Patrick     "
Edmond      "
Susan       "
John        "
Elizabeth Mathews
Bridget Mathews
Anne Mathews
Catherine Mulany
Catherine Sullivan
Mary Brown
Andrew Sanderson
Mary Donovan
Thomas Hughes
Patrick     "
John        "

---

List of Passengers
on Ship SHARON
from Liverpool to
New York,
4 October, 1845.

Helena Nagle
Mary Charlot Nagle
Richard Tyler
Catherine Ohara
John McNight
Ann Weeks
Susannah FitsSimmon
Catherine Corr
Alexander Robinson
Jane McClusky
Susan       "
Thomas Woods
Ann Brena
Mary Cochrane

---

List of Passengers
on Ship NEW YORK
from Liverpool to
New York,
3 November, 1845.

William Maxwell
Mary Shanley
Ann         "
George Dickse
Jane        "
Thomas Manning
Bridget Gaynor
Judy        "
Mary Sweeny
Charles McKeon
Mary Patterson
Mary A. Reynolds
Mr. Corcoran
Mrs.        "
Mary        "
Ann         "
John Boyle
Owen Philben
John Henry
Honora Clifford
Mary Mead
Bridget Carr
Mary Mulligan
Peter Ennis
Ann Fitzpatrick

---

Passengers on Ship
ST. PATRICK from
Liverpool to New
York, 3 December,
1845.

Thomas McCarty
Margaret    "
Julia       "
Mary        "
Margaret    "
Catherine Kelly
Ann Reilly
Edward Byrne

---

Mary Freel
Sarah       "
Martha Lewis
Christopher Delany
Rachel      "
John Richardson
Mrs. Elizabeth
Richardson
Christopher Lawless
Bridget     "
Mary        "
Patrick     "
Bridget Carlin
Mary A. Fitzpatrick
James McMahon
Mary McDermott
John Riggs
Mrs. Riggs
Mary Reilly
Mathew Kirby
Ellen       "
Bridget     "
John        "
William Byrne

---

List of Passengers
on Ship STEPHEN
WHITNEY from
Liverpool to New
York, 6 April, 1846.

James Mahon
Ann         "
John        "
Joseph      "
James       "
Margaret    "
Madge       "
Mary Leary
Catherine Magan
Catherine Hannigan
Anne Harrison
Thomas Finnan
Anne Doyle
Mary Connor
Anne Sheridan
Thomas Donohoe
Patrick Reynolds
Mary Murray
Rose Boylan
Rose Smith
Margaret Shanky
Thomas      "
Mary Malone
Margaret Good

---

Passengers on Ship
JUNIUS from Liverpool
to New York, 1 May,
1846.

Dennis Lyons
Marcilla Lyons
James Doyle
Sally Noble
John Mourne
Christopher McCormack
Ann         "
Christian   "
Helen       "
Margaret    "
Patt Farrell
Margaret Farrell
Patt Farrell
Ann Casey
Catherine Casey
Mary        "
Biddy       "
Mary Hanlon
Mary        "
Ann McCormack
Dennis Sullivan
Dennis      "
Jeremiah    "
Dennis Farrell
Michael Connor
Jeremiah Casey
Mary McMahon

---

Florence Sullivan
William White
Dorothy Reilly
William Ryan
Lawrence Cooney
William Butler
Walter Madden
Mary        "
Richard     "
Alice       "
John Walsh
Johanna Walsh
Mary        "
Patt        "

---

List of Passengers
on Ship ALHAMBRA
from Dublin to New York,
1 June, 1846.

Patt Costigan
Cathrine Conway
Bridget Quinn
Michael Whelan
Julia Cuff
Bridget Madden
Thomas      "
John        "
Julia       "
Ellen       "
Mary        "
Susan       "
Michael     "
Sarah Leonard
Hugh        "
Bridget Carey
Michael Dunne
Catharine Lyons
Mary Donelly
Julia O'Neal
Bridget Farrelly
Thomas Fallon
Michael McDonal
Ann Lynch
Bridget Hely
James Lawless
James McLaughlin
Mary        "
Patt        "
Patt McCaffry
Mary Treacy
Malachy Treacy
Richard Scot
John Brenan
Miles McNulty
Patt Flanagan
Bridget Flanagan

---

List of Passengers on
Ship MILICETE from
Liverpool to New York,
13 July, 1846.

Thomas McDonnell
Mrs.        "
Mary        "
Pat Maher
Julia Maher
Julia Doorly
Margaret Brophy
Patrick Moore
Pat Maloney
Mrs.        "
George Slack
George Hall
M. Cunningham
Mary Collins
Michael Dooley
Mary        "
Mary Wise
Martin Sullivan
Mrs.        "
William Martin
William Stephen
George Dalzel
Patrick McDon...
Mrs.        "
Mary        "

Pat Whelan
John Hennessy
Mrs.          "
Michael Cosgrove
Mrs.          "
Abraham Thomas
James McNulty
Mrs.          "
Frederick     "
Henry         "
Emily         "

List of Passengers
on Ship ST. GEORGE
from Liverpool to
New York, 3 August,
1846.

Edward Moriarty
Bridget       "
Ellen         "
Catherine     "
Henry         "
James         "
Thomas Brennan
Mary          "
Margaret      "
Sarah         "
Patrick Curren
Michael Kelly
Michael Brannigan
Catherine Madden
Michael       "
Patrick Lavell
James Garrity
Anne          "
Daniel Ennis
Hugh White
Bernard McCullen
Patrick Quinn

List of Passengers
on Ship SARACEN
from Glasgow to
New York,
1 September, 1846.

Michael Benny
M. Fleury-Cash
James Lee
Agnes Lee
Elizabeth Lee
Thomas        "
James         "
Mary          "
Agnes         "
Charles Melone
Agnes         "
Cathrine Denny
Harriet McGlocken
Margaret Colwell
Benjamin Guthrie
Martha        "
Mary          "
Ann           "
Jane          "
Elizabeth     "

Passengers on Ship
PANAMA from
Liverpool to New
York, 12 October,
1846.

Christopher Carroll
Hohn Naughton
Catharine Naughton
Bridget McCauley
Mary Noon
John Nally
Mrs.          "
Patrick Nally
Mary Anne Nally
Mary Langan
Mary Smith
Jane Mitchell

Patrick Heslin
Maria         "
Margaret      "
Pat Lynch
William McNamara
Catherine Burns
Brien Golding
Eliza Brien
Andrew Brien
Cormick McGarry
Ellen         "
Catherine Brennan
Dennis Ryan
Margaret Lynch
Mary          "

Passengers on Ship
JOHN R. SKIDDY from
Liverpool to New
York, 4 November,
1846.

Bridget Mathews
James         "
Patrick       "
Margaret      "
Margaret McKeone
Patrick       "
Catherine McGuire
Ann Gray
Mary Gray
Catherine Gunning
Ann Hickey
Michael Shanley
Mary Ann      "
Maurice Connor
Ellen         "
Ellen Driscoll
Catherine McGuire
Ann Bohan
Thomas Searles
William Buckley
Dominick Brady

Passengers on Ship
WESTMINSTER from
London to New York,
4 December, 1846.

Edward Graham
Mary Fitzgerald
Joseph Cavena
William Nappier
Mary Ann Tallon
William       "

Passengers on Ship
AMERICAN from
Liverpool to New
York, 4 December,
1846.

Mary Waters
Patrick Waters
Edward Hollywood
Pat Clarke
Cathrine Oates
Bridget Tracy
Ailis         "
Mary Morris
Mary McLean
Mary Curley
Michael Madden
Thomas Donlen
John Hoban
Mary Connell
Peggy Fahee
Jude Quinlon
Margarett Quinlon

List of Passengers
on Ship SARDINIA
from Liverpool to
New York, 6 February,
1847.

Ann Cannon
Bridget Cannon
Peter         "
Nellie        "
Anna          "
Patrick Sheehan
John Lyons
Mary          "
Mary          "
Catherine Lyons
Andrew        "
Biddy         "
John          "
William Brown
Mary          "
A. Davis
Michael Lundy
Margrate Lundy
John          "
Thomas McNicholas
Margrate      "
John          "
Charles O'Dougherty
John Glynn
Eliza         "
Eliza         "
Mary Ann Glynn
Henry Marman
Margaret Plunkett
Julia         "
Mary Brady
Terence Molloy
Catherine Molloy

List of Passengers
on Ship ST. GEORGE
from Liverpool to
New York, 8 April,
1847.

Charles Gildea
Phillip       "
William Bishop
David Hogan
Ann           "
Morris Whittey
Margaret Whittey
Bessy McDonald
Theresa McDonald
Mary McGafney
James Curren
Honora Drew
Honora Dundon
Richard Wall
Mary          "
Abby          "
Margaret Parker
Mary Casey
Laurence Casey
Owen McCarthy
Briget Cummins
Patrick Early
Bridget       "
Thomas Flanery
John Kelly
Michael Hanley
Patrick King
Michael Nelan
Martin Fetherston
Bridget Smith
Catherine Mileagh
Letty Corrigan
Peter Cormick
John Carroll
Thomas Riley
Bridget Monaghan
Martin Crane
Thomas Collyer

Passengers on Ship
FREE TRADER from
Cork to New York,
25 June, 1847.

Thomas Bass
Margaret Bass
Mary Bigley
Catherine Sullivan
John          "
Michael Roche
Johanna Foley
John Munday
Maurice Munday
Thomas Kenedy
Bridget Kirby
Daniel Sweeney
John Brian
Arthur McGuire
Hermione Harris
Timothy Murphy
Hannah Connell
Thomas Good
William Deane
Mary Desmond
Dennis Callaghan
Maria Townley
William Flynn
Bridget Scannell

List of Passengers
on Ship EMMA PRESCOTT
from Galway to New
York, 10 August,
1847.

Michael Burke
Pat Grady
Susan Tierney
Thomas Tiernan
Pat Joyce
Mary Lyons
Peter Rooney
Pat Hegarty
Austin Carrigg
Biddy         "
Mary Leyden
Bridgit Ahern
Mary McDonagh
Thomas Conroy
Martin Cosgriffe
Pat Crow
Mary          "
Edward Folan
Mary          "
Dominick Spelman
Anne Edwards
Mary Ready
James Connole
Mary O'Brien
Hanna         "

List of Passengers
on Ship YORKSHIRE
from Liverpool to
New York,
27 October, 1847.

John Irving
Ann Leonard
Mary Spencer
Ellen Carrol
Johannah Scanlan
Mary McCarty
William Longhead
Francis Farrel
Peter McHugh
Pat Dailey
Michael Gillooly
Mary Black
Mary Griffin
Thomas Brady
Bess Flinn
Catharine McGowan
Thomas McMahan
John Wall
John Griffin
Edmond Quin

Joseph Brown
Catharine Coile
Catharine Coleman
Ann Morrison

Passengers on Ship
LANCASHIRE from
Liverpool to New York,
13 December, 1847.

Mrs. O'Brien
Elizabeth O'Brien
John          "
Thomas        "
Mary Mahaffy
Anna          "
John          "
Sally McGarty
Mary Doyle
Michael Welch
William Clarey
John Purcell
John Moore
Ellen         "
Mary          "
James         "
John McGough
Michael Donnely
Alice Deary
Ann           "
Dan Darcy

Passengers on Ship
SARAH SANDS from
Liverpool to New York,
10 February, 1848.

Archibald Montgomery
James. B. Gamble
John McBride
James Ross
Mary Flannagan
John Thompson
Henry Quinn
Mary Ann Quinn
William H. Culloston
John Myers
William Russill
James Murphy
Pat Malony
James Smith
Jane          "
Martin Lardner
Bernard Murty
Ann           "
John Johnston
John Prentice
Andrew McKinny
John Davies
John Wilson
Owen O'Connor
Peter Smith

List of Passengers on
Ship SIR ROBERT PEEL
from Liverpool to New
York, 30 March, 1848.

Catherine Hughes
Mary          "
Ann           "
Dennis Driscoll
Jane          "
Bernard Brady
John          "
Ann           "
Edward Reilly
John McGowan
Susan         "
Richard Hickey
David O'Keefe
John Thompson
John Flannery
Patrick Kearney
James Cavanagh
Michael Duane

Bridget Duane
John Quin
Timothy Collins
Hugh McGrinnis
Bridget Connaughton
James Barret

---

List of Passengers
on Ship CONSTITUTION
from Belfast to New
York, 8 May, 1848.

John Blake
Catherine Blake
George "
Jane "
James "
William "
John "
Henry "
Thomas "
William McBride
Ann "
Thomas "
Mary "
Jane "
Anne "
William "
John "
George "
Joseph "
Eliza Smith
Isabella Crozier
Arabella Ferguson
Mary "
Hugh "
George "
Sophie "
Anne Johnston
Eliza Richardson
John Simpson
William Campbell
James Robinson
John Mullen
Eliza Love
Jane "
James Donaldson
David Reed
Jane Todd
Robert Toben

---

List of Passengers
on Ship AGENORA
from Liverpool to
New York, 10 July,
1848.

William Laing
Mrs. "
William "
Margaret "
Robert "
Andrew "
Walter "
Charles "
Emphemia "
Elizabeth "
Isabella "
Andrew Haggart
Margaret Davis
Walter "
Josee Scott
Helen Moore
William Clarke
Robert Lamb
George Kennedy
Henry Spencer
Mary Corcoran
William Graham
John Nowlan
Mathew Stokes
James Lavelle
Catharine Dowling
Pat Murtagh
Thomas Halpin
Pat Conway

---

List of Passengers
on Ship NICHOLAS
BIDDLE from
Liverpool to New
York, 7 September,
1848.

Peter Scott
Michael O'Connor
Miss Carroll
Patrick Hickey
Richard Barrington
Mrs. "
Henry "
Mr. Cassidy
John Lahy
William Allen
Ann Tansey
Mary Keane
Patrick Johnston

---

Passengers on Ship
INTRINSIC from
Liverpool to New
York, 6 November,
1848.

John Rian
John Toban
Mary McPartan
Mary McDermott
Judith Coffee
Honora Flin
David Platt
Martin Tain
Edward Fullerton
Patrick McPartin
James Brady
James McBrian
Daniel Barr
Morgan Brean
Richard Hamphrey
Michael Gallacher
Jeremiah Sulivan
William Morgan
Mary "
Bridget Higgins
James Rice
Patrick Collins
James Gibbon
Stephen Duggan
James Hunter
Laurie Ward
John Biggly
Catherine Hay
Thomas Mangan
Robert Evans
Bridget Cane
James Flemin
Patrick Clifford
John Scully

---

List of Passengers
on Ship GLENMORE
from Belfast to New
York, 29 January,
1849.

Mary Donaldson
William Donaldson
Charles Stars
Andrew Largoon
Molly Tatton
Mary Steel
Mary Morton
Andrew Batty
George Scarlett
James McDonald
Thomas Bell
Ann "
Margaret Elliott
Bridget Frazier
Robert Doran
John Whitelock
Biddy Malley
Ellen Rodgers
Ann McVeagh
Thomas Milliga
John English

---

Richard Shephard
William Munroe

---

Passengers on Ship
WEST POINT from
Liverpool to New
York, 6 March, 1849.

Richard Reid
Thomas "
Julia "
Marcella McCormick
Francis Whelan
Thomas Mahon
Charles Reilly
Mary "
Edward Mannin
Edward Daily
Pat Cunningham
Jane Sheil
John Graham
Bernard Banks
Luke Kearney
Mary Taite
Bernard Kennedy
Catherine Donlan
Peter Scully
Pat McCsee
Ann Lynch
James Dimond
Richard Butler
Peter Minhin
Mark Lenehan
John Mansfield
James Heathers

---

Passengers on Ship
ANN HARLEY from
Glasgow to New
York, 29 May, 1849.

Duncan McVean
Anne Hescans
George McMurray
Peter Bird
John Kells
Briget Conroy
Bernard Quinn
Thomas Callihan
John McTaggart
Andrew Haggarty
Batty Creely
Samuel Ross
James Baxter Boyd
James Mooney
Samuel Jones

---

Passengers on Ship
W. H. HARBECK from
Liverpool to New
York, 3 July, 1849.

Denis McMahon
Mary Hogan
Michael Close
Thomas Gannon
Martin Oakley
Mary Ann Armstrong
Niall Battle
Patrick Finn
Arthur Henry
Patrick Gray
Thomas Igo
Mary Ann Wallace
Ellen Reeves
John Cummins
John Neary
Phillip Carberry
Daniel Rack
Thomas Gough
Thomas Penbroke
Garrett Stack
James Downes
Richard Clancy
Patrick Ireland
William Hill
James Mealy

---

Passengers on Ship
ST. PATRICK from
Liverpool to New
York, 3 September,
1849.

Catharine McGarry
Julia Lynch
Mary Cullen
Mary Murray
Eliza Jenkins
Martha Flanagan
Hugh Dyott
Catharine Monaghan
Michael McAuliff
Mary O'Hara
William Tierney
Ann Drury
Patrick Tighe
Joseph Clarke
Catharine Farley
Matilda Hoggs
Thomas Cox
Mary Devlin
Catherine Rock
Ann Ellen McCann
John Hammond
James Creswell
John Noble

---

List of Passengers
on Ship SWAN from
Cork to New York,
4 September, 1849.

Elizabeth Ahern
Mary "
John "
Patrick Hallihan
Mary "
Thomas "
Patrick "
John "
Bridget "
Mary "
Nany "
Michael "
James Kennedy
Maurice Stanton
Johannah Conroy
John Colbert
David "
Timothy Magillacuddy
Thomas Dorgan
Margaret Dorgan
Maurice Dargan
Thomas "
Margaret "
Johanna "
Thomas Cantillion
Bridget "
Mary "
John "
Michael Connor
Patrick Quirk
Pat Crowley
Michael Murphy

---

List of Passengers
on Ship MARIA from
Belfast to New York,
5 November, 1849.

John Jenkins
Nancy Young
Pat Morgan
John Bole
William Harrington
Sarah "
Mary "
Isabella "
Mary Farrell
Thomas Farrell
Isabella Nugent
Biddy Rogers
Eliza McGlone
William McGlone
Gregg "
Joseph "

---

Margaret Waters
James Ritchie
Mary "
Biddy Graham
Thomas Wilson
Nano Wood
Thomas Phillips
James Bole
Thomas Andrews
John Sampson

---

List of Passengers
on Ship NEW WORLD from
Liverpool to New York,
15 January, 1850.

William Morris
Peter McMahon
Ann "
Margaret "
Bridgett "
Catharine "
Anthony "
Bessy "
Mick Riley
Catharine Ginty
John Dickson
Pat Kelly
Thomas Kelly
Owen Dunne
Mary Kelly
Ann "
Bridget "
Michael "
John Jennings
Margaret Armstrong
Farrell Dugan
John Delaney
Michael Kelly
Elizabeth Kelly
Pat McGaw
Margaret McGaw
Peter Whelan
John Kelly
John Donaldson
Catharine Hogan
Maria "
Catherine Gibney

---

List of Passengers
on Ship BRYAN ABBS from
Limerick to New York.
7 March, 1850.

John Slattery
Mary Cahill
Thomas Carroll
Mary "
John "
Biddy "
Hanah Hayes
Johanna Morrissey
Mick Sheehan
Catherine Sheehan
Mary Brazil
Michael Brazil
Patrick Bourke
Mary Begley
Patrick Hassett
Eliza Healey
Mary Quade
Betty Farrell
Catherine O'Dea
Honor Hogan
William Jackson
Ellen Purcell
Thomas "
Abby Nulty
Anne Johnson
Edward Quirk
Patrick Forrestal
Johanna Gleeson
John Darcy

---

List of Passengers
from Co. Roscommon
to New York via
Liverpool on Ship
ROSCIUS,
19. September, 1847.
Age given after the
name.

| | |
|---|---|
| John Carlon or Carlin | 30 |
| Honor " | 40 |
| Bridget " | 18 |
| Ellen " | 9 |
| Mary " | 7 |
| Patrick Colgan | 36 |
| Mary " | 40 |
| Michael " | 19 |
| Patrick " | 8 |
| Anne " | 7 |
| Bridget " | 12 |
| Margaret " | 16 |
| Terence Connor | 50 |
| Mary " | 35 |
| Thomas " | 20 |
| Mary " | 11 |
| Patrick Croghan | 28 |
| John " | 24 |
| Margaret " | 26 |
| Martin Donlan or Donnellan | 32 |
| Hugh McDermott | 50 |
| Eliza " | 48 |
| Bernard " | 28 |
| Hugh " | 12 |
| James " | 26 |
| John " | 24 |
| William " | 18 |
| Anne " | 25 |
| Bessy " | 20 |
| Ellen " | 13 |
| Rosanna " | 14 |
| Susan " | 22 |
| Catherine Mullera, Mullerea or Mulere | 30 |
| Patrick Narry or Neary | 40 |
| Mary " | 28 |
| Bridget ". | 1 |
| Richard Padian | 32 |
| Mary " | 30 |
| James " | 9 |
| William " | 12 |
| Bridget " | 10 |
| Maria " | 6 |
| James Reynolds | 28 |
| Bridget " | 60 |
| John " | 24 |
| Joseph " | 22 |
| Thomas " | 40 |
| Bridget " | 14 |
| Catherine " | 2 |
| James Stuart | 63 |
| Ellen " | 60 |
| George " | 20 |
| Ellen " | 18 |
| Patrick Stuart or Stewart | 18 |
| Catherine " | 25 |

List of Passengers
from Co. Roscommon to
New York via Liverpool
on Ship CREOLE,
18 October, 1847.

| | |
|---|---|
| William Brennan or Brannon | 70 |
| Andrew " | 20 |
| Daniel " | 24 |
| Gilbert " | 7 |
| Roger " | 28 |
| William " | 26 |
| Jane " | 18 |
| John Carrington | 14 |
| Ellen Costello | 55 |
| John Costello | 8 |
| Bridget " | 16 |
| Mary " | 18 |
| Mary Deffely or Deffley | 60 |

| | |
|---|---|
| George Deffely or Deffely | 26 |
| James " | 20 |
| Patrick " | 60 |
| Mary " | 55 |
| Bridget " | 14 |
| Patrick Donlon | 28 |
| Anne " | 27 |
| Patrick Donlan | 60 |
| Edward " | 25 |
| John " | 36 |
| Patrick " | 27 |
| William " | 16 |
| Margaret " | 14 |
| Garret Fallon | 32 |
| Eliza " | 26 |
| Bridget " | 20 |
| Thomas Fallon | 33 |
| Anne " | 32 |
| Martin " | 5 |
| Ellen " | 8 |
| Mary " | 1 |
| Patrick " | 16 |
| Bridget " | 25 |
| Thomas Fallon | 43 |
| Mary " | 18 |
| James Hanly or Hanley | 30 |
| Susan " | 30 |
| John " | 7 |
| Peter " | 5 |
| Thomas Hanly or Hanley | 60 |
| Mary " | 50 |
| Darby " | 16 |
| Edward " | 18 |
| Michael " | 13 |
| Patrick " | 24 |
| Honor " | 22 |
| Mary " | 20 |
| Michael McCormick | 19 |
| Honor " | 17 |
| Margaret " | 19 |
| Sally " | 16 |
| John Magan | 34 |
| Patrick Magan | 22 |
| Anne " | 28 |
| Ellen " | 26 |
| Catherine " | 24 |
| John Maguire | 30 |
| Mary " | 30 |
| Patrick " | 5 |
| Mary " | 3 |
| James Mullera | 50 |
| Bridget " | 50 |
| Denis " | 12 |
| Anne " | 9 |
| Bridget " | 10 |
| Mary Neary | 35 |
| James " | 3 |
| Anne " | 7 |
| John " | 16 |
| Bridget " | 14 |
| Catherine Neary | 24 |
| Catherine Quinn | 30 |
| George Stuart | 40 |
| Bridget " | 32 |
| Charles " | 6 |
| John " | 4 |
| Mary " | 10 |
| John Stuart | 21 |
| William Stuart | 47 |
| Bridget " | 43 |
| Charles " | 14 |
| Michael " | 12 |
| William " | 8 |
| Eliza " | 10 |

List of Passengers
from Co. Roscommon
to New York via
Liverpool on Ship
METOKA, 26 September,
1847.

| | |
|---|---|
| Patrick Colgan | |
| Anne " | 40 |
| Bernard " | 8 |
| Michael " | 4 |
| William " | 1 |
| Anne " | 12 |
| Betty " | 6 |

| | |
|---|---|
| Betty Colgan | 6 |
| Mary " | 15 |
| Patrick Finne or Finn | 35 |
| Margaret " | 24 |
| Michael " | 22 |
| Bridget " | 20 |
| Margaret " | 9 |
| Michael Gallagher | 24 |
| Margaret " | 20 |
| James Hanly or Hanley | 64 |
| Betty " | 54 |
| James " | 14 |
| John " | 18 |
| Martin " | 22 |
| Patrick " | 20 |
| Roger " | 12 |
| Mary " | 17 |
| Catherine McCormack or McCormick | 55 |
| Patrick " | 22 |
| Peter " | 15 |
| Anne " | 9 |
| Ellen " | 30 |
| Edward McCormick | 40 |
| Margaret " | 32 |
| Edward " | 4 |
| James " | 1 |
| Thomas " | 8 |
| Anne " | 14 |
| Catherine " | 6 |
| Mary " | 18 |
| Mary McCormick or McCormack | 26 |
| Anne " | 20 |
| Bridget " | 24 |
| Mary McDermott | 44 |
| John " | 13 |
| Thomas " | 15 |
| Bridget " | 11 |
| Ellen " | 20 |
| Mary " | 17 |
| Patrick McDonnell | 24 |
| John Moran | 56 |
| Winifred Moran | 44 |
| Francis " | 7 |
| John " | 15 |
| Catherine " | 10 |
| James Mullera or Mulera | 22 |
| Thomas " | 20 |
| Bernard O'Neal or O'Neill | 45 |
| Betty " | 40 |
| Bernard " | 13 |
| John " | 16 |
| Anne " | 20 |
| Thomas Reynolds | 33 |
| Mary " | 30 |
| Andrew " | 5 |
| James " | 8 |
| John " | 6 |
| Thomas " | 2 |
| Mary " | infant |
| Andrew " | 27 |
| Bridget " | 60 |
| Honor Winters or Winter | 60 |
| Thomas " | 30 |
| Honor " | 18 |
| Margaret " | 24 |
| Catherine " | 1 |
| John Wynne or Winn | 52 |
| Patrick " | 22 |
| Mary " | 13 |

List of Passengers from
Co. Roscommon to New
York via Liverpool on
Ship CHANNING, 13 March,
1848.

| | |
|---|---|
| William Cline | 58 |
| Margaret Colgan | 66 |
| Thomas Costello | 46 |
| Mary " | 54 |
| Martin " | 12 |
| Michael " | 14 |
| Pat " | 17 |
| Thomas " | 6 |
| Anne " | 16 |

| | |
|---|---|
| Pat Farrell | 55 |
| Mary " | 50 |
| William Farrell | 18 |
| Bridget " | 14 |
| Mary " | 16 |
| Francis Fox | 35 |
| Mary " | 33 |
| Francis " | 4 |
| Pat " | 7 |
| Thomas " | 26 |
| Catherine Fox | 16 |
| Bernard Gill | 30 |
| Michael Hoare | 35 |
| Mary " | 30 |
| James " | 5 |
| John " | 7 |
| Thomas " | 2 |
| Bridget " | 8 |
| Mary " | 11 |
| James Kelly | 45 |
| Mary " | 40 |
| Edward " | 18 |
| James " | 16 |
| John " | 2 |
| Anne " | 12 |
| Catherine Kelly | 14 |
| Eliza " | 10 |
| Ellen " | 7 |
| Mary " | 20 |
| Pat McCormick | 32 |
| Catherine McCormick | 28 |
| Michael " | 4 |
| Pat " | 6 |
| Anne " | 8 |
| Mary " | 20 |
| Andrew McDonnell | 18 |
| Anne " | 22 |
| Ellen " | 16 |
| Michael McDonnell | 50 |
| Michael " | 21 |
| Catherine McDonnell | 24 |
| Mary " | 18 |
| John McGann or McGanne | 24 |
| Atty " | 19 |
| Luke " | 20 |
| Anne " | 26 |
| Mary " | 15 |
| John " | 1 |
| Mary McGann or McGanne | 40 |
| James " | 18 |
| John " | 5 |
| Thomas " | 8 |
| Anne " | 1 |
| Bridget " | 10 |
| Eliza " | 14 |
| Thomas McManus | 29 |
| James " | 20 |
| Thomas McManus | 24 |
| Andrew " | 21 |
| Pat " | 23 |
| Mary " | 18 |
| Mary Madden | 46 |
| Thomas Madden | 13 |
| Catherine Madden | 16 |
| Anne Mullera | 25 |
| Pat " | 29 |
| John Mullera | 35 |
| Sarah " | 30 |
| Francis " | 6 |
| James " | 4 |
| John " | 8 |
| Patrick " | 12 |
| Thomas " | 10 |
| Pat " | 25 |
| Thomas Mullera | 36 |
| Mary " | 30 |
| Thomas " | 6 |
| Anne " | 2 |
| Bridget " | 55 |
| Bartholomew or Bartley Narry | 45 |
| Michael " | 26 |
| William " | 36 |
| Michael Reynolds | 9 |
| Bridget Stewart | 35 |
| James " | 17 |
| Michael " | 5 |
| Bridget8 | 14 |
| Francis Stewart | 56 |
| Anne " | 50 |
| John " | 30 |

| | |
|---|---|
| Bridget Wynne | 30 |
| Michael Wynne | 60 |
| Bell " | 55 |
| James " | 16 |
| Catherine " | 13 |
| Mary " | 18 |

List of Passengers from
Co. Roscommon to New
York via Liverpool on
Ship PROGRESS,
25 April, 1848.

| | |
|---|---|
| Luke Caveney | 46 |
| Mary " | 40 |
| Edward " | 12 |
| Luke " | 10 |
| Patrick " | 17 |
| Thomas " | 15 |
| Anne " | 7 |
| Catherine Caveney | 1 |
| Mary " | 19 |
| James Connor | 45 |
| Honor " | 44 |
| Martin " | 22 |
| John Connor | 37 |
| Catherine Connor | 27 |
| Pat Kelly | 40 |
| Eliza " | 36 |
| Thomas " | 12 |
| William Kelly | 8 |
| Anne " | 10 |
| Bridget " | 1 |
| Maria " | 14 |

List of Passengers from
Galway to Quebec on Ship
SEA BIRD, 15 June, 1848.

| | |
|---|---|
| Michael Brien, Byrne or Bryne | 22 |
| Anne Bryne | 20 |
| Anne Carney | 20 |
| John Carty or McCarthy | 60 |
| Bridget " | 55 |
| Edward " | 12 |
| Martin " | 15 |
| Peter " | 10 |
| Thomas " | 14 |
| Mary " | 25 |
| Peggy " | 21 |
| Ann " | 2 |
| John Casey | 16 |
| Pat " | 15 |
| Michael Coffey | 20 |
| Bridget Conway | 42 |
| Pat " | 16 |
| Mary " | 12 |
| James Conway | 27 |
| Margaret or Mary Conway | 24 |
| Thomas Conway | 7 |
| Pat " | 2 |
| Margaret " | 3 |
| Bridget Cosgrave | 50 |
| James " | 13 |
| John " | 26 |
| Michael " | 16 |
| Pat " | 7 |
| Peter " | 29 |
| Thomas " | 20 |
| Anne " | 18 |
| Margaret " | 17 |
| Mary " | 10 |
| James Cosgrave | 41 |
| Mary " | 37 |
| Pat " | 6 |
| Thomas " | 3 |
| William " | 2½ |
| Catherine " | 2 |
| Maria " | 8 |
| Anne " | 12 |
| Bridget " | 22 |
| John Cosgrave | 24 |
| Francis " | 20 |
| Ann8 " | 34 |
| James " | 1 |
| John " | 4 |
| Thomas " | 11 |
| Bridget " | 12 |

| | |
|---|---|
| Julia Cosgrave | 22 |
| Pat Cosgrave | 35 |
| Mary " | 32 |
| John " | 4 |
| Bridget " | 3 |
| Thomas Cosgrave | 38 |
| Hannah " | 23 |
| Hannah " | 1½ |
| Peter Craughwell | 40 |
| Winifred " | 36 |
| John " | 4 |
| Patrick " | 6 |
| Bridget " | 14 |
| Catherine " | 18 |
| Ellen " | 11 |
| Kitty " | 20 |
| Mary " | 16 |
| Rose " | 13 |
| Thomas Craughwell | 20 |
| Pat " | 15 |
| Honoria " | 14 |
| Mary " | 16 |
| Thomas Daw or Dawe | 32 |
| Bridget " | 28 |
| Pat " | 2 |
| Biddy " | 4 |
| Mary Ann " | ½ |
| James " | 20 |
| John " | 18 |
| Anne " | 20 |
| Mary " | 16 |
| Pat Kennedy | 28 |
| Anne " | 24 |
| Bridget " | 24 |
| Catherine Kennedy | 19 |
| Pat " | 10 |
| Pat (John) Kennedy | 48 |
| Mary " | 40 |
| John " | 16 |
| Thomas " | 6 |
| Ann " | 14 |
| Biddy " | 16 |
| Bridget " | 20 |
| Catherine " | 18 |
| Hannah " | 12 |
| Mary " | 10 |
| Peggy " | 4 |
| Anthony Kilcannon | 17 |
| Bridget Killalea | 35 |
| John " | 8 |
| Mark " | 1 |
| Margaret " | 7 |
| Mary " | 11 |
| Bridget Killalea | 16 |
| Darby Killalea | 46 |
| Margaret " | 44 |
| John " | 15 |
| Bridget " | 9 |
| Mary " | 16 |
| John Killalea | 19 |
| Mathias Killalea | 45 |
| Sally " | 40 |
| Lawrence " | 8 |
| Mathias " | 10 |
| Michael " | 19 |
| Thomas " | 14 |
| Peggy " | 16 |
| Patrick Killalea | 42 |
| Patrick " | 17 |
| Henry Dempsey | 50 |
| Catherine " | 47 |
| Henry " | 4 |
| John " | 13 |
| Michael " | 10 |
| Patrick " | 21 |
| Anne " | 13 |
| Catherine " | 1½ |
| Margaret " | 18 |
| Mary " | 15 |
| John Dempsey | 57 |
| Bridget " | 55 |
| John " | 30 |
| Biddy " | 30 |
| Ann " | 5 |
| Catherine Dempsey | 1 |
| Margaret " | 6 |
| Michael Dempsey | 32 |
| Catherine " | 31 |
| Pat " | 5 |
| Bridget " | 8 |
| Bryan Dolan | 17 |

| | |
|---|---|
| John Dolan | 15 |
| Thomas Dolan | 15 |
| Catherine Donnellan, Donolan or Donlon | 55 |
| John " | 26 |
| Pat " | 20 |
| Thomas " | 30 |
| Bridget " | 17 |
| Catherine " | 33 |
| Thomas Dooley | 1 |
| Mary Dowd | 20 |
| Mary Egan | 20 |
| Nicholas Flannery or Flanary | 40 |
| Nancy " | 38 |
| John " | ½ |
| Michael " | 12 |
| Pat " | 13 |
| Catherine " | 8 |
| Ellen " | 5 |
| Margaret " | 7 |
| Mary " | 10 |
| Winifred " | 4 |
| John Foster | 20 |
| Michael Golden | 24 |
| Hannah " | 24 |
| Thomas " | 1 |
| Mary " | 3 |
| Margaret Gormally | 37 |
| Mary Gormally or Gormley | 36 |
| John " | 13 |
| Thady " | 4 |
| Bridget " | 11 |
| Catherine " | 9 |
| Denis Grady or Gready | 30 |
| John " | 21 |
| Honoria " | 20 |
| Mary Gready | 18 |
| Thomas Guinnessy | 22 |
| Bridget " | 20 |
| Judy Hambury or Hansbury | 23 |
| Michael Horan | 38 |
| Anne " | 34 |
| Michael " | 6 |
| Thomas " | 2 |
| Catherine " | 4 |
| Eliza " | 16 |
| Catherine Jennings | 19 |
| Bryan Kelly | 21 |
| Ellen C. Rafferty | 22 |
| John Rafferty | 50 |
| Mary Ann Rafferty | 50 |
| John " | 15 |
| Pat " | 18 |
| Bridget " | 24 |
| Catherine " | 20 |
| Mary Ann " | 22 |
| Mary Rafferty | 40 |
| John Jun. Rafferty | 20 |
| Pat " | 16 |
| Thomas " | 12 |
| Catherine " | 15 |
| Mary Spencer | 13 |
| Anne White | 16 |
| John 'Black' White | 50 |
| Bridget " | 41 |
| John " | 16 |
| Martin " | 12 |
| Michael " | 6 |
| Pat " | 14 |
| Biddy " | 15 |
| Jane " | 3 |
| Mary " | 20 |
| Nancy " | 18 |
| Pat White | 26 |
| Biddy Loftus | 40 |
| John " | 15 |
| Michael " | 15 |
| Thomas " | 6 |
| Biddy " | 9 |
| Ellen " | 3 |
| Mary " | 22 |
| Mary Ann " | 16 |
| Bridget Lynskey | 25 |
| Michael Lynskey | 50 |
| Judy " | 40 |
| John " | 16 |
| Thomas " | 21 |
| Catherine " | 10 |

| | |
|---|---|
| Mary Lynskey | 12 |
| Timothy Lynskey | 40 |
| Richard Manly | 48 |
| Bridget " | 40 |
| James " | 9 |
| John " | 12 |
| Richard " | 3 |
| Bridget " | 16 |
| Ellen " | 18 |
| Mary " | 14 |
| John Morrissey | 40 |
| Hannah " | 33 |
| Pat " | 3 |
| Bridget " | 2 |
| Catherine " | 4 |
| Ellen " | 11 |
| Maria " | 10 |
| Thomas (Roger) Morrissey | 37 |
| Peggy " | 36 |
| John " | 12 |
| Bridget " | 6 |
| Mary " | 8 |
| Mary Mullen or Mullin | 45 |
| John " | 14 |
| Catherine Naughton | 26 |

List of Passengers from
Galway to Quebec on Ship
NORTHUMBERLAND,
17 August, 1849.

| | |
|---|---|
| Mary Byrne | 20 |
| Michael Byrne or Birne | 41 |
| Bridget " | 38 |
| John " | 8 |
| Michael " | 11 |
| Timothy " | 4 |
| Ellen " | 18 |
| Pat Byrne | 15 |
| Bridget Byrne | 26 |
| Thomas Byrne | 21 |
| Ellen " | 20 |
| Mary " | 19 |
| Thomas Carroll | 31 |
| Bridget " | 23 |
| John " | 22 |
| Michael " | 24 |
| Bridget " | 15 |
| Mary Ann " | 18 |
| Ann Rafferty | 21 |
| Mary " | ½ |
| Owen Carty | 22 |
| Catherine Carty | 20 |
| John Conway | 31 |
| Biddy " | 20 |
| Catherine Conway | 36 |
| Mary " | 25 |
| Mary Ann " | 41 |
| Ellen Cosgrave | 24 |
| William " | 21 |
| Ellen " | 19 |
| Michael Craughwell or Croghell | 20 |
| Ann " | 22 |
| Ellen " | 16 |
| Nancy Craughwell | 41 |
| Pat " | 20 |
| Margaret " | 17 |
| Peggy Kennedy | 40 |
| John " | 15 |
| Thomas " | 7 |
| Margaret Curley | 30 |
| Biddy " | 5 |
| John Kelly (Sen.) | 52 |
| Barney " | 21 |
| John Kelly (Jnr.) | 24 |
| Michael Kelly | 18 |
| Thomas " | 19 |
| Ann " | 17 |
| Bridget " | 8 |
| Mary " | 11 |
| Margaret Kelly | 35 |
| Catherine " | 9 |
| Margaret " | 7 |
| Mary Connolly | 18 |
| Mary Kennedy | 24 |
| Thomas Kennedy | 30 |
| Biddy " | 20 |
| Honoria " | 18 |

| | |
|---|---|
| Peggy Kennedy | 17 |
| Ellen " | 3 |
| Kennedy | 33 |
| Daniel Kennedy | 18 |
| Michael " | 17 |
| Pat " | 12 |
| Ann " | 15 |
| Bridget " | 9 |
| Catherine " | 9 |
| Mary Ann " | 6 |
| Abegail Killalea | 27 |
| Biddy " | 25 |
| Catherine " | 20 |
| Ellen " | 17 |
| Catherine Killalea | 45 |
| Ann " | 20 |
| Catherine " | 7 |
| Margaret " | 15 |
| Bridget Egan | 51 |
| John " | 18 |
| Michael " | 10 |
| Pat " | 14 |
| Michael Glynn | 55 |
| Julia " | 53 |
| Michael " | 21 |
| Pat " | 16 |
| Timothy " | 8 |
| Bridget " | 26 |
| Margaret " | 19 |
| Mary " | 24 |
| Peggy " | 23 |
| Leonard | |
| Peter Grady or Gready | 31 |
| Mary " | 27 |
| Thomas " | ½ |
| Catherine8 " | 2 |
| Thomas Grady or Gready | 41 |
| Catherine " | 36 |
| John " | 14 |
| Michael " | 3 mths. |
| Pat " | 6 |
| Thomas " | 2 |
| Ann " | 11 |
| Bridget " | 4 |
| John Guinnessy | 27 |
| Hanora " | 25 |
| John " | 2 |
| Thomas " | 3 mths. |
| Pat " | 55 |
| Mary " | 51 |
| James " | 20 |
| Malachy " | 16 |
| Pat " | 13 |
| Ann " | 14 |
| Catherine Guinnessy | 3 |
| Catherine Hanbury, | |
| Hambury or Hamberry | 36 |
| Michael Hart | 36 |
| Pat " | 2 |
| Mary " | 8 |
| Catherine Hart | 32 |
| James " | 23 |
| John " | 1 |
| Michael " | 17 |
| Thomas " | 16 |
| Catherine " | 14 |
| Catherine Kelly | 21 |
| Ellen Rafferty | 24 |
| Catherine " | 15 |
| Mary " | 20 |
| Bridget White | 36 |
| John " | 6 |
| Pat " | 16 |
| Bridget " | 8 |
| Margaret " | 10 |
| Mary " | 16 |
| Bridget White | 39 |
| Ann " | 14 |
| Catherine " | 6 |
| Mary " | 15 |
| Sally " | 19 |
| Michael White | 21 |
| Margaret " | 22 |
| Thomas White | 26 |
| Honor | |
| or Harriet White | 28 |
| Michael " | 6 |
| Bridget " | 3 |
| Margaret " | 7 |
| John Looby, Luby | |
| or Lubey | 15 |

| | |
|---|---|
| Margaret or | |
| Mary Lynskey | 61 |
| Mary " | 20 |
| Thomas McLoughlin | 37 |
| Ellen " | 35 |
| Bridget " | 4 |
| Catherine " | 1 |
| Anthony Manahan or | |
| Monaghan | 20 |
| Pat Mannion | 38 |
| Peggy " | 40 |
| John " | 17 |
| Malachy " | 10 |
| Pat " | 13 |
| Thomas " | 8 |
| Mary " | 5 |

List of Passengers from
Cork via Liverpool to
New York on board
COLUMBUS, 7 September,
1849.

| | |
|---|---|
| John Casey | 56 |
| Michael Casey | 13 |
| Bab or Barbara Casey | 19 |
| Johanna " | 18 |
| Rosean " | 16 |
| David Connell | 45 |
| Margaret " | 35 |
| Dan " | 15 |
| Jerry " | 10 |
| John " | 13 |
| Pat " | 3 |
| Eileen " | ½ |
| Johanna " | 8 |
| Margaret " | 9 |
| Mary " | 5 |
| Patrick Connell | 50 |
| Ellen " | 44 |
| Dan " | 16 |
| John " | 13 |
| Philip " | 19 |
| Johanna " | 4 |
| Judy " | 15 |
| Margaret " | 7 |
| Mary " | 22 |
| John Cremin | 28 |
| Kitty " | 25 |
| Timothy " | 3 mths. |
| Daniel Daly | 50 |
| Margaret Daly | 50 |
| John " | 26 |
| Bessy " | 25 |
| Judy " | 20 |
| Margaret " | 19 |
| Denis (Daniel) Danihy | 40 |
| Johanna " | 40 |
| Con " | 15 |
| Dan " | 17 |
| Denis " | 7 |
| Matt " | 5 |
| Michael " | 13 |
| Mary " | 19 |
| Mary " | 13 |
| Denis (Matt) Danihy | 60 |
| Johanna " | 50 |
| Daniel " | 19 |
| Denis " | 7 |
| John " | 17 |
| Matt " | 21 |
| Michael " | 11 |
| Tade " | 3 |
| Bridget " | 15 |
| Eileen " | 10 |
| Mary " | 23 |
| Tim Danihy | 40 |
| Mary " | 42 |
| Con " | 3 |
| Dan " | 13 |
| Michael " | 8 |
| Tade " | 5 |
| Nelly " | 10 |
| Daniel Fenigan | 55 |
| Johanna " | 48 |
| Johanna " | 20 |
| Judy " | 7 |
| Kitty " | 10 |
| Mary " | 22 |
| John Foley or Fowley | 52 |
| Eileen " | 50 |

| | |
|---|---|
| Dan Foley or Fowley | 18 |
| John " " | 21 |
| Pat " | 16 |
| Eileen " | 28 |
| Johanna" | 11 |
| Julea " | 8 |
| Mary " " | 24 |
| John Galvin | 32 |
| Margaret Galvin | 30 |
| Patrick " | 2 |
| Tade " | 4 |
| Biddy " | 6 |
| Tade " | 30 |
| Margaret Keeffe or | |
| O'Keeffe | 50 |
| Eugene " | 17 |
| Jeane " | 13 |
| Johanna " | 21 |
| Nano " | 23 |
| Daniel Kelleher | 69 |
| Dan " | 29 |
| Kitty " | 26 |
| Tade " | 2 |
| Kitty " | 3 |
| Mary " | 21 |
| John " | 36 |
| Connor or Daniel Leary | 55 |
| Ellen Leary | 50 |
| Jerry " | 11 |
| John " | 18 |
| Eileen " | 16 |
| Johanna " | 20 |
| Mary " | 13 |
| Peggy " | 5 |
| Matthew Leary | 50 |
| Mary " | 45 |
| Dan " | 6 |
| Darby " | 18 |
| John " | 16 |
| Matt " | 1 |
| Pat " | 13 |
| Johanna " | 4 |
| Judy " | 20 |
| Denis McAuliffe | 28 |
| Michael " | 22 |
| Robert " | 17 |
| Johanna " | 24 |
| Margaret McCarthy | 22 |
| John Sullivan | 35 |
| Ellen " | 30 |
| John " | ½ |
| Mary " | 25 |

List of passengers from
Galway to New York on
ship BARK CARACTACUS
4 May, 1849

| | |
|---|---|
| James Morgan, labourer | 24 |
| James Lawless, do. | 50 |
| Rose Lawless, spinster | 41 |
| John Keely, labourer | 33 |
| Judy Murphy, spinster | 40 |
| Biddy Murphy, do. | 21 |
| Peter Higgins, labourer | 30 |
| Martin King, do. | 21 |
| Honor Fury, spinster | 25 |
| Michael Morris, carpenter | |
| Thomas Murphy, labourer | 19 |
| Margaret Cahill, child | 14 |
| Honor " do. | 11 |
| Patrick Tynan, mason | 41 |
| Peter Scully, labourer | 19 |
| John Tracey, do. | 21 |
| Thomas Donoghue, do. | 18 |
| Thomas Killen, do. | 20 |
| Dudley Ridge, do. | 21 |
| Sabina Dolan, spinster | 17 |
| John Burke, child | 5 |
| Mary Kelly, spinster | 18 |
| Catherine Kelly, do. | 16 |
| Judy Burke, spinster | 30 |
| John Cunniff, labourer | 45 |
| John Fagan, " | 25 |
| Biddy Connors, spinster | 19 |
| Conor Brodie, labourer | 27 |
| John Burke, do. | 27 |
| James Nolan, labourer | 22 |
| James Shaughnessy, | 18 |

List of passengers from
Belfast to New York on
ship Emma Pearl, 4, May,
1849

| | |
|---|---|
| Andrew McClelland, labourer | 60 |
| Sarah " do. | 55 |
| Margaret " spinster | 27 |
| Richard " labourer | 23 |
| Mary McKnight, spinster | 60 |
| William McKnight, | 22 |
| Elizabeth " | 21 |
| Mary " infant | |
| Thomas Clegg, labourer | 35 |
| Sarah " | 21 |
| David " infant | |
| Thomas Boyd | 28 |
| Margaret Boyd | 26 |
| John Rogan | 24 |
| Rose Rogan | 25 |
| Patrick Bannon | 56 |
| Mary " | 40 |
| Cecily " | 19 |
| James " | 17 |
| Mary " | 9 |
| Betty " | 7 |
| Anne " | 3 |
| Catherine " 10 months | |
| Daniel Comb | 21 |
| John McComb | 26 |
| John Moreland | 29 |
| Eliza " | 29 |
| Thomas " infant | |
| William Bryen | 25 |
| Catherine Bryen | 25 |
| Margaret " | 3 |
| Eliza " infant | |
| Francy Wallace | 26 |
| John Fox | 26 |
| Bernard Lally | 24 |
| Bridget " | 24 |
| Henry Hollan, labourer | 40 |
| Eliza " | 35 |
| Sarah " | 12 |
| Rachel Hogg, spinster | 17 |
| John Donaghy | 38 |
| William Donaghy | 3 |
| John " infant | |
| Daniel McDonald | 21 |
| Bernard McNally | 20 |
| Biddy Canavan | 16 |
| William Boyle | 20 |
| James Hamilton | 20 |
| Nancy McDonald | 20 |
| Isabella Anderson | 34 |
| Robert " | 14 |
| Rebecca " | 7 |
| William " | 5 |
| John Donley | 24 |
| Jane " | 22 |
| Thomas Maguire | 25 |
| Mary Maguire | 17 |

LIST of passengers from NEWRY,
Ireland, to New York on Ship
JAMES 10 May, 1849

| | |
|---|---|
| Michael Vallely, labourer | 30 |
| Margaret " wife | 28 |
| James McKeon, labourer | 20 |
| Sally McKenna, servant | 20 |
| Margaret O'Neill do. | 23 |
| Susan " do. | 19 |
| John Hanvey, labourer | 18 |
| Pat " do. | 15 |
| Bridget Hanvey, servant | 11 |
| Jane McNally, do. | 19 |
| Hugh McGeogh, labourer | 21 |
| Jane McCartin, servant | 19 |
| Bridget Quin, " | 17 |
| Mary Fanning, " | 23 |
| Mary McGrory, " | 18 |
| William Dongan, shoemaker | 30 |
| Jane " wife | 25 |
| Anne McDermott, servant | 24 |
| Roger White, labourer | 20 |

Passengers on Ship
MARCHIONESS OF BUTE
from Newry to New
York, 15 May, 1850.

Rosanna Halligan
Eliza          "
James Wilson
Samuel Todd
Edward Cassidy
Patrick        "
John Quinn
Peter Connor
James McShane
Rose Garvey
Christy Garvey
William Kennedy
Jane Hamilton
James Devlin
Patrick McDonnell
Alice Cassidy
Margaret Sinclair
Alice Simms
Thomas McBride
Stephen Sloan
Betty Managhan
Margaret Toal
John Hanratty
Michael Donaghy
Alice McVeigh
Ann Collins
Francis Stephens
Bridget Delan
James Wright
Catharine Dunlop

Passengers on Ship
INFANTRY from
Liverpool to New
York, 29 July,
1850.

Biddy Doyle
Patrick Doyle
John           "
Kitty          "
Michael Walsh
Ellen          "
Thomas McCartney
James Rooney
William Carberry
Mary Curley
Thomas Plunkett
Sara Dunn
Patrick Byrne
Bridget McGee
Alice Cullan
Ann Kinlan
Patrick Riley
Patrick Haley
Patrick Lanagan
Michael Doran
Philip Ready
Daniel Heaney
Ann Ashley
Ann McCuskin
Thomas Dawson
Philip         "
Sarah Franklin
William Stewart
June Whyte
Biddy McGlone
Thomas Kearney
William Carroll
Daniel Meehan

List of Passengers
on Ship ADAM CARR
from Glasgow to New
York, 2 September,
1850.

William Glendinning
Catherine       "
Richard Henderson
Ellen           "
John Stewart
Robert Davis
Mary Ann Shearer

John Shearer
Thomas Foster
Michael McNally
Daniel Fitzpatrick
Dennis Dee
James Laden
Michael Donhay
Ann            "
Elizabeth Banks
Thomas Miller
James Dowdall
David Meagan
William Phillips
James Scott
Robert Maxwell
Jane Breen
Margaret Robinson
William Robertson
Rose McGraw'
Peter McGuire
John Downey
Conn Connor
Hugh McLaughlin
Ellen McCue
Margaret White

List of Passengers
on Ship ISAAC WRIGHT
from Liverpool to
New York,
1 November, 1850.

Mary Scanlon
Patrick Scanlon
Francis McManus
Bridget Eagan
Julia Dailey
Mary Coffey
Elizabeth Connell
Daniel Sullivan
John Finegan
Bella Hughes
John Smithwick
Johanna Higgins
Martin Gleeson
Ann Haligan
Catherine Thornton
Pat Pender
James Lapan
John Cahill
P. Garvey
James Degan
Patrick Kirby
Judy Quigley
Mary Blake
Maria Ellis
Mary Devane
Thomas Hanley
Malachy Collins
Ann Flaherty
Margaret Usher
John Monaghan
Thomas Sheady
Eliza Reardon

List of Passengers
on Ship COLONIAL
from Liverpool
to New York,
23 January, 1851.

John Grady
Michael Cargan
Thomas Martin
James Bruton
Michael Earley
Edward Shilley
John Fagan
Margaret Foley
Patrick Watson
James· Carey
Mary Mackham
John Cotter
James Flemming
Eliza Kernan
Bridget Bransfield
Catherine Callahan
John Donlan
Catherine Hopkins

Michael Whelan
Ann Mullins
Ellen Luby
Edward Butler
Maria Fox
Ellen Coffee
Jane Miller
Mary Arnold
John Drew
James Haggerty
Michael Ahern
Catherine Rogers
Margaret Slattery
Dennis Graham
Owen Cosgrave

List of Passengers
on Ship WILLIAM
from Westport to
New York, 30 April,
1851.

Hugh Bones
Honor          "
John Salmon
Bridget Brogan
Ann            "
Michael Gannon
Mary Malley
James Coleman
Nancy Handers
Martin Flannery
Philip Gibbons
Patrick Heraghty
Winny Garravan
Maria McEneely
Honor Joyce
John Loftus
Honor Kerigan
Elizabeth Murtagh
Ellen Scully
Frank Quin
Patrick Durkan
Michael Beckett
Edward Gough
Ann Short
Daniel Murdock
Mary Cain
Patrick McNally
John Timlin
Patrick Magan
Honor Langan
Patrick Gibbons
James Gill

Passengers on Ship
VICTORIA from
Limerick to New
York, 23 August,
1851.

John Fitzgibbon
Connor Ward
Margreth Griffin
Mary Nolan
Ellen Murray
Peter Sweeney
Mathias Nester
Bridget Fury
Thomas Kildeay
John Tierney
Margaret Conway
Mary Tracy
Martin Rooney
Thomas Noon
Catharine Burt
Bridget Finn
Hanna Hayes
John Morris
James Matthews
Bridget Mullin
Catharine Forde
Mary Brady
Bridget Lynch
Patrick Deigan
Catharine Commans
Bridget Carr
Martin Shanahan
Patrick Conneally

Margareth Joyce
Susan McMan
Anthony Puniard

List of Passengers
on Ship NATHANIEL
G. WEEKS from
London to New York,
1 November, 1851.

John Driscole
Ellen Ager
Amos Hinckley
James Wright
Patrick Roach
Patrick O'Connor
William O'Brien
William Taylor
John Tucker
Soloman Cohen
Catherine Hickey
John Cunningham
George Caxon
John Roan
Enorah Dowling
Ellen Sullivan
Michael Regan
Mary Buckley
Ellen Donoghue
William Buckman
Timothy Carron
William Altyn
John Brown
Louis Cohen
Samuel Henry
Aaron Moses
Joseph Ellis
Michael Redman
Caroline Wilmore
Catherine Hurley
Edward Evershed
John Ireland
Ellen Dillon

List of Passengers
on Ship RODERICK
DHU from Liverpool
to New York,
6 January, 1852.

Matt Douglas
Tipperary
John Maher
Killkelly
Judith Maher
Mick Mullin
Mayho
James Cunningham
Roscommon
Pat O'Neil
Limerick
John Cummin
Limerick
Mick Hardman
Galway
Alice Barry
Tipperary
Ellen Neilson
Co. Clare
Joseph Russell
Co. Clare
Laurence Millvihill
Co. Clare
James Murphy
Co. Mayo
William Byrne
Wick      "
C  .   rine Connor
_xford
Alice Carlin
Tyrone
Sarah Carlin
Tyrone
Ann Riley
Mayo
Mary Leslie
Donegal
Margaret Cassidy
Tyrone

Dennis Mahony
Kerry
Catherine Delany
Kilkenny
Ellen Slevin
Tyrone
Pat Healey
Furghmenagh
Mick Redman
Furghmenagh
Pat Murphy
Wexford
Robert Elliot
Furmannah
Dennis Carroll
Co. Kerry
Bridget Bennett
Roscommon

List of Passengers
on Ship ODESSA from
Dublin to New York,
2 April, 1852.

Michael Kenney
Jno. Archer
Jno. Wilson
William Lennox
Edward Collins
John Ford
Patrick Duffy
Charles Hurley
William Dalton
James Daly
Edward Gibney
Patrick Gallagher
John Kelly
James Bulger
William Moffatt
Thomas Hinly
Margaret Rowe
John Plunkett
Charles Long
Ann Cooleghan
James Markey
Ann Rogers
James Kavanagh
Bridget Lynch
Owen Hammond
Mary Flynn
Bridget Darby
Charles Egan
William Norris
James Corrigan

List of Passengers
on Ship RAJAH from
Liverpool and Tralee
to New York, 2 September
1852.

J. Maloney
M. Connor
B. Griffin
M. Moriarty
J. Boyle
J. Hanihan
W. Kerby
P. Egan
C. Carroll
D. Callahan
J. Quirk
M. Sheahan
E. Jefcott
M. Brusnan
D. Keating
C. Lucy
E. Plowman
J. Lovett
M. Lean
E. Devine
D. Whelan
E. Barrett
D. Hurlehy
J. Morris
B. Corbett
M. Driscoll
M. Cahilan
M. Sears

List of Passengers
on Ship MARCHIONESS
OF CLYDESDALE from
Glasgow (passengers
embarked at Greenock)
to New York,
6 December, 1852.

Mary Taggart
Hugh Flinn
Hugh Gallacher
Robert Quigley
Ellen Sweeney
John Mullan
Martha Richard
John Carr
Margaret Livingstone
George Kelly
Joseph Docherty
Jane Devlin
Rebecca Young
James Mowbray
Patrick O'Hara
Michael McSwegon
John Simpson
John Marshall
James Mehan
William Armstrong
Charles McHugh
Stephen McIntyre
Thomas Moore
Mary Kane
John Feeney
James McIlver
Samuel McDermott
Mary Johnstone
Margaret Rourke
Patrick McGroharty
Isabella McDaid
Sally McAvana


List of Passengers
on Ship COLUMBIA from
Liverpool to New
York, 3 March, 1853.

William Welsh
Laurence Quinlan
Hugh Higgins
Michael Evans
Catherine Gibbons
Patrick Scales
James Dillon
Pat Brown
Catherine Garity
Susan Blacker
Alexander Gamble
Daniel Lunney
Laurence Martin
Thomas Whelan
Laurence Ward
Edward Fitzpatrick
James Tyrrol
Henry Blake
William Green
James Power
Michael Summers
Oliver Bower
Patrick Laurence
Henry Cooper
Patrick Coffey
John Mortimer
Bessey Gaffney
Ann Oates


List of Passengers
on Ship PRINCETON
from Liverpool to
New York, 18 July,
1853.

Ellen Grany
Co. Kerry
John Connor
Co. Kerry
Mary Dunlevy
Co. Kerry
Mary Welsh
Co. Kerry
Mary Sullivan

Co. Kerry
Philip Brady
Fermanaugh
Margaret Brady
Fermanaugh
Peter Gavican
Roscommon
Ann Cunningham
Roscommon
Kitty Radir
Clare
Johanna Welsh
Limerick
Johanna Calligan
Cork
Ann Cullum
Longford
Margaret McDavatt
Tyrone
Bridget Tiernan
Leitrim
Patrick Gaynor
Leitrim
Catherine Butler
Tipperary
Ellen Dower
Tipperary
Julia Tobin
Limerick
Mary Brown
Roscommon
John Ward
Galway
Catherine Murray
Galway
Margaret Norton
Galway
Catherine Tierney
Galway
Mary Higgin
Queens
Rosana Quin
Queens
Mary Callaghan
Armaugh
Michael Manly
Mayo
Julia Tynan
Queens
Betsy Dargan
Westmeath
Mary Mahoney
Cork


Passengers on Ship
TELEGRAPH from
Liverpool and
Tralee to New York,
25 October, 1853.

Bridget Fitzgerald
Jeremiah Foreham
Patrick Casey
Patrick Higgins
David Ready
Mathew Moriarty
Catherine Dalton
Catherine Courteray
Mary Keating
William Joy
Peggy Joy
Mary Spillane
Daniel Dowd
Francis Abott
Kate Conway
Mary Rice
Maurice Burns
Daniel Flynn
Catherine Flaherty
Maurice Cuonihan
Denis Barton
William Shanahan
Denis Quill
Catherine Stack
Honora Cusack
William Costello
Johanna Scanlon
Thomas Evans
May Day
Robert Baker

Passengers on Ship
HERMAN ROOSEN from
Dublin to New York,
23 January, 1854.

Patrick Smith
John Ryan
Mary Woods
Michael Conlan
Laurence Rutledge
John Keogh
Peter Noonan
Mark Scott
James Dean
Judith Dunn
Ann Neale
Bridget Morrison
John Redmond
James Masterson
Eilen Walker
Bridget Keeffe
Bridget Lynch
John Keyne
Eliza Wallengood
John Dwyer
Thomas Atkinson
Anne Heusen
Patrick Magee
Bridget Darling
Mary McGuinness
Gabriel Warner
Rosa Thompson
Richard Monks
Ann Roe
Margaret Sheridan
Mary Farrelly
Ellen Malone


Passengers on Ship
STAR OF THE WEST
from Liverpool to
New York, 3 April
1854.

Anne Horan
Patrick Nowlan
Patrick Delany
James Litton
John Mockler
Martin Carroll
John Bushell
Bessy Cosgrove
James Cleary
Joseph Newton
Philip Grimes
David Thomas
James Stone
William Glass
Thomas Carmody
Catherine Dolphin
Michael Rooney
Mary Seymour
John Nagle
James Cawley
Andrew Dudley
Michael Finn
James Gash
Bridget Behan
Abraham Cooke
Margaret Coughlin
Julia Crowley
John Devaney
Andrew Heffernan


Passengers on Ship
WILLIAM TAPSCOTT
from Liverpool to
New York, 14 August,
1854.

James Lane
Mary Madden
James Boyle
Patrick Boyle
Mary Kane
Alice Murray
Pat Gilmartine
Thomas McCord
Ellen Hagan

Mary Wall
Ellen Quigley
Mary Cox
Mary Hiney
Peter Gilroy
Brid Sheehan
Thomas Burns
David Lynch
John Clinton
Hugh Morris
Mary Fountain
Margaret Gannon
Mary Broderick
John Donlan
Kerry
Jno. Casey
Kerry
Pat Loughrea
Kerry
Michael McCanary
Kerry
Catherine Curley
Kerry
Pat Healey
Kerry
Jeremiah Sullivan
Kerry
Thomas Connolly
Kerry


List of Passengers
on Ship WEBSTER
from Liverpool to
New York, 20 November,
1854.

Peggy Barrett
Alexander Chambers
Michael Havey
Edward Brothers
William Ward
Margaret Devine
Mary McGowan
James Baines
Thomas Mulhall
Ellen Rourke
Barney Donnelly
Richard Savage
James Tighe
Mary McGarry
Ellen Mulligan
Margaret Coddingham
Anne Coffey
Judy Collins
Ellen Higgins
Bridget McEvoy
James Beardsley
Johanna Hanlon
Maria Clay
Mary Slattery
Margaret McInerny
Honora Norton
Margaret Cussack
Catharine Bowers


List of Passengers
on Ship NEW WORLD
from Liverpool to
New York, 19 March,
1855.

Bernard Cain
Catherine Connell
Charles Cooney
Edward Fay
John Hyland
Pat Keenan
Catherine Gregan
Ann Healy
James Chamberlain
Hamelton Smith
Mary Birmingham
Michael O'Keefe
Hannah Glenn
Margaret Cassidy
Mary Lockart
Thomas Burke
Delia Rush
Richard Cullen

Stephen Eason
Fanny Frain
Matt Farrell
James Lyons
Mary Curly
Jno. Sweeny
Michael Corcoran
Michael O'Hara
Connell Duggan


Passengers on Ship
KATHERINE from Belfast
to New York, 1 June, 1855.

William Boyd
William Ross
James Bell
James Lowrey
William Knowles
Samuel Taylor
Susanna Rodgers
William McCartney
John Caughey
George Andrews
Margaret McComb
Jane Jameson
Amelia Palmer
Robert Nisbett
John Harper
Henry Rowane
Alexander McGlade
Sarah Carson
William Redment
David Maxwell
Hugh Flinn
John Johnstone
Catherine Smith
Ellen McGee
Mary McFurson
William Williamson


Passengers on Ship WEBSTER
from Liverpool to New York,
3 September, 1855.

Terence McGarraty
Ann Pickering
John Shorten
Ann Corrigan
Jane Faulkener
Ann Welsh
Christian Durgan
Henry Maher
John Leahey
Ellen Delaney
Margaret Cox
Catharine Gilmore
Patrick Nolan
Edward Hughes
William Dryden
William Caughlan
Hugh Sinclair
Matilda Brown
Barbara Doyle
David Gillespie
Agnes Devlin
William Farley
Joshua Oldroyd
John Heffron
Eliza Brophy
Winny Ford
Catharine Harrington

# Record Repositories and their Contents

## Public Record Office, Dublin

List Based on Reports of Deputy Keeper, Public Record Office, Dublin and *Short Guide to Public Record Office in Ireland.*

### Marriage Licence Bonds

Indexes to:

Armagh, 1727-1845.
Cashel and Emily 1664-1807.
Clogher, 1711-1866.
Clonfert, see Killaloe.
Cloyne, 1630-1867.
Cork and Ross, 1623-1845.
Derry (five bonds), 1702, 1705, 1722.
Dublin (Marriage Licence Grant Books) 1672-1741.
Dublin (Marriage Licence Bonds), 1718-46.
Elphin, 1733-1845.
Kildare, 1790-1865.
Killala and Achonry, 1787-1842.
Killaloe, 1719-1845.
Kilmore and Ardagh, 1697-1844.
Limerick, 1827-1844.
Meath, 1665, 1702-1845.
Ossory, Ferns and Leighlin, 1691-1845.
Raphoe, 1710-1755, 1817-1830.
Tuam, 1769-1845.
Waterford and Lismore, 1649-1845.

### Valuation and Tax Records

Land Commission —
Tithe applotment books, i.e. books containing particulars of holdings subject to tithe, giving occupiers' names, compiled to provide a basis for tithe commutation, under the Tithe Composition Acts, 1823 and following.

Valuation Office —
Mainly books compiled 1826-51, in the course of work on the general valuation, giving various particulars of holdings and tenants, viz —field books (4578), house books (4262), record of tenure books (470)

Quit Rent Office —
Records transferred on the removal of the office to the Land Commission in 1943, dealing with quit rents and other land revenues of the crown, management of crown property and related matters, from the 17th century onwards. Includes much material on the 17th century surveys and forfeitures, especially a set of certified copies of the Civil Survey of 1654-56 (originals destroyed, 1922)

83 original Down Survey and Distribution (in which the changes of ownership brought about by the 17th century land settlement are summed up), the crown rental of 1706, numerous series of letter-books, account-books, correspondence, memoranda and files of documents, ranging from 1689 to 1942, with 15 boxes of copies and extracts from deeds, patents and other records from the 15th century onwards. Much of the 17th century material was formerly in the Headford collection, belonging to the descendants of Sir Thomas Taylor, the colleague of Sir William Petty in the making of the Down Survey, and was bought in 1837 by the Commissioners of Woods and Forests, under whom the Quit Rent Office was at the time functioning. Much of the earlier material originated in the Forfeiture Office, which functioned from 1703 to 1823, in succession to the Commissioners of Forfeitures, appointed to administer the forfeited estates.

### Parish Church Records

The position with regard to the custody of parochial records is that under the Parochial Records Acts of 1875 and 1876 records of baptisms and burials prior to 1871 and marriages prior to 31 March, 1845, of the late Established Church, were constituted public records, but where an adequate place of storage was available locally they were allowed to remain in the custody of the incumbent by the authority of a retention order made by the Master of the Rolls. In 1922 the pre-1871 records of 1006 parishes were in the Public Record Office, while the remaining 637 were in local custody under retention orders (see table in P.R.I. rep. D.K. 28, appendix). A revised version of this appendix, indicating known copies of destroyed registers, is available in the search room.

**Material now in the Public Record Office is as follows —**

Original registers —
Nineteen parishes: Clogherny, dioc. Armagh, Corkbeg & Inch, Ballyclough, Castletownroche, Cloyne, Fermoy, Macroom, dioc. Cloyne; St. Mary Shandon, dioc. Cork, vol. 1861-78 only; Killinick, dioc. Ferns; Inch, dioc. Glendalough;

Clane, Curragh Camp and Newbridge Garrison, Ballysax, marriages from 1845, dioc. Kildare; Dungarvan, Templemichael, dioc. Lismore; Clonard, dioc. Meath; Athenry, dioc. Tuam.

Copies of registers —
Twenty seven parishes: Aghabullog, Carrigtwohill and Mogeesha, Castletownroche and Bridgetown, Killeagh, Magourney, Midleton, dioc. Cloyne; Ahascragh, dioc. Clonfert, formerly Elphin; Ardcanny and Chapel Russell, Fedamore, dioc. Limerick; Ashfield, dioc. Kilmore; Ballymartle, Fanlobbus or Dunmanway, dioc. Cork; Cloghran, Crumlin, St. Paul, dioc. Dublin; Clonmore, dioc. Ferns; Clonmore, dioc. Ossory; Doon, Toem, dioc. Cashel and Emly; Dromod and Prior, dioc. Ardfert; Drumcliff, dioc. Elphin; Drumcree, Killochonogan, dioc. Meath; Glengariff, dioc. Ross; Killeigh, dioc. Kildare; St. Peter (Drogheda), dioc. Armagh; Templemichael, dioc. Ardagh.

Parochial returns
Returns of baptisms, marriages and burials made by incumbents on the occasion of a visitation — parishes of Innismacsaint, dioc. Clogher, 1660-1866; Inniskeel, dioc. Raphoe 1669-1700 & 1818-64; St. Mary's, Dublin, 1831-70.

Extracts from registers
Appreciable quantity for eight parishes only — Ballingarry, dioc. Cashel; Carne and Kilpatrick, dioc. Ferns; Castlerickard, dioc. Meath; Churchtown, dioc. Cloyne; Durrow, dioc. Ossory; St. Andrew's and St. Kevin's, dioc. Dublin.

## Census Records

Antrim County
Census Returns 1851, parishes — Tickmacrevan, Carncastle, Grange, Kilwaughter, Larne, Craigs, Ballymoney, Donaghy, Rasharkin, Killead, Aghagallon, Aghalee, Ballinderry.

Cavan County
Census Returns 1821, parishes — Annageliffe, Ballymacue, Castlerahan, Castleterra, Crosserlough, Denn, Drumlummon, Drung, Larah, Kilbride, Kilmore, Kinawley, Lavey, Lurgan, Munterconaght, Mullagh. Census returns 1841, parish Killeshandra.

Derry County
Census Returns 1831, parishes — Agivey, Macosquin, Ballyaghran, Killowen, Aghanloo, Tamlaght, Finlagan, Templemore, Arboe, Termoneeny, Banagher, Glendermot.

Fermanagh County
Census Returns 1821, parishes — Derryvullen, Aghalurcher. Census returns 1841, parish Currin. Census returns 1851, parish Drumheeran.

Galway County
Census Returns 1821, baronies — Arran and Athenry.

Meath County
Census Returns 1821, baronies — Upper and Lower Navan.

Offaly County (King's Co.)
Census Returns 1821, barony of Ballybritt including town of Birr formerly Parsonstown.

Waterford County
Census Returns 1841, parish — Lismore.

1901 & 1911 Census Returns
Complete for all Ireland.

## Wills (Diocesan)

Indexes to:
Ardagh, 1695-1858. Ardfert and Aghadoe, 1690-1858.
Armagh, 1677-1858. (And Drogheda District, 1691-1846).
Cashel and Emly, 1618-1858. Clogher, 1661-1858.
Clonfert, 1663-1857. Cloyne, 1621-1858 (damaged).
Connor, 1622-1858 (and an entry of 1859).
Cork and Ross, 1548-1858 (and two probates, 1454,1470).
Derry, 1612-1858. Down, 1646-1858.
Dromore, 1678-1858. (damaged).
Dublin, 1536-1858 (fragments). (Printed in appendices to 26th and 30th Reports of the Deputy Keeper of the Records).
Elphin, 1650-1858 (fragments).
Ferns, 1601-1858 (fragments).
Kildare, 1661-1857 (fragments).
Killala and Achonry (fragments).
Killaloe and Kilfenora (fragments).
Kilmore, 1682-1857 (badly Damaged).
Leighlin, 1682-1858 (fragments).
Limerick, 1615-1858.
Meath,1572-1858 (fragments).
Newry and Mourne, 1727-1858 (fragments).
Ossory, 1536-1858 (very badly damaged).
Raphoe, 1684-1858 (very badly damaged).
Tuam, 1648-1858 (very badly damaged).
Waterford and Lismore, 1648-1858 (very badly damaged).

## Collections of Family Papers

Edgeworth papers
Late 17th to early 19th century, relating to family property in Co. Longford and the town of Kinsale, including a volume of copies of documents dealing with the management of the family property compiled by Maria Edgeworth in continuation of the Black Book of Edgeworthstown.
Sarsfield Vesey papers
Dealing with the property of the Sarsfield and Vesey families in counties Dublin, Wicklow,

Kildare and Carlow, mainly late 17th and 18th centuries (deeds 1414-1808). Memo in P.R.I. rep. D.K. 56, p.342, with list of deeds, index to correspondence, and some items printed in full.

Carew papers
 Relating to Carew family of Castle Boro, Co. Wexford, 18th and early 19th centuries. Calendared for the Irish Manuscripts Commission by A.K. Longfield ( *Shapland Carew Papers* Dublin, 1946).

Monteagle papers
 Relating to the families of Spring and Rice and their property in counties Kerry and Limerick, 1669-1925.

Grenville papers
 Relating to the estates of the Grenville family in Co. Cavan, early 19th century. Memo in P.R.I. rep. D.K. 57, p.468.

Hamilton papers
 Relating the property of the Hamilton family in counties Armagh and Down, 17th and 18th centuries.

Bateman papers
 Relating the property of the Bateman family in Co. Kerry, 1648-1848.

King-Harman papers
 Relating to the King-Harman estates in counties Longford, Kildare, Queen's County and Westmeath, 1656-1893.

Fitzpatrick papers
 Relating to the property of Fitzpatrick (barons of Upper Ossory and Gowran), mainly in counties Leix and Kilkenny, 1574-1842.

Wyche documents
 Papers of Sir Cyril Wyche, chief Secretary to the Duke of Ormonde, 1676-82, and Viscount Sidney, 1692-93, and also Lord Justice, 26 June 1693-9 May 1695 and for some time one of the Trustees for the sale of Forfeited Estates. Consists of correspondence, King's letters, memoranda, accounts and miscellaneous, military and ecclesiastical affairs and the administration generally. Detailed catalogue in search room. Memorandum with partial catalogue and some documents printed in full P.R.I. rep. D.K. 57, pp. 479-518.

Frazer collection of papers
 Relating to the 1798 period and after. Most of this appears to have originated with the firm of Kemmis, who for some generations acted as solicitors for the crown in criminal causes. It consists of miscellaneous papers relating to the rising of 1798, including a series of reports from an informer, 'J. Smith', and copies of minutes of evidence at courts martial in connection with the rising in Wexford, reports of trials of Ribbon Men in 1840, a series of letters of Sir Jonah Barrington

and his family dealing mainly with his money difficulties, and a brief information in the case of the Queen v. William Smith O'Brien and Thomas Francis Meagher, 1848. Special catalogue in search room. Memorandum in P.R.I. rep. D.K. 55, p.145.

Prim papers
 Collection of miscellaneous papers relating to the history of Kilkenny in the 17th and 18th centuries. Catalogue in P.R.I. rep. D.K. 58.
 A large collection of papers (reports, accounts and correspondence) presented by the Religious Society of Friends, dealing with the work of the society in relieving distress, 1847-65.

The Lindsay collection
 Consisting mainly of material relating to the family of Bermingham of Athenry, Co. Galway, and the claim by Edward Berminghan to the Athenry peerage in 1824, and including a set of copies of parliamentary writs, a visitation book of the diocese of Meath, 1762, a volume of letters and memoranda relating to the Irish Record Commission of 1819-30, and the 8th report of the Maynooth College Commission, 1834. Catalogue in P.R.I. rep. D.K. 56, pp. 58 and 397.

Clifden papers
 Relating to the property of the Agar family (viscounts Clifden) in and near Gowran, Co. Kilkenny, 1670-1895.

Lenigan papers
 Relating to the property of the Lenigan family and related families of Evans, Armstrong and Fogarty, in and near Thurles, Co. Tipperary, 18th and 19th centuries.

Osborne papers
 Relating to the property of the Osborne family, mainly in Co. Waterford, mid. 17th to late 19th century.

## Genealogical Collections

Betham genealogical abstracts
 214 volumes of abstracts compiled by Sir William Betham for genealogical purposes, mainly from prerogative wills prior to 1800.

Betham correspondence
 Eight volumes, dealing with his genealogical researches, including memoranda and extracts from records.

Thrift genealogical abstracts
 Twenty six bundles of abstracts made by Miss. G. Thrift. Names in testamentary and ecclesiastical documents abstracted in this collection are included in indexes forming appendix Ib to P.R.I. rep. D.K. 57 and appendices IIc and IId to P.R.I. rep. D.K. 55.

Groves genealogical abstracts

Fifteen boxes of abstracts compiled by the late Tenison Groves. List and index of names in search room.

Grove-White parish register extracts

Forty three volumes of extracts from registers, mainly from Co. Cork.

Crossle genealogical abstracts

Nineteen parcels of abstracts made by the late Philip G. Crossle. Card index in search room.

## Miscellaneous Matter

List of inhabitants of the baronies of Newcastle and Uppercross, Co. Dublin, c. 1652. M 2467. Copy of a book of survey, Co. Dublin, 1658. M.2475.

Copies of 24 proclamations, miscellaneous subjects, 1652-1691, from originals in the Public Library, Philadelphia. M.3144-3167.

Copy list of forfeiting proprieteors, from commonwealth council book no. A 35. M.752.

Copies of, and extracts from, subsidy rolls, hearth money rolls, and poll-tax assessments and accounts, 1634-99, various places, counties Dublin, Armagh, Fermanagh and Tyrone. M. 2468-74.

Volume of notes relating to receipts of revenue and payments, Dec. 1682-Mar. 1683, by John Price, receiver general. M.2539.

Volume of copies being ecclesiastical instruments and proceedings, principally for the diocese of Dublin, 17th century, with other miscellaneous extracts, including a description of counties Sligo, Donegal and Fermanagh and Lough Erne, by the Rev. William Henry, 1739. M.2533.

Three volumes of copies being petitions, King's letters, bills, acts and correspondence, temp. Chas.II-Wm.III. M.2458-60.

Volume of correspondence, petitions, etc. (20 items), c. 1678-97, some originals, some copies, including original letter from inhabitants of Belfast declaring readiness to submit to James II, 14 March, 1689. M 2541.

Belturbet corporation minute books, 1708-1798, 4 sheets of corporation minutes, 1660-1664 and a volume of miscellaneous records relating mainly to charitable bequests, mid. 18th century. M.3571-3573, 3606 and 3607.

Copies from parliamentary returns, bundle 73, formerly in P.R.O, relating to the Franciscan order in Ireland, 18th century. M.2928.

Volume containing lists of salaries and pensions payable on 26 October, 1729. M.2480.

Copy notebook of Bishop Tension of Ossory, describing the state of the diocese, 1731. M.2462.

Diocesan Census of Elphin, prepared for bishop Edward Synge, 1749, arranged by parish, giving the name of each householder, religion, profession, number of children and others in household. M.2466.

Twenty-three volumes, with a small quantity of papers, relating to the civil administration of the parish of St. Thomas, Dublin, 1750-1864 (mainly applotment books for assessment of taxation), 1823-64, also minute book of directors of the watch, 1750-1770, grand jury cess book, 1772, register of cholera cases, 1832, deserted children's account book, 1842-64, declarations of finding of deserted children, 1852-63, and applotment warrants and notices to applot, 1764-1832) M.4940-4964.

Volume of copies of material on the history of the liberty of St. Sepulchre, Dublin, 18th century. M.2545.

Extracts from returns of the 1766 religious census for parishes in the dioceses of Armagh, Cashel and Emly, Clogher, Cloyne, Connor, Derry, Dromore, Down, Dublin, Ferns, Kildare, Kilmore & Ardagh, Ossory, Raphoe and Cork & Ross. M.2476, 2478, 3582 and 3585.

Test book, 1775-76, containing names of Catholics taking the oath of allegiance under Acts 13 and 14 Geo.III, c. 35 from a vol. formerly in P.R.O. M.3092. Printed rep. D.K. 59 app.III.

List of freeholders, Co Meath, 1781, from Headford MS. M.1364.

Register of popish clergy , diocese of Meath, 1782-3. M.551.

List of electors, Co. Longford 1790. M.2486-88.

Irish civil lists, 1803 and 1818. M.2425 and 2426.

Visitation books, early 19th century

Diocese of Armagh, 1819-51, Cashel and Emly 1816, Clogher 1826-61, Dublin and Glendalough 1821-30, Kildare 1823 and n.d., Kilmore 1823, Meath 1823 and 1826, and Ossory 1823 and 1829. M.2491-1529.

Letter books of Lord Francis Leveson-Gower, Chief Secretary, 1829-30 M.736-38.

A number of volumes dealing with army administration in the 18th and 19th centuries, acquired from various sources, including 7 volumes dealing with the Sligo militia, 1855-7 (M.2558-63), an entry book from the Adjutant General's office, Dublin, 1763-65 (M.2554), an entry book of the Lords Justices relating to marital affairs, 1711-13 (M.2553), and 10 vols, relating to the Longford militia, 1791-1860 (M.3474-3483).

Accounts of Byran Bolger, quantity surveyor, Dublin, 1758-1834, of interest for architectural history.

Volume of copies and abstracts of charters and grants, temp. Hen.II — Hen.VIII (Armagh, Cork, Dublin, Drogheda, Kilkenny, Leitrim, Trim, Waterford, Holy Cross Abbey and Melifont). M.2531.

Volume of transcripts of Dublin charters, Hen.II — Eliz., by W. Monck Mason. M.2546.

Volume containing abstracts of entries relating to Ireland in various records now in P.R.O., London, transcript of cartulary of St. Thomas, abstracts of some Irish plea rolls, copy of rental of the Lords of Lisnaw, temp. Hen.III. etc. M.2542. Memo in P.R.I., rep. D.K. 57, p.522.

Volume of extracts from statute, justiciary, de banco and memoranda rolls, temp. Edw. I — Edw.IV, in 17th century hand. M.2551.

Volume of abstracts relating to history of Dublin, temp. Hen.III, 17th century, by W. Monck Mason. M.2459. Memo in P.R.I. rep. D.K. 57, p.518.

Letter from an Irish chieftain, Cormacus Thadei, to Thomas, Earl of Ormond, n.d., c. 1485-95, asking for funds and various favours. M.2427.

Volume of extracts, in 17th century hand, from patent roll 3 Edw.II and memoranda rolls and

council books, c. 1536-95, dealing with submissions of chiefs, maintenance of troops in Ireland (county cess, hostings, etc.) and copy of instructions from Queen Mary to Lord Deputy Sussex, 20 March, 1557. M.2532.

Small collection of petitions to Lord Deputy Bellingham, 1548-9. M.2439. Replies of the freeholders of the Queen's County to queries regarding remedies for disorders in the county, 1576. M.2440.

Bond of William O'Carroll, chief of his name, to Sir Henry Sidney for a debt of 13 score beeves to the captain of Her Majesty's gallowglasses. M.742.

Desmond Survey, 1586
Survey of the forfeited lands of the Earl of Desmond, formerly in P.R.O. — copy of portion relating to Co. Kerry (printed) and Co. Limerick (MS). M.5037,5038.

Peyton's Survey, 1586
Survey of forfeited lands in Co. Limerick, formerly in P.R.O. — calendar by J.M. McEnery, formerly of the P.R.O. M.5039.

Volume of abstracts of inquisitions
Counties Dublin and Wicklow, Hen.VI — Chas. II, by W. Monck Mason. M.2543.

Volume of extracts from records
Illustrating the history of the Earldom of Ulster (De Lacy and De Burgo), also Kildare, Louth, Ormond, Desmond.

## Royal Irish Academy

Book of Lecan
Illuminated 15th century book on Gaelic Law, traditions and genealogy by Giolla Iosa MacFirbis. M.535.
Book of Genealogies
by MacFirbis, O'Curry transcript, M.583.
O'Donnell Genealogy, with poems. M.545.
Book of Munster
Genealogies of principal southern families M.484.
Roscommon Co. Deeds, 1812. M.24.
Fitzgeralds (Tree of Life of the)
With notes on allied families, Roche, Barry, Butler. M.673.
Book of O'Connor Don
Poems, topography on allied Connaught families. M.625.
Westmeath Co. 1741. (A survey of) M. H.1.2.
Purcell Family papers, Co. Tipperary. M.4.A.42.
Notebook of John Philpot Curran M. 12.B1.10.
Dublin City
Memoranda Rolls, 1447-1745. M. 12C.18.
Clonmel Freeholders, 1776. M. 12.D36.
Burke family notes
Cos. Mayo, Galway, Sligo. M.1001.

Sarsfield family of Co. Cork
(Papers relating to) M. 12K.20.
Cavan Co. (Survey of) c. 1835. M. 14B.7.
O'Reilly & Maguire family Genealogies.
O'Lees of Hy-Brasil. (Book of the) M.454.
O'Connor & MacDermot Genealogical papers M.1219
O'Clery Book of Genealogies
Story of the Irish race. M.790.
O'Reilly Papers
Genealogy and the House of O'Reilly. M.1038.
Genealogy of Anglo-Irish families.
M.247.
MacNamaras of Tulla, Co.Clare (papers of) M.1040.
Pedigrees of —
O'Neill, MacSweeney, O'Cathain, O'Hagan MacLochlainn, O'Ferguson, etc. M.621.
Clare genealogies —
MacNamara, Clancy, O'Grady, O'Quin, O'Dea, MacCoghlan. M.1212.
Genealogical poem on the
O'Rourkes, O'Reillys, McGaurans, etc. M.471.
Munster Families
Dal gCais and derived families. M.622.
Kings of Ireland
Lists, notices, history. M.667.

## Public Record Office, Belfast

List based on Reports of Deputy Keeper, P.R.O., N.I., various years, principally 1951-53, with approximate dates covered by records, together with year and page of relevant report.

### Collections of Family Papers

Acheson family notes, 17c., 1939-45, p.15.

Adair of Co. Antrim, pedigrees and notes, 17c., 18c., 19c., 1935, p.8.

Adams family records, Co. Armagh, 18c., 1951-53, p.30.

Agnew of Cos. Antrim and Armagh 17c., 1951-53, p.31.

Agnew of Co. Down, 17c., 1924, p.10.

Aldworth Papers, 17c., 1949-50, p.20.

Alexander of Tyrone, family tree, 18c., 1951-53, p.31.

Alexander of Fermanagh, notes and tree, 1933, p.10. Allen family of Armagh, 18c., 1951-53, p.32.

Anderson of Cos. Down and Tyrone, 17c., 1951-53. p.33.

Andrews of Antrim and Armagh, 18c., 1951-53. p.33.

Armstrong family notices, 17c., 1951-53, p.17, 35.

Arundell and associated families, 17c., 18c., 1926, p.8.

Ashe of Derry, notes and history, 1948, p.21

Atkinson of Tyrone, 17c., 1951-53, p.37.

Atkinson family pedigree of Co. Down, 18c., 1934, p.28.

Auchmuty genealogy, 17c., 18c., 1951-53, p.38.

Bacon family of Derry, notes and genealogy, 17c., 18c., 1951-53, p.38.

Baillie family history from wills, 17c., 18c., 1951-53, p.39.

Baker of Cos. Tyrone and Armagh, 17c., 18c., 1951-53, p.39.

Barton rentals, 17c., 18c., 19c., 1930, p.10

Batt historical notes, 17c., 18c., 1951-53, p.19.

Beatty family anecdotes, 1924, p.10.

Beck pedigree, 1600-1900, 1930, p.10.

Becker notes, 17c., 18c., 1951-53, p.44.

Bell historical notices, 18c., 19c., 1951-53, p.45.

Bellew family tree, 1951-53, p.46.

Bellingham genealogy, 17c., 18c., 1951-53, p.46.

Benson family notes, 17c., 18c., 1951-53, p.47.

Berry of Cavan, Westmeath and King's Co., 1951-53, p.48.

Bigger of Co. Antrim, (1650-1850), 1949-50, pp.35, 351.

Bird family notes, (1740-1900), 1951-53, p.50.

Black family genealogy, 1951-53, p.51.

Blackwood history, (1660-1900), 1938-45, p.19.

Blair family notices, 1929, p.10.

Blennerhasset historical notes, 17c., 1927, p.19.

Bolton of Derry and Antrim, 17c., 18c., 1926, p.8.

Bond of Armagh, 1948, p.29.

Boyd genealogical notes, 1951-53, p.55.

Breden family notes, 17c., 18c., 1951-53, p.58.

Bristow genealogical notes, 17c., 18c., 19c., 1951-53, p.58.

Bullock history and notes, 16c., 17c., 18c., 1928, p.36, 1931, p.32.

Burrows family notes, 17c., 18c., 19c., 1951-53, p.64.

Bury notices, 18c., 1951-53, p.64.

Caldwell family notes, 18c., 1951-53, p.18.

Carson of Co. Monaghan, 1931, p.15.

Cary of Derry, pedigree, 1951-53, p.71.

Caulfield genealogy, 17c., 1951-53, p.72.

Chambers family history, 17c., 1951-53, p.72.

Chapman of Armagh history, 17c., 1951-53, p.73.

Christy family of Co. Down, 17c., 18c., 1951-53, p.74.

Clarke family of Antrim and Armagh, notes, 1951-53, p.75.

Cowley genealogy. 15c.,-18c., 1934, p.9.

Colvin of Armagh, various records, 18c., 1951-53, p.79.

Cooke family records, 16c., 17c., 1951-53, p.82.

Cooper records, lists, Armagh, 17c., 1951-53, p.82.

Cope genealogies, Armagh, 18c., 1951-53, p.82.

Crawford family of Co. Antrim, 17c., 18c., 1949-50, pp.69-70.

Cunningham of Co. Donegal, (1100-1800), 1951-53, pp.10-90.

Darley family records, 18c., 1926, p.31.

Davenport family notices, 17c., 18c., 1951-53, p.92.

Davidson of Co. Down, pedigree, 17c., 18c., 1938-45, p.47.

Delafield family history, 1946-47, p.9.

Delap of Cos. Derry and Armagh, 17c., 18c., 1951-53, p.95.

Despard genealogy, 17c., 18c., 1951-53, pp.18-96.

Dickson, Dixon, notes on family of; Derry, Down and Armagh, 1951-53, pp.96, 97, 98.

Dobbin family notices, 17c., 18c., 19c., 1926, pp.9, 25.

Dobbs family papers, 1951-53, pp.98, 99.

Dobson genealogy, 17c., 1927, p.35.

Douglas history, Tyrone, Armagh, Antrim, 17c., 18c., 19c., 1951-53, pp.98, 99.

Downing family deeds, pedigree, 1800, 1951-53, p.101.

Dowse family history, 1927, p.10.

Drennan family deeds, letters, 1928, pp.8, 9, 10.

Drought notes and pedigree, 1928-45, p.15.

Druit of Co. Armagh, 18c., 1951-53, p.102.

Dunbar of Fermanagh, notes, history, genealogy, 1951-53, p.103.

Eames family notices, 17c., 18c., 1951-53, p.105.

Echlin family genealogy 1100-1800, 1951-53, pp.106, 107.

Edwards of Co. Derry, pedigree, 1936, p.9.

Elder of Donegal, family notices 19c., 1951-53. pp.10, 108.

Ellis records, 1951-53, p.107.

Emison family records, lists, 1946-47, p.9.

Ewarts genealogy, (1700-1900). 1930, p.10.

Faris family records, (1600-1800), 1951-53, p.110.

Fawcott of Antrim and Armagh, 1951-53, p.111

Ferrard family papers, 16c., 17c., 18c., 1926, p.8.

Finnis notices, (1600-1800), 1951-53, p.113.

Fisher of Co. Armagh, 17c., 1951-53, p.114.

Fletcher family notes, 1951-53, pp.114, 115, 116.

Forsythe of Derry County, 18c., 1951-53, pp.117, 118.

Fox family records, Co. Armagh, 18c., 1951-53, p.118.

Frith lists, notes, (1600-1800), 1951-53, p.120.

Getty family of Belfast, bible and notes, 19c., 1951-53, p.123.

Gibson records, Cos. Armagh and Down, 1951-53, p.123.

Gilbert family records, Co. Armagh, 1951-53, p.123.

Gorden Clan of Co. Antrim, 1935, p.12.

Graham family notices, 1934, pp.56, 57.

Greer genealogy, various counties, 17c., 18c., 1951-53, pp.17, 130, 131.

Gregg of Derry and Antrim, various dates, 1951-53, p.132.

Grierson of Scotland and Ireland, (1500-1800), 1951-53, p.132.

Hall of Cos. Antrim and Monaghan, 18c., 1951-53, p.123.

Hamilton family history, *in extenso,* 1951-53, pp.136, 137.

Hanna family tree, 1946-47, p.6.

Hare genealogical records, 17c., 1951-53, p.139.

Harman notices, 1951-53, p.140.

Harrison family of Co. Armagh, 18c., 1951-53, p.141.

Haughton records, Antrim and Armagh, 1951-53, p.142.

Heather family notices, 18c., 1951-53, p.144.

Henderson family tree, various counties, 18c., 1927, p.7.

Hewitt of Antrim and Armagh, 17c., 18c., 19c., 1951-53, p.146.

Hill of Cos. Antrim and Down, 17c., 18c., 1951-53, p.148.

Hillary etc., of Armagh and Down, 1951-53, p.148.

Hobson family records Tyrone, Antrim, Armagh, 1951-53, p.150.

Hogg of Cos. Armagh and Antrim, 18c., 1951-53, pp.150, 151.

Holmes genealogy, 17c., 18c., 1951-53 p.19.

Houston family records, 1927, pp.7, 41.

Hughes genealogy, 17c., 18c., 1932, p.9.

Hull family of Co. Down, 1932, p.12.

Hume records, 1951-53, p.155.

Hunter of Cos. Antrim, Down, and Armagh, 1951-53, p.155.

Irwin, Irvine, etc., genealogy, various dates 1951-53, pp.20, 158.

Jackson family documents, early dates, 1951-53, pp.20, 159.

Johnston of Co. Down, genealogical notes, (1000-1800), 1946-47, p.68.

Johnstone family records, 16c., 17c., 18c., 1928, p.65.

Jones genealogy, 17c., 18c., 1851-53, p.165.

Kellett family history, 18c., 1951-53, p.165.

Kenah, notes and history, 1951-53, p.166.

Kennedy of Clogher and Derry, family trees 1938-45, p.16.

Kerr genealogy, (1100-1900), 1951-53, p.167.

Kilpatrick family of Donegal, 18c., 19c., 1981-53, p.10.

King family notices, various dates, 1951-53, pp.16, 18, 168, 169.

Kirk of Cos. Antrim and Armagh, 18c., 1951-53, pp.170, 171.

Kirkpatrick pedigree etc., (1300-1800), 1951-53, p.170.

Knight family records, 18c., 1951-53, p.170.

Knox genealogy, various dates, 1948, p.6.

Langtree family notes, 18c., 1951-53, p.172.

Lecky genealogical notes, Donegal, 18c., 1951-53, p.10.

Lewis family records, 18c., 1951-53, p.15.

Lombard history, 17c., 1951-53, p.180.

Lowry family genealogy, (1600-1900), 1931, p.13.

Luther genealogy, 17c., 1951-53, p.182.

Lynas etc., of Armagh, various dates, 1951-53, pp.178, 182.

McDonald of Fermanagh, pedigree, 18c., 19c., 1938-45, p.60.

McNeill, notes and pedigree, (1400-1900), 1951-53, p.21.

Magennis etc., 1951-53, p.199.

Magrath family chronicle, 17c.-19c., 1951-53, p.199.

Maitland of Co. Down, pedigree, 18c., 1938-45, p.6.

Marsh family chronicle, 17c., 18c., 1951-53, p.202.

Marshall of Armagh and Antrim, various dates, 1951-53, p.203.

Matthews family notices, various dates, 1951-53, pp.204, 205.

McAskie family, notes etc., 18c., 1951-53, p.184.

McBride records, Armagh, 16c., 17c., 1951-53, p.184.

McCance and allied families, early dates, 1925, pp.7, 8, 9.

McGready of Co. Down, family tree, (1700-1900), 1930, p.10.

McCullogh genealogy and notices, 18c., 19c., 1951-53, pp.18, 188.

McGusty family records, (1600-1850), 1951-53, p.192.

McNeil etc., family chronicle and notes, (1400-1900), 1951-53, p.196.

McQuiston family, births, and deaths, 1690-1883.

McTier of Belfast, notes etc., 17c., 18c., 1929, pp.10, 28.

Mercer family of Down and Armagh, various dates, 1951-53, p.207.

Meredith of Cos. Antrim and Down, assorted records, 1951-53, p.207.

Miller family records, some early, 1951-53, p.209.

Millikin chronicle, Down and Armagh, 1951-53, p.210.

Montgomery family notices and pedigrees, most extensive, 1951-53, pp.212, 213; 1946-47, p.95; 1938-45, pp.16, 17.

Moore pedigree, 17c., 18c., 1951-53, p.215.

Morrison of Cos. Tyrone and Armagh, various dates, 1951-53, p.217.

Mulholland family notices, extensive, 1951-53, pp.21, 219.

Nesbitt genealogy, (1600-1850), 1951-53, p.223.

Nicholson of various northern counties, early date, 1951-53, pp.225, 226.

Nixon family documents, middle dates, 1924, p.10.

Parkinson family papers, Co. Louth, 1951-53, p.233.

Patterson Records, some early, mainly Armagh, Antrim and Tyrone, 1951-53, pp.234, 235.

Person family of Armagh, early dates, 1951-53, p.237.

Phillips of Derry, notes, early date, 1927, p.4.

Pillar of Armagh, Tyrone and Down, middle date, 1951-53, p.238.

Pim family tree, (1600-1900), 1951-53, p.17.

Porter of Armagh, various records, early date, 1951-53, p.240.

Purdy of Co. Tyrone, notes, early date, 1951-53, p.243.

Ray or Rea or Ray of Cos. Down and Armagh, early date, 1951-53, pp.224, 245, 246, 247.

Reade family chronicle, (1600-1900), 1951-53, pp.246, 247.

Richardson of Cos. Armagh, Down and Tyrone, various dates, 1951-53, pp.248, 249.

Robinson records, assorted, middle date, 1951-53, p.250.

Rodgers family records, Antrim, Tyrone, Down, and Armagh, various dates, 1951-53, p.252.

Rowan of Co. Antrim, family tree, (1500-1900), 1938-45, p.19.

Savage family records, very extensive, 1951-53, pp.79, 125, 257.

Shaw family documents, various dates, 1951-53, p.260.

Smyth records, notes, pedigree, 18c., 1951-53. p.264, 265.

Stephens of Armagh, pedigree, 18c., 1951-53, p.269.

Stephenson family records, middle dates, 1925, pp.7, 8; 1937, p.8.

Stewart genealogical notices, very extensive, 1946-47, p.118; 1938-45, pp.13, 16.

Stone family pedigree, (1300-1800), 1951-53, pp.19, 271.

Stouppe documents, middle dates, 1925, pp.7, 8.

Swanzy deeds and notes, middle dates, 1951-53, pp.19, 274.

Tandy family notices, (1600-1800), 1951-53, p.275. Taylor documents, notes, etc., early dates, 1951-53, pp.19, 276.

Thompson family documents, extensive, 1951-53, pp.16, 21, 278.

Travers family charts, 17c., 18c., 1951-53, p.283.

Turner of Armagh and Down, middle dates, 1951-53, p.285.

Van Homrigh genealogy, 17c., 18c., 1951-53, p.287.

Walker family records, Cos. Down, Tyrone and Monaghan, 1951-53, p.289.

Wardell genealogy, 18c., 1951-53, p.293.

Watson documents, early dates, 1925, pp.7, 8.

Webb family records, 17c., 18c., 1951-53, p.294.

West family tree, 1951-53, p.296.

Wilkinson family notices, Cos. Antrim & Armagh, 1951-53, p.301.

Wilson papers, pedigrees etc., very extensive, 1925, pp.8, 9; 1951-53, pp.303, 304.

Wray documents and history, early dates, 1946-47, p.9.

Young historical notices, 1924, p.10; 1951-53, p.308.

## Major Collections

**Antrim Deeds**

Papers of the Earl of Antrim covering the period 1610-1784; contains 360 documents relating to his estates in Cos. Antrim and Derry. Index to deeds in D.K.'s Report, 1928, Appendix B.

**Armagh Manor Rolls — (microfilm)**

Original collection in Armagh Library; contains accounts of court cases held on manors or estates.

**John Mitchel Letters**

Copies of letters written by Mitchel while in exile first in Van Dieman's Land (Tasmania) and later in America.

**Downshire Letters, 18th century**

Marquis of Downshire collection; records relating to the rise of the United Irishmen.

**Paterson Collection 1737-1888**

Papers relating to the affairs of the Irwin family of Carnagh, Co. Armagh.

**Massereene Tithe Book, 17th century**

Mainly a register of deeds affecting the estate of Viscount Massereene and Ferrard.

**Findlay and Williams Collection**

Military records, consisting of militia and army lists.

## Library of Trinity College, Dublin

List based on Catalogue of MSS. in the Library of Trinity College, Dublin, compiled by T.K. Abbott.

Book of Kells
9th cent. illuminated manuscript, made and long preserved in Columcille's monastery at Kells, Co. Meath, where it remained till 1541 when the last abbot, Richard Plunket was forced to give up the abbey and it's property. In 1568 the MS. was in the hands of Gerald Plunket, a harbour-master at Dublin. Later it was acquired by Richard Ussher, the primate, and from his library it entered Trinity College. This manuscript consists of 339 leaves of thick glazed vellum written in red, black, purple and yellow inks by at least two artists. It contains the four gospels, a short account of Hebrew names and charters bestowing grants of land on the Abbey of Kells. Has been described as the most beautiful book in the world. M.58.

Book of Armagh
Made in 807 by the scribe Ferdomnach. MS. contains the New Testament in Latin, the confession of St. Patrick and an account of the life of St. Martin of Tours. M.52.

Book of Durrow
From Durrow in Co. Offaly, like Kells, a Columban institution. MS. dates from 6th-7th cent. and is the oldest known Irish book. It contains a copy of the Gospels in Latin, an explanation of Hebrew names, epistle of St. James and summaries of the Gospels with symbols of the Evangelists. Book of Durrow used to possess a cover now lost, made by Flann, son of Malachy, King of Ireland. M.57.

Genealogical & historical tracts —
Descent of Fitzpatrick, genealogy of Kavanagh, notice of Birmingham who changed their name to MacFeorais, genealogy of Reynolds from Milesius to a chief called Megranall, a catalogue of the Kings of the race of Ir who ruled over all Ireland. M.804.

de Burgos (Burke)
Historia et Genealogia Familiae de Burgo, with an account of the high connections of the Burkes in England, France and Ireland, and description of the property and the rights of MacWilliam Burke. Contains nine pictures full-length portraits of Burkes in complete armour, the first being Richard Mor, also a roll of arms of various branches of the de Burgos. M.1440.

Collection of romances, historical poems and genealogies with pedigrees of —
O'Duffy, O'Murrigan, O'Donnellan, O'Hamill. M.1280.

Caithreim Turlough
Pedigrees of various branches of the O'Brien family, also O'Gorman, O'Loughlin & MacBrody. M.1294.

Medical Treatise -
With the names of Physicians O'Fergus, O'Callanan and O'Cannavan, noted physician of West Connaught. M.1326.

Brehon (Old Irish) Law Tracts -
Relative duties of the chieftian and his subjects: Laws relating to property, theft, evidence, article on the rights of poets; scripture genealogies; list of women celebrated in Irish history; pedigrees of O'Dooley, O'Linchy, O'Coffey, O'Driscoll, O'More and other families of Leix. M.1336.

History Of O'Rody family -
Poems, songs and notes. M.1419.

Collection of Irish Deeds
With details of wills, mortages, covenants, indentures, early 16th century. M.1429.

History of the Irish Race
Account of the Milesians; pedigrees of M'Carthy, O'Sullivan Mor, Beare and Moyle; O'Keeffe, MacGillicuddy and O'Cahill family trees; pedigrees of the O'Donoghues for twenty seven generations showing stems of the two main branches, O'Donoghue of the Glens and O'Donoghue of the Lakes; a short account of English families in Ireland; article on the early inhabitants of Ireland; genealogies of the following — O'Moriarty, O'Donovan, O'Cullen, O'Brien, MacMahon, O'Kennedy, MacNamara, O'Dea, MacGrath, MacCoghlan, MacConry, O'Quin, MacClancy, O'Carroll, O'Meagher, O'Hara, O'Gara, Magennis, lord of Iveagh, O'Conor Kerry, O'Conor Corcamroe, O'Loughlin of Burren, O'Neill, MacSweeney of Fanad, of Doe and of Bannagh; O'Donnell, O'Shaughnessy, Mac Donnell, Earl of Antrim, Maguire, MacMorough, MacGiollapatrick, O'Mulloy, O'Mulvey, Mac Allin, now Campbell. M.1296.

Scottish Records
Pedigrees of various Scottish families including MacLeoid; description of the Shrine of Adamnan, 9th abbot of Iona. M.1079.

Journal of events in Ireland in 1641 by O'Mellan, chiefly those in which O'Neills were concerned but list of names include many other families. M.1071.

Yellow Book of Lecan
Historical poems about many Irish families including MacMahon of Oriel and O'Kelly of Hy-Maine; sketch of the history of the Jews from Abraham to David; account of celebrated trees of Ireland knocked by a storm in 665; description of Cruachan, ancient palace and cemetery. M.1318.

## Registry of Deeds, Dublin

Land Index Volumes in sequence arranged by Counties and Cities with dates

1.  Cos. Antrim, Armagh, 1708-1738.
2.  Cos. Armagh, Cavan, 1739-1810.
3.  Co. Clare, 1708-1738.
4.  Cos. Clare, Kerry, 1739-1810.
5.  Co. Cork, 1810-1819.
6.  Cos. Clare, Kerry, Limerick, 1811-1820.
7.  Cos. Antrim, Down, 1811-1820.
8.  Co. Cork, 1780-1809.
9.  Co. Cork Towns, 1780-1809.
10. Co. Antrim, 1739-1810.
11. Co. Down, 1739-1810.
12. Co. Cork, 1820-1828.
13. Cos. Tipperary, Waterford, 1708-1738.
14. Cos. Kerry, Limerick, 1808-1738.
15. Cos. Carlow, Dublin, 1708-1738.
16. Cos. Carlow, Laois, 1739-1810.
17. Cos. Clare, Kerry, Limerick, 1821-1825.
18. Cos. Meath, Laois, 1811-1820.
19. Cos. Donegal, Sligo, 1739-1810.
20. Cos. Cavan, Down, 1821-1825.
21. Co. Galway, 1826-1828.
22. Cos. Clare, Kerry, Limerick, 1826-28.
23. Cos. Down, Cavan, 1826-1828.
24. Co. Galway, 1811-20.
25. Co. Leitrim, 1811-20.
26. Co. Cork, 1739-1779.
27. Co. Kildare, Kilkenny, Offaly, 1708-1738.
28. Co. Offaly, 1739-1810.
29. Co. Kildare, 1739-1810.
30. Co. Kilkenny, 1739-1810.
31. Cos. Kilkenny, Kildare, Offaly, 1811-1820.
32. Cos. Kilkenny, Kildare, Offaly, 1821-1825.
33. Cos. Kilkenny, Kildare, Offaly, 1826-1828.
34. Co. Dublin, 1739-1806.
35. Dublin Liberties, 1739-1810.
36. Co. Dublin, 1807-1819.
37. Co. Dublin, 1820-1828.
38. Cos. Mayo, Roscommon, Sligo, 1708-1738.
39. Cos. Mayo, Roscommon, Sligo, 1739-1810.
40. Cos. Mayo, Roscommon, Sligo, 1811-1820.
41. Cos. Donegal, Sligo, Mayo, 1821-1825.
42. Cos. Donegal, Sligo, Mayo, 1826-1828.
43. Cos. Fermanagh, Derry, Monaghan, Tyrone, 1708-38.
44. Cos. Fermanagh, Derry, City, 1739-1810.
45. Cos. Monaghan, Tyrone, 1739-1810.
46. Cos. Monaghan, Tyrone, 1811-1820.
47. Cos. Fermanagh, Derry, 1811-1820.
48. Cos. Fermanagh, Derry, Monaghan, 1821-1825
49. Cos. Derry, Tyrone, Fermanagh, 1826-1828.
50. City Of Cork, 1810-1819.
51. City of Cork, 1820-1828.
52. Cities of Kilkenny, Derry, Drogheda, 1780-1810.
53. Cities of Limerick, Waterford, 1780-1810.
54. Cos. Leitrim, Longford, 1729-1810.
55. Co. Galway, 1708-1738.
56. Co. Galway, 1739-1810.
57. Cos. Leitrim, Longford, Galway, 1821-25.
58. Co. Tipperary, 1739-1810.
59. Co. Tipperary, 1739-1810.
60. Cos. Waterford, Tipperary, 1811-1820.
61. Cos. Waterford, Tipperary, 1821-1825.
62. Cos. Waterford, Tipperary, 1826-1828.
63. Cos. Westmeath, Wexford, Wicklow, 1708-1738.
64. Cos. Wicklow, Waterford, 1739-1810.
65. Co. Wexford, 1739-1810.
66. Co. Westmeath, 1739-1810.
67. Cos. Wexford, Wicklow, 1811-1820.
68. Co. Westmeath, 1811-1820.
69. Athlone, Mullingar, 1821-1825.
70. Cos. Westmeath, Wexford, Wicklow, 1825.
71. Cos. Louth, Meath, Leix, 1708-1738.
72. Co. Meath, 1739-1810.
73. Co. Louth, 1738-1810.
74. Cos. Carlow, Louth, Meath, Leix, 1821-25.
75. Cos. Meath, Louth, Leix, 1826-1878.
76. Co. Limerick, 1739-1810.
77. Cos. Armagh, Cavan, 1811-1820.
78. Cos. Antrim, Armagh, 1821-25.
79. Cos. Armagh, Antrim, 1826-28.
80. City of Cork, 1739-1779.
81. Co. Carlow, 1811-1820.
82. Cos. Cavan, Donegal, Down, 1707-1738.
83. City of Cork, 1779-1810.
84. Cities Limerick, Waterford, Derry, 1811-1820.
85. Cities Waterford, Drogheda, Limerick, 1821-25.
86. Cities Kilkenny, Waterford, Derry, 1826-28
87. City of Dublin, 1708-1738.
88. City of Dublin, A-J, 1739-1799.
89. City of Dublin, K-Z, 1739-1799.
90. City of Dublin, A-J, 1780-1792.
91. City of Dublin, K-Z, 1780-1792.
92. City of Dublin, 1793-1806.
93. City of Dublin, 1807-1819.
94. City of Dublin, 1820-1828.
95. Co. Antrim, 1828-1832.
96. Co. Armagh, 1828.
97. Co. Carlow, 1828-1832.
98. Co Cavan, 1828-1832.
99. Co. Clare, 1828-1832.
100. Co. Cork, 1828-1832.

## Representative Church Body Library

Extracts from the catalogue of manuscripts in the possession of the Representative Church Body Library prepared by Rev. Chancellor J.B. Leslie D. Litt. (O.) Original, otherwise copy. (C.) Copyright reserved.

Aghalow and Carnteel Parishes
  Religious Census, 1766, with names of house-holders, (Groves Tr.)
Ahoghill Religious Census, 1766
  With names of Dissenters, Papists & Church-people, (do.).
Ardagh Diocese
  Summary of Religious Census, 1766, some names given, (do.).
Ardbraccan Parish
  Religious Census, 1766, giving names of Protestants, (do).
Ardee Parish
  Religious Census, 1766, names, (do.).
Ardtrae Parish
  Religious Census, 1766, names by townlands, (do.).
Armagh County
  Hearth Money Return, 1640, of Lurgan, Derrynoose & Tynan, (do.).
Armagh Diocese
  Parliamentary Return re. Churches, 1768, (Groves Tr.).
  Religious Census of 1766 under Parishes, (do.).
  See Rent Rolls, 16th & 17th Cent., (Groves Tr.).
  Drogheda Rural Deanery Return, 1802.
Aughnamullen Parish
  Religious Census, 1766, by townland, (Groves Tr.).

Bagot Family, see Drury Papers.
Ballinlanders Marriage Register, 1852-77.
Ballyburr (Ossory)
  Tithe Composition Book, 1828, (O.).
Ballymakenny (Armagh)
  Religious Census, 1766, giving names (Groves Tr.).
Ballymodan (Cork)
  Copy Baptismal Registers 1695-1793, by Rev. W.W. Stewart.
Ballynascreen (Derry)
  Religious Census 1766, giving names of Protestants, (Groves Tr.).
Ballynaslaney, Co. Wexford
  Religious Census 1766, some names given, (Groves Tr.).
Beaulieu (Armagh)
  Religious Census 1766, with names, (Groves Tr.).
Boho (Clogher)
  Religious Census, 1766, with names, (Groves Tr.).

Bovevagh (Derry)
  Religious Census, 1766, names by townlands, (Groves Tr.).
Butler, Isaac
  1744 Journal, in Armagh Library, extracts re. Clergy, Monumental Inscriptions, & c., (Groves Tr.).

Carlingford (Armagh)
  Religious Census, 1766, names by townlands, (Groves Tr.).
Carte Papers
  Extracts showing the names of Clergy in Ireland 1647.
Cassidy, William
  Inscriptions on Tombstones in Lambeg Churchyard, (printed copy).
Castledawson (Derry)
  Religious Census, 1766, (in Ardtrea Lists, Groves Tr.).
Charlestown (Co. Louth)
  Religious Census, 1766, names, (Groves Tr.).
Clergy of Church of Ireland
  Biographical index by Canon J. B. Leslie. 4 volumes. (O.).
Clerical Obituaries
  18th Century, (Lodge MS. in Armagh Library).
Clonkeehan Parish, Co. Louth
  Religious Census, 1766, names. (Groves Tr.).
Clonmore (Ossory)
  Religious Census, 1766, two names & numbers, (Groves Tr.).
Cong (Tuam)
  Combined Register, 1745-1759, (O.).
Conor Diocese
  Parliamentary Return re. Churches, 1768, (Groves Tr.).
Cork Diocese
  Religious Census, 1766, (Groves Tr.).
Creggan (Armagh)
  MS. History of Parish by Rev. Samual Nelson, Presbyterian Minister.
Crumlin (Dublin)
  Religious Census, 1766, names of families (Groves Tr.).

Darver, Co. Louth
  Religious Census, 1766, names, (Groves Tr.).
Derry Diocese
  Parliamentary Returns 1768.
Derry Diocese
  Religious Census, 1766 by parishes, giving names of Church Clergy & other Ministers, (Groves Tr.).

Derryloran (Armagh)
list of Protestant Householders, 1740, from Hearth Money Return, (Groves Tr.).
Religious Census,1766, names by townlands, (Groves Tr.).

Derrynoose (Armagh)
List of Protestant Householders, 1740, (do.).

Derryvullen (Clogher)
Religious Census, 1766, names by townlands, (do.).

Desertcreat (Armagh)
List of Protestant Householders, 1740, (do.).

Desertmartin (Derry)
Religious Census, 1766, names of Protestants, Dissenters & Papists given.

Donaghcloney (Dromore)
Extracts from Parish Register, (Swanzy Collection).

Donaghmore (Armagh)
Copy of Parish Register with index, 1741-1825, made by Capt. Ynyr A. Burges, D.L.

Donnybrook Parish (Dublin)
Religious Census, 1766, summary by townlands, (Groves Tr.).

Drogheda Rural Deanery Return, 1802,
Dromiskin, Co. Louth
Religious Census, 1766, names, (Groves Tr.).

Dromore Diocese
Religious Census of Seapatrick, 1766, names & summary of other parishes (do.).

Drumachose (Derry)
Religious Census, 1766, names of Dissenting and Popish families, by townlands (Groves Tr.).

Drumglass, Armagh
Religious Census, 1766, names by townlands, (do.).
Extracts from Parish Register, 1685-1799.

Drury Family Papers
Including entries from Parish Registers of Ballysonnan, Durrow, Fountstown, Nurney, re. Baggot, Gatchell, Harte, Hoysted, Kelly, Phillips, Stack & Toomey families, and biographical notices of 24 clergy.

Dublin Diocese
Grant Book, 1660-97, Calendar of, (C.), (Leslie Collection from Records lost in P.R.O.).
Twenty one Marriage Licences early 18th Cent. St. Mary's Parish, and Arklow. Memoranda & Plea Rolls, 1464-1546, extracts. Religious Census, 1766, summaries by Parishes.

Duganstown Churchyard
Plan of same made by Prof. Stanley Lane Poole, with names of families buried, 1643-1908.

Dunleer Parish Register (now lost)
Extracts from, (Swanzy Collection).

Durrow (Ossory)
Parish Registers (lost), extracts copied by late Canon P.B. Wills.

Edermine (Ferns)
Religious Census, 1766, names of Protestant families, (Groves Tr.).

Eglish (Armagh), Parish Registers 1803-1935.

Ematris (Clogher)
Religious Census, 1766, by townlands, (Groves Tr.).

Great Connell (Kildare)
Tithe Composition Book, 1833, (O.).

Groves Transcripts of Hearth Money Returns, 1740, 1766, & Subsidy Roll, 1634, made by Tenison Groves, B.E., fully indexed, bound in 1 vol., 4to.

Hearth Money Returns
1664-5, 1740 & 1764, indexed under Dioceses & Parishes.

Kilbroney (Dromore)
Religious Census, 1766, names, (Groves Tr.).

Kildemock (Co. Louth)
Religious Census, 1766, with names, (Groves Tr.).

Kildress (Armagh)
Religious Census, 1766, names by Townlands, (do.).

Killaloe
Bp. Worth's Account Book of the Diocese 1661, considerable information about Clare families. (O.).

Killeagh Parish Register
Extracts from (Swanzy Collection.)

Kilmore Diocese
Parish Register of Kilmore, Co. Cavan, extracts from, 1705-1875.
Religious Census, 1766, summary of Parishes, (Groves Tr.).

Kilrush (Killaloe)
Parish Registers, 1741-1841. (O.).

Kilshanning Church and Churchyard, Co. Cork
Copy of Inscriptions in (Swanzy Collection).

Kinawley (Kilmore)
Religious Census, 1766, names of Protestants, (Groves Tr.).

La Touche Family
genealogy (MS copy of printed work).

Leck (Derry)
Religious Census, 1766, names by townlands, (Groves Tr.).

Long MSS.
Deeds & old newspapers deposited by late Mrs. Long of St. Michan's, Dublin.

Lurgan (Kilmore)
Religious Census, 1766, names of Protestant families, (Groves Tr.).

Magharafelt (Armagh)
Religious Census, 1766, with names, (Groves Tr.).

Midleton (Cork)
Parish Register (lost), extracts from, (Swanzy Collection).

Militia Chaplains in 1761 (Groves Tr.)
Modreeney Tithe Payers
    1839. (O.).
Monaghan
    Religious Census, 1766, by townlands,
    (Groves Tr.).
Mullabrack Marriage Register
    1767-1811

Newtownhamilton
    Baptismal Register 1823-26 (typed copy).

Offerlane Tithe Composition Book
    1828. (O. in Ossory Collection).
Omeath, Co. Louth
    Copy of Parish Register, 1845-1936, by Rev.
    E.G. Ward, M.A.
Ossory Grant Book
    Marriage Licences, 1738-1804.

Philipstown, Co. Louth
    Religious Census, 1766, names, (Groves Tr.).
Preban (Ferns)
    Tithe Composition book, 1824.

Raphoe Diocese
    Religious Census, 1766, with names of Clergy
    & Summary, (Groves Tr.).

St. Peter's, Dublin
    Marriage Licences, 1787-1824.
Seapatrick (Connor)
    Religious Census, 1766, names, (Groves T.r).
Seaver Pedigree, in Swanzy Collection.

Shankill (Lurgan)
    Dromore Diocese:-
    (1) Protestant Householders, 1740, (Groves
    Tr.).
    (2) Subsidy Roll 1634, names by townlands.
Shanlis, Co. Louth
    Religious Census, 1766, (Groves Tr.).
Shrule, Co. Longford
    List of Protestant Parishioners, 1731,
Shrule (Ardagh)
    Religious Census, 1766, (Groves Tr.).
Smarmore, Co. Louth
    Religious Census, 1766, names, (Groves Tr.).
Stickillen, Co. Louth
    Religious Census, 1766, names, (Groves Tr.).
Swanzy Collection
Transcripts & c., made by late Very Rev. H.B.
Swanzy, M.A., M.R.I.A., Dean of Dromore,
including:-
    (I) Chancery Bills, 1667-1839, names of
    Parties, 1 vol.
    (II) Chancery & Exchequer Bills, surnames of
    3 vols.
    (III) Down & Connor, First Fruit Returns,
    1675-9.
    (IV) Exchequer Bills, 1676-1834, names of
    Parties 1 vol.
    (V) Prerogative Marriage Licences A to D,
    list of, 2 notebooks.
    (VI) Registry of Deeds, extracts with Index of
    names 1 vol.
    (VII) Wills, 800 summaries, typed in diction-
    ary order.

## National Library of Ireland

Pedigrees of Irish Families
    by Madden and Betham. M.110.
Nugent and Dillon family notes. M.122
Magee genealogies (extensive). M.127.
Book of Irish Felonies. M.1597.
Dodwell-Brown Diary, 1788, M.1597.
Convict Register, 19th century. M.3016.
Mayo Co. Stafford Survey (copy) M.5160.
Clonmel assises
    17th and 18th centuries, 2 vols. M.4908-9.
Bulmer family chronicle. M.5220.
Limerick Co. estate maps, 1747, M.1790.
Dublin guilds, history, (Evans), M.738
Society of Friends Minutes 1673-1708, M.94.
Derry, Book of Plantation, 1609, M.27.
Tipperary Co. 'Down Survey', 1655-56. M.95.
Nugent Pedigrees. M.126.
Wills and Administrations, 1632-1894, 2 vols.
    M.142-3.

Leitrim estate rental, 1844. M.179.
Longford Co., Cromwellian Settlement, M.768.
Dublin voters lists, 1832, M.783.
Meath Co., Freeholders list, c. 1775, M.788.
De Angelo (Nangle) Family Pedigree
    Also Nagle, Peppard, Jordan, Costello. M.475.
Ballymodan, Bandon, Co. Cork
    History (Knox) 1834. M.675.
Lenihan family history book. M.763.
Down Co., Estate rolls, 18th century. M.784.
Donegal, Poll of Electors, 1761, M.787.
Loughrea, Co. Galway
    Town Rate book, 1854, 1887. M.92.
Cork & Tipperary Cos.
    Statistical survey 18th, 19th centuries. M.96.
Limerick, city assembly book
    18th century. M.89.
Cusack family history, (extensive). M.2116.
Wexford, Quit Rents, early date. M.1782.

## Presbyterian Historical Society

Adair Narrative
Progress of Pres. Ch. in Ireland (1623-1670).

Aghadowney, Co. Derry
Commonplace Book, Rev. J. McGregor.

Antrim Book by Rev. R. Magill
Bapt. and Marr. Regs. for parish Millrow, Co. Antrim, 1820-39.

Antrim County
Hearth Money Rolls, 1669, transcript copy. Protestant householders, 1740, transcript copy.

Antrim Town
Bapt. and Marr. Regs. 1674-1736.

Army lists, 1642.

Armagh Town
Bapt. and Marr. Regs. 1707-1728, 1796-1808. Aughnacloy, Co. Tyrone: Committee Book, 1743-82.

Ballina, Co. Mayo
Subscription list for erection of church at Ballina, 1849.

Ballymoney, Co. Antrim: Bapt. Reg. from 1817.

Banbridge, Co. Down: Marr. Reg. 1753-1794.

Bangor, Co. Down
Marr. Reg. from 1808 and outline history of congregation.

Belfast
Rosemary St. Ch. Bapt. Reg. from 1722.

Campbell Mss.
Campbell genealogical table by Dr. Campbell.

Carnmoney, Co. Antrim
Bapt. Reg. from 1708, Marr. Reg. from 1708, also memoranda and session books containing Bapt. and Marr. Registers from 1776.

Carrigart, Co. Donegal
Bapt. Reg. 1844-84 with history of congregation by Rev. Francis McClure.

Castledawson and Magerafelt, Co. Derry
Registers and session books, some very early.

Castlereagh, Co. Down
Bapt. Reg. from 1809, Marr. from 1816.

Coleraine, Co. Derry
Meeting house account book, 1802-35, Marr. Regs. 1809-1840.

Cullybackey, Co. Antrim: Bapt. Reg. from 1812.

Down County — Subsidy Roll, 1663.

Drumual, Randalstown, Co. Antrim
List of seat holders 1842.

Drumbo, Co. Down
Bapt. Regs. from 1764, Marr. from 1787.

Dublin (Abbey Church)
Bapt. Regs. from 1779, Marr. from 1805.

Derry County
List of Protestant householders, 1740.

Dissenters lists 1704-1782
1775 list very comprehensive. Donegal County — Hearth Money Rolls, 1669.

Derryvalley, Co. Monaghan: Bapts. from 1816.

Donegore, Co. Antrim
Bapts. and Marr. from 1806.

Dromara, Co. Down — Marr. from 1817.

Donacloney, Co. Down — Bapts. from 1798.

Derry County — Hearth Money Rolls, 1663.

Dundalk, Co. Louth
Bapt. and Marr. Regs. from 1819.

Dungannon, Co. Tyrone
Bapt. and Marr. from 1790.

Enniskillen, Co. Fermanagh
Marr. Reg. from 1819.

Fourtowns, Co. Down
Notices of Marriages 1845-61.

Frankford of Castleblaney, Co. Monaghan
Marr. Reg. 1820-34.

Gervagh, Co Derry
Bapt. and Marr. Regs. from 1795.

Hamilton Estate — Rent Rolls, 1670
With lists of tenant holders in parishes of Bangor, Holywood, Dundonald, Ballywalter and Killyleagh, Co. Down.

Killeshandra, Co. Cavan
Bapt. and Marr. Regs. from about 1740.

Killyleigh, Co. Down
Transcript copy Regs., from c. 1692.

Larne, Co. Antrim, poll list 1833.

Lisburn
Bapt. Regs. from 1692, Marr. from 1688.

Lurgan, Co. Armagh: Bapt. Regs. from 1746.

Maghera
Sketch of its history by Rev. R.L. Marshall.

Muster Rolls 1631.

Mountmellick, Co. Laois
Regs., history, statistics, bapt. 1849-96.

Rathfriland, Co. Down
Marr. Regs. from 1763, bapt. from 1804.

Reid Mss.
Misc. papers relating to Irish affairs and history of Pres. Ch. in Ireland.

Rowan — Genealogical tree from 1660.

Scarva, Co. Down
Bapt. Reg. 1807-34, Marr. Reg. 1825-45.

Templepatrick
Session book 1688-97 with names of donors.

Tyrone County
Hearth Money Rolls, 1666.

Ulster Plantation
List of Scottish Freeholders, notes on the plantation of Ulster.

Waterford
Bapt. Reg. 1770, Marr. Reg. from 1761.

Workman
History of the Workman family of Belfast by Rev. A. Rose, 1920.

Wills
Copies of certain wills from originals in P.R.O. Dublin by Rev. J.E. Boggis.

Copy of Mulligan Wills, Diocese of Conor, 18th century.

Copy of will of Thomas Fulton, of Co. Derry, 1688.

# Genealogical Office, Dublin.

Kings, Princes, Chieftains.....
A book of pedigrees and notes on Gaelic families including O'Brien, O'Connor, O'Melaghlin, MacMurrough, O'Neill, O'Donnell, Mac Donlevy, MacLoughlin, O'Carroll, MacCarthy, MacDermott, O'Phelan, O'Farrell, Magennis, Maguire, O'Kelly, O'Moore, O'Reilly, O'Rourke, O'Sullivan, Brennan, Callaghan, O'Donoghue, O'Donavan, O'Gorman, Murphy, O'Shea, O'Toole, Fox and Fitzgibbon. M.610.

Prerogative marriage licences, 1600-1800 M.605-607.

Limerick freeholders with extact addresses and occupations, 1829. M.623.

Genealogical collections
A book of pedigrees, families include Cusack, Dillon, Lee, Sarsfield, Redmond, Arthur, Mac Cartney, Taaffe, Mitchell, French, Hamilton, Gravett, Butler, Armstrong, Birchenshaw, Griffith, Bathe, St. John, Beckford, Cambell, Tuite. M.540.

The Palatines.....
A book of notes on the German colony in Co. Limerick. M.540.

Obituaries from newspapers, Mainly 17th, 18th centuries. M.546-551.

Co. Down wills, 1646-1858. M.472.

Kilkenny, Tipperary, Limerick families
Pedigrees and notes — Andrews, Baker, Brereton, Briscoe, Cave, Cochrane, Comerford, Dodwell, Drew, Eaton, Elliot, George, Greene, Haughton, Hoare, Holmes, Langley, Lewis, Lloyd, Nelligan, Nixon, Osborne, Pigott, Rothe, St. Leger, Southwell, Sweetman, Walker, Walsh, Wheeler, Whitehall, Wilson. M.708.

Wills
Abstracts from prerogative wills of Ireland by Sir William Betham, very extensive, 17th, 18th, 19th centuries. M.223-256.

Freeholders
Co. Clare, 1829; Queen's County, 1758; Kilkenny, 1775; Donegal, 1761; Fermanagh, 1788; Meath, 1775; Roscommon, 1780; Tipperary, 1775; Longford, 1836; Armagh (Poll Book), 1753; Westmeath (Poll Book), 1761. M.442-444.

Genealogies and Pedigrees
Book of the genealogies and pedigrees of the following families — Armit, Brabazon, Benn, Bowen, Bray, Bloomfield, Beatty, Carney, Cuthbert, Cox, Cain, Dorman, D'Olier, Davys, Erck, Eager, Edgeworth, Fleming, Ford, Gregg, Gahan, Gamble, Greene, Gilbert, Goslin, Hearn, Humphry, Henchy, Hatch, Hendrick, Jones, Lloyd,

Little, Latham, Loughnan, Lambert, McGusty, Meadows, Mason, Manley, Noy, Parsons, Purcell, Preston, Pim, Redmond, Ridgeway, Rowan, Smith, Sloan, Talbot, Wilson, Wallis, Walker, Wall. M.384.

Funeral books
Arms and genealogies of thousands of families, mainly 16th, 17th centuries. M.64-79.

Directories for year 1809
Covering the following towns — Belfast, Cork, Waterford, Limerick. M.542.

Freemen, roll for city of Dublin, 1468-1744.

Louth county poll tax, 17th century
Transplantation lists, 1656
Book of postings and sales, 1703
Book of survey and distribution, 1659
Grand Jury members, 1861, 1879. M.541.

Religious census 1766
Returns for over sixty parishes in various counties. M.536-537.

Ossory (mainly Co, Kilkenny)
Marriage licence bonds index, mainly 17th and 18th centuries. M.612-617.

Pedigrees of O'Dwyer, Grace, Heard, Cummins, Power, Slack. M.412.

Grants of arms etc. from 1552;
Card index in office.

Walker pedigree
With tabulated pedigrees of associated families — Cooper, Sisson, Turner, Crampton, Marsh, Wall, Roper, Thompson, Garston, Digby, French, Verner, Jervis, Meredyth, Ribton, Sale. M.505.

Linea Antiqua (Roger O'Ferrall)
Original plus copy in three volumes by Sir William Betham, most extensive work containing genealogies and arms of Irish families.

Book of wills, pedigrees, notes etc.
On the following — Farmer, Gamble, Nicholls, St. Leger, Weekes, Purdon, Leader, Donovan, Chinnery, Jephson, Aldworth, North, Hansard, Llyod. M.523-524.

Dublin marriage licences
With dates and places of marriage, mainly 17th and 18th century. M.473-5.

Anglo-Irish families
Short pedigrees based on wills (originals destroyed), about 3,000 families, 16th, 17th, 18th centuries. M.215-219.

Crown Jewels

Report of the commission into disappearance of Irish crown jewels from Dublin Castle, 1907. M.507.

Book of genealogies

Several families including — Rodgers, Esmonde, Codde, Phaire, Hill, Jacob, Symes, Newton, King, Naper, Redmond, Moore. M.279.

Gordon family, extensive history, biography, notes. M.702.

Militia lists, 1761

Covering the following counties — Limerick, Cork, Tipperary, Kerry, Derry, Louth, Wicklow, Monaghan, Roscommon, Down, Donegal, Dublin, Tyrone. M.680.

Butler of Ormond

Memoirs and commentary. M.711.

Army lists, 1746-1772   Reviews at Tullamore, 1770; Dublin, 1771; Bandon, 1769; Cork, 1772; Drogheda, 1770; Birr, 1769; Thurles, 1772; Galway, 1771; Gort, 1769; Athlone, 1770. M.579.

Notices and wills of -

Blain, Nixon, Gaven, Bowyer, Rolleston, Spunner, Bingham, Becher, Martin, Brett, Orr. M.520.

Blennerhasset pedigree

15th C. onwards, with allied families — Bayley, Conway, Herbert, Peppard, Lacy, Babington, Brown, Spring. M.562.

Davys, Co. Longford, notes and history. M.653.

Donnellan family, family tree, 1500-1900. M.467.

# Pedigrees in Printed Books

Printed pedigrees relating to Irish Families from Burke's Colonial Gentry and pedigrees from notes in Lodge's Peerage.

| | |
|---|---|
| Agnew | Donegore, B.C.G., 592 |
| Alcock | Wilton, Co. Wexford, Ir.B., 1888 |
| Alen | St. Wolstan's, Kild.J., IV., 95 |
| Archdall | Castle Archdall, Fermanagh, L.P. III., 280 |
| Armstrong | King's County, Kild.J. III., 160. |
| Aungier | Cambridge, L,P. III., 377 |
| Aylmer | Balrath, Meath, B.C.G., 754 |
| | Donadea, Kild.J. III., 178 |
| Bagot | Nurney, Kild.J. VII., 317 |
| Barnewall | Bt. Crickstown, Meath, L.P. V., 30 |
| | Rowstown, L.P. V., 35 |
| Barron | Ballyneal Waterford, B.C.G., 708 |
| Barry | Knt. Santry, The Rock, Cork, L.P. VI., 303, |
| Barton | Straffan, Kild.J. IV., 112 |
| Bealing | Knt. Tirrelstown, Dublin, L.P. I., 67 |
| Bellew | Bellewstown, KIld.J. VII., 250 |
| Bernard | Castle Mahon, Cork, L.P. V., 152 |
| Blake | Corbally, Galway, B.C.G., 413 |
| Bolton | Brazeel, Dublin, L.P. V., 141 |
| Borrows | Bt. L.P. I., 103 |
| Bowen | Ballyadams, Queen's Co., Kild.J. VII., 3 & B.C.G., 511 |
| Boyd | Mayo, B.C.G., 511 |
| Brabazon | L.P. II., 271 |
| Bradstreet | Bt. L.P. IV., 75 |
| Brook | Knt. Magherabeg, Donegal, L.P. VI., 35 |
| Browne | Bt. Kenmare, L.P. VII., 57 |
| Bulkely | Old Bawn, Kild.J. VII., 223 |
| Burton | Burton Hall, Carlow, L.P. VII., 176 |
| Butler | Grantstown, Tipperary, L.P. IV., 29 |
| | Kilcash, L.P. IV., 28-40 |
| | Nodstown, L.P. IV., 28 |
| | Roscrea and Cloughgrennan, L.P. IV., 26 |
| Chadwick | Ballinard, B.C.G., 586 |
| Chetwood | Woodbrook, Kild.J. IX., 226 |
| Clayton | Moyallo, Cork, L.P. II., 247 |
| Clibborn | Moate, Westmeath, B.C.G., 72 |
| Connolly | Castletown, L.P. VII, 184 |

| | |
|---|---|
| Cooke | Cookesborough, Co. Westmeath, Ir.B., 1888 |
| Corry | L.P. II., 194 |
| Cosby | Stradbally, Kild.J. V., 317 |
| Cramer | Ballyfoile, L.P. II., 400 |
| Crofton | Bt. Moate Park, Roscommon, L.P. VII., 252 |
| Cruise | Grallagh, L.P. IV., 309 |
| Cudmore | Limerick, B.C.G., 674 |
| Daly | Carrownekelly, Galway, L.P. III., 396 |
| | Galway, B.C.G., 492 |
| Davis | Carrickfergus, L.P. II., 150 |
| Dawson | New Forest, Tipperary, L.P. VI., 79 |
| Deane | Crumlin, Dublin, L.P. II., 364 |
| D'Arcy | L.P. I., 121 |
| | Ireland, B.C.G., 459 |
| Darley | Dublin, B.C.G., 514 |
| Denny | Tralee, L.P. I., 298 |
| Dering | L.P. I., 316 |
| Dever | Ballyshannon, B.C.G., 291 |
| Dillon | Ardnegragh, L.P. IV., 175 |
| | Balgeeth, L.P. IV., 143 |
| | Drumraney, L.P. IV., 171 |
| | Huntstown, Dublin, L.P. IV., 144 |
| | Lismullen, Meath, L.P. IV., 147 |
| | Newtown, Meath, L.P. IV., 154 |
| | Riverstown, Meath, L.P. IV., 142 |
| | Trinity Island,Cavan, L.P. IV., 160 |
| | Knt. Proudstown, L.P. IV., 138 |
| Dixon | Kilkea, Co.Kildare, Kild.J. IX., 392 |
| Donne | Picton, L.P. IV., 96 |
| Dowdall | Knt. Kilfinny, Limerick, L.P. IV., 16 |
| Doyne | Wells, Co.Wexford, Ir.B., 1890 |
| Eastwood | Castletown, Co.Louth, Ir.B., 1888 |
| Edgeworth | Longford, B.C.G., 745 |
| Elwood | Dublin, L.P. VII., 201 |
| Eustace | Clongowes wood, Kild.J. III., 210 |
| | (Viscount) Baltinglass, Kild.J. V., 395 |
| | Craddockstown, Kild.J. V., 44 |
| | Harristown, Kild.J. V., 406 |
| | Coghlanstown, Kild.J. VII., 302 |
| Fagan | Feltrim, Co.Dublin, Ir.B., 1888 |
| Falkiner | Abbotstown, Kild.J. VIII., 331 |

| | |
|---|---|
| Fanshaw | Ware Park, Herts., L.P. IV., 276 |
| Fenton | Bt. Mitchelstown, Cork, L.P. IV., 228 |
| Fitzgerald | Ballyshannon, Kild.J. III., 426 |
| | Belan, Kild.J. V., 241 |
| | Castle Dodd, Cork, L.P. II., 238 |
| | Glassealy, Kild.J. V., 85 |
| | Leixlip, Kild.J. V., 149 |
| | Morett, Kild.J. IV., 289 |
| | Rathagan, Kild.J. V., 151 |
| Fleming | Staholmoc, Meath, L.P. VI., 311 |
| Forrest | Dublin, B.C.G., 746 |
| Foster | Dunleer, Louth, L.P. III., 361 |
| | Louth, B.C.G., 57 |
| Fownes | Woodstock, Kilkenny, L.P. II., 280 |
| Fox | Gragie, Tipperary, L.P. VI., 311 |
| Freke | Bt. Castle Freke, Cork, L.P. IV., 169 |
| French | Frenchpark, L.P. III., 113 |
| Fuller | Kerry, B.C.G., 655 |
| Fulton | Bellasize, Antrim, B.C.G., 714 |
| | Lisburn, B.C.G., 338 |
| Giffard | Castle Jordan, King's County, Ir.B., 1890 |
| Gore | Barrowmount, Kilkenny, L.P. III., 115 |
| | Clonrone, Clare, L.P. III., 113 |
| Gorges | Somerset House, Derry, L.P. VI., 312 |
| Grattan | Co.Cavan, Ir.B., 1888 |
| Gresson | Swanlinbar,Cavan, B.C.G., 705 |
| Hamilton | L.P. III., 5 |
| | Bangor, L.P. III., 9 |
| | Caledon, L.P. I., 197 |
| | Keelagh, Cavan, L.P. VI. |
| | Monella, Armagh, L.P. I., 270 |
| | Glenawley, L.P. II., 300 |
| Harman | Newcastle, Longford, L.P. III., 237 |
| Hanon | Pirton, Hereford, L.P. II., 391 |
| Hartpole | Shrule, Kild.J. VI., 301 |
| Hearn | Correagh, Westmeath, B.C.G., 107 |
| Henry | Lodge Park, Kild.J. II., 388 |
| Hill | Knt. Hounston, Somerset, L.P. II., 211 |
| Hone | Dublin, Ir.B., 1888 |
| Hore | Harperstown, Wexford, L.P. III., 122 |
| Hort | Hortland, Kild.J. VII., 207 |
| | Hortland, Kildare, L.P. II., 204 |
| Houghton | Kilmannock, Co.Wexford, Ir.B., 1888 |
| Hume | Bt. Castle Hume, Fermanagh, L.P. II., 112 |
| Hungerford | The Island, Cork, B.C.G., 858 |
| Hussey | Knt. Doddlington Pigot, Lincoln L.P. VII., 232. |
| | Baron, Galtrim, L.P. VII., 45 |
| Jackson | Kilmore, Monaghan, B.C.G., 434 |

| | |
|---|---|
| Jacob | Bt. Bromley, Middlesex, L.P. I., 302 |
| Jones | Headford, Co. Leitrim, Ir.B., 1888 |
| | Wexford, Kild.J. III., 469 |
| | Obertstown, Co.Kildare, L.P. II., 395 Ir.B., 1888 |
| Kavanagh | Co. Kildare, Kild.J. V., 358 |
| Keating | Narraghmore, Kild.J. VII., 410 |
| Kennedy | Camus, Derry, B.C.G., 280 |
| Kerdiff | Kerdiffstown, Kild.J. VII., 184 |
| Kirkpatrick | Clonsilla, Dublin, B.C.G., 280 |
| | Dublin & Co.Kildare, Ir.B. , 1888 |
| Lattin | Morristown, Kild.J. III., 190 |
| La Touche | L.P. II., 402 |
| | Dublin, Kild.J. VIII., 174 |
| Lee | Lee, L.P. IV., 197 |
| Lefoy | Carrigglass, Longford, B.C.G., 646 |
| Legge | Tipperary, B.C.G., 357 |
| Leslie | Bishop, L.P. VII., 179 |
| | Tarbert, Co.Kerry, Ir.B., 1890 |
| Lightburne | Co. Meath, Ir.B., 1888 |
| Lismore | Lord. Refer to O'Callaghan, Ir.B., 1890 |
| Litton | Dublin, B.C.G., 614 |
| Lowther | Kilrue, Meath, L.P. II., 301 |
| Ludlow | Earl Ludlow, Ir.B., 1890 |
| Lye | Clonaugh, Kild.J. II., 354 |
| Lynch | The Knock, Kild.J. VI., 265 |
| Macartney | Lish, Armagh, B.C.G., 472 |
| McDonnell | Antrim, Kild.J. IX., 325 |
| | Tinnakill, Kild.J. IV., 208 |
| Madden | Cork, B.C.G., 610 |
| Magrath | Archbishop of Cashel, Kild.J. VII., 15 |
| Mahon | L.P. VI., 317 |
| Marley | Crevagh, Leitrim, L.P. VI., 303 |
| Martin | Bishop, L.P. V., 22 |
| | Galway, B.C.G., 812 |
| Marward | Baron of Skryne, L.P. VI., 186 |
| Minchin | Tipperary, B.C.G., 352 |
| Molesworth | B.C.G., 67 |
| Molyneux | Bt. Dublin, L.P. VI., 86 |
| Monck | St.Stephen's Green, L.P. V., 138 |
| Montgomery | Killaghter, B.C.G., 460 |
| Moore | Knt. Croghan, King's Co., L.P. II., 84 |
| | Ballymacarne, Cavan, B.C.G., 318 |
| | Rhoddens, B.C.G., 489 |
| | Roscarbery, Cork, L.P. VI., 256 |
| Morgan | Cotletstown, Sligo, L.P. VI., 303 |
| | Co. Limerick, Ir.B., 1888 |
| Myhill | Killarney, Kilkenny, L.P. VII., 269 |
| Nugent | Bracklin, L.P. I., 217 |
| | Culvin, L.P. I., 217 |
| O'Callaghan | Lord Lismore, Ir.B., 1890 |
| O'Carroll | Ely O'Carroll, Kild.J. V., 142 |

O'Connor   Leixlip, Kild.J. VI., 241
Offaly, Kild.J. V., 142
Kerry, B.C.G., 381

O'Dempsey   Viscount Clanmalier, Kild. J. II., 421

Ogle   L.P. IV., 129 O'Halloran
Limerick, B.C.G., 81

O'Kelly   Cadamstown, Kild.J. II., 450
O'Loghlen   Port, Clare, B.C.G., 155
O'More   Leix, Kild.J. VI., 88
Ballyna, Kild.J. IX., 377
O'Neill   The Fews, Kild.J. IX., 325
Orpen   Kerry, B.C.G., 401
Osborne   Ballyntayler, Waterford, L.P. VII., 70

O'Toole   Fercullen, Kild.J. VI., 137

Palmer   Kilkenny, B.C.G., 47
Pennefather   Cashel, Tipperary, L.P. II., 299
Perceval   Knightsbrook, Meath, L.P. II., 395
Percival   Meath, B.C.G., 817
Piers   Bt. Tristernagh, L.P. II., 201
Plunket   Knt. Bewley, L.P. VI., 162
Knt. Killeen, L.P. VI., 175
Knt. Kilsaran, L.P. VI., 164
Pole   Ballyfin, Queen's Co., L.P. III., 69
Ponsonby   Bishopscourt, Kild.J. VIII., 4
Pratt   Cabra, Kild.J. VII., 223
Prendergast   Tipperary, B.C.G., 773
Preston   Gormanstown, L.P. III., 75
Prior   Rathdowney, Queen's Co., B.C.G., 51

Reynell   Co.Westmeath, Ir.B., 1890
Rice   Mount Rice, Kildare, L.P. III., 203
Robinson   Dublin, Ir.B., 1888
Rosmead, Westmeath, B.C.G., 757
Rochfort   Carrick, L.P., 15
Rowan   Antrim, B.C.G., 594
Rowe   Hackney & Shacklewell, L.P. II., 331
Ryan   Kilgera, Kilkenny, B.C.G., 192
Ryves   Rathsallagh, Co.Wicklow, Ir.B., 1888

St. George   Bt. Carrick-on-Shannon, L.P. I., 114
Knt. Dunmore, Galway, L.P. III., 284
Sarsfield   Lucan, Kild.J. IV., 116
Saunders   Saunders' Court, Co. Wexford Ir.B., 1890
Saunders' Grove, Kild.J., IX., 125, 133
Shane   Bt. Kilmore & Bishopstown, L.P. I., 104
Shaw   Dublin, B.C.G., 456
Southwell   Knt. Mereworth, Kent., L.P. VI., 4
Woodrising, Norfolk, L.P. VI., 6
Barnham, L.P. VI., 14

Span   Longford, B.C.G., 745
Staunton   Galway, Ir.B., 1888
Stewart   Bt. Newtown Stewart, Tyrone, L.P. VI., 243
Stopford   Bishop, L.P. III., 121
Sutton   Castletown, Kild.J. II., 366

Talbot   Belgard, Kild.J. IV., 131
Carton, Kild.J. IV., 5
Taylor   Swords, Co. Dublin, Ir.B., 1888
Temple   Mount Temple, Westmeath, L.P. V., 234
Tennison   Donoughmore, Wicklow, B.C.G., 508
Tuite   Bt. Sonna, L.P. III., 25
Tynte   Ballycrenane, Kild.J, VIII., 223

Usher   Dublin, L.P. IV., 311
Ussher   Mt. Ussher, Co. Wicklow, Ir.B., 1888

Vernon   Clontarf, Dublin, B.C.G., 198
Vincent   Dublin, Kild.J. V., 79

Wall   Johnstown, Co.Wicklow, Kild.J. VI., 382
Warburton   Garryhinch, King's Co., B.C.G., 804
Waring   Pottlerath, Kilkenny, B.C.G., 757
Waterhouse   Castlewaterhouse, L.P. II., 391
Wemys   Knt. Danesfort, Co.Kilkenny, L.P. VI., 74
Danesfort, Co.Kilkenny, Ir.B., 1888
Wentworth   Fyanstown, Meath, B.C.G., 95
Wesley   Dangan, Meath, L.P. III., 67
Wheeler   Grenan, Kilkenny, L.P. II., 247
Whaley   Whaley Abbey, L.P. VI., 71
White   Pitchfordstown, Kildare, L.P. I., 48
Whyte   Leixlip, Kild.J. II., 397
Redhills, Cavan, L.P. II., 296
Williams   Lord, Thame, L.P. IV., 281
Wogan   Blackhall, Kild.J. III., 87
Rathcoffey, Kild. J.III., 79 V., 110
Wolfe   Kildare, B.C.G., 723
Worth   Rathfarnham, L.P. VI., 245
Dublin, Kild. J. VI., 233
Wilson   Ballycloughan, Antrim, B.C.G., 61
Scarr, Wexford, B.C.G., 662
Winter   Agher, Meath, B.C.G., 792
Wray   Castle Wray, B.C.G., 642
Wrixon   Ballybiblin. Cork, B.C.G., 143
Wybrants   Danesfort, Co.Kilkenny, Ir.B., 1888

## List of Pedigrees contained in *Visitation of Ireland*
### Edited by F. A. Crisp, privately printed, 1911

### Volume 1

Belmore, Earl of
Bowen-Colthurst
    of Oakgrove & Dripsey Castle, Co. Cork.
Burke of Elm Hall, Co. Tipperary.
Burtchaell of Brandondale, Co. Kerry.
Cooke-Trench of Millicent, Co. Kildare.
Cooper of Cooper Hill, Co. Limerick.
Drever
Gillman of Clonteadmore, Co. Cork.
Greene
    formerly of Greenville, Co. Kilkenny.
Greer of Sea Park
    Carrickfergus, Co. Antrim.
Greeves of Strandtown, Co. Down.
Hore of Pole Hore, Co. Wexford.
Jackson of Tighnabruaich
    Belfast, Co. Antrim.
Lowry of Pomeroy House, Co. Tyrone.
Macpherson, formerly of Londonderry.
Massey-Westropp of Attyflin.
O'Callaghan-Westropp of Maryfort.
Paterson, formerly of
    Plaister and Swillymount, Co. Donegal.
Powerscourt, Viscount.
Roberts of Glassenbury, Co. Kent, Britfields
    Town, Co. Cork, and of the City of Cork.
Somerville of Clermont, Co. Wicklow.
Stackpoole of Eden Vale, Co. Clare.
Stubbs of Danby, Co. Donegal.
Tuthill, formerly of Kilmore, Co. Limerick.
Vigors of Burgage, Co. Carlow.
Whitla of Ben Eadan, Co. Antrim.

### Volume 2

Ardilaun, Baron
Blood of Ballykilty, Co. Clare.
Butcher of Danesfort, Killarney, Co. Kerry.
Carroll
    of Hyde Park, and Carrollina, Co. Cork.
Chevenix-Trench, Archbishop of Dublin
Crawford
    of Stonewold, Ballyshannon, Co. Donegal.
Crozier of Gortra House, Co. Fer-managh.
Cullen of Corry, Co. Leitrim.
Grierson of Baldonell, Co. Dublin.
Guinness of Dublin.
Hudson-Kinahan of Glenville, Co. Cork.
Iveagh, Baron
Longworth-Dames of Greenhill, King's County.
Macartney
    formerly of Rosebrook, Co. Armagh.
Monck, Viscount
Montgomery of Grey Abbey, Co. Down.
Montgomery
    of New Park, Moville, Co. Donegal.

O'Connell
    of Lakeview and Ballybeggan, Co. Kerry.
Peacocke, Archbishop of Dublin.
Pigott of Tincurry, Co. Tipperary, and the Manor
    House, Dundrum, Co. Down.
Sharman-Crawford
    of Crawfordsburn and Rademon, Co. Down.
Stony of the Downs, Co. Wicklow.
Westropp of Ballyvolane, Co. Cork.
White of Lough Eske Castle, Co. Donegal.

### Volume 3

Alexander of Ahilly, Co. Donegal.
Ashtown, Baron
Ball
Barry of Sandville, Co. Limerick.
Bayly of Ballyarthur, Co. Wicklow.
Berry
    formerly of Eglish Castle, King's Co.
Clements of Ashfield Lodge, Co. Cavan.
Coote of Ballyfin, Queen's County.
Deane-Drake of Stokestown, Co. Wex-ford.
Filgate of Lissrenny, Co. Louth.
Galt of Ballysally, Co. Derry.
Grogan of Moyvore, Co. Westmeath & Ballyntyre
    Hall, Co. Dublin.
Harman
    of Palace and Carrigbyrne, Co. Wex-ford.
Hatton of Clonard, Co. Wexford.
Homan-Mulock of Bellair, King's County.
Hussey-Walsh
    of Cranagh and Mulhussey, Co. Roscommon.
Lefroy of Carrig-glas Manor, Co. Long-ford.
Leitrim, Earl of
L'Estrange of Moystown, King's County.
Mansergh of Grenane, Co. Tipperary.
Orpen-Palmer of Killowen, Co. Kerry.
Smyth of Ardmore, Co. Derry.
Vincent of Summerhill, Co. Clare.
Westropp of Fortanne, Co. Clare.
Wright, formerly of Golagh, Co. Monaghan.

### Volume 4

Annesley, Earl
Athlumney, Baron
Bewley
Blake of Corbally, Co. Galway.
Bowen of Bowen's Court, Co. Cork.
Cavan, Earl of
Casey of The Donaghies, Raheny, Co. Dublin.
Dillon, Viscount
Dillon, formerly of Rathmoyle, Co. Dublin.
Fuller of Glashmacree, Co. Kerry.
Gosford, Earl of
Greene
    of Milbrook and Hallahoise, Co. Kildare.

Heaton-Armstrong of Roscrea, King's County.
Kelly of Mucklon, Co. Galway, & Kilcash, Co.
    Roscommon.
Kirkpatrick of Mohill, Co. Leitrim.
Lyons of Old Park, Belfast, Co. Antrim.
Moloney of Cragg, Co. Clare.
Moore formerly of Kilcurry, Tagh-shinny, Co.
    Longford.
O'Donovan of Clan Cathal, Co. Cork.
O'Reilly, formerly of Baltrasna, Co. Meath.
Reeves of Besborough, Co. Clare.
Sandes of Greenville, Co Kerry.
Shackleton of Ballitore, Co. Kildare.
Swanzy of Newry, Co. Armagh. Wade of Clone-
    braney, Co. Meath.
West
Wicklow, Earl of
Wilson of Currygrane, Co. Longford.

**Volume 5**
Battersby of Loughbawn, Co. West-meath.
Bingham of Bingham Castle, Co. Mayo.
Borrowes of Gilltown, Co. Kildare, Baronet.
Bourke
Burke of Ballydugan, Co. Galway.
Crookshank
    of Drumhalry and Birrenagh, Co Longford.
De Burgh of Oldtown, Co. Kildare.
Delaney of Bagnalstown, Co. Carlow.
Edgeworth of Kilshrewly, Co. Long-ford.
Finny of Leixlip, Co. Kildare.
Guillamore, Viscount
Henn of Paradise Hill, Co. Clare.
Honan
Lucan, Earl of
Maturin and Maturin-Baird of Newtown Stewart,
    Co. Tyrone.
Morony of Odell Ville, Co. Limerick.
O'Connor of Rockfield, Co. Dublin.
O'Grady of Kilballyowen, Co. Limerick.
Persse
Sligo, Marquess of
Smythe of Barbavilla, Co. Westmeath.
Spedding of Ballynamudagh, Co. Wicklow.
Swanzy of Avelreagh, Co. Monaghan.
Taaffe of Smarmore, Co. Louth.
Talbot of Castle Talbot, Co. Wexford.
Uniacke.

**Volume 6**
Ashbourne, Baron
Barry of Castle Cor, Co. Cork.
Bellew, Baron
Boyle of Limavady, Co. Londonderry.
Brown (now Gardner-Brown)
Farran
Fox of Kilcoursey, King's County
    & Galtrim, Co. Meath.
Higginson of Lisburn, Co. Antrim.
Hurley, formerly of Bridge House, Co Kerry.
Inchiquin, Baron
Lecky of Beardiville, Co. Antrim.
Leslie of Glasslough, Co. Monaghan, Baronet.
Lisle, Baron.

M'Cance of Knocknagoney, Holywood.
M'Cance of Suffolk, Dunmurry, Co. Antrim.
Macauley
MacDermot of Coolavin, Co. Sligo.
Magee
Meadows of Thornville, Co. Wexford.
Morgan of Old Abbey, Co. Limerick.
Ogilby of Ardnargle, Limavady,
    & Pellipar, Dungiven, both Co. Londonderry.
Plummer
Scott of Castle House
    Lisburn, Co. Antrim, Baronet.
Shawe-Taylor of Castle Taylor, Co. Galway.
Westropp of Mellon, Co. Limerick.
Wilson of Daramona House, Co. Westmeath.
Wolseley of Mount Wolseley
    Co. Carlow, Baronet.

### The Irish Genealogist
Aylward of Ireland, Vol.4, No.3, 1970.
Birch family of Birchgrove, parish of Tullylish,
    Vol.3, No.5, 1960.
Boyle-Roche family pedigree, Vol.2, No.8, 1950.
Charleton of Clonmacnoise, Vol.4, No.2, 1969.
Conron family of Co. Cork, Vol.3, No.9, 1964.
Cusack family of Cos. Meath & Dublin, Vol. 6,
    No. 2, 1981.
Dillon family of Roscommon, Vol.2, No.12, 1955.
Elrington family of Ireland, Vol.1, No.9, 1941.
Goodall of Co. Wexford, Vol.3, No.12, 1967.
Grierson of Co. Meath, Vol.3, No.4, 1959.
Herrick family of Co. Cork, Vol.3, No.8, 1963.
Irwin of Roxborough, Co. Roscommon
    Vol.1, No.2, 1937.
Kavanagh 1400-1700, Vol.6, No.2, 1981.
Lambert of Brookhill, Co. Mayo
    Vol.3, No.10, 1965.
Lennon of Cloncullen, Co. Westmeath
    Vol.2, No.2, 1944.
Mulloy of Kells, Co. Meath, do.
Nicholson of Brickeen, Co. Sligo
    Vol.2, No.2, 1944.
Peyton of Co. Roscommon Vol.2, No.2, 1944.
Phibbs of Cos. Sligo and Leitrim
    Vol.2, No.2, 1944.
Wood of Co. Sligo, Vol.3, No.8, 1963.

### The Irish Ancestor
Bevan of Co. Limerick, Vol.6, No.1, 1974.
Blaney of Co. Armagh, Vol.3, No.1, 1971.
Brereton of Cos. Kildare and Carlow
    Vol.3, No.2, 1971.
Brewster of Co. Kerry, Vol.3, No.2, 1971.
Chinnery of Co. Cork, Vol.7, No.2, 1975.
Crone family of Co. Cork, Vol.1, No.2 1969.
Dexter of Dublin and Kildare
    Vol.2, No.1, 1970.
Hillas of Co. Sligo, Vol.4, No.1, 1972.
Odell of Co. Limerick, do.
O'Higgins of Ireland and Chile
    Vol.2, No.2, 1970.
Moncton of Co. Limerick, Vol.4, No.1, 1972.

# Published Family Histories

*Irish Families*

Dr. E. MacLysaght, Dublin, 1972. Articles on the 300 best known Irish names — Ahearn, Athy..... MacWard, Woulfe.

*More Irish Families*

Dr. E. MacLysaght, Dublin, 1982, history of more than 1,000 Irish families, companion volume to Irish Families above.

*Memoirs of the Archdales*

Henry Archdale, Enniskillen, 1925, pedigrees of the following — Archdale, Audley, Barrington, Blackwood, Damer, Dawson, Dunbar, Edwards, Gore, Humphreys, Mervyn, Montgomery, Porter, Price, Sexton, Stewart.

*Families of French and Nixon*

Henry B. Swanzy, 1908. Historical notes on the following families — French, Nixon, Erskine, Meade, Enery, Swanzy.

*An Account of the Families of Lennard and Barrett*

Thomas Barrett-Lennard, 1908, contains history of Lennard, Barrett, Fynese.

*History of the Warren Family: A.D. 912-1902*

Rev. Thomas Warren, 1982. A History and Genealogy of the Warren Family in Normandy, Great Britain and Ireland, France, Holland, Tuscany, United States of America, etc., with numerous family pedigrees.

*Umma - More: The Story of an Irish Family*

William Magan, 1983. History of Magan and allied families.

*Granuaile: The Life and Times of Grace O'Malley. c.1530-1603*

Anne Chambers, 1983. The story of Grace O'Malley with extensive history of the O'Malley clan.

*Roots in Ulster Soil*

T. H. Mullen, Belfast, 1967. Commentary on the following — Mullen, Barbour, Black, Forsythe, Wallace, Brown, Henderson, Anderson, Holdom.

*The Leslies and their Forebears*

Pierce Leslie Pielou, Dublin, 1935. Contains history of Leslie, Pielou and allied families.

*History of Maunsell or Mansel*

Robert G. Maunsell, Cork, 1903, genealogy of the following — Crayford, Gabbett, Knoyle, Persse, Toler, Waller, Warren, White, Winthrop.

*History of the County Dublin*

F. E. Ball, Dublin, 1902.

Vol 1. Families dealt with — Allen, Archibold, Bee, Byrne, Cheevers, Crehall, Bathe, Dungan, Espinasse, Fitzsimons, Goodman, Hacket, Jessop, Kennedy, Mapas, Plunkett, Proud, Powell, Pocklington, Talbot, Walsh, Watson.

Vol 2. Borr, Bret, Brigg, Burns, Cusack, Deane, Dobson, Downes, Harold, Loftus, Moenes, Ussher, Walsh, North.

Vol 3. Allen, Bulkelley, Clinch, Curran, Dawe, Domville, Howell, Preston, Purdon, Roberts, Russell, Taylor.

Vol 4. Annesley, Brereton, Browne, Carberry, Deane, Fagan, Finlay, Forster, Gallane, Harte, Luttrell, Miles, Molyneux, Says, Scurlock, Sedgrave, Slingsby, White, Wilkinson.

*History of Armstrong*

William R. Armstrong, Pittsburg, Pennsylvania, 1969, with accounts of the following — Stevenson, Bell, Johnston, Dunlap, Duncan, Browne.

*History of Clonmel*

William P. Burke, Waterford, 1907, with historical notes on — Alcocke, Bagwell, Baron, Brenock, Burke, Butler, Foley, Hamerton, Hely-Hutchinson, Leynagh, Moore, Osborne, Perry, Riall, Vaughan, Wall, White.

*The Book of McKee*

Raymond W. McKee, Dublin, 1959, with history of Mackey, O'Neill and McKee families.

*History and Genealogy of the Pomeroy family*

W. Pomeroy, U.S.A., 1958, contains genealogy of — Pomeroy, Holmes, Smyth, Gilbourne, Deane, Togwood.

*The Seagrave Family 1066-1935*

Charles W. Seagrave, London, 1936, with extensive history of Seagrave and allied families.

*Memorials of Adare Manor*

Earl of Dunraven, Oxford, 1865, contains pedigrees of — Edwin, O'Donovan, Quin, Scrope, Wyndham.

*History of the Town and County of Wexford*

Philip H. Hore, London, 1911, among the families treated — Kavanagh, Peppard, Devereux, Masterson, Codd, Wadding, Roche, O'Byrne, Kinselagh, Colclough, Cox, Meadows, Chambers, White, McCarte, MacMurrough, Anglesey, Harvey, Stafford, Harper.

*Pedigrees from Ulster*

R. M. Sibbett, Belfast, 1931. Families treated —Baird, Wauchop, Cochran, Gibson, Wasson.

*The Wrays of Donegal*

C. V. Trench, Oxford, 1945, with history of — Wray, Donnelley, Johnston, Waller, MacDaniel, Atkinson, Jackson.

*The History of the County of Monaghan*

E. P. Shirley, London, 1879, with notices and family trees of — MacKenna, Leslie, Ancketill, Dawson, Corry, Madden, Burnet, Cairns, Westerna, Lucas, Fleming, Foster, Owen, Montgomery, Blaney, Devereux, Shirley, Ferrer, Seymour, MacMahon.

*History of County Mayo*

Hubert T. Knox, Dublin, 1908, with genealogy tables of the following families — O'Connor, Donnell, McWilliams, Bourke, Gibbons, Walter, Barrett, Jordan, Costello, MacEvilly, Staunton.

*History and Topography of County Clare*

J. Frost, Dublin, 1883. Contains history of three hundred Clare families including, O'Davoren, O'Loughlin, O'Hynes, MacNamara, MacClancy, O'Grady, O'Dea, O'Griffin, O'Quin, MacBrody, MacGorman, MacCurtin, O'Brien, O'Connor.

*Three Hundred in Innishowen*

A. Young, Belfast, 1879, with pedigrees, trees, engravings, portraits, arms of Young, Hart, Harvey, Doherty, Knox, Montgomery, Cary, Davenport, Benson, Vaughan, Latham, MacLaughlin, Hamilton, Skipton, Richardson, Stuart, Gage, Boyd, Crofton, Day, Staveley, Laurence, Homan, ffolliott, Cuff, Synge, Nesbitt, Ball, Chichester, Smith, Ussher, Torrens.

*The Fermanagh Story*

Peter Livingstone, Enniskillen, 1969, with history of over three hundred County Fermanagh families — Aiken, Bannon, Breen..... Winslow.

*History and Antiquities of the Diocese of Kilmacduagh*

J. Fahy, Dublin, 1893, with history and legends of the following families — O'Connor, O'Loughlin, O'Daly, O'Shaughnessy, Burke.

*Annals of Westmeath*

James Woods, Dublin, 1907, with accounts of the following — Petit, Nugent, Delamer, Ledwith, Naper, O'Melaghlin, MacGeoghegan, Tyrrell, O'Connor, Malone, Piers, Tuite, de Lacy, Fenelon, Fallon.

*Blake Family Records*

Martin Blake, London, 1905, with genealogies and arms of the tribes of Galway:- Athy, Blake, Bodkin, Browne, D'arcy, Deane, Font, French, Joyce, Kirwan, Lynch, Martin, Morris, Skerritt.

*History of the Corry Family*

Earl of Belmore, London and Dublin, 1891. Contains historical notes on — Corry, Crawford, Johnston, Anketill, Meryvn, Leslie, Armour, Lowry, Eccles, Shepherd, Dawson.

*The Pooles of County Cork*

R. ffolliott, pr. pr., 1956, with history and anecdotes of — Poole, Bernard, Hungerford, Hewitt, Baldwin, Morris, Lackey, Barry, Townsend, Jellett, Morgan, Wynn, Waring, Lucas, Hayman, Holmes, Meade, Casey, Daunt, Nesbitt, Becher, Moore, Boyle, Somerville.

*The History of Sligo, Town and County*

O'Rorke, Dublin, n.d., with historical notes on — O'Hara, Filan, Jones, Fibbs, MacDonagh, O'Connor, Meredith, O'Gara, MacDermott, O'Dowd, MacDonnell, MacSweeney, Crofton, O'Rorke.

*History of Enniskillen*

W. C. Trimble, Enniskillen, 1921, with much genealogical information on the following — Frith, Gamble, Quinton, Kerr, Dundas, Edmonson, Crook, Walmsley, Whitten.

*The Ulster Clans*

T. H. Mullin, Belfast, 1966, contains extensive history of — O'Neill, MacLoughlin, O'Kane, McCloskey, O'Mullan, Magilligan, O'Mellan, O'Hagan, O'Quin.

*A Genealogical History of the Tyrrells*

Joseph H. Tyrrell, pr. pr., with chart pedigrees of the following — Ashe, Aylmer, Blood, Carlisle, de Clare, Edgeworth, Giffard, Hassard, Haughton, Head, Loftus, Longcake, Lucas, de Nogent, O'Reilly, Pilkington, Rochford, Sarsfield, Senlis, Tuite, Thompson, Warren.

*Old Kerry Records*

Mary A. Hickson, London, 1872, with notes on — Aylmer, Blennerhasset, Brown, Daly, Fagan, Gould, Hussey, Nagle, Sigerson, Skiddy, Tuohy, Wall.

*O'Kief Coshe Mang, Slieve Lougher and Upper Blackwater, Ireland*

Albert Casey, Alabama, U.S.A. A most extensive work running to 14 vols. on Cork and Kerry families, based on baptismal records, deeds, wills, gravestone inscriptions etc.

*History of Queen's County*

Daniel O'Byrne, Dublin, 1856. Contains a history of the ancient septs of that county — Brennan, Byrne, Delaney, Dempsey, Duff, Dunne, MacEvoy, Gorman, Fitzpatrick, Kelly, Lawlor, More.

*History and Antiquities of Kilkenny*

William Healy, Dublin, 1893, with histories of the following families — Archdeacon, Archer, Bryan, Butler, Blanchfield, Blake, Comerford, Dalton, Fitzgerald, Forstall, Grace, Lincoln, Leslie, O'Neil, St. Ledger, Lawless, Purcell, Ryan, Rochford, Shortal, Strange, Sweetman, Walsh.

*Ball Family Records*

William Ball Wright, York, 1908, with genealogical memoirs of — Ball, Blackall, Delahoyd, Feltus, Paumier, Wright.

### The Roll of the House of Lacy

de Lacy — Ballingari, Baltimore, 1928, with pedigrees, military memoirs and notices of the following families — Browne, Croke. Harnett, Odell, de Lacy, Naughton/Norton.

### The History of the Moore Family

Countess of Drogheda, Dublin, 1906, contains chart pedigrees of — Moore, Clifford, Loftus.

### History of Ely O'Carroll etc.,

John Gleeson, Dublin, 1915. Contains much information on north Munster families including O'Carroll, O'Meagher, Ryan, Kennedy, Butler, Hogan, MacEgan, O'Meara, Jordan, Foyle and Fitzpatrick.

### The Barringtons

Amy Barrington, Dublin, 1917. Contains pedigrees of the following families — Barrington, Bewley, Malone, Shackleton, Mark, Strangman, Pim, Wakefield, Grubb, Abraham, Leadbeater and Carleton.

### Memoirs of the Binghams

Rose McCalmont, London, 1915, with notices of - Bingham, Ramsey, Carden, Mills, Yelverton, Wake, Trenchard.

### The Tiernan and other Families

Charles B. Tiernan, Baltimore, 1901, with genealogy of the following — Tiernan, Somerville, Bolling and Bernard.

### Vicissitudes of Families

Bernard Burke, London, 1896, with commentary on several families including — Percy, Neville, Cromwell, Stuart, O'Neill, de Vere, Doddington, Lindsay, Mitton, Baird and Maguire.

### Families of Ballyrashane (Ulster)

T. H. Mullin, Belfast, 1969, with family trees of the following — Simpson, Rankin, Greer, Stuart, McCollum, Atchison, Reid, Huston, McConaghy, MacAfee, McCurdy, Norris, Lynn, Barr, Curry, Parkhill, Eaton, Chestnutt, Anderson, Stirling, McIntyre, Ross, Boyce, Jamison, Quin, Carson, Workman, Morrow, Campbell, Moore, Williamson, McClelland, Pollock, Eccles, Irvine, Withrow, Patton, McKinley, Blair, Ferguson, Godfrey, Calvin, Dunlop, Logan, Nevins, Walker, Sloan, Lees, Hemphell, Sinclair, Lyly, Getty, Boyd, Auld, Watton.

### History of the Irish Brigades in the Service of France

John C. O'Callaghan, London, 1885. Most extensive; among families treated — Barrett, Bellew, Cantillon, Drumgold, Grattan, Lally, Luttrell, MacSheehy, O'Farrell, Shortall, Williams, Wogan.

# Common Elements in Irish Placenames

Ath, Agh, *ath:* a ford, shallow part of a river.

Agha, *achadh:* a field, level meadow.

Alt, *alt:* an eminence, high place, side of a glen.

Anna, Annagh, *eanach:* a moor, marsh, soft terrain.

Ard, *ard:* a height, top, summit, lofty, higher ground.

Bally, *baile:* town, village, homestead.

Ballagh, *bealach:* a roadway, passage, gap, pass.

Barn, Barna, *bearna:* pass or gap in hill or mountains.

Barr, *barr:* top, head, summit.

Bawn, Baun, *ban:* small field, enclosure, white coloured.

Beagh, *beithe:* abounding with birch trees.

Bell, *beal:* mouth, entrance, estuary.

Ben, *beann:* peak, pointed hill.

Boher, *bothar:* road, way, passage, lane.

Boley, *buaile:* place for milking cows, booley or dairy place.

Brack, *breac:* speckled, spotted, (with stones, furze) hill.

Bun, *bun:* end, bottom, of hills or mountains.

Caher, Cahir, *cathair:* stone fort, abode, city.

Cam, *cam:* crooked.

Cappa, Cappagh, *ceapach:* plot of ground laid out for tillage.

Carn, *carn:* heap of stones, rocky summit.

Carrick, Carrig, *carraig:* a rock, crag or stone.

Carrow, Carhoo, *ceathramadh:* quarter, measure of land.

Cashel, *caiseal:* wall, bulwark, castle.

Cavan, *cabhan:* a hollow plain.

Clar, *clar:* plain, flat piece of land.

Clash, *clais:* furrow, deep ditch.

Clogh, *cloch:* stone, rock, cliff.

Clon, Cloon, *cluain:* plain, lawn, meadow.

Cool, *cul:* back, corner, angle.

Cor, Corr, *cor:* a round hill.

Cosh, Cush, *cos:* leg, foot, at the foot of, beside.

Creeve, *craobh:* branch, bough, tree, bush.

Croagh, Crogh, *cruach:* rick, stack, piled-up hill.

Cross, *cros:* a cross.

Cuil, Cuill, *coill:* a wood.

Curra, Curragh, *currach:* bog, marsh, soft plain.

Derry, *doire:* an oak, oak wood.

Doo, *dubh:* black.

Doon, Dun, *dun:* a fortress.

Dreen, Drin, *draighean:* blackthorn.

Drom, Drum, *druim:* the ridge of a hill.

Eden, *eadan:* the forehead, brow of a hill.

Esker, *eiscir:* ridge of sand hills, ridge of mountains.

Farn, *fearn:* alder trees, place abounding in alders.

Farren, *fearann:* land, ground, country.

Freagh, *fraoch:* heather, heath, a healthy place.

Gal, Gall, *gall:* stranger, foreigner.

Garran, Garraun, Garrane, *garran:* grove, wood, copse.

Garry, *garrdha:* garden.

Glas, *glas:* green; of mountain, stream or meadow.

Glan, Glen, *gleann:* valley, glen.

Gol, Goul, Gowl, *gabhal:* fork, the fork of a hill.

Gort, Gurt, *gort:* a field or a garden.

Graigue, *graig:* village, manor.

Greenan, *grianan:* sunny place, bower, summer house.

Illan, Illaun, *oilean:* island.

Innis, Inish, Inch, *inis:* an island, a field near a river or a lake.

Kell, *caol:* narrow, slender, straight.

Kil, Kill, *cill:* a church or small monastery.

Knock, *cnoc:* hill, hillock.

Lack, Leck, Lick, *leac:* stone, flagstone, slate.

Laght, *leacht:* a grave, pile of stones in memory of the dead.

Lis, Liss, *lios:* earthen fort, fortified place, ancient place.

Lough, *loch:* a lake.

Lag, Leg, Lug, Lugg, *lag:* a hollow, glen.

Lear, Lyre, *ladhar:* a fork, forking of glens or rivers.

Maghera, *machaire:* a plain, level ground.

Maul, Meel, *meall:* a hillock, eminence.

Meen, *min:* a smooth spot on a hill presenting a green surface.

Mon, *moin:* turf, peat, bog.

Money, *muine:* brake, shrubbery, a hillock.

Moy, *magh:* a plain, plain of hills.

Muck, *muc:* a pig or boar.

Mullagh, *mullach:* top, summit, height, top of a hill.

Park, *pairc:* field, meadow.

Poll, Pol, Poul, *poll:* hole, pit, a measure of land.

Port, *port:* a harbour, bank or landing place.

Rath, *rath:* earthen fort with trees, a fortress.

Ring, Rin, Rinn, *rinn:* a headland, promontory.

Roe, Roo, *ruadh:* red, gorse-clad hill.

Ros, Ross, *ros:* a promontory, isthmus, a grove or wood.

Scart, *scairt:* a thick tuft of shrubs or bushes.

Shan, *sean:* old, e.g. Shanbally, 'old Town'.

Sra, Sragh, srah, *srath:* a field on the bank of a river.

Tawnagh, Tawny, *tamhnach:* a small field.

Temple, *Teampall:* a church or temple.

Ti, *tigh:* a house.

Tir, *tir:* land, country, region.

Tober, *tobar:* well, fountain, spring, source.

Tom, *tuaim:* a grave or tumulus.

Ton, *toin:* backside.

Toor, *tuar:* a place for bleaching clothes.

# Useful Addresses

Department of Folklore,
University College,
Belfield,
Dublin 4.

Genealogical Office,
2 Kildare Street,
Dublin 2.

General Register Office,
8-11 Lombard Street East,
Dublin 2.

Government Publications Sales Office,
Molesworth Street,
Dublin 2.

Linen Hall Library,
17 Donegal Square North,
Belfast BT1 5GD.

Marsh's Library,
St. Patrick's Close,
Dublin 8.

Maynooth College Library,
Maynooth,
Co. Kildare.

National Library of Ireland,
Kildare Street,
Dublin 2.

Ordnance Survey (Maps),
Phoenix Park,
Dublin 8.

Presbyterian Historical Society,
Church House,
Fisherwick Place,
Belfast BT1 69W.

Public Record Office,
The Four Courts,
Dublin 7.

Public Record Office of Northern Ireland,
66 Balmoral Avenue,
Belfast BT9 6NY.

Registrar General of Northern Ireland,
Oxford House,
Chichester Street,
Belfast.

Registry of Deeds,
King's Inns,
Henrietta Street,
Dublin 1.

Representative Church Body Library,
Braemor Park,
Rathgar,
Dublin 14.

Royal Irish Academy,
19 Dawson Street,
Dublin 2.

Society of Friends' Library,
6 Eustace Street,
Dublin 2.

State Paper Office,
Lr Yard,
Dublin Castle,
Dublin 2.

Trinity College Library,
College Street,
Dublin 2.

University College Library,
Galway,
Co. Galway.

University College Library,
Western Road,
Cork.

# INDEX